Federal Income Taxation of Decedents, Estates and Trusts

2019 Edition

DAVID A. BEREK

Editorial Staff

Editor .... Barbara L. Post, Esq.
Production .... Jennifer Schencker, Gokiladevi Sashikumar,
Prabhu Meenakshisundaram

This publication is designed to provide accurate and authoritative information in regard to the subject matter covered. It is sold with the understanding that the publisher is not engaged in rendering legal, accounting, or other professional service and that the authors are not offering such advice in this publication. If legal advice or other expert assistance is required, the services of a competent professional person should be sought.

ISBN 978-0-8080-5036-0

©2018 CCH Incorporated and its affiliates. All rights reserved.
2700 Lake Cook Road
Riverwoods, IL 60015
800 344 3734
CCHCPELink.com

No claim is made to original government works; however, within this Product or Publication, the following are subject to CCH Incorporated's copyright: (1) the gathering, compilation, and arrangement of such government materials; (2) the magnetic translation and digital conversion of data, if applicable; (3) the historical, statutory and other notes and references; and (4) the commentary and other materials.

Printed in the United States of America

MIX
From responsible sources
FSC www.fsc.org **FSC® C103993**

Preface

At the death of the decedent, a separate taxable entity, the decedent's estate, is created. A fiduciary is appointed to take over administration of the decedent's estate. The representative gathers the assets, files the decedent's final income tax return, satisfies tax liabilities, and oversees creation and funding of any testamentary trusts, which become separate taxpaying entities. The estate is liable for the tax on the income received during the period of its administration, and the fiduciary oversees preparation of all tax forms required including the final income tax return and any estate and gift tax returns that are due.

Federal Income Taxation of Decedents, Estates and Trusts provides concise, plain-English coverage of the fundamental rules for practitioners involved in the preparation and review of a decedent's final income tax return and the fiduciary income tax returns that follow. Fundamental fiduciary income tax topics are covered in detail, including trust accounting income (TAI) and distributable net income (DNI). The fiduciary taxation of specialty trusts is reviewed, including grantor trusts, charitable remainder trusts (CRTs) and charitable lead trusts (CLTs), qualified small business trusts (QSSTs) and electing small business trusts (ESBTs), as well as grantor and non-grantor foreign trusts and the fiduciary duties involved, including liability for filing a return and paying any taxes due on behalf of the estate or trust. Also, thoroughly discussed is the state fiduciary income taxation of trusts. Examples illustrating these rules are provided throughout.

Among the subjects covered in this quick answer reference are:

- Application of the 3.8% net investment income tax to trusts and estates
- Decedent's final income tax return including pre- and post-mortem planning elections
- Treatment of partnership items for a deceased partner
- Fiduciary income tax return fundamentals
- Trust accounting income and distributable net income
- Distributing capital gains as part of distributable net income
- Beneficiary's tax liability
- Grantor trust rules and grantor trust reporting
- Split-interest trusts: CRTs and CLTs
- S corporations and trusts: QSST and ESBT rules
- Taxation of foreign trusts
- State fiduciary income taxation of trusts
- Fiduciary duties and liabilities
- Consistency of basis reporting rules
- Partnership audit rules promulgated under the Bipartisan Budget Act

- Congress's recent effort to repeal and replace the Affordable Care Act
- Presidential Executive Order on identifying and reducing tax regulatory burdens
- *Kaestner* and the residence of the beneficiary
- *Bank of America* and trust administration in a state
- The Tax Cuts and Jobs Act of 2017 (TCJA) including the limitation ofm certain deductions for taxable years 2018 through 2025
- CRAT and CRUT payments

Latest changes to the Internal Revenue Code, as well as new regulations, rulings and cases, are reflected throughout the text through date of publication.

David A. Berek

July 2018

About the Author

David A. Berek is a Partner in private practice with Baker & McKenzie LLP in Chicago. He focuses his practice on Family Office Structuring and Administration, Wealth Transfer Planning, Income Tax Planning, and Trusts & Estates.

Prior to re-entering the practice of law, Mr. Berek was a Director at a global private bank in its family office group as a family CFO, and ran the Wealth Planning group in the Central U.S. region advising clients of the private bank on family office and wealth transfer techniques. Prior experience includes practicing trusts and estates law with large- and mid-size law firms; income, transfer tax and trust planning with two big 4 public accounting firms; and, estate tax compliance and administration with a large Chicago-based trust company.

Mr. Berek is currently the editor of the two-volume treatise *Illinois Estate Planning, Will Drafting and Estate Administration Forms with Practical Commentary* published by LexisNexis. Mr. Berek is also an adjunct professor at DePaul University where he teaches Estate Planning; Estate, Gift and GST Tax; and Income Taxation of Decedents, and Estates and Trusts in the Masters of Science in Taxation program; and previously at The John Marshall Law School where he taught Fiduciary Income Taxation and Advanced Income Taxation in the LL.M. Graduate Tax program. He is the co-Director of a new Masters of Science in Wealth Management offered through the Finance Department at DePaul University where he teaches Transfer Tax Planning for Wealth Management, and Family Office and Multigenerational Estate Planning.

Mr. Berek earned a Bachelor of Science in Accountancy degree from DePaul University, a Juris Doctorate degree, *cum laude* (Law Review, Moot Court), and an LL.M. in Employee Benefits degree, *with honors*, from The John Marshall Law School. Active with bar associations, he is a John S. Nolan Tax Law Fellow of the American Bar Association, Tax Section, a former chair of the Tax Practice Management Subcommittee, current chair of the Fiduciary Income Tax Subcommittee, and a former Current Developments reporter of the Estate and Gift Tax Subcommittee. He is past chair of the Illinois State Bar Association Trusts & Estates Section Council, and a past co-chair of the Chicago Bar Association Estate Planning Committee Young Lawyers Section.

Mr. Berek has been recognized by various independent organizations on their lists of top attorneys. Leading Lawyers Network named Mr. Berek one of the Top Attorneys in Illinois in two areas: (1) Trusts, Wills & Estate Planning, and (2) Tax Law (Individual). Mr. Berek is licensed to practice law in Illinois and Florida and has been awarded an AV® Preeminent™ 5.0 out of 5 peer review rating by Martindale-Hubbell for both legal abilities and ethical standards. Mr. Berek is also a Certified Public Accountant (Illinois), and a Certified Financial Planner.™

Table of Contents

	Paragraph
Chapter 1: Introduction and Fiduciary Income Tax Trends	
Fiduciary Income Tax—In General...................	101
Post Mortem Tax Elections	102
Post Mortem Tax Elections Affecting the Decedent's Final Income Tax Return	102.01
Tax Elections Affecting the Decedent's Estate and Trust Income Tax Return	102.02
Impact of the Net Investment Income Tax on Trusts and Estates	103
Basics of the Net Investment Income Tax	103.01
Estates and Trusts Not Subject to the NIIT	103.02
Income Included as Net Investment Income for Estate and Trusts	103.03
Investment Expenses Deductible in Computing NII...	103.04
Regulations and Elections	103.05
Status of the Affordable Care Act	103.06
Miscellaneous Itemized Deductions for Trusts and Estates	104
Passive Activity Losses and Material Participation for Fiduciaries and Beneficiaries	105
Distributing Capital Gains in Distributable Net Income	106
State Fiduciary Income Taxation for Resident and Nonresident Trusts	107
Trust Charitable Deduction for Contributions by Pass-Through Entities	108
FATCA and Developments Regarding Foreign Trusts	109
Look to Any Applicable IGAs	109.01
Classify Trust in Accordance with Final Regulations ..	109.02
Determine and Comply with Reporting Requirements .	109.03
Consistency of Basis Reporting Rules...................	110
Chapter 2: Decedent's Final Income Tax Return	
Introduction	201
Determining Whether a Return Must Be Filed	202
Filing Requirements: Standard Deduction	202.01
Gross Income Threshold	202.02
Dependents	202.03
Additional Taxes Due	202.04
Refunds or Credits	202.05
Form 1310 Claim for Refund....................	202.06
Filing the Final Returns	203

	Paragraph
Gathering Financial Information	204
Sources of Information	204.01
Decedent's Tax Returns	204.02
Financial Institutions	204.03
Insurance and Annuities	204.04
Monitor Mail	204.05
Safe Deposit Box	204.06
Form to File	205
Filing of Joint Returns	206
Disaffirmance of Joint Returns	206.01
Change to Joint Return	206.02
Due Date of Final Return	207
Extensions for Income Tax Returns	207.01
Longer Extension of Time for Form 1040	207.02
Form 709 Gift Tax Return	207.03
Form 706 Estate Tax Return	207.04
Form 8971 and the Consistency of Basis Rules	207.05
Payment of Tax	208
Signing the Return	209
Where Return Should Be Filed	210
When a Refund Is Due	211
Special Benefit for Surviving Spouse	212
Continuation of Estimated Tax Payments	213
Estimated Tax Liability of Estate	213.01
Personal Exemptions on Final Return	214
Dependency Exemptions	215
Income Taxes of Deceased Armed Forces Members and Terrorist Victims	216
Joint Returns	216.01
Missing in Action Status	216.02
Procedure for Claiming Relief	216.03
Tax Obligations for Foreign Assets	217
W-2 Filers	217.01
Foreign Bank Accounts	217.02
FinCEN Reporting and FBAR	217.03

Chapter 3: Fundamentals of Decedent's Final Return

Accounting Method of Decedent	301
Constructive Receipt Rule Applies	302
Amounts Taxable to Estate or Survivors	303
Treatment of Decedent's Income by Recipient	304
Income in Respect of a Decedent	305
Installment Obligations Acquired from Decedent	306
Unrealized Profits Not Taxed	307
Farmers	307.01
Postponement-of-Gain Benefits	308

	Paragraph
Post-Death Transactions	308.01
Sale of Principal Residence	308.02
Payments by Employers to Surviving Spouse or Estate	309
Deductions Not Allowable on Final Return	310
Expenses, Interest, and Taxes	310.01
Debt in Respect of a Decedent	310.02
Decedent's Losses	311
Deduction for Decedent's Medical Expenses	312
Amend Prior Individual Returns for Decedent's Medical Expenses	312.01
Deduction Limitations	312.02
Treatment of Depreciation and Depletion	313
Estate Tax Deduction for Recipient of Decedent's Income	314
Consistency of Basis Reporting	315
Special Deduction for Survivor Annuitant	316
Passive Activity Losses	317
Suspended Losses	317.01
Disposal of Taxpayer's Entire Interest	317.02

Chapter 4: Income and Deductions Reported on a Decedent's Final Return

Interest and Dividends	401
Interest on U.S. Savings Bonds	402
Taxation of Dividends	403
Stock Options and Employee Stock Purchase Plans	404
Statutory Stock Options	404.01
Employee Stock Purchase Plans	404.02
Incentive Stock Options	404.03
Stock Options Held by a Decedent	404.04
Nonstatutory Stock Options	404.05
Agreements to Sell Stock at Stockholder's Death	405
S Corporation Income	406
Regulated Investment Company Stock	407
Alimony	408
Life Insurance Proceeds Are Not Subject to Tax	409
Accelerated Death Benefits	409.01
Installment Payments	409.02
Policy Transfers	409.03
Flexible Premium Policies	409.04
What Is Insurance?	409.05
Unrecovered Investment in Annuity Contracts	409.06
Death Benefits Resulting from Terrorist Attacks	409.07
Death Benefits for Astronauts	409.08
Employee's Group-Term Life Insurance	410
Qualified Retirement Plans and Individual Retirement Accounts (IRAs)	411

	Paragraph
Treatment of Medical, Health and Education Savings Accounts	412
Medical Savings Accounts	412.01
Health Savings Accounts	412.02
Education Savings Accounts	412.03
Charitable Contributions	413
Split-Dollar Insurance Transactions	413.01

Chapter 5: Fiduciary Income Tax Return

Overview	501
Term of an Estate or Trust	502
Estate Administration	502.01
Trust Creation	502.02
Rule Against Perpetuities	502.03
Qualified Revocable Trusts Election Sec. 645	503
Taxation of Estates and Trusts	504
Multiple Trusts	504.01
Tax Computation	504.02
Personal Exemptions and Tax Rates	504.03
Code Sec. 1411 Medicare Tax	504.04
Alternative Minimum Tax Rules	504.05
Income Test for Filing	505
Nonresident Aliens	505.01
Domestic Estates and Trusts with Nonresident Alien Beneficiaries	505.02
Fiduciary Capacity of Guardian	505.03
Due Date for Return	506
When Tax Is to Be Paid	507
Calendar Year or Fiscal Year	507.01
Estimated Tax	507.02
Filing Extensions	508
Interest	508.01
Penalties	508.02
Duties of Ancillary Representatives	509
Separate Return for Each Trust	510

Chapter 6: Fiduciary Income Tax Return Fundamentals

General Types of Income to Be Reported	601
U.S. Saving Bond Interest Reported by an Estate	602
Section 454 Election	602.01
Individual Beneficiary Receiving Bonds from Estate	602.02
Estate Holding the Bonds	602.03
Types of Estate Income in Respect of a Decedent	603
Interest Income Received	603.01
Income from Real Property	603.02

	Paragraph
Income from Personal Property	603.03
Farm Loss Property and Farm Land	603.04
Sales of Crops	603.05
Gain or Loss When Legacy Satisfied in Property	604
Capital Gains and Losses	605
Capital Gains Tax Rates	605.01
Depreciable Real Estate	605.02
Collectibles	605.03
Netting of Gains and Losses	605.04
Basis of Estate or Trust Property	606
Adjustments to Basis	606.01
Deductions and Credits	607
Credits	607.01
Expenses of Administration	607.02
Miscellaneous Itemized Deductions and Section 67	608
Deductibility of Litigation Expenses	609
Deductions in Respect of a Decedent	610
Deductibility of Interest	611
Deduction of Taxes by an Estate or Trust	612
Double Deductions for Certain Items Not Allowed	613
Depreciation Deduction Is to Be Apportioned	614
Trusts—Depreciation Deduction	614.01
Estates—Depreciation Deduction	614.02
Treatment of Depletion Deduction	615
Deductible Losses of an Estate or Trust	616
Casualty Losses	616.01
Capital Losses	616.02
Losses Sustained by Decedent or Estate	616.03
Related Parties	616.04
Net Operating Loss Deduction Allowed	617
At-Risk Limitations	617.01
Unused Loss Carryovers	618
Excess Deductions on Termination	619
Limitation on the Deductibility of Excess Deductions on Termination	619.01
Allocation in Year of Termination	620
Alimony and Separate Maintenance Payments	621

Chapter 7: Fiduciary Accounting Income and Distributable Net Income

Conduit Nature of Fiduciary Income Taxation	701
Fiduciary Accounting Income (FAI)	702
Total Return Legislation	703
Distributable Net Income (DNI)	704
Distributing Capital Gains in Distributable Net Income	705
Distinction between Simple and Complex Trusts	706
Simple Trust: All Income Distributed	706.01

	Paragraph
Complex Trust: Any Principal Distributed	706.02
Complex Trust: Income Accumulated	706.03
Distributions in Kind	706.04
Decedent's Estate—Complex Trust Treatment	706.05
How to Determine Distributable Net Income	707
Simple Trust's Deduction for Distributions to Beneficiaries	708
Estate's and Complex Trust's Deduction for Distributions to Beneficiaries	709
Character of Amounts Distributed	709.01
Limitation of Distribution Deduction	709.02
Illustration of an Estate and Complex Trust Deduction Computation	710
Income—FAI	710.01
Distributable Net Income	710.02
Character of Distribution	710.03
Taxable Income	710.04
Distributions in Kind	711
Gain or Loss	711.01
Election to Recognize Gain	711.02
Mandatory Recognition of Gain or Loss	711.03
Holding Period	711.04
65-Day Election Rule Under Section 663(b)	712

Chapter 8: Beneficiary's Tax Liability

SIMPLE TRUSTS

Amounts Included in Beneficiary's Gross Income	801
Income Required to Be Distributed	801.01
Character of Income and Allocation of Expenses	801.02
Tax Years of Beneficiaries and Trusts	802
Death of a Simple Trust Beneficiary	802.01

ESTATES AND COMPLEX TRUSTS

Income Taxed on a "Tier" Basis	803
Tier 1: Income Required to Be Distributed	803.01
Tier 2: Other Amounts Properly Paid, Credited, or Required to Be Distributed	803.02
Comprehensive Example	804
Trust Accounting Income	804.01
Distributable Net Income	804.02
Distribution Deduction	804.03
Character of Income	804.04
Taxable Income	804.05
Tier 1: Income Required to Be Distributed	804.06
Tier 2: Other Amounts Required to Be Distributed	804.07
Depreciation	804.08
Interest Paid on Deferred Legacies	805

	Paragraph
Elective Shares	806
Separate Shares Treated as Separate Trusts	807
Calendar-Year Requirement; Complex Trust	808
Gifts and Bequests May Be Exempt	809
Charitable Contributions Not Allowed as Part of Distribution Deduction	810
Double Deductions Are Denied	811
Treatment of Gain from Sale of Life Interest	812
Assignment of Trust Interest vs. Trust Income	813
Throwback Rules—In General	814
Accumulation Distributions	815
Undistributed Net Income	816
How the Throwback Rule Operates	817
Computation of Beneficiary's Tax	818
Multiple Trust Distributions	818.01
Foreign Trusts	818.02

Chapter 9: Grantor Trusts

History of the Grantor Trust Rules	901
Helvering v. Clifford	901.01
Clifford Trusts	901.02
The Clifford Regulations	901.03
Contemporary Planning and Rate Compression	901.04
Overview of the Grantor Trust Rules and the Use of Grantor Trusts	902
Returns	902.01
Adverse and Nonadverse Parties—Code Sec. 672	903
Adverse Parties	903.01
Nonadverse Parties	903.02
Related or Subordinate Under Code Sec. 672(c)	903.03
Reversionary Interests in Grantor Trusts—Code Sec. 673	904
Power to Control Beneficial Enjoyment—Code Sec. 674	905
Independent Trustees	905.01
Permissible Powers	905.02
Exercise of Administrative Powers—Code Sec. 675	906
Power to Make Loans	906.01
Actual Borrowing from the Trust	906.02
Other Powers	906.03
Power of Substitution—Code Sec. 675(4)	907
Power to Revoke Grantor Trusts—Code Sec. 676	908
Postponement of Beneficial Enjoyment	908.01
Income for Benefit of Grantor—Code Sec. 677	909
Constructive Distributions	909.01
Uses of Trust Income	909.02
Payment of Gift Tax and Net Gift	909.03
Payment of Income Taxes and Revenue Ruling 2004-64	909.04

	Paragraph
Private Annuity	909.05
Reversionary Interests in Excess of 5%	909.06
Discharge of Legal Obligation	909.07
Income Taxable to Person Other than Grantor—Code Sec. 678	910
Crummey Powers and Code Sec. 678	910.01
Certain Types of Trusts—Code Secs. 679 and 685	911
Foreign Grantor Trusts—Code Sec. 679	911.01
Pre-need Funeral Trusts	911.02
Trusts Holding S Corporation Stock	911.03
Specialty Non-Grantor Trusts—Alaska, Divorce Settlement, Cemetery	912
Alaska Native Settlement Trusts	912.01
Alimony and Separate Maintenance Payments	912.02
Cemetery Perpetual Care Funds	912.03
Overview of Grantor Trust Tax Reporting	913
The Grantor Trust Reporting Regulations	914
Alternative Filing Methods for Grantor Trusts	915
First Alternative Method of Reporting—All by Grantor Directly on Form 1040	916
Second Alternative Method of Reporting—All on Form 1099 with a Statement	917
Traditional Method of Reporting—Blank Form 1041 with Grantor Tax Letter	918
Changing Methods of Reporting	919
Changing from Filing Form 1041 to Methods 1 (Grantor) or 2 (Form 1099)	919.01
Changing from Method 1 (Grantor) to Filing Form 1041 (Traditional)	919.02
Changing from Method 2 (Form 1099) to Filing Form 1041 (Traditional)	919.03
Changing from Method 1 (Grantor) to Method 2 (Form 1099)	919.04
Changing from Method 2 (Form 1099) to Method 1 (Grantor)	919.05
Grantor Trusts that Cannot Report Under an Alternative Method	920
Tax Identification Numbers: Must the Trustee Obtain a Separate Number	921
Tax Reporting for Grantor Trusts and Disregarded Entities	922
Irrevocable Life Insurance Trust	922.01
Term Trusts: GRAT and QPRT	922.02
Husband and Wife who File a Joint Return—One Grantor	922.03
Revocable Joint Trust Grantor Trust Tax Reporting	922.04
Revocable Trust but Grantor Not a Trustee	922.05
Coordinating Other Disregarded Entities with Grantor Trusts	923

Paragraph

Chapter 10: Death of a Partnership Member

Income on Deceased Partner's Final Return	1001
Death of a 50% Partner	1001.01
Final 1040 Reporting	1001.02
Treatment of Self-Employment Tax in Final Year	1001.03
Electing Large Partnerships	1002
Partnership Representative	1003
Partnership Accounting Periods	1004
Transfer of Decedent's Entire Partnership Interest to Spouse	1005
Payments to Deceased Partner's Successor in Interest	1006
Allocation of Payments	1007
Partner Receiving Income in Respect of a Decedent	1008
Partnership Goodwill	1009
Payments for Goodwill	1009.01
Formula for Valuing Goodwill	1009.02
The 754 Election	1010
The Election	1010.01
Termination of the Election	1010.02
Coordination of the 754 Election and Mandatory Basis Adjustment Rules	1010.03
Mandatory Basis Adjustment Rules	1011

Chapter 11: Charitable Deduction and Split-Interest Trusts: CRTs and CLTs

Overview of the Fiduciary Charitable Deduction	1101
Charitable Contribution Deduction Limited to Sums Paid Out of Gross Income	1102
Distributions Pursuant to the Terms of the Governing Instrument	1103
Charitable Deduction for Section 691 IRD Property	1104
Charitable Contribution Deduction for Distributions from Flow-Through Entities	1105
Charitable Distributions Not Allowed as Part of Distribution Deduction	1106
Charitable Contribution Substantiation Requirements	1107
Split-Interest Charitable Trusts—Overview	1108
Grantor v. Non-Grantor Trust Status	1108.01
Charitable Remainder Trust (CRT)	1108.02
Charitable Lead Trust (CLT)	1108.03
Initial Interest: Annuity or Unitrust	1108.04
Additional Contributions to Unitrust, Not to Annuity Trust	1108.05
Definition of Trust Income	1108.06
Funding of Split-Interest Charitable Trusts	1109
Current 7520 Rate and Two Months Preceding	1109.01
Charitable Deduction Present Value	1109.02

	Paragraph
Annuity and Unitrust Interests	1110
Sum Certain Annuity or Fixed Percentage Unitrust	1110.01
CRAT Payment	1110.02
CRUT Payment	1110.03
Division of Trust	1110.04
Taxation	1110.045
Tax Reporting	1110.06
Charitable Remainder Trusts—Distributions to Beneficiaries	1111
Income Beneficiary	1111.01
Remainder Beneficiary	1111.02
Trust Term	1111.03
Valuation of the Remainder Trust	1111.04
Assets to Consider for Funding a CRT	1111.05
Ordering Rules of Distributions	1111.06
Charitable Lead Trusts	1112
Grantor Charitable Lead Trusts	1112.01
Qualified Non-Grantor Charitable Lead Trust	1112.02
Payments of Annuity or Unitrust Amounts	1112.03
Trust Term	1112.04
Valuation of the Remainder Interest	1112.05
Assets to Consider for Funding a CLT	1112.06
CLT Tax Reporting	1113
CLT Distribution Income Ordering Regulations	1114
Pooled Income Trusts	1115

Chapter 12: S Corporation and Fiduciary Income Tax

S Corporation Rules—In General	1201
Taxation of S Corporation Shareholders	1201.01
Duty of Consistency	1201.02
At-Risk and Passive Activity Rules	1201.03
Passive Activity Loss Rules Apply	1201.04
Small Business Stock	1201.05
Eligible S Corporation Shareholders	1202
Individuals	1202.01
Estates	1202.02
Trusts	1202.03
Exempt Organizations as Shareholders	1202.04
QSSS	1202.05
Qualified Subchapter S Trusts—QSST	1203
Electing Small Business Trusts—ESBT	1204
QSST Election	1205
Sample QSST Election	1205.01
ESBT Election	1206
Sample ESBT Election	1206.01

Paragraph

Chapter 13: Foreign Trusts

Foreign Trust Defined—In General 1301
Inbound Foreign Grantor Trusts 1302
Outbound Foreign Grantor Trusts 1303
Nongrantor Foreign Trusts 1304
    United States Taxation of the Trust 1304.01
    United States Taxation of the U.S. Beneficiaries 1304.02
    Accumulation Distributions 1304.03
    Undistributed Net Income 1304.04
    How the Throwback Rule Operates 1304.05
    Computation of Beneficiary's Tax 1304.06
    Anti-Deferral Provisions of the Internal Revenue Code . 1304.07
Reporting Requirements 1305
FATCA and Other Related Developments Regarding Foreign
  Trusts 1306
    Look to Any Applicable IGAs 1306.01
    Classify Trust in Accordance with Final Regulations .. 1306.02
    Determine and Comply with Reporting Requirements . 1306.03
Offshore Voluntary Disclosure Programs (OVDP) 1307
    Prior OVDP Campaigns and Administration 1307.01
    Goals of the Campaign 1307.02
    Selection for Audit 1307.03

Chapter 14: Fiduciary Duties and Liabilities

Fiduciary's Personal Liability for Tax 1401
    The Federal Priority Statute 1401.01
Enforcement of Fiduciary Liability 1402
Executor Can Be Discharged from Liability 1403
Notice of Fiduciary Relationship 1404
    Written Notice 1404.01
Identification Numbers 1405
Claims for Credit or Refund 1406
Assessment and Collection Period Can Be Shortened 1407
Transferee Liability of a Beneficiary 1408
Lien for Taxes—Insurance Proceeds 1409
Fiduciary Liability for Self-Employment Tax 1410

Chapter 15: State Fiduciary Income Taxation of Trusts

Overview of State Fiduciary Income Taxation for Resident And
  Nonresident Trusts 1501
    Resident State Taxation 1501.01
    Nonresident State Taxation 1501.02
The *Linn* Example: Introduction to the Issue 1502
How is the "Residence" of a Trust Determined 1503
    Mobility and Multi-Jurisdictional Contacts 1503.01

	Paragraph
Factors the States Apply to Determine State Fiduciary Taxation	1504
Constitutional Basis for State Taxation—Perspective on Supreme Court Analysis	1505
The Commerce Clause	1506
The Substantial Nexus Test	1506.01
The Due Process Clause	1507
Minimum Contacts and Due Process	1507.01
Quill Corporation and Minimum Contacts for State Law Taxing Power	1508
Swift, Founder Criteria and Present Benefit Minimum Contacts for State Trust Laws: Six Points	1509
Blue, Founder Criteria and Ongoing Protection Minimum Contacts Required for State Law Taxing Power	1510
Bank of America and Trust Adminitration in a State	1511
Mercantile Safe Deposit and Control over the Property Necessary by New York Beneficiaries	1512
Kassner and New Jersey Testamentary Trusts with Undistributed S Corporation Income	1513
Pennoyer and Probate Administration for Testamentary Trust Not Enough	1514
D.C. v. Chase Manhattan Bank and Probate Is Enough to Withstand Challenge	1515
McNeil and the Importance of Discretionary Beneficiaries under the Pennsylvania Statute	1516
Gavin and Treatment of Non-Contingent Beneficiaries	1517
Kaestner and the Residence of the Beneficiary	1518
Trends Practitioners Should Plan For	1519

	Page
Case Table	16,001
Table of Internal Revenue Code Sections	17,001
Table of Treasury Regulations	18,001
Table of Revenue Rulings and Other IRS Releases	19,001
Index	20,001

Chapter 1

Introduction and Fiduciary Income Tax Trends

¶ 101   Fiduciary Income Tax—In General
¶ 102   Post Mortem Tax Elections
¶ 103   Impact of the Net Investment Income Tax on Trusts and Estates
¶ 104   Miscellaneous Itemized Deductions for Trusts and Estates
¶ 105   Passive Activity Losses and Material Participation for Fiduciaries and Beneficiaries
¶ 106   Distributing Capital Gains in Distributable Net Income
¶ 107   State Fiduciary Income Taxation for Resident and Nonresident Trusts ~Exclude
¶ 108   Trust Charitable Deduction for Contributions by Pass-Through Entities
¶ 109   FATCA and Developments Regarding Foreign Trusts
¶ 110   Consistency of Basis Reporting Rules

By way of introduction, this first chapter is intended to capture two broad topics that would be most useful to practitioners: (1) a review of commonly considered elections relevant to fiduciary income taxation, and (2) important and continuing developments in fiduciary income taxation that deserve separate and distinct coverage. Perhaps the most pressing issue in fiduciary income tax currently is the impact of the "Trump Tax Plan" known as the "Tax Cuts and Jobs Act" or "TCJA" that was signed by the President on December 22, 2017.[1] Of considerable interest is how the individual income tax changes carry over to fiduciary income tax. For example, as discussed in ¶ 607, an estate or trust is entitled to the same deductions for expenses as an individual in the production of income, including deductions for interest and taxes.[2] However, the current legislation incorporates reforms such as "doubling the standard deduction" for individuals and otherwise limiting Schedule A deductions for those individual taxpayers but what is the impact on trusts and estates. Fiduciary income tax practitioners must assess the consequences of this legislation and, specifically, the impact of the limitation on deductions by estates and trusts.

---

[1] The Tax Cuts and Jobs Act ("TCJA") (P.L. 115-97) is actually titled "An Act to provide for reconciliation pursuant to titles II and V of the concurrent resolution on the budget for fiscal year 2018," which is why it is "known as" the TCJA.

[2] Reg. § 1.641(b)-1.

Another development in the transfer tax area that impacts fiduciary income tax practitioners is the consistency of basis rules.³ Although not a fiduciary income tax requirement, its implementation will affect the filing and reporting of fiduciary income tax returns. Furthermore, Treasury's guidance under Code Sec. 67 regarding the application of the 2% AGI limitation, Treasury's guidance under the 3.8% Medicare surtax, imposed as of January 1, 2013, as it relates to trusts and estates, and material participation with regard to the passive loss rules as applied to trusts and estates continue to be important developments that practitioners must monitor, even though there have been no new noteworthy developments on these topics since their initial release. Finally, the state fiduciary income taxation of trusts is an evolving area as states seek to capture more tax revenue, and Paragraph 107 introduces this topic, and Chapter 15 on State Fiduciary Income Taxation for Resident and Non-Resident Trusts evaluates the topic in greater detail. We now begin with a survey of fiduciary income tax elections and a general introduction to the topic.

A final point applies to the status of the regulatory process. On April 21, 2017, the Trump Administration released a Presidential Executive Order on Identifying and Reducing Tax Regulatory Burdens, and on July 2017, the IRS issued Notice 2017-38⁴ in response to Executive Order 13789, which required the Treasury Department to reduce regulatory burdens by identifying any regulations issued from January 1, 2016, through April 21, 2017, that: (a) impose undue financial burdens on taxpayers; (b) add "undue complexity" to federal tax laws; and (c) exceed the IRS's statutory authority. Treasury Secretary Steven Mnuchin has directed Treasury staff to review significant tax regulations issued in 2016 to determine if any of them impose an undue financial burden on American taxpayers, add undue complexity, or exceed statutory authority.⁵ Given this rather comprehensive review, it is uncertain whether practitioners will see new guidance from Treasury in the short term, yet guidance will likely be produced, and therefore a close watch as to Treasury efforts is warranted in the near term.

¶ 101 Fiduciary Income Tax—In General

A common element regarding the income tax treatment of the combination of (i) a decedent's final return, (ii) an estate income tax return, and (iii) a trust income tax return, is the premise that the income tax laws are applied on behalf of or for the benefit of another individual or group of individuals. This "applied on behalf of or for the benefit of another individual" conveys a fiduciary relationship. The definition of a "fiduciary" is a person who is vested with rights and powers to be exercised for the benefit of another person.⁶ Thus, final income tax return and estate and trust income tax returns fall under the description of fiduciary income taxation because someone other than the individual or entity receiving the benefit of the property is responsible for tax filings.

---

³ Proposed Regulations issued on March 4, 2016, under Code Secs. 1014(f) and 6035 regarding basis consistency between estates and persons acquiring property from a decedent.

⁴ 2017-30 IRB 147.

⁵ In its review, the Treasury Department found eight regulations that it believes meet the criteria of either undue financial burdens or undue complexity including proposed, temporary and final regulations under Code §§ 103, 337(d), 367, 385, 752, 987, 2704, and 7602.

⁶ Black's Law Dictionary Online (2d ed. 2013).

¶ 102 Post Mortem Tax Elections[7]

Post mortem elections affect more than just the decedent's final income tax return and fiduciary income tax returns. Provided below is a summary of various post mortem elections that fiduciary income tax practitioners should be aware of, including elections beyond the scope of this treatise (such as estate settlement and administration matters) because those elections may arise during the settlement process.

It is important to note that while some elections involve only timing, other elections involve more significant ramifications, and not all beneficiaries are likely to be affected in a similar fashion. In most cases, the personal representative will have to decide the most advantageous manner to proceed and on which return to report a particular item. It should be noted that failing to make an election to the detriment of a beneficiary can subject the personal representative to fiduciary liability—thus, these are important decisions.

An example highlighting the importance of these decisions involves the decedent's unpaid medical expenses. If deducted on the estate tax return, those deductions potentially offset a 40% federal estate tax, if estate tax is payable. If deducted on the decedent's final income tax return as discussed in ¶ 312, those deductions might offset a 37% plus 3.8% (40.8%) income tax.[8] Additionally, the impact of state taxes (both income and estate taxes) greatly affects the calculation. Thus, the answer of where to report income or deduct expenses is not always obvious and must be carefully considered. The following is a "quick" summary of the rules and where more information can be found within the book.

.01 Post Mortem Tax Elections Affecting the Decedent's Final Income Tax Return

The treatment of the decedent's final income tax return is discussed in Chapters 2, 3, and 4. The following is a summary of special income and deduction treatment that can be reported on either the decedent's final income tax return, Form 1040, the estate's fiduciary income tax return, Form 1041, or estate tax return, Form 706.

Savings Bond Interest. Interest received by a decedent is covered in detail in ¶ 402. Interest received by a taxpayer or credited to a taxpayer's account is includible in income, unless an exception applies.[9] The interest on current issues of U.S. savings bonds generally is fully taxable. Series EE bonds, for example, are bonds that are issued at a discount and increase in value each year until maturity. The increase in value each year is taxable as interest, except that a cash-basis taxpayer has the option of reporting the increase in the current year or deferring the interest until the bonds are redeemed. After death, a personal representative may elect to report all previously deferred or unreported Series E or EE Bond interest as income under Code Sec. 454(a) on a decedent's final Form 1040.[10] The

---

[7] The author would like to recognize the contribution of Carol A. Cantrell of Cantrell & Cantrell, PLLC, for input on post mortem planning recommendations.

[8] Code Sec. 213(c).

[9] Code Sec. 61(a)(4).

[10] Rev. Rul. 68-145, 1968-1 CB 203; Rev. Rul. 79-409, 1979-2 CB 208.

additional income on the decedent's final income tax return may increase the decedent's final income tax liability, which will be a deduction on the estate tax return, Form 706, thereby reducing federal estate tax.[11] The election to report the interest at death does not impact the prospective reporting requirements of recipients of the bonds who may again choose to defer income recognition.[12]

Medical Expenses. Medical expenses are covered in detail in ¶ 312. If the decedent had unpaid medical expenses incurred prior to death and paid within one year of death, then the personal representative may elect to deduct some or all of those medical expenses that are paid within one year after the date of death either on the decedent's final income tax return, Form 1040 or on the federal estate tax return, Form 706.[13]

The election can be made to forgo the estate tax deduction and deduct on the final personal income tax return. If the election is made, the personal representative must attach a statement that the amount has not been allowed as a deduction on the estate tax return and the personal representative must irrevocably waive the right to deduct these expenses on the 706.[14] Note that expenses that are not deductible on the final income tax return due to the 10% AGI limitation are also not allowed as a deduction on the estate tax return.

Installment Sales. The personal representative may elect out of installment sale treatment in the year of death and report the gain on the decedent's final income tax return to increase the personal income tax liability to correspond to an additional claim against the estate for estate tax purposes. Otherwise, when the proceeds are recognized after death, an income tax deduction under Code Sec. 691(c) for estate taxes paid on the installment sale is available to the recipient of the property when the note payments are collected (see ¶ 314).

.02 Tax Elections Affecting the Decedent's Estate and Trust Income Tax Return

Fiscal Year-End. Fiscal year filing is covered in ¶ 507. Currently, income from an estate, like that of an individual, can be reported on either a calendar year or fiscal year basis.[15] Estates are permitted to select tax years in order to defer income tax because (i) estates generally are not administered as long as trusts, and (ii) estate fiduciaries need to select an accounting period to coincide with the administration of the estate. Trusts, however, generally must use a calendar year.[16] Selecting a fiscal year-end for an estate can produce deferral of income recognition for the calendar year beneficiary.[17]

If an estate selects a fiscal year, it must qualify as a permissible accounting period.[18] A permissible period includes (i) a calendar year or (ii) a fiscal year that ends on the last day of the month.[19] Once chosen, the tax year can only be changed by permission from the IRS. The regulations provide that neither Form SS-4 nor a

---

[11] IRS Letter Ruling 9232006 (April 17, 1992).
[12] Reg. § 1.454-1(a).
[13] Code Sec. 213(c); Rev. Rul. 77-357, 1977-2 CB 328.
[14] Reg. § 1.213-1(d)(2).
[15] Code Sec. 441.
[16] Code Sec. 644(a).
[17] Reg. § 1.662(c)-1.
[18] Reg. § 1.441-1(c).
[19] Reg. § 1.441-1(b)(1)(iv).

return extension determines the year-end.[20] The taxable year for a new taxpayer is adopted by filing the first federal income tax return.[21]

Qualified Revocable Trust. Although a trust generally must select a calendar and an estate may elect a fiscal year, if the Code Sec. 645 Election is made, the trust will be treated and taxed for income tax purposes as part of the estate rather than a separate trust pursuant to Code Sec. 645(a) (see ¶ 503). The election period begins on the date of the decedent's death and terminates on the earlier of (1) the day on which the electing trust and related estate have distributed all of their assets, or (2) the day before the applicable date.[22] The Code Sec. 645 election once made is irrevocable.[23]

A "qualified revocable trust" is any trust (or portion thereof) that was treated under Code Sec. 676 as owned by the decedent by reason of a power in the decedent to revoke, determined without regard to Code Sec. 672(e).[24] The Code Sec. 645 election allows such a trust to take advantage of tax rules that apply to estates, including: the charitable set aside deduction under Code Sec. 642(c) (see Chapter 11); the reasonable extension of time to hold subchapter S stock under Code Sec. 1361(b)(l) (see ¶ 1202); the allowance of a $25,000 passive loss deduction for rental real estate activities under Code Sec. 469(i)(4)[25] (see ¶ 316); a fiscal year election which will be allowed in this case but which is not available to a trust generally; avoidance of related party rules under Code Sec. 267, including recognition of loss upon the satisfaction of a pecuniary bequest with assets that have a fair market value less than basis pursuant to Code Sec. 267(b)(3), as well as other loss limitations (PAL's, NOL's Capital, see ¶ ¶ 616-618); relief of Code Sec. 6654(l)(2) estimated tax payment requirements for two years.[26]

Charitable Contributions Made After Year-End. The fiduciary may elect to treat a charitable contribution as paid in a particular tax year if the contribution is actually paid after the close of that year but on or before the end of the succeeding year.[27] Careful tax planning to make maximum use of the charitable contribution deduction is necessary.[28]

Disallowance of Double Deductions. As provided in Chapter 6, ¶ 613, for estate tax purposes, the Code allows certain deductions from the gross estate in computing the taxable estate.[29] Of these, administration expenses and losses during administration might include items that would also be deductible from gross income for income tax purposes. To prevent duplication of the deductions, the law provides that amounts that qualify for estate tax purposes under Code Sec. 2053 or 2054 may not be used in computing the taxable income of the estate (or any other person) for income tax purposes unless the deduction for estate tax purposes is waived.[30] Code Sec. 642(g) (the disallowance of double deductions rule) in turn

---

[20] Reg. § 1.441-1(c).
[21] Reg. § 1.441-1(c).
[22] Reg. § 1.645-1(f)(1).
[23] Reg. § 1.645-1(e)(1).
[24] Code Sec. 645(b)(1).
[25] Reg. § 1.645-1(e)(2).
[26] *See* Chapter 5, ¶ 510.
[27] Code Sec. 642(c)(1); Reg. § 1.642(c)-1(a)(1).
[28] *See* Chapter 11. *See also* ¶ 108 below regarding charitable deductions for trusts from pass-through entities.
[29] Code Sec. 2051.
[30] Code Sec. 642(g); Reg. § 1.642(g)-1.

¶102.02

prohibits deductions on Form 706 *unless* a statement is attached to Form 1041 waiving the right to claim the deduction on Form 706[31] or the deductions are allocated between the two returns.[32]

The rule against double deductions does not apply to deductions for taxes, interest, business expenses, or other items accrued at the date of the decedent's death, such as deductions in respect of a decedent (also referred to as "DRD") which are deductible on both returns.[33] Consequently, such items are deductible from the gross estate as claims against the estate and also from gross income as "deductions in respect of a decedent" for income tax purposes.[34]

Estimated Tax Payments. Estates and trusts, like individuals, must pay estimated income tax. However, estimated tax payments from an estate are not required for any tax year ending before the second anniversary of the decedent's death.[35] Also, in the case of a trust that was treated as owned by the decedent that will receive the residue of the decedent's estate under the will (or, if no will is admitted to probate, that will be primarily responsible for paying debts, taxes, and administration expenses), estimated tax payments are not required for any tax year ending before the second anniversary of the decedent's death.[36] Qualified revocable trusts that make the Code Sec. 645 election may take advantage of the two-year exemption from paying estimated taxes that is available to estates.[37] Trusts may also elect to treat any part of an estimated tax payment as having been made by a beneficiary.[38] Estates may also make this election, but only for their final year.

In the case of a trust, for any tax year or, in the case of an estate, for the estate's final year, the fiduciary (or executor) may elect to treat any portion of estimated tax payments for the tax year as payments made by a beneficiary and not as payments made by the trust or estate. Such an amount is treated as payment of the estimated tax made by the beneficiary that would otherwise be due January 15 of the following tax year. The fiduciary must make the election on Form 1041-T (Allocation of Estimated Tax Payments to Beneficiaries). The election must be filed on or before the 65th day after the close of the tax year of the trust or estate.[39] Once made, the election is irrevocable.[40]

65-Day Election Rule. The fiduciary of a complex trust or the executor of an estate may elect to treat any distribution or any portion of any distribution to a beneficiary within the first 65 days following the end of a tax year as an amount that was paid or credited on the last day of the tax year.[41]

The election allows the fiduciary to balance out the income tax rates between the trust and the beneficiaries. To make the election, the executor or trustee must check the box on page 2 of Form 1041 filed on or before the extended due date of the return.[42]

---

[31] Code Sec. 642(g); Reg. § 1.642(g)-1.
[32] Reg. § 1.642(g)-2.
[33] Code Sec. 691(b).
[34] Reg. § 1.642(g)-2.
[35] Code Sec. 6654(i).
[36] Code Sec. 6654(l)(2); Instructions for Form 1041, U.S. Income Tax Return for Estates and Trusts.
[37] Reg. § 1.645-1(e)(4).
[38] Code Sec. 643(g).
[39] Code Sec. 643(g)(2).
[40] Reg. § 301.9100-8(a)(4)(i). *See* Chapter 5, ¶ 510.
[41] Code Sec. 663(b); Reg. § 1.663(b)-1(a)(1).
[42] *See* Chapter 7, ¶ 712.

¶102.02

¶ 103 Impact of the Net Investment Income Tax on Trusts and Estates

.01 Basics of the Net Investment Income Tax

The Net Investment Income Tax ("NIIT"), effective January 1, 2013, is imposed under Code Sec. 1411 and applies a tax rate of 3.8% to certain net investment income of individuals, estates and trusts that have income above the statutory threshold amounts. The NIIT affects income tax returns of individuals, estates and trusts.

Estates and trusts are subject to the NIIT if they have undistributed net investment income and also have adjusted gross income over the dollar amount at which the highest tax bracket for an estate or trust begins for such taxable year (for tax year 2018, this threshold amount is $12,500). Note that for estates and trusts, the 3.8% surtax will apply at the first dollar of taxable income. There are special computational rules for certain unique types of trusts, such as Charitable Remainder Trusts and Electing Small Business Trusts.

.02 Estates and Trusts Not Subject to the NIIT

Not all estates and trusts are subject to the NIIT, including:

1. trusts that are exempt from income taxes imposed by Subtitle A of the Code (charitable trusts and qualified retirement plan trusts exempt from tax under Code Sec. 501 and Charitable Remainder Trusts exempt from tax under Code Sec. 664),
2. charitable trusts in which all of the unexpired interests are devoted to one or more of the purposes described in Code Sec. 170(c)(2)(B), and
3. grantor trusts classified under Code Secs. 671-679 (because the grantor is subject to the NIIT at the individual level, see Chapter 9).

.03 Income Included as Net Investment Income for Estate and Trusts

In general, investment income includes, but is not limited to: interest, dividends, capital gains, rental and royalty income, non-qualified annuities, income from businesses involved in trading financial instruments or commodities, and businesses that are passive activities to the taxpayer (within the meaning of Code Sec. 469). To calculate NIIT, investment income is reduced by certain expenses properly allocable to the income.

Some common types of income are not considered to be Net Investment Income, including: wages and unemployment compensation, operating income from a nonpassive business, Social Security Benefits, alimony (prior to 2019),[43] tax-exempt interest, self-employment income, Alaska Permanent Fund Dividends[44] and distributions from certain Qualified Plans (those described in Code Sec. 401(a), 403(a), 403(b), 408, 408A, or 457(b)).

---

[43] For payments required under a divorce or separation instrument that is executed after December 31, 2018, the new 2017 TCJA eliminates the deduction for alimony payments, thus the payor will no longer receive a deduction, and the recipient will no longer include the alimony in taxable income. See ¶ 408.

[44] See Rev. Rul. 90-56, 1990-2 CB 102.

Generally, capital gains are included in Net Investment Income to the extent they are not otherwise offset by capital losses. Gains from the sale of interests in partnerships and S corporations, are included in Net Investment Income to the extent the estate or trust is a passive owner.

.04 Investment Expenses Deductible in Computing NII

In order to arrive at Net Investment Income, gross investment income is reduced by deductions that are properly allocable to items of gross investment income including investment interest expense, investment advisory and brokerage fees, expenses related to rental and royalty income, and state and local income taxes properly allocable to items included in Net Investment Income.

For estates and trusts, the Net Investment Income Tax is reported on, and paid with, the fiduciary income tax return, Form 1041, and thus such additional tax is subject to the estimated tax provisions. Estates and trusts that expect to be subject to the tax should adjust their income tax withholding or estimated payments to account for the tax increase in order to avoid underpayment penalties.

.05 Regulations and Elections

The proposed regulations are effective for tax years beginning after December 31, 2013. Taxpayers were able to rely on the proposed regulations for purposes of compliance with Code Sec. 1411 until the effective date of the final regulations. Any election made in reliance on the proposed regulations will be in effect for the year of the election, and will remain in effect for subsequent taxable years. Since the final regulations provide for a similar election, taxpayers who opted not to make an election in reliance on the proposed regulations were not precluded from making that election pursuant to the final regulations.

.06 Status of the Affordable Care Act

It should be noted that Congress's recent effort in 2016 to repeal or replace parts or all of the Affordable Care Act could have a direct impact on Code Sec. 1411, and practitioners should track the status of this tax in relation to the fate of the Affordable Care Act.

¶ 104 Miscellaneous Itemized Deductions for Trusts and Estates[45]

The 2017 Tax Act (TJCA)[46] eliminates the miscellaneous deduction for individuals, which in turn eliminates that portion of deductions for trusts and estates deemed to be subject to the 2% floor under Code Sec. 67(a).[47] Deductions available to an estate or trust for miscellaneous fees and expenses (including investment advisory fees) are discussed in detail in Chapter 6, ¶ 608. This topic has received a good amount of attention in recent years, and is now settled with the promulgation of regulations.[48] The regulations clarify how costs, such as investment advisory and

---

[45] The author would like to recognize the contribution of Sharon L. Klein, Managing Director of Family Office Services & Wealth Strategies at Wilmington Trust, NA, for analysis of the new regulations under Code Sec. 67.

[46] See supra footnote 1 (Tax Cuts and Jobs Act dated December 22, 2017).

[47] Code Sec. 67(g).

[48] Reg. § 1.67-4 issued May 9, 2014 (effective date January 1, 2015).

bundled fiduciary fees, incurred by estates and (non-grantor) trusts are exempt from the 2% floor for miscellaneous itemized deductions under Code Sec. 67(e). Notice 2011-37 extended the existing interim guidance providing that taxpayers were required to determine the portion of a "bundled fiduciary fee" that is subject to the 2% floor under Code Sec. 67 for taxable years that began before the publication of final regulations. A bundled fiduciary fee is likely most commonly utilized by a corporate fiduciary where multiple services are combined or bundled into one fiduciary fee, which might include some fees subject to the 2% floor, such as investment advisory, and others that are clearly not, such as trustee fees. The final regulations define the class of deductions allowed in computing the AGI of a trust or estate, as opposed to being potentially classified as "miscellaneous itemized deductions" subject to 2% of AGI under Code Sec. 67. The regulations provide that if a "bundled" fee is attributable both to costs that are subject to the 2% floor and costs that are not, the fee must be allocated between the two. However, if the bundled fee is not computed on an hourly basis, only the investment management component of the fee is subject to the 2% floor. To allocate a bundled fee between costs subject to the 2% floor and costs that are not, "any reasonable method" may be used, including determining the portion of a bundled fee allocable to investment advice.

Note that the exception for trusts and estates under Code Sec. 67(e) only applies to deductions that could not have been incurred if the property were held by an individual. If the exception under Code Sec. 67(e) does not apply, perhaps because of an "unbundled" portion, then the general rule under Code Sec. 67(a) applies, and the deduction is eliminated under new Code Sec. 67(g) titled "Suspension for taxable years 2018 through 2025" enacted by the TCJA.[49]

¶ 105 Passive Activity Losses and Material Participation for Fiduciaries and Beneficiaries[50]

The topic of material participation of estates and trusts has been evolving since Code Sec. 469 was enacted in 1986, and more so recently with the promulgation of Code Sec. 1411 regarding the tax on net investment income. The Department of Treasury has requested guidance from practitioners with regard to Treasury Regulation 1.469-5T(g), which remains reserved for rules on the "material participation of estates and trusts."[51] Generally, Code Sec. 469 prevents certain taxpayers, including estates and trusts, from deducting losses from passive activities against positive sources of income, such as salary and investment income. Under Code Sec. 469, a passive activity is a trade or business in which the taxpayer does not materially participate[52] or a rental activity.[53] Although the Treasury Regulations provide extensive guidance as to what constitutes material participation by an individual under Code Sec. 469, those regulations include no rules for estates or trusts. Moreover, despite the passage of nearly thirty years since the enactment of

---

[49] P.L 115-97.
[50] The author would like to recognize the contribution of Richard L. Dees of McDermott Will & Emery for input on passive activity losses and the application to trusts and estates.
[51] Fed. Reg. Vol. 78, No. 231, p. 72393 (Dec. 2, 2013).
[52] Code Sec. 469(c)(1).
[53] Code Sec. 469(c)(2).

Code Sec. 469, there exists only a brief discussion of the topic in the legislative history[54] and two published cases, *Frank Aragona Trust v. Commissioner*[55] and *Mattie Carter Trust v. United States*.[56] There is little authoritative guidance on fiduciary material participation for purposes of Code Sec. 469.

Furthermore, the application of Code Sec. 1411 to the taxpayer's "net investment income," including income from a passive activity, has alerted the government and motivated commentators to acknowledge the need for guidance. It is generally accepted that such guidance should be provided in new Code Sec. 469 regulations, rather than in the Code Sec. 1411 regulations.

Perhaps the most important consideration in drafting regulations in this area for estates and trusts is the identification of whose participation is relevant to determine whether a trust or estate materially participates in a trade or business or related activity. The legislative history identifies the participation of the fiduciary of the trust or estate as relevant in determining whether the entity's income or loss is active or passive. Once the fiduciary is identified, is it important to determine whether that person's actual title (just a trustee, or a trustee and beneficiary, or a trustee and an officer of the trade or business) makes a difference, or whether actual discretionary decision-making power over the trade or business of the trust or estate is the relevant issue. Alternatively, is the trust beneficiary's material participation relevant?[57] Or should the material participation rules apply when an event (such as an individual's death) results in a potential change in tax status or the identity of the taxpayer? Resolution of these issues will be an important part of any written determination by the Treasury.

Note that the Trump Administration has asked Treasury Secretary Steven Mnuchin to review significant tax regulations issued in 2016 to determine if any of them impose an undue financial burden on American taxpayers, add undue complexity, or exceed statutory authority. Given this rather comprehensive review, it is unlikely practitioners will see new guidance regarding the passive loss rules in the short term.

¶ 106 Distributing Capital Gains in Distributable Net Income[58]

Gains from sale or exchange of capital assets are generally excluded from distributable net income to the extent that such gains are allocated to principal. The regulations under Treas. Reg. 1.643(a)-3(a) provide that capital gains are ordinarily excluded from distributable net income. However, the regulations under Treas. Reg. 1.643(a)-3(b) specifically acknowledge that capital gains may be allocated to distributable net income under: (1) a state unitrust statute, (2) when allocated to

---

[54] S. Rep. No. 313, 99th Cong., 2d Sess. 735 & n. 287, reprinted at 1986-3 CB 735.

[55] 142 TC No 9 (Mar. 27, 2014).

[56] 256 FSupp2d 536 (N.D. Tex. 2003).

[57] Under the QSST rules, because the beneficiary is treated as the tax owner of the S corporation, the focus is only on the beneficiary's material participation. Under the ESBT rules, because the trust always pays the tax on the S corporation income, the focus is only on the trustee's material participation. Thus, the S corporation rules consistently focus on the identity of the taxpayer to determine whether the income is active or passive. On the other hand, when income from a partnership interest held by a trust is distributed to a beneficiary, the beneficiary pays the tax on that income.

[58] The author would like to recognize the contribution of Gregory V. Gadarian of Gadarian & Cacy, PLLC for input on distributing gains in DNI and the application to trusts.

corpus but treated consistently by the fiduciary on the trust's books, records, and tax returns as part of a distribution to a beneficiary, or (3) when allocated to corpus but actually distributed to the beneficiary or utilized by the fiduciary in determining the amount that is distributed or required to be distributed to a beneficiary. An allocation of capital gains to income will generally be respected if the allocation is made either pursuant to the terms of the governing instrument and applicable local law, or pursuant to a reasonable and impartial exercise of a discretionary power granted to the fiduciary by applicable local law or by the governing instrument, if not prohibited by applicable local law. This is a trend among certain states that have amended local law (North Carolina and Alaska) or are considering changes (Arizona and New York).[59]

¶ 107 State Fiduciary Income Taxation for Resident and Nonresident Trusts

In addition to Federal fiduciary income taxation, trusts are also subject to a particular *state's* income tax regime, if such state imposes a state fiduciary income tax. If a trust is determined to be a "resident" of a particular state, that state will tax all of the trust's income (potentially forever). Alternatively, if the trust is not determined to be a resident as to a particular state, then various states may apportion the tax based on only that amount of income attributed to such state.

The determination of whether the trust will be treated as a resident trust, and thereby subject a trust to full state taxation, is based on the level of contacts that exist with the state.[60] Five commonly reviewed contacts include: (1) contacts with the decedent or decedent's estate that gave rise to the testamentary trust, (2) contacts with the state by the grantor who created an inter vivos trust, (3) contact through the ongoing administration of the trust, (4) contacts with the trustee of the trust, and (5) contacts with the beneficiary of the trust. Under one or more of these factors, a trust may be deemed a statutory resident, and thereby subject to resident state taxation. See Chapter 15 generally, and ¶ 1504 for factors states apply to determine state fiduciary taxation in a quick reference "Summary Chart of State Fiduciary Income Tax Contacts."

Two cases of recent significance discussed in Chapter 15 include *Bank of America*[61] and *Kaestner*.[62] In *Bank of America v. Massachusetts Department of Revenue*,[63] the question was whether the bank qualified as an inhabitant of the state subject to the state fiduciary income tax because the bank served as trustee or co-

---

[59] *See* North Carolina General Statute § 36C-8-816(16) regarding specific powers of trustee. "Without limiting the authority conferred by G.S. 36C-8-815, a trustee may: ... (16) Exercise elections with respect to federal, state, and local taxes including, but not limited to, considering discretionary distributions to a beneficiary as being made from capital gains realized during the year"; Alaska § 13.36.109 (29): "Except as otherwise provided by this chapter, in addition to the powers conferred by the terms of the trust, a trustee may perform all actions necessary to accomplish the proper management, investment, and distribution of the trust property, including the power ... (29) to consider discretionary distributions to a benefici- ary as being made from capital gains realized during the year."

[60] The issue of resident state taxation was most recently considered in Illinois under the decision of *Linn v. Department of Revenue*, 2 NE3d 1203 (Ill. App. Ct. 2013), as well as in Pennsylvania under the decision *McNeil v. Commonwealth*, 67 A3d 185 (Pa. Commw. Ct. 2013), both 2013 decisions, and both discussed below.

[61] *Bank of Am. v. Mass. Dep't of Revenue*, 474 Mass 702 (2016). *See* Chapter 15, ¶ 1511

[62] *Kaestner v. N.C. Dept. of Revenue*, 777 SE2d 61 (N.C. 2015). *See* Chapter 15, ¶ 1517.

[63] 474 Mass 702 (2016).

trustee on 34 inter vivos trusts, and maintained 200 branch offices. Ultimately, the Massachusetts Supreme Court looked to how much trustee administration of the trusts took place within Massachusetts and concluded that the trusts were subject to fiduciary income tax in Massachusetts because of the connections with the state.

In *Kimberly Rice Kaestner 1992 Family Trust v. North Carolina Department of Revenue*[64] North Carolina imposed state fiduciary income tax on income earned and accumulated by an out-of-state trust. The lower court determined and the appellate court affirmed that the North Carolina statute was unconstitutional because of the lack of minimum contacts required under the Due Process Clause of the Constitution. The court noted that the trust lacked a physical presence in North Carolina because it did not custody assets nor did it maintain records in North Carolina – the only connection between the trust and North Carolina was the residence of the beneficiary.[65]

¶ 108 Trust Charitable Deduction for Contributions by Pass-Through Entities

Generally, the governing instrument of a trust must give the trustee the authority to make charitable contributions in order for a trust to claim a charitable deduction under Code Sec. 642(c) for contributions made directly by the trust. However, a trust may claim a deduction for its distributive share of a charitable contribution made by a partnership from the partnership's gross income even though the trust's governing instrument does not authorize the trustee to make charitable contributions.[66] In the case of a trust's investment in a partnership, the partnership may make a charitable contribution from the partnership's gross income, and that income is never available to the trust. For federal tax purposes, however, the trust must take into account its distributive share of the partnership's income, gain, loss, deductions (including charitable contributions), and credits. Under these circumstances, a trust's deduction for its distributive share of a charitable contribution made by a partnership will be allowed even if the trust's governing instrument does not authorize the trustee to make charitable contributions.

¶ 109 FATCA and Developments Regarding Foreign Trusts[67]

Treasury and the IRS issued final regulations on January 17, 2013, regarding the Foreign Account Tax Compliance Act (FATCA).[68] Congress passed FATCA on March 18, 2010, in an effort to curb perceived tax abuses by U.S. persons with offshore bank accounts and investments. Subsequent to the issuance of the final regulations, Treasury and the IRS have issued several correcting amendments to the final regulations, notices, revenue procedures, and announcement in an effort to

---

[64] 777 SE2d 61 (N.C. 2015), aff'd, 789 SE2d 645 (N.C. Ct. App. 2016).

[65] *Quill Corp. v. North Dakota*, 504 US 298 (1992), and *International Shoe Co. v. Washington*, 326 US 310 (1945). *See* Chapter 15 generally and ¶ 1508 in particular regarding the *Quill* analysis.

[66] Rev. Rul. 2004-5, 2004-1 CB 295.

[67] The author would like to recognize the contribution of Rodney Read of Baker McKenzie LLP, for input on the current developments affecting trusts and estates.

[68] *See* Reg. §§ 1.1471-0 through 1.1474-7, T.D. 9610 (Jan. 17, 2013).

provide comprehensive guidelines for the application of the FATCA withholding and reporting rules to foreign trusts.

FATCA generally requires that foreign financial institutions (FFI) and certain other non-financial foreign entities (NFFE) report on the foreign assets held by their U.S. person account holders or be subject to withholding on withholdable payments. An FFI will be subject to 30% FATCA withholding by the payor on withholdable payments (primarily U.S.-source income) made to the FFI unless it enters into an FFI agreement with the United States in which the FFI is obligated to comply with certain requirements (e.g., registration, due diligence, and reporting).

.01 Look to Any Applicable IGAs

Several countries have entered into inter-governmental agreements (IGAs), or are treated as if they have an IGA in effect, with the U.S. as an alternative or supplement to the FATCA regime.

.02 Classify Trust in Accordance with Final Regulations

The final regulations define an FFI as any "financial institution," and generally identify four groups that are considered financial institutions: depository institutions, custodial institutions, investment entities, and insurance companies. Because most trusts use some form of professional money management—sometimes directly—when the trustee is a bank or trust company and sometimes indirectly when the trustee is an individual but hires an investment adviser or money manager, the ultimate conclusion is that most trusts will be categorized as "professionally managed" and therefore as FFIs.

.03 Determine and Comply with Reporting Requirements

The final regulations and subsequently published guidance allow a trust categorized as an FFI to avoid a 30% withholding tax on withholdable payments by entering into an FFI agreement and performing due diligence to identify and report information about its U.S. settlor and/or certain of its U.S. beneficiaries. The trust may be able to avoid entering into a formal FFI agreement if it qualifies as an owner-documented FFI. An owner-documented FFI is an investment entity with a withholding agent that is a U.S. financial institution or participating FFI that agrees to satisfy the reporting requirements on behalf of the FFI.

The key effective dates for foreign trusts subject to FATCA were July 1, 2014 when required withholding began and March 31, 2015 when the first information report was due.

¶ 110 Consistency of Basis Reporting Rules[69]

The consistency of basis rules were included in the Surface Transportation and Veterans Health Care Choice Improvement Act of 2015[70] (the "Act"). The Act created new Code Sec. 1014(f) and Code Sec. 6035 which implement new basis consistency rules for taxpayers acquiring property from a decedent. These rules

---

[69] The author would like to recognize the contribution of George D. Karibjanian of Franklin, Karibjanian & Law, PLLC, Hannah W. Mensch of Ehrenkranz Partners LP, and, Stacey Delich-Gould of The Capital Group Companies, Inc. for their input on the consistency of basis reporting rules.

[70] P.L. 114-41, 129 Stat. 443.

impose additional information reporting requirements for executors. The Act also included new Code Sec. 6662(b)(8), which incorporates the basis consistency rules into the accuracy-related penalties provisions, and also provides that certain returns and statements are subject to the return penalty provisions of sections 6721 and 6722. Thus, the failure to comply with these requirements and to provide the necessary returns and statements may subject the estate to penalties, and the time period has passed for adoption and retroactivity purposes.

The Regulations enacted under these provisions are presently in proposed form, and were expected to be finalized soon. However, as noted above, on April 21, 2017, the Trump Administration released a Presidential Executive Order on Identifying and Reducing Tax Regulatory Burdens, which directs Treasury Secretary Steven Mnuchin to review significant tax regulations issued in 2016 to determine if any of them impose an undue financial burden on American taxpayers, add undue complexity, or exceed statutory authority. Given this rather comprehensive review, it is unlikely practitioners will see new guidance regarding consistency of basis from Treasury in the short term. However, the Priority Guidance Plan lists "Regulations under §§ 1014(f) and 6035 regarding basis consistency between estate and person acquiring property from decedent." The "reporting" portion of the proposed and temporary regulations was published on March 4, 2016 (relating to Form 8971 and its Schedule A), and is widely viewed as burdensome and controversial. These regulations needed to be finalized by January 31, 2017 in order to be retroactive under section 7805(b)(2) and they have not been so finalized.

Chapter 2

Decedent's Final Income Tax Return

¶ 201 Introduction
¶ 202 Determining Whether a Return Must Be Filed
¶ 203 Filing the Final Returns
¶ 204 Gathering Financial Information
¶ 205 Form to File
¶ 206 Filing of Joint Returns
¶ 207 Due Date of Final Return
¶ 208 Payment of Tax
¶ 209 Signing the Return
¶ 210 Where Return Should Be Filed
¶ 211 When a Refund Is Due
¶ 212 Special Benefit for Surviving Spouse
¶ 213 Continuation of Estimated Tax Payments
¶ 214 Personal Exemptions on Final Return
¶ 215 Dependency Exemptions
¶ 216 Income Taxes of Deceased Armed Forces Members and Terrorist Victims — *Exclude*
¶ 217 Tax Obligations for Foreign Assets — *Exclude*

¶ 201 Introduction

Individuals die, but liability for their unpaid taxes does not. The responsibility for filing a decedent's last final income tax return and for paying (or claiming a refund for) income taxes on the decedent's behalf fall to the decedent's personal representative (i.e., the executor, administrator, or anyone who is in charge of the decedent's property).[1] In fact, the personal representative may have to file two income tax returns, depending, in part, on when the decedent died. If the death occurred after the close of the tax year, but before the decedent filed a return for that year, a return for the year just closed must be filed. That return is not the decedent's last return; rather, it is treated as a regular return.

> **Example 1:** Decedent, a calendar-year taxpayer, died on April 1, 20X1, without having prepared her income tax return for the previous year (20X0). Her personal representative must prepare and file her return for the previous

---
[1] Code Sec. 6012(b)(1); Reg. § 1.6012-3(b)(1).

year 20X0 (or request an extension of time to do so) by April 15, 20X1. Moreover, her personal representative must prepare and file the decedent's final return for 20X1, the first three months of the year of Decedent's death (January 1 through and including April 1), by April 15, 20X2, the year following her death.

When an individual dies, a series of questions must be asked to determine how tax matters will be handled. Below is a checklist of some items to consider:

- ☐ Does an income tax return even have to be filed? Income tax returns do not have to be filed for taxpayers whose income is below the standard deduction and the personal exemption. See ¶ 202.
- ☐ If an income tax return must be filed, who will prepare and file it? A personal representative must be designated. See ¶ 203.
- ☐ Has the personal representative collected all of the information and documents needed to prepare the return? All sources of income, deductible items, etc. must be found. See ¶ 204.
- ☐ What forms must be filed? In addition to the standard Form 1040, accompanying Schedules and Forms may be required. See ¶ 205.
- ☐ If the decedent was married, can (and should) a joint return be filed? If the surviving spouse has remarried before the end of the relevant tax year, this option will not be available. If a joint return is allowed, computations must be made to determine which type of filing would result in the greatest tax savings. See ¶ 206.
- ☐ Does the personal representative have enough time to collect the necessary documentation, adequately prepare the return, and file it by the due date? If not, the representative should ask for an extension of time to file the return. See ¶ 207.
- ☐ Are taxes due? If they are not paid, the personal representative may be personally liable for them. See ¶ 1401.
- ☐ Is a refund due? Form 1310 (Statement of Person Claiming Refund Due a Deceased Taxpayer) must be filed with the final return if a refund is being claimed by someone other than the surviving spouse. See ¶ 211.

¶ 202 Determining Whether a Return Must Be Filed

One of the duties of the personal representative (executor, administrator, or anyone else in charge of the decedent's property) of a decedent's estate is to file the decedent's final income tax return and any returns not filed for the preceding years. If an individual died after the close of the tax year, but before the return for that year was filed, the personal representative must file the return for the year before death and the final return for the year in which death occurred. If a personal representative has not been named in the will or assigned by the court, the surviving spouse may be able to file a joint return (see ¶ 206).

.01 Filing Requirements: Standard Deduction

The decedent's final income tax return covers the tax year ending with the date of the decedent's death. The income, age, and filing status of the decedent at the time of death generally determine the filing requirements.

An income tax return for the decedent must be filed if the decedent's gross income *equals or exceeds* the sum of the standard deduction, any additional standard deduction (for individuals over 65 or blind), and the personal exemption, if applicable, before December 31, 2017.[2] The amounts are adjusted each year as published by the IRS in a Revenue Procedure.

Beginning in 2018, there is no personal exemption, and the standard deduction is generally doubled. As a result of the Tax Cuts and Jobs Act ("TCJA")[3], effective January 1, 2018, personal exemptions are eliminated, and the standard deduction is increased to $12,000 for single individuals, $18,000 for head of household, and $24,000 for individuals who are married filing jointly.[4]

Further, exemption amounts for Alternative Minimum Tax are also reflected in the Revenue Procedure along with the graduated phaseout of those amounts.[5] In addition, for taxable years beginning in 2013, ATRA imposed overall limitations to Itemized Deductions under Code Sec. 68(b) that must be taken into account.[6]

.02 Gross Income Threshold

The filing test applies to *gross* income. Thus, items that are not included in the statutory meaning of that term, such as tax-exempt interest, are not to be taken into consideration. However, for filing-test purposes, gross income includes gain from the sale of a principal residence as well as foreign-earned income and housing cost amounts otherwise excludable under Code Sec. 911 relating to U.S. citizens or residents living abroad.[7]

If the decedent was a cash-basis taxpayer, only those assets actually or constructively received before death are included in gross income in the decedent's final return. See ¶ 302.

.03 Dependents

If the decedent was a dependent of another taxpayer, the requirement to file a return is conditioned on (1) the amount of the decedent's earned or unearned income, (2) the amount of the decedent's gross income, and (3) whether the decedent was single or married, 65 or older, or blind.

.04 Additional Taxes Due

A return may be required to be filed even if the decedent's gross income is *less* than his or her filing requirement amount (standard deduction) if the decedent owed other taxes, such as:

- Self-employment tax on net earnings from self-employment.
- Social Security tax on tips not reported to the employer.

---

[2] Code Sec. 6012(a); Reg. §§ 1.443-1(a)(2) and 1.6012-3(b)(1); Code Secs. 63 and 151(d).
[3] P.L. 115-97.
[4] Rev. Proc. 2018-18, 2018-10 IRB 392.
[5] Code Sec. 55(d).
[6] Rev. Proc. 2018-18, 2018-10 IRB 392, as introduced in Rev. Proc. 2013-15, 2013-5 IRB 444.
[7] Code Sec. 6012(c).

- Uncollected Social Security or railroad retirement tax on tips reported to the employer.
- Alternative Minimum Tax.
- Tax on an IRA or qualified retirement plan.
- Recapture tax on (1) an investment credit, (2) a low-income housing credit claimed in a previous year, or (3) the disposition of a home purchased with a federally subsidized mortgage.

.05 Refunds or Credits

Even if a decedent does not meet the above filing requirements, a return should be filed if income tax has been withheld or estimated tax has been paid. A refund may then be obtained (see ¶ 211). A return should also be filed if the earned income credit or some other refundable credit entitles the decedent to a refund. Refundable credits claimed by a taxpayer are treated as an overpayment of tax only to the extent such credits exceed the taxpayer's income tax liability after reduction by nonrefundable personal credits, the tax credits under Code Secs. 27 through 30C, business-related credits, any credit claimed under Code Sec. 53 for a prior year minimum tax liability and, after 2005, any credit claim under Code Sec. 54 on renewable energy bonds.[8]

.06 Form 1310 Claim for Refund

In general, persons claiming a refund due a deceased taxpayer must file Form 1310 (Statement of Person Claiming Refund Due a Deceased Taxpayer). Surviving spouses filing a joint return and court-appointed or certified personal representatives filing an original return for the decedent do not have to file Form 1310. In the latter case, the personal representative must attach to the return a copy of the court certificate showing his or her appointment.

¶ 203 Filing the Final Returns

Ordinarily, a decedent's last federal and state income tax returns are filed by the estate's executor or administrator (personal representative). Because the returns are for the decedent rather than for the estate, they are prepared and signed on the decedent's behalf. If an executor or administrator has not been appointed (e.g., when the estate is not probated), the returns are to be filed by some person charged with the disposition of the decedent's property (frequently the surviving spouse). The heirs could act jointly, or appoint one heir, to take charge of the estate for this purpose. Such parties must assume responsibility for filing the returns or they will be subject to penalties for willful neglect or tax evasion.

In the case of the death of a minor or mentally incapacitated person, the legal guardian (presumably the guardian of the estate if separate guardians of the estate and person were appointed) or conservator should file the last returns.

Final returns will need to be filed in each state where required by local law.

---

[8] Code Sec. 6401(b)(1).

¶ 204 Gathering Financial Information

Unless the personal representative was a close family member or business associate—and maybe even then—he or she will lack some knowledge, at least initially, of the decedent's financial affairs. These gaps in knowledge must be closed before preparing the decedent's income tax return. The personal representative will need to marshal all types of documents to create a full picture of the decedent's financial position. In addition to collecting paycheck stubs and other paperwork showing transactions occurring in the year of the decedent's death, the personal representative will have to research necessary documentation to prepare the income tax return. For example, to compute capital gains on the sale of the decedent's house in the year of the decedent's death, all other paperwork documenting the value of the house must be collected. With respect to the deduction for medical expenses, medical bills, perhaps covering the decedent's last illness, must be gathered together as well. These amounts may be deducted from income if they meet eligibility requirements and are paid within one year of a decedent's death to the extent that they exceed 10% of the decedent's adjusted gross income in 2014 and beyond.[9] If the decedent made any charitable gifts valued at $250 or more, deductibility will depend on proper written substantiation.[10]

> *Note:* There was a temporary exemption for individuals age 65 and older until December 31, 2016 (which has been extended under the 2017 TCJA). If an individual was 65 years or older, he or she could continue to deduct total medical expenses that exceed 7.5% of adjusted gross income through 2016. If the individual was married and only one of the spouses was age 65 or older, they could still deduct total medical expenses that exceeded 7.5% of adjusted gross income. This exemption was temporary. Beginning on January 1, 2017, the 10% threshold applies to all taxpayers, including those over age 65.

.01 Sources of Information

In general, the following items are among the important records that should be located and examined by the personal representative:

- ☐ Bank passbooks
- ☐ Certificates of deposit
- ☐ Savings bonds
- ☐ Stock certificates
- ☐ Financial statements
- ☐ Profit-sharing information
- ☐ Promissory notes
- ☐ Cancelled checks
- ☐ Checkbooks
- ☐ Income tax returns for the last several years
- ☐ All prior gift tax returns

---

[9] *See* ¶ 312.　　[10] *See* ¶ 411.

☐ Securities and brokers' statements

☐ Deeds, mortgages, etc.

Depending on how well (or poorly) the decedent's records were organized, the personal representative, with the assistance of the decedent's family, should be prepared to rummage through every room, closet, desk drawer, and "secret hiding place" of the decedent's home(s), and office, if appropriate, in search of the pertinent documents. This will have to be done, in any case, to identify and evaluate the decedent's assets for settlement of the estate, and the payment (if any) of estate, gift, and/or generation-skipping transfer taxes.

.02 Decedent's Tax Returns

The decedent's income tax returns for the last several years before death contain valuable information. These returns should list most income-producing assets and a wealth of other information about the decedent's financial affairs. Furthermore, other substantiating records are often kept in the vicinity of the tax returns.

If the returns are unavailable, a court appointed representative of an estate may request copies of a decedent's more recent income tax returns. The representative needs to file Form 56, Notice Concerning Fiduciary Relationship, along with a copy of the Letters of Office or Letters Testamentary to inform the IRS of the appointment and establish that the representative has a material interest to obtain the returns.[11] Form 4506, Request for Copy of Tax Return, can then be filed by the representative, along with the required fee. Processing time is approximately 60 days. The representative could request a transcript using Form 4506-T, but a transcript likely will not produce the information needed by the representative.

.03 Financial Institutions

The decedent's checkbook and file of cancelled checks for the previous year is another excellent source of information. Many individuals are doing their banking on-line, so the personal representative may be able to contact the decedent's bank to get copies of cancelled checks and bank statements. The personal representative should look for payments made for investments, insurance, debts, mortgages, medical expenses, tax payments, and safe-deposit box rental fees. The checkbook ledger may reveal the name of an accountant who may have prepared the decedent's prior tax returns.

The decedent's credit card statements may reflect repeated charges for the purchase of an item. For example, some term life insurance is purchased on a monthly basis through credit card charges.

The personal representative should also search the state treasurer's website in each state that the decedent has resided in the last ten years to determine whether there are any assets deemed to have been abandoned by the decedent that the personal representative can claim. Examples include odd-lots of stock or abandoned bank accounts.

---

[11] Code Sec. 6103(e).

.04 Insurance and Annuities

The National Association of Insurance Commissioners (NAIC) provides a national service to consumers with search capabilities to help them find a deceased person's lost life insurance policies and annuities. Consumer requests are encrypted and secured to maintain confidentiality. Participating insurers will compare submitted requests with available policyholder information and report all matches to state insurance departments through a locator. Companies will then contact beneficiaries or their authorized representatives. The NAIC can be accessed at www.naic.org.

.05 Monitor Mail

Monitoring the decedent's incoming mail is also a good idea for at least six months and possibly a full year after death if time constraints for filing permit. The personal representative should look for dividends, pension payouts, promissory note repayments, and bank or brokerage statements, among other things. Keep in mind that many statements are now electronic and "paperless" so monitoring the decedent's incoming e-mail is also a good idea.

.06 Safe Deposit Box

The personal representative must also locate and inventory the contents of the decedent's safe-deposit box(es), if any. This can be done by looking for a small flat key with a number imprinted on it among the decedent's personal belongings, or for a statement or a cancelled check for the yearly rental fee. If these cannot be found, and there is good reason to believe that safe-deposit boxes were rented, a canvas of banks and savings institutions will be necessary. The American Safe Deposit Association (TASDA), a national organization located in Franklin, Indiana, will canvas its over 2,000 member banks and savings institutions nationwide for boxes in the decedent's name or in an alias name.[12] As a result of the Patriot Act, a person may open a safe deposit box only at a bank in which the individual has an account, so contacting each bank where the decedent had an account to request a search is suggested.

Safe-deposit boxes are the usual receptacle for important papers such as deeds, stocks and bonds, and promissory notes. Ordinarily, the box will be opened only for the surviving joint tenant, or for the court-appointed personal representative. Even then, a representative of the state treasury department may have to be present to inventory the contents. A bank officer can help make the necessary arrangements.

¶ 205 Form to File

The final return of a decedent should be filed on Form 1040, which is the regular income tax return for an individual. All necessary supporting schedules (Schedules A, B, C, etc.) should be attached. Thus, for example, if the decedent had

---

[12] TASDA may be reached at P.O. Box 519, Franklin, IN 46131. The phone number is (317) 738-4432 and its e-mail address is TASDA1@aol.com. The cost is $75, plus $5 for each alias or variation in spelling of name, and the service is available only to personal representatives who provide written proof of their appointment, a certified copy of the death certificate, and a completed form provided by the organization.

been a farmer, Schedule F (Profit or Loss From Farming) would be attached to report the decedent's income from farming operations. If requirements are otherwise met, Form 1040A or Form 1040EZ may be filed instead of Form 1040.

If the decedent was a nonresident alien, Form 1040NR (U.S. Nonresident Alien Income Tax Return) must be filed.

¶ 206 Filing of Joint Returns

Generally, a joint return for a decedent and the decedent's surviving spouse (who has not remarried before the end of the year of the decedent's death) may be filed by the executor or administrator and the surviving spouse. The surviving spouse alone, however, may file the joint return if all of the following requirements are met:

- No return was made by the decedent for the tax year for which the joint return is made.
- No executor or administrator was appointed before the time the joint return was made.
- No executor or administrator was appointed before the last day prescribed for filing the return of the surviving spouse, including any extensions.[13]

It should be remembered that marriage is not the sole factor governing the filing of a joint return. Not only must the decedent and the surviving spouse have been married at the time of the decedent's death, but they must have had the same accounting period, both must have been U.S. citizens or residents for the tax year, and the surviving spouse must not have remarried before the close of the tax year in which the decedent died. The requirement that both spouses have the same accounting period means that their tax years must have begun on the same day and would have ended on the same day except for the death of the decedent.

An election to treat a nonresident alien individual as a resident of the United States for joint return purposes is terminated by the death of either spouse.[14] Such termination is effective as of the beginning of the first tax year of the surviving spouse following the year in which such death occurred unless the surviving spouse is a U.S. citizen or resident who is entitled to surviving spouse filing status. In the latter case, the termination is effective at the close of the last tax year for which such individual is entitled to the surviving spouse filing benefits (see ¶ 212).

> *Example 2:* Husband and wife, are on a calendar-year basis. Husband dies on September 15. If a joint return is filed, the return will cover husband's income and deductions for the period January 1 through September 15 and wife's income and deductions for the full calendar year.

No joint return may be filed when the tax year of either spouse is a fractional part of a year resulting from a change of accounting period.[15]

> *Example 3:* Husband and wife, make their returns on a calendar-year basis. Wife dies on May 16, and husband, thereafter, receives permission to

---

[13] Code Sec. 6013(a)(3); Reg. § 1.6013-1(d).
[14] Code Sec. 6013(g)(4).
[15] Code Sec. 6013(a)(2); Reg. § 1.6013-1(d)(2).

change his accounting period to a fiscal year beginning July 1. A joint return cannot be made under these circumstances.

.01 Disaffirmance of Joint Returns

Even though the surviving spouse complies with all of the conditions set forth above and files a valid joint return with the decedent, an executor or administrator who is subsequently appointed may disaffirm the joint return. Such a disaffirmance must be made within one year after the last day prescribed for filing the return of the surviving spouse, including any extensions. The disaffirmance is made by filing a separate return for the decedent. If a disaffirmance is made, the survivor's return will be considered to be the survivor's separate return. The tax will be computed on the basis of the joint return filed, with all the items properly includible in the return of the deceased spouse deleted from it.[16]

The executor or administrator of a deceased spouse does not necessarily have to disaffirm a joint return made by the survivor. However, in making this decision, certain factors should be considered. If the joint return is allowed to stand, the administrator may work out an agreement with the survivor under which a division of the joint tax may save money for the estate. On the other hand, when a separate return for the decedent is initially prepared, it may be found that the estate can save money by disaffirming the joint return and filing the prepared separate return. Generally, the executor or administrator and the surviving spouse will decide whether a joint return made by the survivor should be allowed to stand.

A joint return may be filed even when the decedent and the surviving spouse were not living together at the date of the decedent's death. However, a joint return cannot be filed if they were legally separated under a decree of divorce or separate maintenance on such date.[17]

.02 Change to Joint Return

If a separate return was originally filed for the decedent and the due date for filing the return has expired, a change to a joint return can be made only by the decedent's executor or administrator. Thus, when no executor or administrator has been appointed, a joint return cannot be filed.[18] In addition, a switch from a separate return to a joint return *cannot* be made if with respect to the tax year at issue:

- three years have passed from the last date prescribed by law for filing the return for such tax year (determined without regard to any extension of time granted to either spouse); or
- a notice of deficiency under Code Sec. 6212 was mailed to either spouse, and the spouse responded to the notice by filing a petition with the Tax Court within the time prescribed in Code Sec. 6213; or
- either spouse has commenced a suit in any court for the recovery of any part of the tax; or

---

[16] Reg. § 1.6013-1(d)(5).
[17] Code Sec. 6013(d)(2); Reg. § 1.6013-4(a).
[18] Code Sec. 6013(b); Reg. § 1.6013-2(a)(3).

- either spouse has entered into a closing agreement under Code Sec. 7121 for such tax year, or any civil or criminal case arising against either spouse with respect to such tax year was compromised under Code Sec. 7122.[19]

¶ 207 Due Date of Final Return

Death does not change the due date of an individual income tax return. Thus, unless an extension is requested or the deadline would fall on a Saturday, Sunday, or legal holiday, the final return of a decedent must be filed on or before the 15th day of the fourth month following the close of the 12-month period that began on the first day of the tax year in which the decedent died.[20] For a calendar-year decedent, this means that the final return is due on or before April 15 following the close of the calendar year in which he or she died. If the due date falls on a Saturday, Sunday, or legal holiday, the return may be filed on the next succeeding day that is not a Saturday, Sunday, or legal holiday.

.01 Extensions for Income Tax Returns

A taxpayer can obtain an automatic six-month extension to file Form 1040, 1040A, 1040EZ, 1040NR or 1040NR-EZ by filing a timely and properly completed Form 4868 (Application for Automatic Extension of Time to File U.S. Individual Income Tax Return) and paying the balance of the estimated tax for the year.[21] The extension application must be filed on or before the regular due date for the return. The automatic extension provisions extend the time for filing the return only; they do not extend the time for payment of the tax. Thus, interest will be due on any unpaid portion of the final tax. However, the late payment penalty will not apply when the balance of the tax still due on the final return is no greater than 10% of the total final tax and the balance due is remitted with the final return.[22]

.02 Longer Extension of Time for Form 1040

The IRS can grant a reasonable extension of time for filing any return, declaration, statement or other document. The extension cannot exceed six months, unless the taxpayer is abroad. As noted above, the representative can receive an automatic six-month extension for filing a decedent's income tax return by requesting the extension on Form 4868.

.03 Form 709 Gift Tax Return

If the representative files Form 4868, a six-month extension of time to file a decedent's United States Gift (and Generation-Skipping Transfer) Tax Return, Form 709, is automatic to October 15. Alternatively, the representative may file Form 8892 to extend time to file Form 709, but not for an individual's income tax returns.

.04 Form 706 Estate Tax Return

An executor can receive up to a six-month extension for filing the United States Estate (and Generation-Skipping Transfer) Tax Return, Form 706 (the "estate tax return"), upon a showing of good cause. The application for the extension is filed on

---

[19] Code Sec. 6013(b)(2)(A)-(D).
[20] Reg. § 1.6072-1(b).
[21] Temp. Reg. § 1.6081-4T.
[22] Reg. § 301.6651-1(c)(3).

Form 4768 (Application for Extension of Time to File a Return and/or Pay U.S. Estate (and Generation-Skipping Transfer) Taxes).

Discretionary extensions may also be granted for gift tax returns, employee and pension benefit plan returns, partnership returns, fiduciary returns and information returns. However, extensions cannot be granted for withholding tax returns by employers.

.05 Form 8971 and the Consistency of Basis Rules

As discussed in greater detail under ¶ 110, Consistency of Basis Reporting Rules, the basis consistency provisions for property received from a decedent provide that a beneficiary's basis of property acquired from a decedent will be no higher than the finally determined estate tax values as provided under new Section 1014(f).The information is reported on Form 8971 (Information Regarding Beneficiaries Acquiring Property from a Decedent).

A personal representative or other person required to file Form 706 or Form 706-NA under Sections 6018(a) and 6018(b), beginning after July 2015, is required to file Form 8971 with attached Schedule A with the IRS and to provide each beneficiary listed on the Form 8971 with that beneficiary's Schedule A. Form 8971 is not required when (1) the gross estate plus adjusted taxable gifts is less than the basic exclusion amount; (2) Forms 706-QDT, 706-CE, and 706-GS(D) are filed; (3) the estate tax return is filed solely to make an allocation or election respecting the generation-skipping transfer tax; or (4) the estate tax return is filed solely to elect the deceased spouse's unused exclusion (DSUE) amount.

Penalties may be imposed if the required information statements are not furnished to the IRS and to estate beneficiaries.[23]

¶ 208 Payment of Tax

The tax shown due on the decedent's final income tax return usually must be paid in full when the return is filed. However, if no deduction or exclusion is claimed in connection with working abroad, and taxable income for the decedent's final tax year was less than $100,000 and consisted of wages, salary, tips, interest, dividends, taxable Social Security benefits, unemployment compensation, IRA distributions, pensions, and annuities only, and the taxpayer does not itemize deductions, the person filing the return may elect to have the IRS compute the tax due.[24]

As noted above, persons claiming a refund due a deceased taxpayer must file Form 1310 (Statement of Person Claiming Refund Due a Deceased Taxpayer). Most states have a state version of Form 1310 as well. Surviving spouses filing a joint return and court-appointed or certified personal representatives filing an original return for the decedent do not have to file Form 1310. In the latter case, the personal representative must attach to the return a copy of the court certificate showing his or her appointment. However, a surviving spouse not filing a joint return, or, a personal representative filing an amended return would be required to file a Form 1310. See also ¶ 211, When a Refund Is Due, for more detail.

---

[23] Code Secs. 6721 and 6722. [24] Reg. § 1.6014-2.

¶ 209 Signing the Return

If a return is required and an executor or administrator has been appointed, that person must sign the return. This may be done, for instance, as follows: "John Smith, Administrator of the Estate of Harry Roe, Deceased," or "John Doe, Executor of the Last Will and Testament of John Brown, Deceased."

If no legal representative has been appointed, the surviving spouse should sign the return as the taxpayer and write in the signature area "Filing as surviving spouse." The filer of the return should write "Deceased" after the decedent's name and indicate the date of death in the name and address space. The word "DECEASED," the decedent's name, and the date of death must also be written across the top of the return.

If the final return is a joint return (see ¶ 206) and an executor or administrator has been appointed, both the executor or administrator and the surviving spouse must sign the return. The surviving spouse should write "Filing as surviving spouse" in the area for signing the return.

¶ 210 Where Return Should Be Filed

In general, a decedent's final return may be mailed to the IRS Center for the area in which the person filing it lives. A hand-carried return may be filed with any District Director's Office within the filer's district.

However, if the decedent was a nonresident alien for whom Form 1040NR (U.S. Nonresident Alien Income Tax Return) must be filed, Form 1040NR should be filed with the IRS Service Center, Austin, TX 73301-0215, U.S.A. If enclosing a payment, Form 1040NR should be filed with the Internal Revenue Service, P.O. Box 1303, Charlotte, NC 28201-1303, U.S.A.

¶ 211 When a Refund Is Due

If the final return of a decedent shows that a refund is due, and the person claiming the refund is not a surviving spouse, Form 1310 (Statement of Person Claiming Refund Due a Deceased Taxpayer) must be filed with the final return. Form 1310 is not to be used for claiming a refund of income taxes that have been paid on a previously filed return.

A claim for refund of previously paid income taxes is to be made on Form 1040X (Amended U.S. Individual Income Tax Return). A taxpayer not otherwise required to file a return may obtain a refund of non-refunded backup withholding by filing a Form 843 (Claim for Refund and Request for Abatement) for the quarter in which the tax was erroneously withheld.[25]

The Code Sec. 6511 statute of limitations period applicable to refund claims may be suspended ("tolled") during any period that an individual is "financially disabled."[26] An individual is financially disabled if the individual is under a medically determinable mental or physical impairment that (1) can be expected to result in death or which has lasted or can be expected to last for a continuous period of not

---

[25] Rev. Proc. 84-80, 1984-2 CB 758. [26] Code Sec. 6511(h).

less than one year, and (2) renders the person unable to manage his or her financial affairs. The tolling of the statute of limitations, however, does not apply for any period during which the taxpayer's spouse or another person is authorized to act on behalf of the individual in financial matters. Thus, if the surviving spouse is not financially disabled, regardless of the capacity of the decedent before his or her death, the limitations period will not be tolled.

The U.S. Supreme Court has held that the limitations period cannot be equitably tolled. The high court reversed a decision of the U.S. Court of Appeals for the Ninth Circuit that applied equitable tolling principles to permit a decedent's estate to recover, several years after the limitations period had expired, income tax overpayments made by a senile taxpayer.[27]

¶ 212 Special Benefit for Surviving Spouse

A surviving spouse may use the joint return tax rates for the two tax years following the year of death of the deceased spouse. But such rates can be used only if the surviving spouse maintains as a home a household that, for the entire tax year, is the principal place of abode of the survivor's dependent child, stepchild, or foster child.[28] Furthermore, the surviving spouse must not have remarried and must have been entitled to file a joint return with the deceased spouse for the year of death, but the fact that a joint return was not actually filed for such year is immaterial.

It should be emphasized that the "surviving spouse" provision merely makes the joint return tax rates available; it does not authorize the surviving spouse to file a joint return or claim any personal exemptions (prior to December 31, 2017) other than for dependents.

¶ 213 Continuation of Estimated Tax Payments

The IRS issued final regulations regarding the treatment of joint estimated tax payments under Code Sec. 6654. These regulations clarify and adopt additional instructions for determining estimated tax payments and additional guidance for nonresident aliens that are required to make estimated tax payments. The IRS has clarified that married taxpayers may make a joint estimated tax payment, even if they are living separate and apart.[29] Joint estimated payments are not allowed if: (1) there is a decree of separate maintenance or divorce; (2) the married taxpayers have different tax years; or (3) the taxpayer's spouse is a non resident alien (including a bona fide resident of Puerto Rico or U.S. possession to which Code Sec. 931 applies for the entire tax year), unless an election under Code Sec. 6013(g) or (h) is in effect.

Joint estimated payments are based on the aggregate taxable income. In the event that estimated self-employment taxes are required, the amount of estimated self-employment tax is based on the separate income of that individual. If, after making a joint estimated tax payment, the spouses decide to file separate returns, they may allocate the estimated payment amount in any manner upon which they

---

[27] *M. Brockamp*, SCt, 97-1 USTC ¶ 50,216, 519 US 347, rev'g CA-9, 95-2 USTC ¶ 50,551, 67 F3d 260.

[28] Code Sec. 2(a); Reg. § 1.2-2.

[29] Reg. § 1.6654-2(e)(5)(i).

both agree.[30] If they cannot agree, the payments will be allocated based on the ratio that the taxpayer's separate tax liability, including any self-employment tax, bears to the total tax liability of the taxpayer and spouse. This treatment is similar to the treatment provided under the removed Reg. § 1.6015(b)-1(b).

Similar treatment is given to the surviving taxpayer in the event that a joint estimated tax payment is made and the spouse dies during the tax year.[31] The taxpayer can continue to make estimated payments in the year of death based on the aggregate total income if they reasonably believe they will be filing a joint return. The self-employment exception still applies here; each taxpayer must pay estimated self-employment tax based on their income only. In the event the surviving taxpayer and the estate representative decide to file separate returns, the allocation rules as outlined above apply. This guidance is similar to removed Reg. § 1.6015(b)-1(c).

Clarification of how to determine the amount of estimated tax is provided.[32] The taxpayers must assume that their income stream will remain constant throughout the year when determining the amount of income that will be taxable. This means that, if dividends, interest, rents or royalties have been paid on a consistent basis for a number of years and the taxpayer has no reason to believe a change will occur, these amounts must be included in income when determining estimated income tax payments. The rule of each taxpayer being responsible for the determination of their estimated self-employment tax remains, except that the estimate must reflect the best information available at the time the estimated payment is due.

.01 Estimated Tax Liability of Estate

Although no estimated taxes are required on behalf of a deceased individual, if the decedent's estate stays open for more than two years after the date of death, estimated taxes will be required of the estate from that time until the time when the estate is closed. These estimated payment requirements are discussed in greater detail at ¶ 507.01.

¶ 214 Personal Exemptions on Final Return

All of a decedent's personal exemptions (prior to December 31, 2017) may be taken on the decedent's final return. Furthermore, the exemption amount is not required to be prorated even though the tax year may have been cut short by death.[33] Thus, for example, if a calendar-year individual dies on June 30, full personal exemptions are allowed on the decedent's final return even though the decedent was alive for only one-half of the tax year.

As indicated above in ¶ 202, the amount of a decedent's available personal exemption is typically published in a Revenue Procedure issued in the year of death.[34] As a result of ATRA, personal exemptions are phased out as indicated in ¶ 202 and the referenced Revenue Procedure and pursuant to the 2017 TCJA,

---

[30] Reg. § 1.6654-2(e)(5)(ii).
[31] Reg. § 1.6654-2(e)(7).
[32] Reg. § 1.6654-5.

[33] Reg. § 1.443-1(a)(2).
[34] *See, e.g.,* Rev. Proc. 2013-35, 2013-47 IRB 537, for tax year 2014, where the standard personal exemptions were published in Rev. Proc. 2013-35.

personal exemptions have been eliminated beginning in 2018. The standard deduction is increased for persons over the age of 65 and/or blind persons[35] and those amounts are also included in the applicable Revenue Procedure.[36]

If the decedent was married at the time of death and a joint return is filed by the surviving spouse, either alone or with the decedent's executor or administrator (see ¶ 206), both the decedent's and the surviving spouse's exemptions and the standard deduction available for married couples may be claimed on the joint return. If the executor or administrator files a separate return on behalf of the decedent, no personal exemption for the surviving spouse may be taken on the decedent's return unless the surviving spouse did not have gross income and was not the dependent of a person other than the decedent. Likewise, if the surviving spouse files a separate return, no personal exemption for the decedent may be claimed on that return unless the decedent did not have gross income and was not the dependent of another person.

A surviving spouse who has no gross income and who remarries during the same calendar year of his or her spouse's death may be claimed as an exemption on both the final separate return of the deceased spouse and the separate return of the new spouse. However, if the surviving spouse files a joint return with the new spouse, the exemption can only be claimed on that return.[37]

¶ 215 Dependency Exemptions

Death does not change the rules for dependency exemptions[38] that may be taken on the decedent's final return prior to 2018. Thus, if the decedent furnished more than half of the support of a person otherwise qualifying as a dependent during the calendar year in which the tax year of the decedent began, an exemption for the dependent can be taken on the decedent's final return.

> *Example 4:* George supported his aged father, furnishing full support until the date of George's death on September 1. Assuming that George's support constituted more than half of the father's support for the calendar year, a dependency exemption for the father would be allowed on George's final return.
>
> However, if George died on April 1 and his brother, James, supported the father for the balance of the year, incurring a larger expense than George did during the first part of the year, James would be entitled to the dependency exemption for the father.
>
> If the support for the father were furnished equally by James and a sister, Helen, from April 1 on, and if neither George, James, nor Helen furnished over half of the father's support for the year, any one of them (including the executor or administrator on George's final return) could take the dependency exemption for the father if each of the other two executes Form 2120 (Multiple Support Declaration) and gives it to the one claiming the exemption. The

---

[35] The additional standard deduction for people who have reached age 65 or who are blind for 2018 is $1,300 for each married taxpayer or $1,600 for unmarried taxpayers.

[36] *Id. See also* Code Sec. 151(d).

[37] Rev. Rul. 71-159, 1971-1 CB 50.

[38] Code Sec. 68(b).

individual claiming the exemption would file the Form 2120 with his or her return. There is no limit on how many persons may aggregate their support to meet the more-than-50-percent test so long as each taxpayer alone could claim the dependency exemption except for the percentage test. However, the taxpayer claiming the exemption must have provided more than 10% of the dependent's support and filed a Multiple Support Declaration provided by each contributor of more than 10% of the dependent's support.

Regardless of the amount of support, no exemption would be allowed for the father if he had gross income above a certain amount, which amount is typically published in a Revenue Procedure at the end of the year for the following year.

Although, for the year of death, a taxpayer's death will not deprive a surviving spouse of any dependency exemptions, it may affect income, deductions, or credits. Therefore, in some cases, a working spouse may find it desirable to adjust withholding allowances by submitting a new Form W-4 (Employee's Withholding Allowance Certificate) to his or her employer.

¶ 216 Income Taxes of Deceased Armed Forces Members and Terrorist Victims

The tax liability of an Armed Forces member who dies while in active service or as a result of wounds, disease, or injury sustained in a combat zone is cancelled for the year of death and for any prior year ending on or after the first day of service in a combat zone.[39] The designation of an area as a combat zone is made by the President.[40] Forgiveness extends to the full calendar year in which the individual dies, not just to the death-shortened tax year.[41]

For qualifying military or civilian employees who die from wounds or injuries incurred outside the United States in a terroristic or military action (not including training exercises), income tax liability is excused for the year of death and for any tax year falling within the one-year period preceding the year of the injury that caused death. Effective for tax years ending on or after September 11, 2001, this provision is broadened to apply wherever the action takes place.[42]

The exemption from U.S. income tax applies to "specified terrorist victims": individuals who die from wounds or injuries incurred in the April 19, 1995, terrorist attack in Oklahoma City or the September 11, 2001, terrorist attacks, or individuals who die from an anthrax-related attack occurring on or after September 11, 2001, and before January 1, 2002.[43] These victims are entitled to a minimum benefit of $10,000. If the amount of tax not imposed under the relief provision is less than $10,000, the victim will be treated as having made a payment of $10,000 over the amount not imposed for the victim's last tax year.[44]

The IRS is authorized to issue regulations that would except from the income tax exemption the tax on certain death-related payments and payments that are

---

[39] Code Sec. 692(a)(1).
[40] Code Sec. 112.
[41] Reg. § 1.692-1(a).
[42] Code Sec. 692(c).
[43] Code Sec. 692(d).
[44] Code Sec. 692(d)(2).

made as a result of an action taken after the September 11, 2001, attacks. Specifically, the exemption would not apply to tax attributable to (1) deferred compensation paid after death, regardless of how death occurs and (2) amounts paid in the tax year because of an action taken after September 11, 2001, that would not have otherwise been taken.[45]

The exemption from income tax liability for members of the Armed Forces has been extended to any astronaut who dies in the line of duty after December 31, 2002.[46] This exemption applies to the astronauts who lost their lives in the space shuttle Columbia disaster on February 1, 2003. The income tax exemption applies to income tax liability for the year of death as well as the prior year.

If the tax of a prior year has been previously paid and the period for filing a claim has not ended, the tax paid may be claimed as a refund. If any tax is still due, it will be cancelled. The normal period provided under Code Sec. 6511(a) for filing a claim for credit or refund—three years from the time the return was filed or two years from the time the tax was paid, whichever ends later—is extended under Code Sec. 7508(a) by the amount of time served in a combat zone and the period of continuous hospitalization outside the United States from an injury received in a combat zone, plus the next 180 days, plus the unexpired portion of time for filing (or paying tax) that existed at the time when the decedent entered the combat zone. In addition to the above, any unpaid tax liabilities against the service member for years before service in a combat zone will be cancelled or abated.[47]

.01 Joint Returns

The above provisions apply only to the deceased service member's tax liability. If a joint return has been filed, the only tax affected is that portion of the joint tax equal to the same percentage that the tax on the service member's separate income bears to the combined tax on the separate incomes of the service member and his or her spouse. For years before the service member's entry into a combat zone, the abatement applies only to the amounts unpaid as of the date of the service member's death.[48]

If a service member and his or her spouse filed a joint declaration of estimated tax for the tax year ending with the service member's death, the estimated tax paid may be treated as the estimated tax of either of them, or may be divided between them, in such manner as the service member's legal representative and the spouse may agree. Should they agree to treat the estimated tax, or any portion thereof, as the estimated tax of the service member, the estimated tax so paid is to be credited or refunded as an overpayment for the tax year ending with the service member's death.[49]

The above allocation procedures given by Reg. § 1.692-1 apply to combat zone forgiveness under Code Sec. 692(a).[50] The IRS has ruled that they also apply in the case of terroristic or military action forgiveness under Code Sec. 692(c).[51] Moreo-

---

[45] Code Sec. 692(d)(3).
[46] Code Sec. 692(d)(5).
[47] Code Sec. 692(a)(2).
[48] Reg. § 1.692-1(b).
[49] Reg. § 1.692-1(c).
[50] Reg. § 1.692-1(a)(1).
[51] Rev. Rul. 78-1, 1978-1 CB 199, as amplified by Rev. Rul. 85-103, 1985-2 CB 176.

ver, the IRS will apply the allocation procedures in the case of "specified terrorist victims" under Code Sec. 692(d).[52]

.02 Missing in Action Status

Similar rules govern Armed Forces members who were declared missing in action and were subsequently determined to have died. In such case, the date of death for the abatement-of-tax provisions is the date on which a determination of death is made. The tax abatement for qualifying Vietnam service members and their spouses is permanent.[53]

.03 Procedure for Claiming Relief

The procedures for claiming tax relief under Code Sec. 692(a) and (c) are set forth in Rev. Proc. 2004-26, 2004-1 CB 890. Representatives of employees who qualify for the benefits of Code Sec. 692(c), and for whom no Form 1040, U.S. Individual Income Tax Return, has been filed, may claim those benefits, or claim a refund of withholding or estimated tax payments, by filing a Form 1040. The representatives should file those forms at the address provided in Publication 3920, Tax Relief for Victims of Terrorist Attacks. In the case of any employee for whom a Form 1040 already has been filed, claims for refund should be made by filing Form 1040X, Amended U.S. Individual Income Tax Return, with IRS at the address provided in Publication 3920.

On joint returns reporting taxable income of the surviving spouse, taxpayers must make an allocation of the tax liability between spouses.[54] If the surviving spouse or other person filing the joint return cannot determine the proper allocation, he or she should attach a statement of all income and deductions allocable to each spouse and the IRS will make the proper allocation. The representative must attach the employee's Form W-2, Wage and Tax Statement.

All returns and claims for refund should be identified by writing "KITA" in bold letters on the top of page 1 of the return or claim for refund.

Returns and claims for refunds must be accompanied by the following documents:

1. Form 1310, Statement of Person Claiming Refund Due a Deceased Taxpayer, unless: (a) the surviving spouse is filing an original or amended joint return, or (b) the decedent's personal representative is filing an original Form 1040, in which case the personal representative must attach a copy of the court certificate showing his or her appointment;

2. For military and civilian employees of the Department of Defense, a certification made by the Department of Defense on DD Form 1300 that includes the name and social security number of the individual, the date of injury, the date of death, and a statement that the individual died as the result of a military or terrorist action and was an employee of the United States on the date of injury and on the date of death;

---

[52] IRS Publication No. 3920, Tax Relief for Victims of Terrorist Attacks (Feb. 2002), p. 2.

[53] Code Secs. 692(b), 6013(f).

[54] Reg. § 1.692-1(b).

3. For United States government employees killed in the United States (who are not employees of the Department of Defense), a death certificate stating the nature of the injury causing death or, if the cause of death is not apparent from the death certificate, a letter from the treating physician, medical examiner, or hospital stating the cause of death, and a certification from the federal employer that includes the name and social security number of the decedent, the date of injury, the date of death, a statement that the decedent was an employee of the United States on the date of injury and the date of death and, if the death was associated with an event that the Secretary has identified as a military action or terrorist activity in published guidance, a statement identifying the action or activity associated with the death. This certificate may be a form or letter from the employing agency's personnel department to the decedent's representative; and

4. For United States government employees killed overseas (who are not employees of the Department of Defense), a certification from the Department of State that the death was the result of terrorist or military action outside the United States. The certification must be made in the form of a letter signed by the Director General of the Foreign Service, Department of State, or his or her delegate. The certification must include the name and social security number of the individual, the date of injury, the date of death, and a statement that the individual died as the result of a military or terrorist action outside the United States and was an employee of the United States on the date of injury and on the date of death.

In a case in which a representative of a decedent who died as the result of terrorist or military action does not have enough tax information to file a timely claim for refund, the representative may stop the running of the period of limitations for making such a claim by filing Form 1040X with the IRS at the address provided in Publication 3920, attaching Form 1310, any other available documentation required by this revenue procedure, and a statement that an amended claim will be filed as soon as the additional requisite information is ascertained.

If an event occurs in the United States that the representative of a decedent who was not an employee of the Department of Defense at the time of injury and death believes was a terrorist or military action, and the Secretary has not published a determination that the event was a terrorist or military action, the representative may submit a request for a determination with the return or claim for refund of the decedent's estate and any other documentation required by this revenue procedure. The surviving spouse or personal representative should submit the following information with their determination requests: (a) date and location of incident, (b) type of incident (terrorist or military), (c) number of taxpayers thought to be affected, (d) a description of the facts on which the personal representative bases the claim that a terrorist or military action has occurred, including the facts relating to any alleged international dimension of a terrorist action, and (e) a completed Form 8821, Tax Information Authorization, that will permit the IRS to disclose to the Department of Justice (for terrorist attacks), the

Department of State (for terrorist attacks with an alleged international dimension), or the Department of Defense (for military actions) return information relating to the return or claim for refund. Taxpayers should complete the form as instructed, listing the Department of Justice as the appointee if the request relates to an alleged terrorist attack, the Department of State if the request relates to an alleged terrorist attack with an international dimension, or the Department of Defense if the request relates to an alleged military action. The appointee's address is not required in this instance. Taxpayers should check the box on the line of Form 8821 that indicates that the tax information authorization is for a specific use and not recorded on the Centralized Authorization File (CAF).

¶ 217 Tax Obligations for Foreign Assets

As a U.S. citizen, dual citizen or resident alien, a taxpayer (decedent) would be required to report income from all worldwide sources to the IRS, even if the decedent did not receive a Form W-2, 1099 or foreign equivalent. Income from offshore sources is required to be reported.

.01 W-2 Filers

If a decedent worked abroad in and was out of the country on the April 15 filing deadline, a two-month extension would be available to file the return. To qualify, the taxpayer must be (1) a U.S. citizen, a dual citizen, or a resident alien living overseas, or (2) serving in the military outside the U.S. on the regular due date of his or her tax return. A taxpayer can only qualify for this automatic two-month extension by attaching a statement to the return explaining which of the two situations applies.

.02 Foreign Bank Accounts

Many taxpayers receive income from foreign sources, including income from foreign trusts, foreign banks and securities accounts. All such income must be reported to the IRS. In most cases, such taxpayers must complete Schedule B of their tax return. Part III of Schedule B requests information about the existence and location of all such foreign income sources.

Some taxpayers must also file Form 8938, "Statement of Foreign Financial Assets," if the aggregate value of those assets during the tax year exceeds certain thresholds.

.03 FinCEN Reporting and FBAR

In addition to reporting these assets to the IRS, there is a separate reporting requirement under certain circumstances. In this instance, the taxpayer must electronically file a Financial Crimes Enforcement Network (FinCEN) Form 114, "Report of Foreign Bank and Financial Accounts" (FBAR) with the U.S. Treasury on or before June 30 of the year following the year of reporting.

A taxpayer is required to file an FBAR if: (1) he or she is a U.S. Person (any citizen or resident of the U.S. and any domestic partnership, corporation, estate or trust); (2) has a financial interest in or signature authority over even one qualifying account in a foreign country; and (3) the aggregate value of the foreign account(s) is greater than $10,000 at any time during the tax year.

For purposes of the FBAR, "foreign accounts" include a bank account, brokerage account, mutual fund, unit trust and certain other types of financial accounts held in a foreign country.

The FBAR must be filed electronically on or before June 30th following the tax year. There is no extension of time to file available and severe penalties will apply for failing to file the FBAR. In *U.S. v. Zwerner*, the jury found that the taxpayer in *Zwerner* willfully failed to file accurate FBARs for three years and the Court imposed the maximum 50% FBAR penalty for each year.[55] The penalty totaled 150% of the account balance, an unusual and substantial result.

---

[55] *U.S. v. Zwerner*, 13-cv-22082, 2014 U.S. Dist. LEXIS 192271 (S.D. Fla. Apr. 29, 2014).

Chapter 3

Fundamentals of Decedent's Final Return

¶ 301	Accounting Method of Decedent
¶ 302	Constructive Receipt Rule Applies
¶ 303	Amounts Taxable to Estate or Survivors
¶ 304	Treatment of Decedent's Income by Recipient
¶ 305	Income in Respect of a Decedent
¶ 306	Installment Obligations Acquired from Decedent
¶ 307	Unrealized Profits Not Taxed
¶ 308	Postponement-of-Gain Benefits
¶ 309	Payments by Employers to Surviving Spouse or Estate
¶ 310	Deductions Not Allowable on Final Return
¶ 311	Decedent's Losses
¶ 312	Deduction for Decedent's Medical Expenses
¶ 313	Treatment of Depreciation and Depletion
¶ 314	Estate Tax Deduction for Recipient of Decedent's Income
¶ 315	Consistency of Basis Reporting
¶ 316	Special Deduction for Survivor Annuitant
¶ 317	Passive Activity Losses

¶ 301 Accounting Method of Decedent

Death often suspends transactions. Whether money collected after death is income taxable to the decedent or to the estate or other person receiving it is a problem that often confronts the executor or the administrator.

If the deceased individual used the cash method of accounting, which is typical, only the items of income actually or constructively received up to and including the date of death are to be accounted for in the final return. If the decedent used the accrual method of accounting, which would be unusual, only the income items accrued to the date of death are to be accounted for in the final return. But income that accrues only by reason of the decedent's death is not to be included. If the taxpayer did not follow an approved method, only amounts received during that year are to be included.[1]

---

[1] Code Sec. 451(b); Reg. § 1.451-1(b)(1).

All amounts of gross income that are not properly includible in the final return but that the decedent had a right to receive and could have received had he or she continued to live are treated as income in respect of the decedent or "IRD." These amounts must be included in gross income for the tax year when received by the estate or person receiving such amounts by reason of inheritance or survivorship through the decedent, regardless of whether such recipient reports income on the cash or accrual method of accounting.[2] For further discussion of amounts taxable to the decedent's estate, heirs, or beneficiaries, see ¶ 303.

Example 1: Decedent, who used the cash method of accounting, was employed by a small factory and earned $500 per week. He worked 14 weeks during the tax year before he died. For the eight weeks preceding his death, Decedent was not paid because the factory was unable to pay at that time. Two months after his death, the factory paid Decedent's executor the eight weeks' wages, $4,000 less deductions. Decedent's final return will include the six weeks' wages of $3,000 that he actually received prior to his death. His final return will not include the eight weeks' wages of $4,000 (considered IRD) that were paid to the executor after his death, but the estate's income tax return will include this amount.

Example 2: Decedent, a broker, kept his books on the accrual basis. Under a contract that he had with one firm, the firm agreed, in the event of his death, to pay his estate 25% of his last year's commissions by way of settlement for deals in process but uncompleted. Decedent died, and, under this clause, the firm paid his estate $4,000. The firm also paid his estate $2,000 for commissions on deals completed prior to his death. The $2,000 is includible on Decedent's final income tax return. The $4,000 is not includible on the final income tax return but on the return of the estate. Although Decedent was on the accrual basis, the settlement commissions were paid by reason or death, not accrued during life. (Under the cash method of accounting, both amounts would have been taxable to the estate only.)

Unless a cash-basis decedent has completed a sale of property and received the proceeds of the sale before death, gain on the sale is not includible in the decedent's final return. If the sale has been completed and the estate receives the proceeds after death, the gain is income in respect of a decedent and is taxable to the estate. If the executor of the estate completes a sale that the decedent had negotiated, gain on the sale is taxable to the estate (see ¶ 307) although it is not income in respect of a decedent.[3] On the other hand, presumably, if a decedent on the accrual basis completes a sale before death and the proceeds are received after death by the estate, the gain will be included in the decedent's final income tax return and the proceeds will not be income in respect of a decedent taxable to the estate.

Because the basis of property acquired from a decedent is generally stepped up to fair market value, the stakes are likely to be high in controversies over the income tax treatment of death interrupted transactions. In one such dispute, the

---

[2] Code Sec. 691(a)(1); Reg. § 1.691(a)-2.   [3] Reg. § 1.691(a)-2(b), Example (5).

Tax Court listed four criteria (not challenged on appeal by the IRS) that must be met before an accrual-basis decedent, as of the date of death, had a right to the proceeds from a sale of livestock:

1. The decedent entered into a legally significant contract.
2. The decedent performed the substantive preconditions to the sale.
3. No economically material contingencies existed at the time of the decedent's death that might have disrupted the sale.
4. The decedent would have received the sale proceeds (actually or constructively) if he had remained alive.[4]

As only about two-thirds of the livestock eventually delivered by the decedent's estate met the age requirements of the contract, the second requirement was not satisfied, and the proceeds from the sale were not income in respect of a decedent (see ¶ 303).[5]

Further elaborating on application of the "right-to-income" (or "entitlement") test, the Tax Court expressly endorsed a "substantial certainty" approach. Thus, in the context of a firmly established company practice, the fact that a bonus was not formally awarded until after an executive's death did not preclude such payments from being treated as income in respect of a decedent.[6]

With respect to the "ripening" of a decedent's right to income during his or her lifetime, the Tax Court has held that, where a condition precedent to the sale of a decedent's house was not met before the decedent's death, proceeds from the eventual sale of the house were not treated as income of a decedent for determining basis in computing the amount of gain on the sale since the decedent had no right to the proceeds of the sale on the date of death.[7] Noting that a decedent may have the right to the proceeds of a sale even though he had not completed every act required of him by the contract on the date of death, the Tax Court went on to say that in order for such proceeds to constitute income in respect of a decedent, the only remaining acts must be ministerial rather than substantive.[8]

¶ 302 Constructive Receipt Rule Applies

Usually, a taxpayer using the cash method of accounting must actually receive income before incurring tax liability. However, the doctrine of "constructive receipt" of income provides an exception to this general rule. Under this doctrine, a taxpayer is taxed on income that is credited to him or her without restriction and made available to the taxpayer during the tax period, to the extent that it may be drawn upon and brought immediately within the taxpayer's possession or control. There must be no substantial limitations or conditions on this right. The construc-

---

[4] *C.W. Peterson Est.*, 74 TC 630, CCH Dec. 37,046, aff'd, CA-8, 82-1 USTC ¶ 9110, 667 F2d 675.

[5] *V. Gavin Est.*, CA-8, 97-1 USTC ¶ 50,417 (decedent's fully vested right at time of death to receive rent income was income in respect of a decedent).

[6] *E.D. Rollert Residuary Trust*, 80 TC 619, CCH Dec. 40,009, aff'd, CA-6, 85-1 USTC ¶ 9139, 752 F2d 1128.

[7] *E.G. Napolitano*, 63 TCM 3092, CCH Dec. 48,260(M), TC Memo. 1992-316.

[8] *Id.*, citing *H.B. Sidles Est.*, 65 TC 873, CCH Dec. 33,636, *C.W. Peterson Est.*, 74 TC 630, CCH Dec. 37,046, aff'd, CA-8, 82-1 USTC ¶ 9110, 667 F2d 675, and *Trust Co. of Georgia*, DC Ga., 67-1 USTC ¶ 9156, 262 FSupp 900, aff'd, CA-5, 68-1 USTC ¶ 9133, 392 F2d 694.

tive receipt doctrine is applicable to a decedent in determining income to be reported on the final return.[9]

Thus, it has been held that interest on bonds, due at the date of death but not collected because of the decedent's illness, was taxable as constructively received by a cash-basis decedent.[10] The same rule was followed where interest coupons matured before a decedent's death and were not presented for payment because of his physical condition.[11]

A dividend is constructively received if it is available for the decedent's use without restriction. If a corporation customarily mails its dividend checks to shareholders, the dividend amount is includible in gross income when the shareholder receives the check. If a shareholder dies between the time the dividend is declared and the time it is received in the mail, the shareholder will *not* be treated as having constructively received it before his or her death, and it is not includible in the final return (see ¶ 403).[12]

The receipt of a check representing income is income in the year received.[13] Thus, a check received before death is income taxable on the decedent's final return even though the check is not cashed or used until after death or another check is given to replace it after death. As to when a check may be taken as a deduction by a deceased payer, see ¶ 310.

¶ 303 Amounts Taxable to Estate or Survivors

Items of income that are not taxable to the decedent on the final return under the rules described at ¶ 301 and ¶ 302 are taxable to:

- the decedent's estate, if the estate receives them;
- a beneficiary, if the right to the income passed directly to the beneficiary and he or she receives the income; or
- any person to whom the estate properly distributes the right to receive the income.

The income items are to be included in the income of the estate or other recipient only *when received* even though the estate or other recipient uses the accrual method of accounting to report its income. This income, which is taxed to the recipient and not to the decedent, is characterized as income in respect of a decedent.[14]

> **Example 3:** Decedent, who kept his books on the cash basis, was entitled, at the date of his death, to a large salary payment to be made in equal annual installments over five years. His estate, after collecting two installments, distributed the right to the remaining installments to the residuary legatee of the estate. Decedent's estate must include in its gross income the two installments received by it, and the legatee must include in his gross income each of the three installments received by him.

---

[9] Reg. § 1.451-2(a).
[10] *E.C. Loose, Exrx.*, 15 BTA 169, CCH Dec. 4818 (Acq.).
[11] *E.C. Loose, Exrx.*, CA-8, 4 USTC ¶ 1362, 74 F2d 147.
[12] *H.W. Putnam Est.*, SCt, 45-1 USTC ¶ 9234, 324 US 393.
[13] Code Sec. 451(a); *U.A. Lavery*, CA-7, 46-2 USTC ¶ 9406, 158 F2d 859.
[14] Code Sec. 691(a)(1); Reg. § 1.691(a)-2(a).

Example 4: A claim owned by Decedent, who reported his income on the cash basis, was in the process of litigation at the time of his death. Before administration of Decedent's estate was complete, the claim was settled for $10,000. The $10,000 is income in respect of a decedent and is required to be included in the income of the estate in the tax year in which received.

Example 5: Assume the same facts as in Example 4, except that Decedent's estate, which makes its returns on the cash basis and for a calendar-year period, received $6,000 on account of the claim on February 15, 2014. On March 20, 2014, before it collects any more, the estate is wound up and the account receivable for the balance is distributed, together with other assets, to Smith, Decedent's sole heir. Smith files his returns on the accrual basis and for a calendar-year period. He collects the balance on February 4, 2015. The estate includes the $6,000 on its 2014 return, and Smith includes the $4,000 on his 2015 return. Smith is not to accrue the $4,000 in 2014, the year it was distributed, because it is taxable to him only in the year he receives the money even though he is on the accrual basis.

Example 6: Jackson, a farmer, uses the cash method of accounting and sells his crop to a processor for $5,000, but did not receive payment before his death. The processor pays the $5,000 to Jackson's estate. The payment is taxable to the estate as income in respect of a decedent. Had Jackson used the accrual method of accounting, however, the $5,000 payment would have been includible on his final return, and the estate would not realize income when it received the payment.

Example 7: Lucas, before his death, acquired 10,000 shares of the capital stock of the Y Corporation at a cost of $100 per share. During his lifetime, Lucas had entered into a contract with Y Corporation or with other shareholders whereby Y Corporation or other shareholders agreed to purchase, and Lucas agreed that his executor would sell the 10,000 shares of Y Corporation stock owned by Lucas at the book value of the stock at the date of his death. Upon Lucas' death, the shares are sold by Lucas' executor for $500 a share pursuant to the agreement. Since the sale of stock is consummated after Lucas' death, there is no income in respect of a decedent based on the appreciation in value of Lucas' stock to the date of his death.

Example 8: Hernandez has an employment contract under which he is to be employed for life at fixed annual salaries, and, after his death, payments are to be made to his widow. The payments are to be based on Hernandez's salary. Payments made under the contract to his widow are income in respect of a decedent.[15]

Example 9: Banks, an inventor, sells the patent rights to one of his inventions. Royalties accruing and paid after his death are income in respect of a decedent. If, however, the transfer of the patent rights is a nonexclusive license (rather than a sale), only royalties accrued and due at Banks' death are

---

[15] *A.V. Bernard*, DC N.Y., 63-1 USTC ¶ 9340, 215 F. Supp. 256.

income in respect of a decedent. Royalties accruing after his death are ordinary income to the recipient.[16]

Example 10: Taylor was entitled to two weeks of vacation at the time of her death, and her employer makes the vacation payment to Taylor's estate. Such payment is income in respect of a decedent.

The rules discussed above also apply to successive decedents, provided the right to the income was acquired by the later decedent by reason of the death of the prior decedent or by bequest, devise, or inheritance from the prior decedent.

Example 11: Wife acquired, by bequest from her husband, the right to receive renewal commissions on life insurance sold by him in his lifetime. The commissions were payable over a period of years. Wife died before she received all of the commissions, and her son inherited the right to receive the remainder. The commissions received by Wife were includible in her gross income. The commissions received by her son were not includible in Wife's gross income but must be included in the son's gross income. The commissions in the son's hands represent a decedent's income, Wife being the decedent for this purpose.

It should be noted that rights to income to be collected after death are usually part of the decedent's estate subject to federal estate tax. Because of the income in respect of a decedent rules, such income is taxed to the recipient even though, for income tax purposes, it has a basis equal to the amount includible for estate tax purposes. However, the law gives partial relief from this duplication of taxes by allowing a deduction to the recipient of the income based on the increase in the estate tax attributable to the inclusion of the value of such income right in the estate.[17]

¶ 304 Treatment of Decedent's Income by Recipient

A decedent's income that is taxed to the recipient retains the same character it would have had in the hands of the decedent if he or she had lived and received the income. Thus, if the income would have been capital gain, exempt income, or dividend income to the decedent, it continues to be the same kind of income to the recipient.[18]

Any person who acquires stock in an S corporation by reason of a bequest, devise, or inheritance from a decedent must treat as income in respect of a decedent the *pro rata* share of any item of income of the corporation that would have been income in respect of a decedent if the income had been acquired directly from the decedent.[19] The stepped-up basis of the stock acquired from a decedent is reduced to the extent that the stock's value is attributable to items consisting of income in respect of a decedent.[20]

If the owner-annuitant of a deferred annuity contract dies before the annuity starting date, and the beneficiary receives a death benefit under the annuity

---

[16] Rev. Rul. 60-227, 1960-1 CB 262, clarifying and distinguishing Rev. Rul. 57-544, 1957-2 CB 361.

[17] For details on this deduction, *see* ¶ 314.

[18] Code Sec. 691(a)(3); Reg. § 1.691(a)-3.

[19] Code Sec. 1367(b)(4)(A).

[20] Code Sec. 1367(b)(4)(B).

contract, the amount received by the beneficiary in a lump sum in excess of the owner-annuitant's investment in the contract is includible in the beneficiary's gross income as income in respect of a decedent. If the death benefit is instead received in the form of a series of periodic payments in accordance with Code Sec. 72(s), the amounts received are likewise includible in the beneficiary's gross income as income in respect of a decedent.[21]

¶ 305 Income in Respect of a Decedent

If a right to receive income in respect of a decedent is transferred by the owner of the right (the estate, heir, or other beneficiary) to another person, the fair market value of the right at the date of the transfer is to be included in the income of the transferor, plus the amount by which any consideration received for the transfer exceeds the fair market value of the right.[22] Thus, if the right to receive the income is disposed of by sale, the fair market value of the right or the consideration received, whichever is higher, is includible in the seller's gross income. If the right is disposed of by gift, the fair market value of the right will be includible in the donor's gross income.[23]

> ***Example 12:*** Decedent bequeaths to his son, Benny, the right to receive rental payments from certain real estate. To obtain immediate cash, Benny sells the right to receive the rental payments to Buyer. The fair market value of the right at the date of transfer is $10,000. The sale price is $8,000. Benny will have to include $10,000, the fair market value of the right, in his gross income in the year of transfer. If Benny had made a gift, the fair market value of the right at the time of the gift, here $10,000, would have been includible in his gross income. If he had done neither, the rental income would have been taxed to him as received.

A transfer of a right to receive income in respect of a decedent includes (1) a sale, exchange, or other disposition; (2) the satisfaction of installment obligations at other than face value; or (3) the cancellation of an installment obligation. It does not include a transfer at death to the estate of the decedent or a transfer to a person who would eventually be entitled to the income by reason of the death of the decedent by bequest, devise, or inheritance.[24]

> ***Example 13:*** Decedent bequeaths his right to certain payments of income to a trust. If the trust terminates and the right to the payments is transferred to the beneficiary, the trust does not have to include the fair market value of the right to receive the payments in its income, but the payments are includible in the income of the beneficiary.

Ordinarily, the basis of property acquired from a decedent is the fair market value of the property on the date of the decedent's death or the alternate valuation date (see ¶ 606 and Code Sec. 1014). However, property that constitutes a right to

---

[21] Rev. Rul. 2005-30, 2005-1 CB 1015.
[22] Code Sec. 691(a)(2).
[23] Reg. § 1.691(a)-4(a).
[24] Code Sec. 691(a)(2).

receive an item of income in respect of a decedent under Code Sec. 691 is expressly excepted from the operation of this rule,[25] and the above-discussed rules apply.

The right to such income, of course, has a value that is includible in determining the value of the estate for estate tax purposes. But the estate tax, if any, attributable to the inclusion of such value may be deducted as explained at ¶ 314.

¶ 306 Installment Obligations Acquired from Decedent

Installment obligations acquired from a decedent are to be treated as items of income in respect of a decedent. Therefore, the estate, heir, or other person receiving the installment payments after the death of the decedent will use the same gross profit percentage that the decedent used to arrive at the portion of each collection that represents taxable income.[26]

If the estate, heir, or other recipient sells or exchanges the installment obligation (as described at ¶ 305), the transferor (estate, heir, etc.) should include in its gross income the fair market value of the obligation at the time of the sale or exchange, or the consideration received for the transfer, whichever amount is greater, reduced by the basis of the obligation (i.e., the decedent's basis, adjusted for all installment payments received before the disposition). The basis of the obligation in the hands of the decedent is the excess of the face value over the amount of income that would be returnable had the obligation been satisfied in full.[27]

> *Example 14:* Beneficiary, the heir of a decedent, is entitled to collect an installment obligation with a face value of $100, a fair market value of $80, and a basis in the hands of the decedent of $60. If Beneficiary collects the obligation at face value, the excess of the amount collected over the basis is considered income in respect of a decedent and is includible in Beneficiary's gross income. In this case, the amount includible would be $40. If Beneficiary collects the obligation at $90, an amount other than face value, the entire obligation is considered a right to receive income in respect of a decedent. The amount required to be included in Beneficiary's gross income is the consideration received in satisfaction of the installment obligation (because it is greater than market value) *less* the amount of the basis of the obligation in the decedent's hands. In this case, the amount includible would be $30.[28]

¶ 307 Unrealized Profits Not Taxed

The increase in value of property that occurs between the date the decedent acquired the property and the date of the decedent's death is not income taxable on the decedent's final return. This is true whether the decedent was on the cash or the accrual method of accounting. The property becomes part of the decedent's estate, and the appreciation is reflected when valuing the property for estate tax purposes only.

---

[25] Code Sec. 1014(c); Reg. § 1.1014-1(c)(1).
[26] Code Sec. 691(a)(4).
[27] Code Sec. 453B(b).
[28] Reg. § 1.691(a)-5.

Example 15: Decedent, who operated on the cash basis, purchased a painting for $1,000. At the date of his death the painting was valued at $5,000. The increase in value of $4,000 is not income to be included on Decedent's final income tax return. The painting would become an asset of his estate. If the estate sold the painting for $6,000, it would have a taxable gain of $1,000 (because the basis of the painting is increased to its fair market value on the date of Decedent's death) unless alternate valuation could be, and was, elected. If alternate valuation was elected and the painting was sold within six months of Decedent's death, the basis of the property would be the same as the sale price and no taxable gain would be realized. If alternate valuation was elected but the painting was not sold within six months of Decedent's death, the taxable gain would be limited to any excess of $6,000 over the value of the painting six months after the decedent's death.

In the above example, there would be no difference with respect to the decedent's final return if there had been a sale and delivery of, or an enforceable agreement to sell, the painting for $6,000 before Decedent's death. This is assuming that before his death he had not received the sale proceeds or evidence of the purchaser's debt, which could be considered receipt of the sale proceeds. No profit would have been includible in his final return. In this situation, however, the estate would be the recipient of a right to income in respect of a decedent, and, therefore, it would have to report the sale proceeds as income in the same manner and amount that the decedent would have had to report them had he lived. Accordingly, the total profit to be reported by the estate would be $5,000, the difference between Decedent's basis of $1,000 and the sale proceeds of $6,000. If Decedent had been on the accrual basis, the $5,000 gain on the sale of the painting would have been included in his final return.

If a decedent operated a sole proprietorship that involved the use of inventories, an accounting would have to be made as of the decedent's death to determine the amount of income from the business includible in the decedent's final return. In fixing inventory values at the date of death, care should be taken to follow the valuation method previously used by the decedent, that is, cost, cost or market (whichever is lower), retail method, etc. It is not proper to adopt the valuation made for estate or inheritance tax purposes, or use other outside appraisals, because those valuations may have no relation to the decedent's opening inventory or the method that must be consistently used in computing income on the inventory basis.

.01 Farmers

For farmers, the mere raising of livestock or growing of crops does not constitute taxable income includible on the decedent's final return nor does it constitute a right to income in respect of a decedent. To constitute income in respect of a decedent, there must have been a sale and delivery of, or at least an enforceable agreement to sell, the livestock or crops before the death of the farmer (assuming the farmer had not received before death the sale proceeds or evidence of the purchaser's debt, which could be considered receipt of the sale proceeds). If there has been no sale or agreement to sell before death, the livestock or crops

¶307.01

become an asset of the estate for estate tax purposes.[29] The person receiving the livestock or crops from the decedent will have as his or her basis the fair market value of the livestock or crops at date of death or other applicable valuation date.

Rents received in the form of crop shares or livestock are to be included in income in the year the crop shares or livestock are reduced to money or the equivalent of money, whether a farmer reports income on the cash or accrual method. Thus, crop shares or livestock received as rent by a farmer and owned by the farmer at death, or which the farmer had a right to receive as rent at the time of death, are not includible as income on the farmer's final income tax return. The net proceeds from the sale or other disposition of such items constitute income in respect of a decedent and are required to be included in the gross income of the estate (or other recipient) in the year in which the crop shares or livestock are sold or otherwise disposed.[30] If the decedent dies during a rental period, only the net proceeds attributable to the portion of the rental period ending with the decedent's death are income in respect of a decedent. The proceeds attributable to the portion of the rental period that runs from the day after death to the end of the rental period are ordinary income to the estate or other recipient. Thus, when crop shares or livestock rentals are received in kind, held by the lessor at the time of death, and sold later by the executor (or by a beneficiary who acquires the property in kind by inheritance), the proceeds from the sale of such crop shares or livestock should be allocated between income in respect of a decedent and gross income of the recipient. The income in respect of the decedent includes the proceeds of the rental period ending with the decedent's death, while the recipient's income includes the proceeds attributable to the portion of the rent period that runs from the day after death to the end of the rent period.[31]

¶ 308 Postponement-of-Gain Benefits

It was noted at ¶ 304 that a decedent's income that is taxed to the recipient retains the same character it would have had in the hands of the decedent. A similar principle applies to provide the decedent or the decedent's estate with the benefit of certain nonrecognition-of-gain provisions, such as in Code Sec. 1033. Gain is not recognized from the involuntary conversion of property if an amount equal to the proceeds from the conversion is invested within a certain time in replacement property similar or related in service or use to the former property and not acquired from a related party.[32]

.01 Post-Death Transactions

The right to use the nonrecognition of gain benefits of the involuntary conversion Code provision does not necessarily end at the death of the taxpayer.[33] A replacement of condemned property may be made either by the decedent or by one acting on the decedent's behalf, and it does not matter if the latter is an executor or

---

[29] Rev. Rul. 58-436, 1958-2 CB 366.
[30] *H. Davidson Est.,* CtCls, 61-2 USTC ¶ 9584, 292 F2d 937, cert. denied, 368 US 939.
[31] Rev. Rul. 64-289, 1964-2 CB 173, modifying Rev. Rul. 58-436, 1958-2 CB 366.
[32] Code Sec. 1033(a) and (i).
[33] *S. Goodman Est.,* CA-3, 52-2 USTC ¶ 9556, 199 F2d 895.

a trustee. The focus is upon whether the replacement merely completes the decedent's plans or is made under the direction and control of another. Nonrecognition of gain was available when replacement of property was made by executors,[34] trustees of the decedent's residuary trust,[35] and the trustee of a grantor (revocable) trust.[36]

.02 Sale of Principal Residence

A taxpayer may exclude up to $250,000 of gain realized on the sale or exchange of a principal residence (up to $500,000 if married filing jointly), provided the taxpayer owned and used it as a principal residence for at least two of the five years before the sale or exchange.[37] A surviving spouse's period of ownership of a residence includes the period during which the decedent spouse owned and used the residence.[38]

A taxpayer who fails to meet these requirements because of a change in employment or health, or other unforeseen circumstances, may exclude the fraction of the exclusion amount ($250,000 or $500,000 if married filing jointly) equal to the fraction of the two years that these requirements are met.[39] The exclusion amount, and not the realized gain, is prorated.

To determine the excludable amount, multiply $250,000 or $500,000 (whichever applies) by the ratio of:

1. the shorter of (a) the aggregate periods that the property was owned and used as a principal residence during the five-year period ending on the date of the sale or exchange, or (b) the period after the date of the most recent prior sale or exchange to which the exclusion applied, *over*

2. two years.

Married individuals filing jointly qualify for the entire $500,000 exclusion if: (1) either spouse meets the ownership test; (2) both spouses meet the use test; and (3) neither spouse is ineligible for exclusion by virtue of a sale or exchange of a residence within the last two years. If spouses do not meet all three requirements, the exclusion is determined on an individual basis and equals the sum of the exclusion limitations to which each spouse would have been entitled had they not been married. Each spouse is treated as owning the property during the period that either spouse owned the property.[40]

A surviving spouse is eligible to file a joint return with the decedent spouse only for the year of the decedent spouse's death. Therefore the surviving spouse will be able to exclude up to $500,000 only if he or she sells the residence in the year of the decedent's death; otherwise, the $250,000 limit applies.[41]

If an individual becomes physically or mentally incapable of self-care, the individual is deemed to use a residence as a principal residence during the time in

---

[34] *Id.*; *C.H. Chichester,* DC Ala., 78-1 USTC ¶ 9458.
[35] *J.E. Morris Est.,* CA-4, 72-1 USTC ¶ 9177, 454 F2d 208 (Nonacq.), aff'g, per curiam, 55 TC 636, CCH Dec. 30,609.
[36] *H.A. Gregg Est.,* 69 TC 468, CCH Dec. 34,784.
[37] Code Sec. 121(a) and (b).
[38] Code Sec. 121(d)(2).
[39] Code Sec. 121(c).
[40] Code Sec. 121(b)(2).
[41] Reg. § 1.121-2(a)(4), Examples 5 and 6.

which he or she owns the residence and resides in a licensed care facility (e.g., a nursing home). In order for this rule to apply, the taxpayer must have owned and used the residence as a principal residence for an aggregate period of at least one year during the five years preceding the sale or exchange.[42]

When an individual acquires a principal residence in a like-kind exchange after October 22, 2004, however, the individual must own the property for at least five years prior to its sale or exchange in order for the exclusion of gain rule to apply.[43]

¶ 309 Payments by Employers to Surviving Spouse or Estate

When the surviving spouse or the decedent's estate receives payments from the decedent's former employer, taxability of the sums received may depend upon the application of several provisions of the tax code. The amounts received may be fully taxable under Code Sec. 61 as gross income, they may be taxable as annuities under Code Sec. 72, or they may be excluded as gifts under Code Sec. 102.

The value of death benefits paid to a deceased employee's beneficiary by an exempt employee's trust (that is, a qualified stock bonus, pension, or profit-sharing plan) is taxed to the beneficiary when received.[44] The taxation of such payments is governed by the rules that are applicable to beneficiaries of such plans. Therefore, if the payments are payable over a period of years, the payments are taxed under the annuity rules. If the decedent had retired prior to dying and was receiving a pension, survivorship annuities are taxable to the survivor.

The IRS generally will characterize payments made by an employer to the surviving spouse of a deceased employee as compensation rather than as gifts. A U.S. Supreme Court decision has played an important role in this area. Although the case did not deal with employer payments to surviving spouses or other survivors, the Supreme Court reviewed and recognized certain principles that are intended to guide trial courts in determining whether a particular transaction is a gift or represents compensation. The court stated that a true gift proceeds from a "detached and disinterested generosity" or out of feelings of "affection, respect, admiration, charity, or like impulses." It also agreed that the transferor's intention is the main consideration in determining whether a true gift has been made and that the findings of the trier of fact will not be disturbed unless clearly erroneous.[45] The Tax Court has used this decision as the basis for consistently finding that payments to a widow by the former employer of her deceased husband are income rather than nontaxable gifts.[46] But several higher courts have ruled that such payments are gifts under certain fact situations.[47]

With respect to bonuses, several courts have taken the liberal position that bonuses may be taxed as income in respect of a decedent even when no right to the

---

[42] Code Sec. 121(d)(7).
[43] Code Sec. 121(d)(10).
[44] Rev. Rul. 71-154, 1971-1 CB 128.
[45] *M. Duberstein*, SCt, 60-2 USTC ¶ 9515, 363 US 278.
[46] *M.H.D. Penick*, 37 TC 999, CCH Dec. 25,371; *M.C. Westphal*, 37 TC 340, CCH Dec. 25,144; *L. Rosen Est.*, 21 TCM 316, CCH Dec. 25,406(M); *J.J. Doumakes Est.*, 22 TCM 1247, CCH Dec. 26,306(M), TC Memo. 1963-249.

[47] *M. Kuntz, Sr., Est.*, CA-6, 62-1 USTC ¶ 9376, 300 F2d 849, cert. denied, 371 US 903; *W.R. Olsen Est.*, CA-8, 62-1 USTC ¶ 9452, 302 F2d 671, cert. denied, 371 US 903; *G.E. Frankel*, CA-8, 62-1 USTC ¶ 9453, 302 F2d 666, cert. denied, 371 US 903; *H.B. Kasynski*, CA-10, 60-2 USTC ¶ 9792, 284 F2d 143; *E.F. Greentree*, CA-4, 64-2 USTC ¶ 9884, 338 F2d 946; *A.P. Grinstead*, CA-7, 71-2 USTC ¶ 9568, 447 F2d 937.

bonus existed at the time of death and the amount of the bonus was not determined until after death.[48] Other types of compensation that are considered income in respect of a decedent are accrued vacation allowances,[49] lump-sum payments of accrued annual leave,[50] and a decedent's interest in fees and commissions.[51] Also, transactions that arise after the decedent's death may receive IRD treatment. For instance, the right to receive renewal commissions is an example of compensation that may be characterized as income in respect of a decedent.[52]

Payments made pursuant to "noncompete agreements" are treated also as IRD. For example, an individual who received the unexpired portion of proceeds from an agreement not to compete entered into by his father prior to his death constituted income in respect of a decedent and were includible in the son's gross income. The son became a successor in interest to the unexpired portion of the agreement and the value of that unexpired portion had not been included in the father's gross income before his death. The funds, which would have been ordinary income in the hands of the decedent, were ordinary income in the hands of the son.[53]

¶ 310 Deductions Not Allowable on Final Return

The deductions of a decedent are treated in the same manner as previously outlined at ¶ 303 for income items. If the decedent was on the cash basis, only those items of expense, interest, and taxes actually paid up to and including the date of death are deductible on the decedent's final return. If the decedent was on the accrual basis, only those deductions properly accruable up to and including the date of death are to be taken on the final return. However, otherwise-deductible amounts accrued only because of the decedent's death are not allowed.[54]

Taxable income is determined by subtracting from adjusted gross income the deduction for personal exemptions and either (1) the total itemized deductions or (2) the standard deduction.

Itemization will be desirable if the decedent's itemized deductions exceed his or her standard deduction amount. The full standard deduction is allowable on the decedent's final return regardless of the date of death. However, if the decedent was married, separate returns are filed, and one of the taxpayers itemizes, the other taxpayer may not claim a standard deduction.

.01 Expenses, Interest, and Taxes

Expenses, interest, and taxes, if not deductible on the decedent's final return, are usually deductible by the decedent's estate when paid. However, if the estate is not liable for their payment, and they are paid by an heir or legatee who received property subject to them, the heir or legatee is entitled to the deduction.[55] If the executor or administrator is not liable for the payment of real estate taxes under state law but pays them anyway, no deduction will be allowed the estate unless the

---

[48] E. O'Daniel Est., CA-2, 49-1 USTC ¶ 9235, 173 F2d 966; E. Bausch Est., CA-2, 51-1 USTC ¶ 9146, 186 F2d 313.
[49] Rev. Rul. 59-64, 1959-1 CB 31; Rev. Rul. 86-109, 1986-2 CB 196.
[50] Rev. Rul. 55-229, 1955-1 CB 75.
[51] J.M. Enright, SCt, 41-1 USTC ¶ 9356, 312 US 636.
[52] Reg. § 1.691(a)-2(b), Example 2.
[53] J.C. Coleman, 87 TCM 1367, Dec. 55,647(M), TC Memo. 2004-126.
[54] Code Sec. 461(b).
[55] Code Sec. 691(b)(1); Reg. § 1.691(b)-1.

payment was made on behalf of a beneficiary who was or would be entitled to income from the estate and made instead of a direct payment to the beneficiary (the deduction would be allowable under Code Sec. 661 for distributions to beneficiaries).[56]

Example 16: Finn, a cash-basis taxpayer, was, at the time of his death, the owner of rental property (real estate). Before his death, Finn incurred certain repair expenses, all of which were allowable deductions. However, the expenses remained unpaid at the time of his death. Also, the general taxes and assessments on the property remained unpaid for several years and were then a lien against the property, in addition to a mortgage lien existing since the date of purchase, on which mortgage interest was in arrears.

The repair expenses would be deductible by the estate when paid by it because they are general expenses. The lien obligations, however, would be deductible only by the heir (or devisee) when paid by him or her, if, under state law, the property passed directly to the beneficiary and the executor or administrator is not liable for their payment. However, if under state law the property became a part of Finn's estate before it passed to the beneficiary, the estate would be liable for the lien obligations and would be entitled to the deduction if paid during administration.

If the decedent in Example 1 had been on the accrual basis at the time of his death, all of the items mentioned would be deductible only on the decedent's final return. However, even on the accrual basis, situations might exist when the items would be similarly deducted as shown in Example 1 (e.g., the current taxes were unpaid at death because of a dispute as to their legality, and they were compromised and paid after the decedent's death). In such case the taxes are deductible by the estate or other person in accordance with the provisions of Code Sec. 691(b)(1).

Similar treatment is given to the foreign tax credit provided by Code Sec. 27.

Example 17: John died and left to his son, Jim, the right to income from a factory he owned in France subject to an income tax imposed by France during John's life, which tax had to be satisfied out of such income. Jim is entitled to the foreign tax credit under Code Sec. 27 when he pays this obligation.

.02 Debt in Respect of a Decedent

Although Code Sec. 691(b)(1) specifically allows a deduction for interest on a debt "in respect of a decedent" when paid by either the estate or the beneficiary, that section applies to only the interest accrued before death, not interest properly deductible in the decedent's final return. It does not apply to debts that arise as a result of or after death, such as the federal estate tax. Such debts are not debts of the decedent. Moreover, in the case of the federal estate tax, the recipient of property distributed from the estate may be subject to transferee liability under Code Sec. 6901. (This liability does not, however, relieve the executor or administrator from liability.)

---

[56] Rev. Rul. 58-69, 1958-1 CB 254.

The deduction by the estate or other person of items unpaid by the decedent does not include all of the allowable deductions. It includes only business expenses and expenses related to the production of income, interest, and taxes. As to medical expenses, see ¶ 312. As to depreciation and depletion, see ¶ 313.

Generally speaking, the mailing of a check constitutes payment or delivery, and the subsequent payment of the check relates back to the date of mailing for purposes of claiming a deduction.[57] Accordingly, if a check in payment of a deductible item is delivered or mailed before the date of the decedent's death, the deduction would be allowable on the decedent's final return even though the check is not cashed or deposited until after the decedent's death. The Tax Court has extended this rule to a charitable contribution even though, in the absence of a pledge, there is no enforceable obligation.[58]

¶ 311 Decedent's Losses

Losses are ordinarily deductible under Code Sec. 165 only for the year in which they are sustained and should be deducted on the decedent's final income tax return. If, for instance, stocks or debts became worthless during the period covered by the decedent's final return, the loss cannot be taken on the estate's return on the ground that worthlessness was not discovered until appraisal was made for estate tax purposes.[59] If necessary, an amended income tax return should be filed for the decedent to claim the loss later discovered.

Other losses that are deductible include those due to fire, storm, shipwreck, or other casualty, or from theft. A casualty loss is to be deducted in the year it occurs if the extent of the damage is fixed. However, any action for damages against another party, or an insurance claim, may postpone the year in which the deduction can be claimed. When a claim for reimbursement exists and there is a reasonable prospect of recovery of all or part of the loss, the deductible loss must be reduced by the amount of the anticipated recovery, even though payment is not received until a subsequent tax year. If the subsequent recovery is less than the amount anticipated, the difference may be deducted for the year in which it is determined that no more reimbursement or recovery can reasonably be expected.[60] Double deductions for losses are not allowed. That is, losses are not deductible for both income and estate tax purposes. For losses that are covered by insurance, no deduction is allowed unless a timely claim is made for reimbursement with the insurer.[61]

A loss from theft or embezzlement is deductible in the year in which it is discovered. Therefore, if such loss is not discovered before death, the loss is deductible by the estate.[62]

---

[57] *A. Bradley, Exr.*, CA-6, 3 USTC ¶ 904, 56 F2d 728; *E.B. Witt Est. v. Fahs*, DC Fla., 56-1 USTC ¶ 9534, 160 FSupp 521; Rev. Rul. 80-335, 1980-2 CB 170.

[58] *M.J. Spiegel Est.*, 12 TC 524, CCH Dec. 16,898 (Acq.).

[59] Rev. Rul. 74-175, 1974-1 CB 52, superseding Rev. Rul. 54-207, 1954-1 CB 147.

[60] Reg. § 1.165-1(d).

[61] Code Sec. 165(h)(4)(E).

[62] Reg. § 1.165-8.

Nonbusiness casualty and theft losses are deductible under Code Sec. 165(h) only to the extent that each loss exceeds $100 and only to the extent that the otherwise deductible amount exceeds 10% of adjusted gross income.

Net Operating Losses ("NOL") are personal to a decedent and cannot be carried over to the estate or to beneficiaries. Thus, if a decedent sustained a net operating loss (other than an eligible farming loss), such loss can generally be carried back to the two immediately preceding tax years of the decedent.[63] Although the general carryback period for an NOL is two years, the portion of an individual's NOL attributable to casualty and theft losses may be carried back three years. The three-year carryback period also applies to the portion of an NOL attributable to a presidentially declared disaster in the case of a taxpayer engaged in the trade or business of farming or in the case of a small business.[64] Any loss still remaining after the carryback must be disregarded since it cannot be deducted by the estate or carried over to subsequent years.[65] The carryback period for a farming loss is five years.[66]

A farming loss is defined as the lesser of:

- the amount of a taxpayer's net operating loss for the tax year if only income and deductions attributable to the taxpayer's farming business are taken into account, or
- the amount of the net operating loss for the tax year.[67]

A taxpayer may elect to forgo the carryback period and use the loss exclusively in the years following the loss year.[68]

¶ 312 Deduction for Decedent's Medical Expenses

Ordinarily, medical expenses are deductible only if paid within the tax year, and this is true regardless of whether the taxpayer is on the cash or the accrual basis.[69] However, under a special provision in the tax code, if medical expenses for the care of a taxpayer are paid by a decedent's estate within one year of death, they are treated as having been paid by the decedent when incurred.[70] This means that a decedent's medical expenses are deductible on the return for the year in which they were *incurred*.

.01 Amend Prior Individual Returns for Decedent's Medical Expenses

Under Code Sec. 213(c)(2), if the taxpayer's medical expenses are paid by a decedent's estate within one year of death, they are treated as having been paid by the decedent when incurred and deductible on the return for the year in which they were incurred.[71] Ordinarily, this will be the year for which the decedent's final return is filed. However, the deduction may be made on an amended return if the filing of an amended return or of a refund claim for a year for which a refund or

---

[63] Code Sec. 172(b)(1)(A).
[64] Code Sec. 172(b)(1)(F).
[65] Code Secs. 172 and 1212; Rev. Rul. 74-175, 1974-1 CB 52.
[66] Code Sec. 172(b)(1)(G).
[67] Code Sec. 172(i).
[68] Code Sec. 172(b)(3).
[69] Code Sec. 213(a).
[70] Code Sec. 213(c).
[71] Code Sec. 213(c).

Fundamentals of Decedent's Final Return 3017

deficiency assessment is not barred by the statute of limitations—ordinarily three years from the due date of the return—is permitted.

Example 18: In 2014, the Decedent incurred but did not pay doctor and hospital bills totaling $1,400 for personal medical treatment. She filed her return for calendar-year 2014 on April 17, 2015, and paid the tax shown to be due. The Decedent died in January 2016 without having paid the doctor and hospital bills. Her estate pays them in April 2016. An amended return (or refund claim) for 2014 can be filed, and the allowable medical expenses can be deducted before expiration of the statute of limitations.

.02 Deduction Limitations

The allowance of a deduction for a decedent's medical expenses in the year in which they were incurred applies only to expenses incurred for the deceased taxpayer. This provision does not apply to medical expenses that a decedent may have incurred on behalf of a dependent. The statute expressly provides such treatment only for "expenses for the medical care of the taxpayer."[72] The above provision also does not apply if the decedent's medical expenses have been deducted for estate tax purposes under Code Sec. 2053. To obtain an income tax deduction for such expenses, therefore, the estate must file a statement to the effect that the medical expenses have not been allowed as a deduction for estate tax purposes, together with a waiver of the right to have such medical expenses allowed at any time as a deduction for estate tax purposes.[73] A sample of such an elections follows:

ELECTION TO DEDUCT MEDICAL EXPENSES ON FORM 1040

The personal representative of the above-named deceased taxpayer hereby elects to deduct the taxpayer's following medical expenses paid within one year of death on the deceased taxpayer's final or amended prior income tax return. [*list medical expenses*]

In accordance with Code Section 213(c) and Treasury Regulation 1.213-1(d)(2), the taxpayer hereby maintains that such medical expenses have not been claimed or allowed as a deduction under Code Section 2053 on Form 706, United States Estate (and Generation-Skipping Transfer) Tax Return in computing the taxable estate of the decedent, and further, the taxpayer waives the right to have such medical expenses allowed at any time as a deduction under Code Section 2053.

The above election to waive the deduction of medical expenses on the estate tax return should be filed in duplicate on the appropriate income tax return (final or amended prior) for any year the expenses are claimed.

Deductions for medical expenses are limited to the amount by which such expenses exceed 10% of adjusted gross income. The amount of medical expenses that is not deductible because of the percentage limitation also is not deductible for estate tax purposes.[74] The IRS bases this position on the "amount paid" language of

---

[72] Code Sec. 213(c)(1).
[73] Code Sec. 213(c); Reg. § 1.213-1(d).
[74] Rev. Rul. 77-357, 1977-2 CB 328.

Code Sec. 213(c)(2). In effect, because the election must be made on the basis of amounts paid under Code Sec. 213(c)(2), the election to deduct the medical expenses on the income tax return precludes an estate tax deduction for the amount disallowed because of the 10% adjusted gross income limitation. The courts have not considered this matter; however, a logical argument can be made for the opposite conclusion. Code Sec. 642(g) provides that a double deduction may not be taken for amounts deductible as income or estate tax deductions, and if Code Sec. 213(c)(2) was enacted solely for the express purpose of denying a double deduction, then there would seem to be no reason to preclude an estate tax deduction of an amount not deductible on income taxes.

> **Planning Point:** Note that the flat 40% estate tax rate is likely higher than the applicable income tax rate for the decedent, especially in the year of death. Although in certain circumstances, it is possible that the current 40% estate tax rate may be lower than the effective income tax rate for a high-income decedent, if the decedent's final Form 1040 is taxed at the highest 43.4% rate (39.6% + 3.8% net investment income tax). The election to use the medical expenses on the income tax return is irrevocable.
>
> It may be more advantageous to file the estate tax return, and extend the income tax return, and delay as long as possible (until the estate tax closing letter is issued) using the expenses as income tax deductions. But note that this is not an all or nothing election analysis—some of the medical expenses can be deducted on the income tax return, and some on the estate tax return.[75]

The above limitation applies only to a decedent's medical expenses that are paid by the estate. If the surviving spouse pays a deceased spouse's medical expenses, the surviving spouse may deduct them on either a joint return or a separate return if he or she was married to the decedent either at the time the expenses were incurred or at the time of payment. Therefore, it does not matter if the expenses were paid before or after the death of the decedent, or if the surviving spouse remarries during the year of death.[76]

Insurance reimbursements received by an estate for previously deducted medical expenses are includible in the estate's gross income for the year of receipt.[77]

A child of divorced parents is treated as a dependent of both parents for the medical expense deduction. Thus, medical expenses incurred with respect to a decedent's child will be deductible on the decedent's return regardless of whether the child was otherwise a dependent.[78]

¶ 313 Treatment of Depreciation and Depletion

The decedent ceases to be a taxable entity for all purposes from the moment of death. Therefore, depreciation allowances on depreciable property are computed to that time, and a deduction is taken for that amount in the decedent's final return. Accordingly, the depreciation deduction of the decedent will be a prorated amount,

---

[75] Johnston, Montana Law Rev., Vol. 42, p. 2
[76] Rev. Rul. 57-310, 1957-2 CB 206.
[77] Rev. Rul. 78-292, 1978-2 CB 233.
[78] Code Sec. 213(d)(5).

based on the proportion that the number of months or, if applicable, parts of months, covered by the final return bears to the total annual depreciation that would have been allowable to the decedent had he or she lived.[79]

After the decedent's death, his or her estate, being a new entity, files a return for the period beginning with the date of death and ending with the close of the calendar or fiscal year elected by it. As far as the estate is concerned, the allowable depreciation deduction is to be apportioned among the estate and the heirs, legatees, and devisees on the basis of the estate's income that is allocable to each.[80]

The estate will also have a new basis for depreciation (see ¶ 606 and ¶ 614). The deduction for percentage depletion is allowable only to the person who receives the income in respect of the decedent to which the deduction relates, whether or not such person receives the property from which such income is derived.[81] Thus, an heir who (by reason of the decedent's death) received income derived from sales of minerals by the cash-basis decedent will be allowed the deduction for percentage depletion, computed on the gross income from such sales as if the heir had the same economic interest in the property as the decedent. The heir need not receive any interest in the mineral property other than an interest in the income. According to the Treasury regulations,[82] if the decedent did not compute his or her deduction for depletion on the basis of percentage depletion, any deduction for depletion to which the decedent was entitled at the date of death would be allowable in computing taxable income for the decedent's last tax year. The depletion deduction allowed to the decedent cannot be claimed by any other person as a "deduction in respect of the decedent."

For information on the deduction of depreciation and depletion allowances by estates, trusts, and beneficiaries, see ¶ 614 and ¶ 615.

¶ 314 Estate Tax Deduction for Recipient of Decedent's Income

An estate or other person taxed on income in respect of a decedent is entitled to a deduction for any federal estate tax (and any generation-skipping transfer tax) imposed on the decedent's estate that is attributable to such income.[83] The deduction must be itemized[84] and, therefore, it does not reduce a recipient's adjusted gross income. The deduction for estate tax paid in the case of income in respect of a decedent is not included in the definition of the term "miscellaneous itemized deductions" and, therefore, is not subject to the 2% floor that is generally applicable to such deductions (see ¶ 608). Computing the deduction requires a determination of the amount by which net income in respect of a decedent exceeds the deductions from the gross estate for claims representing (1) the deductions and (2) the credit in respect of a decedent.[85] The excess is the "net value" of the relevant items of income in respect of a decedent. The estate tax attributable to such "net value" is the actual estate tax (reduced by the credits against it) *less* a "hypothetical" estate

---

[79] Rev. Rul. 67-400, 1967-2 CB 99.
[80] Code Sec. 167(d).
[81] Code Sec. 691(b)(2); Reg. § 1.691(b)-1(b).
[82] Reg. § 1.691(b)-1(b).
[83] Code Sec. 691(c)(1).
[84] Rev. Rul. 78-203, 1978-1 CB 199.
[85] Code Sec. 691(c)(2); Reg. § 1.691(c)-1(a)(1).

tax computed independently of such net value. This amount is apportioned among the various recipients of the income in respect of a decedent. This deduction is available even though part of the income items may qualify for the marital deduction.

> **Example 19:** Decedent, a cash-basis decedent, was entitled to receive a $1,200 fee for professional services at the time of his death. The right to receive this fee was valued at $900 in computing the estate tax. There was also an accrued interest item of $100 in the taxable estate, which was uncollected. The inclusion of these two items increased the estate tax by $200. The estate collects the entire $1,200 fee in its first tax year. In computing the income tax of the estate, there may be deducted $900/$1,000 × $200, or $180.

When income in respect of a decedent is payable to an estate or trust, such income is to be treated as income of beneficiaries who actually receive it rather than as income of the estate or trust for determining the deductibility of estate taxes. It is treated as income to the beneficiaries for this purpose, however, only if it is properly paid, credited, or required to be distributed to them during the tax year.[86]

A beneficiary may deduct the estate tax attributable to income in respect of a decedent before the estate tax is paid. An estate beneficiary who inherited the right to receive the remaining payments from a decedent's annuity was entitled to claim the deduction for estate tax attributable to income in respect of a decedent, even though the estate taxes had not yet been paid. Neither the tax code nor the regulations required that the estate tax be paid before a recipient of income in respect of a decedent could claim the deduction for the amount required to be included in gross income.[87]

An estate was required to allocate income received in respect of a decedent to the marital deduction called for by the trust agreement when computing the deduction under Code Sec. 691. To derive the hypothetical estate tax, the income in respect of a decedent must be subtracted from those items to which it pertains. Because the income in respect of a decedent was part of the residuary estate, which included the marital share, the marital deduction had to be adjusted when the income in respect of a decedent was deducted from the gross estate. Otherwise, the marital deduction would be inflated, thereby creating a lower hypothetical estate tax and a deduction greater than the amount of the IRD itself.[88]

The IRS considered the application of the Code Sec. 691(c) deduction to a similar case that involved items of income in respect of a decedent (a decedent's IRAs) that were not specific bequests to the surviving spouse. An additional fact was that the surviving spouse took an elective share (one-third) of her husband's estate. The IRS concluded that the survivor was entitled to a deduction calculated

---

[86] Code Sec. 691(c)(1)(B).

[87] IRS Field Service Advice 200011023, October 6, 1999.

[88] *W. Cherry Est.*, DC Ky., 2001-1 USTC ¶ 50,223.

using the ratio in Code Sec. 691(c)(1), multiplied by the federal estate tax attributable to the net value of the items of income in respect of a decedent. In turn, at the surviving spouse's death, her interest in the IRAs was includible in her gross estate and constituted items of income in respect of a decedent. Thus, the recipients of the portions of the IRAs that were payable to the wife were entitled to a deduction for the portion of federal estate tax attributable to inclusion of the IRAs in the husband's estate and, in addition, were entitled to a deduction for the portion of federal estate tax attributable to the inclusion of the IRAs in the wife's estate.[89]

¶ 315 Consistency of Basis Reporting

In July of 2015, Congress enacted new Code Sec. 1014(f) and Code Sec. 6035, which implement new basis consistency rules for taxpayers acquiring property from a decedent and new information reporting requirements for executors of estates under the Surface Transportation and Veterans Health Care Choice Improvement Act of 2015 (the "Act").[90] The Act also included new Code Sec. 6662(b)(8), which incorporates the basis consistency rules into the accuracy-related penalties provisions, and also provides that certain returns and statements are subject to the return penalty provisions of Sections 6721 and 6722 (together, these provisions shall be referred to as the "Penalty Provisions"). While the filing of the required statements and returns is generally the responsibility of the executor, the process should be noted in the administration of the final return.[91] Note that the Priority Guidance Plan lists "Regulations under §§ 1014(f) and 6035 regarding basis consistency between estate and person acquiring property from decedent." This is important because the "reporting" section (relating to Form 8971 and its Schedule A) of the proposed and temporary regulations were published on March 4, 2016, and are widely viewed as burdensome and controversial. These regulations needed to be finalized by January 31, 2017, to be retroactive under Section 7805(b)(2), although they were not finalized (adding still to their burdensome nature).

¶ 316 Special Deduction for Survivor Annuitant

Annuity payments received by a surviving annuitant under a joint and survivor annuity contract are treated, to a certain extent, as income of a decedent for the purpose of allowing the deduction for estate tax. This applies, however, only if the deceased annuitant died after the annuity starting date.[92]

The portion of estate tax attributable to the survivor's annuity is allowable as a deduction to the surviving annuitant over his or her life expectancy period. If the surviving annuitant continues to receive annuity payments beyond this period, there is no further deduction. If the surviving annuitant dies before expiration of such period, there is no compensating adjustment for the unused deduction.[93]

---

[89] IRS Letter Ruling 200316008, December 31, 2002.
[90] P.L. 114-41, 129 Stat. 443.
[91] See ¶ 110, "Consistency of Basis Reporting Rules," for continuing changes to the implementation to these rules.
[92] Code Sec. 691(d).
[93] Reg. § 1.691(d)-1(a).

In computing the excludable portion of the survivor's annuity payments, the gender-neutral Table VI (Reg. §1.72-9) is to be used if there was a post-June 1986 investment in the contract.[94] The following example is for a post-June 1986 investment in a joint and survivor annuity contract.

Example 20: Bob and Betty, brother and sister, purchased a joint and survivor annuity contract for $203,800, providing for monthly payments of $1,000 starting on January 28 of Year 1, and continuing for their joint lives and for the remaining life of the survivor. Bob contributed $152,850 to the cost of the annuity, and Betty contributed $50,950. As of the annuity starting date, January 1, Year 1, Bob's age at his nearest birthday was 70, and Betty's age at her nearest birthday was 67.

Bob died on January 1, Year 4, and on January 28, Year 4, Betty began to receive her monthly payments of $1,000. The value of the annuity at the date of Bob's death was $159,000, and the value of the annuity for estate tax purposes was $119,250 (($152,850 ÷ $203,800) × $159,000). As of the date of Bob's death, Betty's age was 70 and her life expectancy, determined by reference to Table V (Reg. §1.72-9), was 16.0 years. Both Bob and Betty reported income by use of the cash receipts and disbursements method and filed income tax returns on the calendar-year basis.

The following computations illustrate the application of Code Sec. 72 in determining the excludable portions of the annuity payments to Betty during her life expectancy period:

Amount of annuity payments per year (12 × $1,000)	$12,000
Times: Multiple in Table VI, ages 67 and 70	22.0
Expected return as of the annuity starting date, January 1, Year 1 ($12,000 × 22.0)	$264,000
Investment in the contract as of the annuity starting date, January 1, Year 1	$203,800
Exclusion ratio ($203,800 ÷ $264,000)	77.2 %
Times: Amount of annuity payments per year	$12,000
Exclusion per year under Code Sec. 72 ($12,000 × 77.2%)	$9,264
Times: Betty's life expectancy period	16.0
Excludable during Betty's life expectancy period ($9,264 × 16.0)	$148,224

The value for estate tax purposes of the amount includible in the survivor's gross income and considered IRD is based on Reg. §1.691(d)-1(e), Example 1, and is arrived at by the following formula:

---

[94] Reg. §1.72-9.

$$\text{Includible annuity value} = \frac{\text{Annuity value at date of death of deceased annuitant} - \text{Amount excludable by surviving annuitant under Code Sec. 72 during survivor's lifetime}}{\text{Value of annuity at date of death of decedent}} \times \text{Value of annuity for estate tax purposes}$$

Includible annuity value = ($159,000 − $148,224) × $\dfrac{\$119{,}250}{\$159{,}000}$

Includible annuity value ($10,776 × .75) = $8,082

The estate tax determined to be attributable to the $8,082 is then allowed as a deduction to the survivor over the survivor's life expectancy (Reg. § 1.691(d)-1(e), Example 2).

For further information on annuity contracts, see ¶ 409.

¶ 317 Passive Activity Losses[95]

If a decedent had passive activity losses (PALs) during the year of death, the person responsible for filing the final return should consider the following general rules.

Deductions from passive trade or business activities are limited.[96] For these rules, a passive activity is defined as any trade or business in which a taxpayer does not materially participate, or a rental activity (without regard to whether the taxpayer participates in the activity or unless the taxpayer satisfies the special "active management" rule). To meet this material participation test, the decedent must have been involved on a regular, continuous, and substantial basis in the business operation.[97] To the extent that PALs exceed income from all such passive activities, they generally may not be deducted from other income.

Accordingly, losses and credits from a passive activity, including expenses such as interest attributable to acquiring or carrying an interest in such an activity, may be applied only against income for the tax year or subsequent tax years from that passive activity or other passive activities and not against salary or other income for services or against "portfolio income," such as interest, dividends, royalties, and gains from the sale of property held for investment.

---

[95] See ¶ 105, "Passive Activity Losses and Material Participation for Fiduciaries and Beneficiaries," for updates to these rules.

[96] Code Sec. 469.

[97] Code Sec. 469(h)(1).

.01 Suspended Losses

To the extent that the total deductions from passive activities exceed the total income from such activities for the tax year, the excess—the PAL—is not allowed to be deducted in that year. Instead, it is "suspended" and is carried forward to reduce passive activity income generated in future years. Similarly, the excess of the credits from passive activities over the regular tax liability for the tax year that is allocable to those activities is likewise suspended. Credits are allowed in an amount equal to their deduction equivalent. The deduction equivalent of a credit from a passive activity for any tax year is the amount that, if allowed as a deduction, would reduce the regular tax liability for such tax year by an amount equal to such credits. However, if the credit involves a property that was previously subject to a downward basis adjustment upon being placed in service, the taxpayer may elect to make a similar upward basis adjustment to the property immediately before disposition.

.02 Disposal of Taxpayer's Entire Interest

Code Sec. 469(g) provides special rules for the treatment of passive activity losses upon the complete disposition, including a transfer because of death, of a taxpayer's interest in a passive activity. Under these rules, suspended PALs are generally deductible in full provided (1) the disposition is fully taxable, that is, all gain or loss on such disposition is recognized and (2) the taxpayer's interest is completely extinguished.

Disallowed passive activity losses allocable to a passive activity are deductible in the year that the taxpayer's interest in the activity is transferred by reason of his or her death. The amount of the deduction may not, however, exceed the amount by which the losses are greater than the excess of (1) the transferee's basis in the passive activity interest over (2) the adjusted basis of the interest immediately before the death of the taxpayer.[98] Thus, a transferee loses the use of any disallowed passive activity losses to the extent he or she receives a step-up in the basis of the interest.[99] Any amount not available as a deduction in the year of the taxpayer's death may never be deducted.[100]

A taxpayer who disposes of a passive activity in a taxable transaction must first apply any net passive loss from the activity against income or gain from his or her other passive activities, with any remaining loss from the activity then classified as nonpassive.[101] Such loss may then be used to offset income from nonpassive activities (e.g., wages and interest income).

Example 21: Shortly before her death, Mattie Carter sold her partnership interest in an oil well. Carter had been a limited partner, and, as a result, her interest in the oil well was classified as a passive activity. Carter's sale of her partnership interest resulted in a gain of $5,000. However, during her

---

[98] Code Secs. 469(g)(2)(A) and 1014.
[99] Code Sec. 1014.
[100] Code Sec. 469(g)(2)(B).
[101] Code Sec. 469(g)(1)(A).

period of ownership, she had accumulated $8,000 in suspended passive losses from the oil well. During the year of her death, Carter had $1,000 in passive income from another activity and wages of $50,000. In preparing Carter's final return, her personal representative must first apply the $8,000 in suspended passive losses against Carter's realized gain of $5,000. Then, $1,000 of the remaining passive loss of $3,000 must be applied against Carter's passive income from the other activity. The remaining passive loss of $2,000 must then be deducted from Carter's wage income.

¶317.02

Chapter 4

Income and Deductions Reported on a Decedent's Final Return

¶ 401	Interest and Dividends
¶ 402	Interest on U.S. Savings Bonds
¶ 403	Taxation of Dividends
¶ 404	Stock Options and Employee Stock Purchase Plans
¶ 405	Agreements to Sell Stock at Stockholder's Death
¶ 406	S Corporation Income
¶ 407	Regulated Investment Company Stock – Exclude
¶ 408	Alimony
¶ 409	Life Insurance Proceeds Are Not Subject to Tax
¶ 410	Employee's Group-Term Life Insurance
¶ 411	Qualified Retirement Plans and Individual Retirement Accounts (IRAs)
¶ 412	Treatment of Medical, Health and Education Savings Accounts – Exclude
¶ 413	Charitable Contributions

Sources of income from a decedent's pursuits as a landowner, employee, and investor (including decedent's income derived from holdings of corporate and other stocks) are examined below. A description of income sources derived from a decedent's membership in a partnership is covered separately in Chapter 10.

¶ 401 Interest and Dividends

Interest received by a taxpayer or credited to a taxpayer's account is includible in income, unless an exception applies.[1] Interest income can be received by means of checks or coupons, in the form of merchandise, in the form of a discount, or by merely being credited to an account. Examples of fully taxable interest include interest on bank accounts, bonds (see ¶ 402), credit union accounts, loans, mortgages, notes, refund of taxes, and savings and loan accounts.

A cash-basis taxpayer is considered to have constructively received interest if it is credited to his or her account, set apart for him or her, or otherwise made available, provided his or her control of its receipt is not subject to substantial limitation or restriction.[2] Under the accrual method of accounting, a taxpayer

---

[1] Code Sec. 61(a)(4).   [2] Reg. § 1.451-2(a).

reports interest income in the tax year in which (1) all events have occurred that fix the right to the income and (2) the amount of income can be determined with reasonable certainty.[3]

Forms 1099, 1099-INT (Interest Income) and 1099-DIV (Dividends and Distributions), should be received for the decedent reporting interest and dividends earned before death and included on the decedent's final return. Separate Form 1099s should show the interest and dividends earned after the date of the decedent's death and paid to the estate or other recipient. IRS Publication 559 provides instructions on how to correctly report the interest and/or dividend income if a Form 1099 includes amounts belonging to both the decedent and another recipient.

For more information on dividends, see Chapter 3.

¶ 402 Interest on U.S. Savings Bonds

The interest on current issues of U.S. savings bonds is generally fully taxable. Series EE, Series HH and Series I are the only types of savings bonds that are available to the public. (The Series EE and HH bonds were formerly offered as Series E and H bonds. Series E and H bonds are all past their maturity dates and no longer earn interest.) Series EE bonds are bonds that are issued at a discount and increase in value each year until maturity. The increase in value is taxable as interest, except that a cash-basis taxpayer has the option of reporting the increase each year on a current basis or waiting until death or redemption (of the bonds) and thereby defer recognition until the bonds are redeemed. Series EE Bonds purchased beginning in May 2005 and after earn a fixed rate of return. Series HH bonds, which are available only in exchange for EE bonds, are issued at par value and pay interest semi-annually. The Series I bonds, available since 1998, accrue interest at a rate indexed to inflation and have a 30-year maturity period.

Interest on Series E, Series EE or Series I bonds that are registered solely in the name of a person is taxable to that person. Interest on Series E, Series EE or Series I bonds that are registered in the names of two persons, but that were purchased with the funds of only one of the co-owners, is taxable to the co-owner who provided the funds to purchase the bonds. If both co-owners provided funds to purchase the bonds, the interest on the bonds is reportable by each co-owner based on the portion of the purchase price that each contributed.[4]

If a cash-basis decedent did not elect to report the incremental accrued interest in value of Series E, Series EE or Series I savings bonds as income, the increment in value up to the date of his or her death becomes income in respect of a decedent under Code Sec. 691.[5] This rule applies to the following types of bonds:

- bonds that were purchased by the decedent and registered solely in his or her name;
- bonds that were registered in the names of the decedent and another person, as co-owners, and that were purchased by the decedent solely with his or her own funds; and

---

[3] Reg. § 1.446-1(c)(1).
[4] Rev. Rul. 54-143, 1954-1 CB 12.
[5] Rev. Rul. 64-104, 1964-1 CB (Part 1) 223, as distinguished by Rev. Rul. 68-145, 1968-1 CB 203.

Income and Deductions Reported on a Decedent's Final Return

- bonds that were acquired by the decedent, as the surviving co-owner, and that were purchased by the other co-owner where neither reported the increment as income.[6]

There are a number of optional ways to report the incremental accrual of interest on the above types of bonds as income:

1. An executor, administrator, or any other person charged with the property of a decedent, may elect to report the increment in value up to the date of the decedent's death on the decedent's final return.[7]

2. The administrator of a cash-basis estate may elect to report on its income tax return all the unreported interest on all of the decedent's bonds from the dates of their purchase to the year of the election. An election by the estate will not preclude the person who ultimately receives the bonds from electing to report the discount as income when the bonds are redeemed or finally mature. The IRS ruled that a testamentary trust that acquired a decedent's savings bonds was not bound by the executor's election and could report any remaining accrued increment upon the bonds' maturity or redemption, even though the executor was also the trustee.[8]

3. A cash-basis beneficiary who acquires savings bonds also has the option of either reporting the incremental accrual of interest up to when he or she acquires the bonds or holding the bonds until maturity or redemption and then reporting the unreported incremental interest as income. However, the IRS has ruled that if a "recipient" acquiring savings bonds from a decedent makes an election to report the increment, the recipient must include in gross income all of the unreported increment in value of all Series E bonds that he or she holds and not just the increment attributable to the decedent's bonds. Thereafter, the recipient should report in each tax year the increment in value actually accruing within such tax year.[9]

The unreported incremental interest that represented part of the consideration paid for Series H or HH bonds (in exchange for Series E or EE bonds), and the interest, if any, payable on the Series H or HH bonds (but not received) as of the owner's death also are income in respect of a cash-basis decedent, where the owner had not elected to report the increment in redemption value as income when it accrued.[10] The unexpired increment in the value of the Series E, Series EE or Series I bonds still held by the decedent at his or her death, as well as any unreported increment in the value attributable to the Series E, Series EE or Series I bonds, which by reason of the exchange constituted a part of the consideration paid for the Series H or HH bonds, is reportable by the estate or beneficiary. Treasury Direct has on-line calculators for each type of bond at www.treasurydirect.gov.

---

[6] Rev. Rul. 58-435, 1958-2 CB 370, as distinguished by Rev. Rul. 68-145, 1968-1 CB 203.
[7] Rev. Rul. 68-145, 1968-1 CB 203.
[8] Rev. Rul. 58-435, 1958-2 CB 370, as distinguished by Rev. Rul. 68-145, 1968-1 CB 203.
[9] Rev. Rul. 64-104, 1964-1 CB (Part 1) 223, as distinguished by Rev. Rul. 68-145, 1968-1 CB 203.
[10] Id.

¶402

The interest payable on the Series H or HH bonds but not received as of the date of the decedent's death is included in income when received by the estate or beneficiary.

¶ 403 Taxation of Dividends

Dividends on corporate stock are subject to tax when unqualifiedly made subject to the demands of the shareholder.[11] Therefore, dividends declared before the death of a decedent but payable by the terms of the declaration to stockholders of record on dates falling after the decedent's death are not income taxable to the decedent on the decedent's final return.[12] This rule applies even though the decedent was on the accrual basis. The dividend will be income to the estate or other person when it becomes the owner of the stock and receives the dividend.

It is possible, however, under the doctrine of constructive receipt, for a decedent to be taxable on a dividend in his or her final return even though the decedent had not actually received the dividend.

> *Example 1:* A dividend check was available to the taxpayer (if he personally appeared and demanded it) prior to the date of his death in sufficient time for him to cash or deposit it. Pursuant to taxpayer's request, however, the check was mailed to him, but it did not reach his home or office until after the date of his death. Under the doctrine of constructive receipt, the dividend would be taxable to the taxpayer on his final return.

It should be noted in connection with the above example that constructive receipt would not apply if the corporation customarily mailed the dividend checks to its shareholders. It has been held that, even though a taxpayer could have received his dividend check on the last day of the year had he appeared in person, the dividend will not be taxable until received if the corporation customarily mails its dividend checks.[13] This rule would appear to be equally applicable in the case of decedents.

Note also that a person reporting a dividend as income in respect of a decedent on a decedent's final return can claim a deduction for estate taxes paid to the extent that the dividend was included in the decedent's gross estate.[14] The recipient of the dividend must also reduce the amount reported as eligible for the reduced dividend rate by the amount claimed as a deduction for estate taxes.[15]

This has the effect of reducing the amount of decedent's income eligible for the reduced dividend tax rate by the deduction attributable to estate taxes. Prior to the amendment by the Working Families Tax Relief Act of 2004, the provision coordinating the estate tax deduction with the capital gains tax rate indicated that the amount of "gain" that was included as income in respect of a decedent and taxed at the net capital gain rate should be reduced by the amount of any applicable deduction for estate taxes attributable.[16] The use of the word "gain" instead of simply referring to the amounts eligible for the net capital gain tax rate caused some confusion over whether qualifying dividends were also included in the rule.

---

[11] Reg. § 1.301-1(b); *S.L. Avery*, SCt, 4 USTC ¶ 1277, 292 US 210.
[12] *H.W. Putnam Est.*, SCt, 45-1 USTC ¶ 9234, 324 US 393.
[13] *S.L. Avery*, SCt, 4 USTC ¶ 1277, 292 US 210.
[14] Code Sec. 691(c); Reg. § 1.691(c)-1.
[15] Code Sec. 691(c)(4).
[16] Code Sec. 691(c)(4).

¶ 404 Stock Options and Employee Stock Purchase Plans

Employee stock options that meet specified requirements are called statutory stock options and may qualify for deferred tax treatment. Nonstatutory stock options—that is, employee stock options not meeting these specified requirements—are taxed under the rules of Code Sec. 83 dealing with property transferred in connection with the performance of services.

An employee stock option is a written offer made to an employee by the employer corporation (or by its parent or subsidiary corporation) to sell its stock at a stated or determinable price for a stated period. The employee is under no obligation to purchase the stock.[17]

.01 Statutory Stock Options

There are two types of statutory stock options: (1) options issued under employee stock purchase plans[18] and (2) incentive stock options.[19] The major difference between the two types of plans is that the incentive stock options can be offered on a selected basis while employee stock purchase plans generally offer options to all employees. An individual is not taxed upon the grant or exercise of a statutory stock option provided that (1) the stock received is neither disposed of within two years of the date of the grant nor within one year after the stock is transferred to the individual, and (2) the option holder is an employee of the corporation (or its parent or subsidiary) from the time the option is granted to a period ending three months before the date the option is exercised.[20] Accordingly, the tax consequences regarding the transfer of the stock are deferred until there is a disposition of the stock. If the shares acquired are held for the long-term capital gain holding period (i.e., for more than one year), any gain eventually realized on disposition of the stock will be long-term capital gain.

If the employee dies while holding a statutory stock option and the option can be transferred by will or the laws of descent and distribution, the option will retain its status as a statutory stock option in the hands of the estate or other person who acquires the option by reason of the death of the deceased employee. Thus, if the option is distributed by the estate to a beneficiary as part of the estate, the option remains a statutory stock option. But if the estate or beneficiary sells the option, the option will cease to be a statutory stock option. The estate or beneficiary who succeeds to the option is subject to the same rules that would have applied to the deceased employee in all but two ways:[21]

1. the employer-employee relationship does not apply to the estate or beneficiary—thereby negating the requirement that a statutory stock option be exercised within three months after the termination of the deceased employee's employment; and

2. the holding period requirements otherwise applicable to stock acquired under a statutory stock option do not apply to the estate or beneficiary.

---

[17] Reg. § 1.421-1(a).
[18] Code Sec. 423.
[19] Code Sec. 422.
[20] Code Secs. 422(a) and 423(a).
[21] Code Sec. 421(c)(1).

The estate or beneficiary, however, is still bound by the holding period applicable under the capital gains provisions to determine whether the gain or loss upon disposition of stock acquired under a statutory stock option is entitled to long-term capital gain or loss treatment.[22]

.02 Employee Stock Purchase Plans

An employee stock purchase plan must meet *all* of the following conditions:[23]

1. The plan must provide that options to purchase stock in the corporation are to be granted only to employees of the employer corporation or of its parent or subsidiary.

2. The plan must receive stockholder approval within 12 months before or after the date the plan was adopted.

3. Under the terms of the plan, no employee may receive an option if he or she owns, immediately after the option is granted, 5% or more of the total combined voting power or value of all classes of stock of the employer, its parent, or its subsidiary.

4. Under the terms of the plan, options are to be granted to all personnel. However, employees may be excluded who have worked less than two years, or whose customary employment is 20 hours or less per week, or who do not work for more than five months a year, or who are highly compensated employees.

5. Under the terms of the plan, all employees who are granted options must receive the same rights and privileges. However, the plan may provide that the maximum amount of stock that an employee may purchase under the option bear a uniform relationship to total compensation, or his or her basic or regular rate of compensation. The plan may also provide that no employee may purchase more than the maximum amount of stock fixed under the plan.

6. Under the terms of the plan, the option price may not be less than 85% of the fair market value of the stock either at the time the option is granted or at the time it is exercised, whichever is less.

7. Under the terms of the plan, the option cannot be exercised after the expiration of (a) five years from the date the option is granted (if, under the plan terms, the option price is not less than 85% of the fair market value of such stock at the time the option is exercised); or (b) 27 months from the date such option is granted (if the option price is not determinable as described in (a)).

8. Under the terms of the plan, no employee may purchase stock in excess of $25,000 per calendar year.

9. Under the terms of the plan, the option must be nontransferable and exercisable only by the employee during the employee's lifetime.

---

[22] Reg. § 1.421-2(c).   [23] Code Sec. 423(b).

.03 Incentive Stock Options

An employer corporation and its related corporations can offer incentive stock options to employees on a selective basis. For an option to qualify as an incentive stock option, the terms of the option itself must meet *all* of the following conditions:[24]

1. The option must be granted pursuant to a plan that includes the aggregate number of shares that may be issued under options and the employees (or class of employees) eligible to receive them and must be approved by the stockholders of the granting corporation within 12 months before or after the plan is adopted.

2. The option must be granted within ten years of the date of adoption or the date of approval, whichever is earlier.

3. The term of the option may not exceed ten years.

4. The option price is not less than the fair market value of the stock at the time the option is granted.

5. The option by its terms must be nontransferable other than at death and must be exercisable during the employee's lifetime only by the employee.

6. The employee does not, at the time the option is granted, own more than 10% of the combined voting power of the corporation (or its parent or subsidiary).

The aggregate fair market value of the stock for which incentive stock options are exercisable for the first time by an employee during any calendar year is limited to $100,000. Options will not be treated as incentive stock options to the extent that the aggregate fair market value (determined when the option is granted) exceeds $100,000.[25]

.04 Stock Options Held by a Decedent

When an employee dies after exercising a statutory stock option but before disposing of the stock, the transfer of the stock from the decedent to his or her estate or beneficiary is not a "disposition" of the stock for income tax purposes.[26] However, for stock acquired under an employee stock purchase plan at an option price between 85% and 100% of the fair market value at the time that the option was granted, ownership of the stock at death may result in compensation (ordinary income) on the employee's final return. In such case, the includible compensation is the lesser of (1) the excess of the fair market value of the stock at the time of the employee's death over the amount paid for it or (2) the excess of the fair market value of the stock at the time that the option was granted *over* the option price. This amount, however, is not taken into consideration in determining the basis of the

---

[24] Code Sec. 422(b).
[25] Code Sec. 422(d).
[26] Code Sec. 424(c)(1)(A); Reg. § 1.424-1(c)(1)(i).

stock to the decedent's estate or beneficiary. Instead, the estate or beneficiary will take the stock's estate tax valuation as its basis.[27]

> *Example 2:* Employee was granted an option under an employee stock purchase plan to purchase 100 shares of stock for $90 each when the stock was selling for $95 per share. He exercised the option and died one year later when the stock was selling for $100 per share. The $5-per-share excess of the $95 value of the stock at the time the option was granted *over* the $90 option price will be included as compensation on Employee's final return because it is less than the $10-per-share excess of the $100 value of the stock at Employee's death *over* the $90 paid for it. Assuming that the stock is valued at $100 per share for estate tax purposes, the estate or beneficiary will take a $100 basis for each share.

For purposes of computing gain or loss on the disposition of stock acquired by an estate or beneficiary under a statutory stock option issued to an employee, the value of the option at date of death (or the alternative estate tax valuation date) is added to the option price to determine its basis to the estate or beneficiary. This is a tentative basis that must be adjusted downward if (and to the extent that) the amount treated as ordinary income is less than the amount that would have been so treated if the employee had exercised the option and held the stock at the date of death. Also, the amount treated as ordinary income is to be added to the basis of the stock if (and to the extent that) this amount exceeds the value of the option for estate tax purposes.[28]

> *Example 3:* On February 1, Year 1, Employee, was granted an option under an employee stock purchase plan to buy one share of her employer's stock for $85. On that date, the fair market value of the stock was $100. Employee died October 1, Year 2, without having exercised the option. On that date, the fair market value of the stock was $105. Federal estate tax was due, and her estate elected to use the alternative valuation date (six months after decedent's death), at which time the fair market value of the stock was $95. On October 6, Year 3, the estate exercised the option and immediately sold the stock for $95. Under the above rules, $10 must be included as compensation in the estate's gross income for the tax year including October 6, Year 3. The basis of the stock to compute gain or loss on its sale is determined as follows:
>
> | | |
> |---|---:|
> | Value (in estate) of option on alternative valuation date ($95 – $85) ... | $10 |
>
> **Basis of stock**
>
> | | |
> |---|---:|
> | Option value | $10 |
> | Plus: Cost of stock (option price) | 85 |
> | Tentative stock basis | $95 |

---

[27] Reg. § 1.423-2(k).   [28] Code Sec. 421(c)(3).

Reduction in basis

Amount that would have been compensation to employee (as of date of death)	$15	
Less: Compensation to estate	10	5
Stock basis after reduction		$90

Addition to basis

Compensation to estate	$10	
Less: Basis of option	10	
Excess of compensation		0
Final stock basis		$90

Gain or loss

Proceeds from sale of stock	$95
Less: Final stock basis	90
Gain	$5

Generally, employee stock options and incentive stock options must, by their terms, be nontransferable. However, this general rule does not apply to transfers by will or the laws of descent or distribution.[29] Statutory stock options may be made exercisable by an employee's estate, and any statutory option will retain its status as such even if an estate or beneficiary disposes of stock acquired pursuant to such an option before the expiration of any otherwise mandatory holding period.[30] For instance, under employee stock purchase plans, shares generally may not be disposed of within two years of the granting of the option or within one year of the acquisition of the shares. The holding period requirements for employee stock purchase plans are distinguishable from the holding period rules for computing capital gain (or loss). Executors who dispose of carryover-basis property within one year of the decedent's death are deemed to have held such property for more than one year.[31]

.05 Nonstatutory Stock Options

For stock options that do not qualify as statutory stock options, the amount of income reportable as taxable compensation and the time for reporting such income depends on whether the option has a readily ascertainable fair market value when it is granted. Generally, an option does not have a readily ascertainable value unless the option is actively traded on an established securities market. However, even if the option is not actively traded on an established market, it will be considered to have a readily ascertainable value if the option (1) is transferable, (2) is immediately exercisable by the recipient, (3) is not subject to any restriction or condition (other than a lien or other condition to secure payment of the purchase price) that

---

[29] Code Secs. 422(b)(5) and 423(b)(9).
[30] Code Sec. 421(c)(1); Reg. § 1.421-2(c).
[31] Code Sec. 1223(10).

has a significant effect upon the fair market value of the option, and (4) the fair market value of the option privilege is readily ascertainable (i.e., whether the value of the entire option privilege can be measured with reasonable accuracy).[32] If the option has a readily ascertainable value, the difference between the fair market value of the option and the amount (if any) the employee paid for it is normally includible as taxable compensation in the employee's income in the year in which the option is granted. However, if the option is both nontransferable and subject to a substantial risk of forfeiture, there is no taxable income until the option becomes substantially vested (that is, the property becomes transferable or the risk of forfeiture ends, whichever event occurs first). At such time, the employee realizes income to the extent of the difference between the value of the option at that time and the amount (if any) he or she paid for the option.[33]

If a nonstatutory stock option does not have a readily ascertainable fair market value at the time it is granted, the employee does not realize income at the time of the grant. Normally, the option will become taxable upon exercise. At such time, income will be realized to the extent of the difference between the fair market value of the stock received and the amount (if any) the employee paid under the option. However, if the stock is both nontransferable and subject to a substantial risk of forfeiture, there is no taxable income until the stock becomes transferable or the risk of forfeiture is removed, whichever event occurs first. At such time the employee realizes income to the extent of the difference between the value of the stock at that time and the amount (if any) he or she paid under the option.[34]

If an "insider" sells stock in his or her corporation and, within six months after that, purchases stock in the corporation, securities law requires the insider to surrender to the corporation any profit realized. For the six-month period, shares that are subject to the short-swing profit provisions (Sec. 16(b) of the Securities Exchange Act of 1934 (15 U.S.C.A. § 78(p))) are regarded as subject to a substantial risk of forfeiture.[35] The short-swing profit provisions apply only to "insiders" such as officers, directors, or more-than-10-percent shareholders of publicly traded corporations. Any taxable gain to such insiders from receipt of their company's shares will be measured by the market price of the shares after passage of the six-month period during which the Securities Exchange Act exposes them to liability (to the corporation) for gain from the sale of the shares.

If an individual dies holding a substantially nonvested, nonstatutory stock option, the option is considered a right to receive income in respect of a decedent. Thus, the above rules regarding the taxation of options are applied to the estate, beneficiary, or other person who receives the option rights.[36]

¶ 405 Agreements to Sell Stock at Stockholder's Death

Stockholders, either between themselves or with the corporation, often enter into a buy-sell agreement whereby, upon the death of a stockholder, the surviving stockholders or the corporation may at their option purchase from the decedent's

---

[32] Reg. § 1.83-7(b).
[33] Code Sec. 83(a); Reg. § 1.83-7.
[34] Code Sec. 83(a); Reg. § 1.83-7.
[35] Code Sec. 83(c)(3).
[36] Reg. § 1.83-1(d).

estate, the decedent's stock at a stipulated price. Frequently, the stock purchase funds are provided by the proceeds of life insurance taken out on the lives of the stockholders. The agreement is only executory in nature. Therefore, no actual sale takes place until after the stockholder's death (if the option is exercised). Moreover, title to the stock does not pass upon death to the surviving stockholders or corporation, which have at best only an action on the contract or for specific performance. Accordingly, no income accrues to the decedent to be included in his or her final return under the contract. Also, if the option is exercised, the money received for the stock by the estate (or person who acquired ownership through the decedent) is not income in respect of a decedent. In other words, the money received by the estate (or other person) would not be taxed in the same manner as if the decedent had lived and received the money.[37] The estate (or other person) would use the fair market value of the stock at the date of the decedent's death (or, if applicable, the alternate valuation date) in determining the gain or loss realized on the sale of the stock under the agreement.[38]

The above rules would apply even though there existed at the date of the decedent's death a binding agreement to buy and sell, not just an option. This is true because the decedent did not receive any money under the contract prior to death, and amounts accrued only by reason of death are not includible in the final return.[39] Also, because the decedent on the date of death had no rights to income under the contract, the money received by the estate or other person acquiring ownership of the stock through the decedent under the contract would not be income in respect of a decedent.

¶ 406 S Corporation Income

The final return of a decedent who owned stock in an S corporation must include as taxable income the decedent's share of S corporation income for the corporation's tax year that ends within or with the decedent's last tax year. The decedent's pro rata share of the S corporation's income for the period between the end of the corporation's last tax year and the date of the decedent's death must also be included in the final return.[40] A shareholder who dies is treated as the shareholder for the day of his or her death.[41] Following the death of a shareholder, the decedent's estate can be an eligible shareholder of the S corporation stock for a reasonable period necessary to administer the estate.[42]

The income that accrued in the portion of the S corporation's tax year after the decedent's death is treated as income to the estate or to any other person who has acquired the decedent's S corporation stock and must be reported by the estate or the acquiring shareholder as such.[43] See Chapter 11 for more information on the treatment of S corporations.

---

[37] Reg. § 1.691(a)-2(b), Example (4).
[38] Reg. § 1.1014-1.
[39] Reg. § 1.691(a)-1(b).
[40] Code Sec. 1366(a)(1); Reg. § 1.1366-1(a).
[41] Reg. § 1.1377-1(a)(2)(ii).
[42] Code Sec. 1361(b)(1)(B).
[43] Senate Committee Report to the Subchapter S Revision Act of 1982 (P.L. 97-354).

¶ 407 Regulated Investment Company Stock

A nonresident, non-U.S. citizen-decedent who died after December 31, 2004 but before January 1, 2012,[44] owning a portion of stock in a regulated investment company (RIC) will not be deemed as owning that property within the United States[45] and the stock will not be includible in the estate of such shareholder for federal estate tax purposes. The portion that is exempt from taxation is determined at the end of the quarter of the RIC's tax year immediately preceding the decedent's date of death or other time to be prescribed by regulation. The exempt amount is the proportion of the RIC's assets that were qualifying assets with respect to the decedent in relation to the total assets of the RIC. Qualifying assets are those assets that, if owned by the decedent, would have been:[46]

1. bank deposits that are exempt from income tax;
2. portfolio debt obligations;
3. certain original issue discount obligations;
4. debt obligations of a U.S. corporation that are treated as giving rise to foreign source income; and
5. other property not within the United States.

¶ 408 Alimony

Prior to December 31, 2018, if a separated or divorced individual makes payments to his or her spouse that qualify as alimony or separate maintenance, the payments will generally be deductible by the payer and taxable to the payee. For payments required under a divorce or separation instrument that is executed after December 31, 2018, the 2017 Tax Cuts and Jobs Act[47] eliminates the deduction for alimony payments. Thus, the payor will no longer receive a deduction, and the recipient will no longer include the alimony in taxable income.

Note, however, a divorce or separation instrument may provide that payments otherwise qualifying for alimony treatment are to be treated as non-alimony payments.[48] Even though payments made under a divorce or separation instrument will not be disqualified from treatment as alimony simply because the instrument does not expressly provide that the payments are to terminate at death, no alimony deduction will be allowed if the payments do not terminate at death.[49]

¶ 409 Life Insurance Proceeds Are Not Subject to Tax

The proceeds of life insurance that are received under a life insurance contract or policy and are paid because of the death of the insured are generally excluded from gross income.[50] The exclusion applies to proceeds of life insurance purchased for employees by employers, whether under a group policy or individual employee policies, as well as life insurance policies purchased by an individual for him or

---

[44] Code Sec. 2105(d)(3).
[45] Code Sec. 2105(d)(1).
[46] Code Sec. 2105(d)(2).
[47] P.L. 115-97.
[48] Code Sec. 71(b)(1)(B).
[49] Code Sec. 71(b)(1)(D).
[50] Code Sec. 101(a)(1).

herself. The exclusion applies regardless of who receives the proceeds, whether it is an individual, a partnership, or a corporation.

The exclusion also applies to proceeds received under an endowment contract when they are payable to a beneficiary if the insured dies before the contract's maturity. However, the IRS has ruled that life insurance proceeds paid to shareholders are taxable as dividends if premiums are paid out of corporate earnings and the corporation has all the incidents of ownership of the policy.[51] This is softened by a further private ruling dealing with a situation in which the beneficiary was a shareholder's surviving spouse.[52] The surviving spouse was not a shareholder, so the proceeds were not deemed a dividend; and since such proceeds are excluded from gross income, they could not be income in respect of a decedent.

.01 Accelerated Death Benefits

If certain requirements are satisfied, accelerated death benefits received under a life insurance contract on the life of an insured, terminally or chronically ill individual may be excluded from gross income. Accelerated death benefits are amounts received by the insured, pursuant to a life insurance contract on his or her life, before, and in anticipation of, death. Similarly, if a portion of a life insurance contract is assigned or sold to a viatical settlement provider (see below), amounts from the provider are excludable from gross income.[53]

A "terminally ill individual" is a person for whom the insurer has obtained certification from a physician that the individual has an illness or physical condition that is reasonably expected to result in death within 24 months of the date of certification.[54] A "chronically ill individual" is any person who is not terminally ill and who is certified within the preceding 12-month period by a licensed health care practitioner as:

- being unable to perform at least two activities of daily living for a period of at least 90 days due to a loss of functional capacity,
- having a similar level of disability, as designated by regulations, or
- requiring substantial supervision to protect the person from threats to health and safety because of severe cognitive impairment.[55]

Accelerated life insurance proceeds, paid on a chronically ill insured, are excludable from gross income in a manner similar to amounts paid for long-term care. Amounts paid under a life insurance contract are excludable by the payee if the payment is for actual costs of qualified long-term care incurred by the payee that are not compensated for by insurance or otherwise. This exclusion is dependent on the satisfaction of two additional requirements: (1) the contract does not pay or reimburse expenses that are reimbursable under Medicare, except when Medicare is a secondary payer, or when the contract makes payments on a per diem or another periodic basis without regard to actual expenses; and (2) the consumer protection provisions of Code Sec. 7702B(g) are met. However, if stan-

---

[51] Rev. Rul. 61-134, 1961-2 CB 250.
[52] IRS Letter Ruling 8144001, September 28, 1978.
[53] Code Sec. 101(g).
[54] Code Sec. 101(g)(4)(A).
[55] Code Sec. 101(g)(4)(B).

dards adopted by the National Association of Insurance Commissioners or by the state where the policyholder resides specifically apply to chronically ill individuals, the analogous standards under the consumer protection provisions do not apply.[56]

Payments made on a per diem or other periodic basis without regard to actual expenses are still excludable from gross income,[57] but subject to the dollar cap applicable under per diem type long-term care insurance contracts.[58] The maximum amount of excludable payments is subject to daily or annual limitations, or the equivalent amount in the case of payments made on a different periodic basis. The amount is adjusted annually for inflation.[59]

> ***Example 4:*** Brown, a chronically ill individual, receives accelerated life insurance proceeds in the amount of $10,000. His qualified long-term care expenses are $14,000, but $8,000 is reimbursed by insurance. Only the unreimbursed expenses of $6,000 are excludable from income. The remaining $4,000 ($10,000 – $6,000) is includible in income. If, instead of receiving a lump sum, Brown received per diem payments of $312 per day, the entire amount would be excludable, regardless of actual costs.

A viatical settlement provider is any person that is regularly engaged in the trade or business of purchasing or accepting assignment of life insurance contracts on the lives of terminally or chronically ill insureds. To qualify as a viatical settlement provider, the person must be licensed in the state in which the insured resides. If licensing is not required in that state, the person must meet other requirements that depend on whether the insured is terminally or chronically ill.[60]

The IRS has issued guidance addressing circumstances under which a viatical settlement provider will be treated as licensed by a state. A viatical settlement provider is treated as licensed in a state, where temporary authority has been granted to the provider to engage in business while the state reviews the provider's pending licensing applications, and in another state, where blanket authority to engage in business has been granted to all viatical settlement providers pending further guidance. However, a provider is not treated as licensed and may not qualify as a viatical settlement provider, in a third state, where the licensing statute is effective, but a procedure is not yet in place for licensing providers, nor has the appropriate regulatory authority granted permission, even temporarily, for providers to engage in business until licensing procedures are in place. Therefore, sellers or assignors residing in that state may not exclude any portion of the amount received from the provider. The provider's failure to qualify as a licensed provider in the state does not affect whether it qualifies as licensed in any other state. The guidance is effective for all amounts received on or after January 1, 1997. However, amounts received pursuant to sales or assignments entered into before June 23, 2003, by residents of any state that requires licensing of viatical settlement providers but has neither issued temporary authority to particular viatical settlement providers nor blanket authority to all viatical settlement providers that are not yet

---

[56] Code Sec. 101(g)(3)(B).
[57] Code Sec. 101(g)(3)(C).
[58] Code Sec. 101(g)(3)(D).
[59] In 2012, for example, the per diem rate was $312 ($113,150 annually) pursuant to Rev. Proc. 2011-52, 2011-45 IRB 701.
[60] Code Sec. 101(g)(2)(B).

individually licensed will be treated as received from a viatical settlement provider if, at the time of the sale or assignment the provider satisfied the requirements of Code Sec. 101(g)(2)(b)(i)(II).[61]

.02 Installment Payments

The manner in which the proceeds are paid is also of no consequence. Lump-sum and installment payments are both excluded. However, if installment payments include an element of interest, the interest will have to be included in income under a special statutory formula.[62]

When life insurance proceeds are held by the insurer under an agreement to pay interest thereon, the interest portion of the payments must be included in gross income.[63] For example, when the proceeds are left with the insurer under an agreement to make annual payments to the beneficiary for life in the form of interest and to pay the principal sum to a second beneficiary on death of the first beneficiary, all of the payments to the first beneficiary are taxable as interest because they consist solely of income from the insurance proceeds, rather than the proceeds themselves.

When a life insurance contract provides for optional modes of settlement at the election of the insured or the beneficiary, it does not matter which party makes the election. The proceeds will be excludable because they will be made under an insurance contract and because of the death of the insured.

If the life insurance policy provides no option, and the beneficiary and the insurer, by supplemental agreement, arrange for the beneficiary to receive installment payments, the installment payments will not be excludable as life insurance death proceeds but will be subject to the annuity rules of Code Sec. 72. The reason for this different treatment is that the installments would not be paid under a life insurance contract because of the death of the insured. They would be paid under the provisions of the supplemental agreement, a reason other than the death of the insured.

.03 Policy Transfers

When a life insurance policy is transferred for valuable consideration, the proceeds of the policy paid to the transferee because of the insured's death are excludable from income only to the extent of the consideration paid for the transfer plus the amount of premiums and other sums subsequently paid by the transferee. This transferee rule, however, does not apply when a policy is transferred as a gift or, generally, in connection with a tax-free exchange. It also does not apply if the transfer of the contract was to the insured, a partner of the insured, a partnership including the insured, or a corporation of which the insured was a shareholder or officer. In such cases, therefore, the proceeds are entirely excluded.[64]

---

[61] Rev. Rul. 2002-82, 2002-2 CB 978.
[62] Code Sec. 101(c) and (d).
[63] Code Sec. 101(c).
[64] Code Sec. 101(a)(2).

.04 Flexible Premium Policies

Flexible premium policies, sometimes called "universal life" policies or "adjustable life" policies, allow policyholders to contribute toward the cash value of a policy without increasing its death benefit. Payments from these types of policies can only be excluded from gross income if the contract was issued prior to January 1, 1985. In addition, death benefits paid under flexible premium life insurance contracts issued before 1985 will only qualify for the exclusion for the proceeds of life insurance purchased for employees by employers if (1) the sum of premiums paid under the contract at any time does not exceed a specifically computed "guideline premium limitation," and any amount payable on the death of the insured is not less than the "applicable percentage" of the contract's cash value as of the date of death; or (2) the cash value does not exceed the "net single premium" for the death benefit (without regard to any additional benefits) at such time.[65] The "guideline premium limitation" is the greater, on any date, of the single premium amount necessary to fund the contract or the sum of level annual payments over the life of the contract (but not less than 20 years).

.05 What Is Insurance?

Concern over the use of insurance to achieve investment objectives led to enactment of a definition of a "life insurance contract." Contracts issued after 1984 that fail to meet this definition expose policyholders to receipt of ordinary income to the extent of any increase in net cash surrender value plus any excess of the cost of life insurance protection over premiums paid (reduced by policyholder dividends). In general, the statutory definition requires a contract to qualify as life insurance under applicable state or foreign law and meet either a cash value accumulation test or a guideline premium/cash value corridor test.

.06 Unrecovered Investment in Annuity Contracts

The entire investment in an annuity contract with a refund feature may be recovered tax free if annuity payments cease because of the annuitant's death. This rule applies to individuals whose annuity starting date is after December 31, 1986.

Generally, if an annuitant dies before receiving the full amount of his or her contributions, the amount that was not recovered (i.e., the unrecovered investment in contract) may be deducted on the annuitant's final tax return.[66] However, if an annuity has a refund feature, the investment in contract must be reduced, under Code Sec. 72(c)(2), by the present value of the refund feature.

.07 Death Benefits Resulting from Terrorist Attacks

Amounts paid by employers as a result of the death of an employee who is a "specified terrorist victim" under Code Sec. 692(d)(4) (see ¶ 216) are generally excluded from gross income.[67] However, payments that would have been payable after death if the employee had died other than as a specified terrorist victim are not excludable from gross income, unless they are incidental death payments as described in Code Sec. 401(a) and exempt from tax under Code Sec. 501(a).[68] The

---

[65] Code Sec. 101(f).
[66] Code Sec. 72(b)(3)(A).
[67] Code Sec. 101(i)(1).
[68] Code Sec. 101(i)(2).

income exclusion applies to both lump-sum and installment payments, and also applies to self-employed individuals (as defined in Code Sec. 401(c)(1)).[69]

.08 Death Benefits for Astronauts

Certain death benefits paid by the U.S. government to the survivors of astronauts who die in the line of duty after December 31, 2002, are excluded from gross income.[70] The exclusion does not apply to benefits that would have been payable if the individual had died by reason of an event occurring outside the line of duty.[71]

¶ 410 Employee's Group-Term Life Insurance

An employee must include in income the cost of group-term life insurance provided by his or her employer, to the extent that such cost exceeds the cost of $50,000 of such insurance.[72] Thus, such income may be includible on a decedent's final return. A former employee covered by a qualifying plan is eligible for the exclusion.

> **Example 5:** Corp. pays the premiums on a $70,000 group-term life insurance policy on the life of its president, Zimmer, with Zimmer's husband as beneficiary. Zimmer is 50 years old. Under the tables in the applicable regulations,[73] the cost per $1,000 of coverage for employees in Zimmer's age bracket is 23 cents per month. Assuming Zimmer dies on October 1, her final return should include income of $41.40 from her group-term life insurance coverage ($41.40 = $0.23 (monthly cost per $1,000 of coverage) × 9 (months in Zimmer's final tax year) × 20 (for each $1,000 of coverage in excess of $50,000)).

If a decedent was a "key employee" (see below) and group-term life insurance was provided under a plan that discriminates in favor of key employees, the cost of the first $50,000 of insurance that would otherwise have been excludable from the key employee's income will be included in gross income.[74]

The term "key employee" has the same meaning as in Code Sec. 416(i).[75] A "key employee" is any participant in an employer plan who, at any time during the plan year, is (1) an officer with compensation in excess of $130,000,[76] adjusted for inflation in increments of $5,000 for plan years beginning after 2002, (2) a five percent owner (no more than 50 employees or, if fewer, the greater of three employees or 10% of the employees are treated as officers), or (3) a one percent owner with compensation in excess of $150,000.[77]

The term "key employee" also includes a decedent or any retired employee who was a key employee in the year of retirement or death or in any of the four preceding years.[78]

---

[69] Code Sec. 101(i)(3).
[70] Code Sec. 101(i)(4).
[71] Code Sec. 101(i)(2)(A). See ¶ 216 for more detailed information.
[72] Code Sec. 79(a)(1).
[73] Reg. § 1.79-3(d)(2).
[74] Code Sec. 79(d).
[75] Code Sec. 79(d)(6).
[76] Notice 2012-67, 2012-60 IRB 671 (the $130,000 figure in (1), above, is adjusted for inflation in increments of $5,000 for plan years beginning after 2002).
[77] Code Sec. 416(i).
[78] Code Sec. 79(d)(8).

A health insurance deduction of 100% of applicable health insurance expenses, including limited long term care insurance premiums, is available to self-employed individuals and to general partners in a partnership (or limited partners receiving guaranteed payments) and to shareholders owning more than 2% of the outstanding stock of an S corporation.[79]

¶ 411 Qualified Retirement Plans and Individual Retirement Accounts (IRAs)

The Internal Revenue Code expressly provides that the surviving spouse of a participant in a qualified retirement plan may make a tax-free rollover contribution to an IRA of all or a part of a lump-sum distribution received on account of the death of the participant.[80] A surviving spouse of a deceased participant in a qualified retirement plan is entitled to make a tax-free rollover of an eligible rollover distribution from the plan to another qualified plan, a Code Sec. 403(b) annuity, or a Code Sec. 457 governmental plan that the surviving spouse participates in, as well as to an IRA.[81]

> **Example 6:** Thomas was a participant in his company's qualified retirement plan when he died. His surviving spouse, Angela, is an employee of a public school, where she participates in a Code Sec. 403(b) tax-sheltered annuity arrangement. She is not a participant in a qualified retirement plan or a Code Sec. 457 governmental plan. After Thomas's death, Angela is entitled to make a tax-free rollover of the eligible rollover distribution from her husband's employer's plan to an IRA or to the Code Sec. 403(b) annuity plan maintained by her employer.

Notwithstanding an IRS contention that the right to roll over a lump-sum distribution was (except with respect to a spouse) personal to an employee, a U.S. district court has ruled that an estate could complete a rollover, where the decedent had received the distribution during life but had not yet effectuated the rollover.[82] In any event, however, the rollover must be completed within 60 days of the distribution.[83] The IRS may waive the 60-day rollover period if the failure to grant such a waiver would be against equity or good conscience, including casualty, disaster, or other events beyond the reasonable control of the individual subject to such requirement.[84] Generally, a taxpayer must apply to the IRS for a hardship exception to the 60-day rollover requirement, accompanied by the appropriate user fee. However, no application is required if (1) a financial institution receives funds on behalf of a taxpayer prior to the expiration of the 60-day rollover period; (2) the taxpayer follows all procedures required by the financial institution for depositing the funds into an eligible retirement plan within the 60-day period and; (3) solely due to an error on the part of the financial institution, the funds are not deposited into an eligible retirement plan within the 60-day rollover period. Automatic approval is granted only if: (1) the funds are deposited into an eligible retirement plan

---

[79] Code Sec. 162(l)(1).
[80] Code Sec. 402(c)(9).
[81] Id.
[82] M.J. Gunther, DC Mich., 83-1 USTC ¶ 9252, 573 FSupp 126.
[83] Code Sec. 402(c)(3).
[84] Code Secs. 402(c)(3) and 408(d)(3)(I).

within one year from the beginning of the 60-day rollover period; and (2) had the financial institution deposited the funds as instructed, it would have been a valid rollover.[85]

To be eligible for a waiver of the 60-day rollover period, either automatic or through application to the IRS, the rules regarding the amount of money or other property that can be rolled over into an eligible retirement plan within the 60-day rollover period apply to deposits made pursuant to a waiver of the 60-day rollover period.[86]

The time for making a rollover may be postponed in the event of service in a combat zone or in the case of a presidentially declared disaster or a terrorist or military action.[87]

Generally, if a decedent's IRA proceeds pass through a third party (e.g., a trust or estate) and are then distributed to the surviving spouse, the IRS will treat the IRA proceeds as having come from the third party, and not from the decedent, making the spouse ineligible to make a subsequent tax-free rollover of the proceeds to his or her own IRA. However, depending on the facts, the IRS may make an exception to this rule, as it did when a surviving spouse was treated as the direct payee or distributee of an amount rolled over from the proceeds of her deceased husband's annuities into an IRA set up and maintained in her name, even though her husband's estate was the designated beneficiary under each of the annuities. The husband's will made his surviving spouse the residuary beneficiary. The only other bequest under the will was to a credit shelter trust. The executor (the decedent's son) funded the trust with an amount from the Code Sec. 403(b) annuities that equaled the federal estate tax exemption at time of the decedent's death and then transferred the remainder of the proceeds, the rollover amount, to the widow. The surviving spouse was not treated as receiving the amount from her deceased husband's estate since the executor of the estate had no discretion in paying over to her, the sole residuary beneficiary, the amount in the annuity that exceeded the amount equal to the federal estate tax exemption (and transferred to the credit shelter trust). No portion of the amount transferred was includible in her gross income.[88]

In another instance, where the surviving spouse was both the sole executrix of the estate with authority to allocate assets to the beneficiaries and the sole residuary beneficiary, she was treated as though she received the IRA proceeds directly from the IRA rather than from the beneficiary estate. The spouse, as executrix, paid the proceeds of the IRA to herself as residuary beneficiary and rolled them over into her own IRA within 60 days from the date she received the IRA distribution as executrix.[89]

The IRS also allowed a surviving spouse's tax-free rollover of IRA proceeds to an IRA set up in her own name after the spouse: revoked a trust to which the

---

[85] Rev. Proc. 2003-16, § 3.03, 2003-1 CB 359.
[86] Rev. Proc. 2003-16, § 3.04, 2003-1 CB 359.
[87] Reg. § 301.7508A-1; Rev. Proc. 2007-56, 2007-2 CB 388.
[88] IRS Letter Ruling 200325008 (December 6, 2002).
[89] IRS Letter Ruling 200236052 (June 18, 2002).

decedent's IRA proceeds were distributed, so that the proceeds passed to her;[90] exercised her power, as executrix of the decedent's estate, to allocate to her own marital share IRA proceeds that passed to the estate pursuant to the decedent's will;[91] and acquired the decedent's IRA proceeds following the execution of qualified disclaimers by all of the beneficiaries.[92]

An "inherited" IRA—one passing by reason of death to someone other than the decedent's spouse—is subject to special rules. If a surviving spouse becomes the owner of an IRA by reason of the death of his or her spouse, the survivor can roll over the inherited amount to another IRA as if the surviving spouse had established the account. Beginning with the Pension Protection Act of 2006, a nonspouse beneficiary of an IRA by reason of the owner's death is also eligible for rollover treatment with respect to the inherited account, and required minimum distributions are made over the recipient's life expectancy.[93]

A lump-sum distribution from an inherited IRA is taxable in the year received as income in respect of a decedent up to the decedent's balance at the time of death, including unrealized appreciation and income accrued to date of death minus any nontaxable basis (nondeductible contributions).[94] Amounts distributed that are more than the decedent's entire IRA balance (which includes taxable and nontaxable amounts) at the time of death are the income of the beneficiary. If the distribution is properly rolled over into another traditional IRA, a qualified plan, a Code Sec. 403(b) annuity, or a Code Sec. 457 governmental plan, the distribution is not currently taxed.[95]

The nondeductible Roth IRA, which offered certain tax advantages not available under the traditional IRA, became available to taxpayers for the first time in 1998. Qualified distributions from a Roth IRA are not includible in the taxpayer's income. A distribution made to a beneficiary or to the Roth IRA owner's estate on or after the date of death will be treated as a qualified distribution if it is made after the five-year period beginning with the first tax year in which a contribution was made to the owner's Roth IRA. Thus, if the first tax year was 2010, only distributions made to a beneficiary or the decedent's estate after 2014 will be treated as qualified distributions.[96]

Generally, the interest in a Roth IRA can be distributed over the beneficiary's lifetime or life expectancy, unless there is no designated beneficiary in which case it must be by the end of the fifth calendar year after the year of the owner's death. If paid as an annuity, the distribution must begin before the end of the calendar year following the year of death. A surviving spouse who is the sole beneficiary can delay the distributions until the decedent would have reached the age of 70½ or can treat the Roth IRA as his or her own Roth IRA.[97]

---

[90] IRS Letter Ruling 9811008 (December 16, 1997).
[91] IRS Letter Ruling 199910067 (December 16, 1998). See also IRS Letter Ruling 9703036 (October 24, 1996).
[92] IRS Letter Ruling 9615043 (January 17, 1996).
[93] P.L. 109-280; Code Sec. 408(d)(3).
[94] Rev. Rul. 92-47, 1992-1 CB 198.
[95] Code Sec. 408(d)(3).
[96] Code Sec. 408A(d)(2)(B); Reg. § 1.408A-6, Q&A 2, Q&A 7.
[97] Reg. § 1.408A-6, Q&A 14(b).

¶ 412 Treatment of Medical, Health and Education Savings Accounts

.01 Medical Savings Accounts

The Archer medical savings account (MSA) was created in 1996 to give eligible individuals a new way of defraying unreimbursed health care expenses that would otherwise be eligible for the medical expense deduction. After 2007, no new MSAs may be established, but contributions to existing MSAs may continue.[98] Availability in the program was limited to individuals who were either self-employed or employed by a small employer having 50 or fewer employees.

If the account holder's surviving spouse acquires an interest in a medical savings account by reason of being the designated beneficiary of such account, at the death of the account holder, the MSA will be treated as if the surviving spouse were the account holder.[99]

If, by reason of the death of the account holder, any person other than the surviving spouse acquires the account holder's interest in the MSA, the account will cease to be a medical savings account as of the date of death, and an amount equal to the fair market value of the assets in the account on the date of death will be includible in such person's gross income for the tax year that includes the date of death.[100]

The amount includible in gross income by any person (other than the estate) will be reduced by the amount of qualified medical expenses that were incurred by the decedent before the date of the decedent's death and paid by such person within one year of the date of death.[101]

An appropriate deduction will be allowed under Code Sec. 691(c) to any person (other than the decedent or the surviving spouse) for amounts included in gross income by such person.[102]

.02 Health Savings Accounts

Health savings accounts (HSAs) are tax-favored savings and investment vehicles that allow taxpayers to use tax-free money to pay medical expenses.[103] HSAs are basically Archer MSAs with the existing eligibility restrictions removed. Contributions to an HSA are generally deductible from the account holder's gross income. Contributions continue to belong to the account holder from year to year, and may be invested to earn tax-free income. Distributions are excluded from gross income if they are used to pay qualified medical expenses.[104] Distributions that are not for qualified medical expenses are included in gross income and are subject to an additional penalty. An HSA beneficiary is the person on whose behalf the account was established, who is covered under a high deductible health plan, and may be the taxpayer, the taxpayer's spouse, or the taxpayer's dependents.

---

[98] Code Sec. 220(i).
[99] Code Sec. 220(f)(8)(A).
[100] Code Sec. 220(f)(8)(B)(i).
[101] Code Sec. 220(f)(8)(B)(ii).
[102] Id.
[103] The Medicare Prescription Drug, Improvement, and Modernization Act of 2003 (P.L. 108-173) created these accounts, which can be established after 2003.
[104] Code Sec. 223.

To be eligible for an HSA, an individual's only health insurance must be provided by a high deductible health plan, rather than comprehensive health insurance.[105] An eligible individual can also be covered by a plan that provides only permitted coverage, permitted insurance, or preventive care insurance. Individuals who receive Medicare benefits or who can be claimed as dependents are not eligible.

Contributions made by an eligible individual to an HSA are deductible in determining adjusted gross income, whether or not the individual itemizes deductions.[106] However, the individual cannot also deduct the contributions as medical expense deductions under Code Sec. 213.[107] Contributions made by a family member on behalf of an eligible individual to an HSA are deductible by the eligible individual in computing adjusted gross income.[108] The maximum annual deductible contribution that can be made to an individual's HSA in 2017 for an individual with self-only coverage under a high deductible health plan is $3,400 and $6,750 for an individual with family coverage. These amounts are adjusted for inflation, typically by a Revenue Procedure.

Distributions from a health account for the account beneficiary's qualified medical expenses are excludable from gross income.[109] Qualified medical expenses generally are those incurred after the HSA has been established and deductible as medical expenses under Code Sec. 213(d). Thus, they include expenses, not compensated for by insurance or otherwise, for diagnosis, cure, mitigation, treatment, or prevention of disease; transportation primarily for and essential to such care; drugs; and qualified long-term care expenses. Nonprescription drugs, subject to limitations, are considered qualified medical expenses.[110] Excludable distributions are not treated as deductible medical expenses under Code Sec. 223(f)(6).

When an account beneficiary dies and the HSA passes to the surviving spouse as the designated beneficiary, the HSA is treated as if the surviving spouse were the account beneficiary. If an HSA passes to someone other than the surviving spouse at the account beneficiary's death, the HSA ceases to be an HSA. If the transferee is the beneficiary's estate, an amount equal to the account assets is included in the beneficiary's gross income in the year of death. If the transferee is someone other than the beneficiary's estate, an amount equal to the fair market value of the HSA assets is included in the transferee's gross income but is reduced by the amount of qualified medical expenses incurred by the beneficiary before death and paid by the transferee within one year of the beneficiary's death. In computing taxable income, the transferee may claim a deduction for the portion of the federal estate tax on the decedent's estate that was attributable to the amount of the HSA balance, computed in accordance with the rules in Code Sec. 691(c).[111]

---

[105] Code Sec. 223(c)(1).
[106] Code Sec. 62(a)(19).
[107] Notice 2004-2, 2004-1 CB 269.
[108] Id.
[109] Code Sec. 223(f)(1).
[110] Rev. Rul. 2003-102, 2003-2 CB 559.
[111] Code Sec. 223(f)(8).

¶412.02

.03 Education Savings Accounts

A Coverdell education savings account (formerly known as an education IRA) is a trust or custodial account created or organized in the United States exclusively for the purpose of paying the qualified education expenses of an individual who is the designated beneficiary of the trust.[112] Although scheduled to sunset in 2012 under EGTRRA, the following Coverdell provisions were made permanent by the American Taxpayer Relief Act of 2012: the annual contribution limit per beneficiary of $2,000;[113] allowing qualified withdrawals to include K-12 expenses in addition to post-secondary education expenses; that distributions will be tax-free only for those taxpayers who do not claim an American Opportunity or Lifetime Learning Credit (if eligible) for the same expenses in the same year.

The annual contribution is phased out for joint filers with modified adjusted gross income at or above $190,000 and less than $220,000 (at or above $95,000 and less than $110,000 for single filers). The phase-outs do not apply to entities; they may make maximum annual contributions regardless of their income.[114] Amounts remaining in the account must generally be distributed within (1) 30 days after the beneficiary reaches age 30 or (2) 30 days after the death of the beneficiary.[115]

Death or divorce of the designated beneficiary need not cause a taxable distribution to the spouse or ex-spouse. The transfer of a beneficiary's interest in a Coverdell education savings account to a spouse or ex-spouse under a divorce or separation agreement is not a taxable transfer and, after the transfer, the interest in the account is treated as belonging to the spouse/ex-spouse.[116]

Similarly, if a spouse acquires a beneficiary's interest in a Coverdell education savings account because the spouse was the designated beneficiary of the account at the death of the original beneficiary, the Coverdell education savings account is treated as if the spouse were the account beneficiary. However, if a person other than a spouse is the designated beneficiary, the Coverdell education savings account terminates at death and the account balance is includible in the beneficiary's income as of the date of death (or, if the beneficiary is the estate, on the deceased's final income tax return).

The rule for survivors who acquire the original beneficiary's interest in a Coverdell education savings account upon the beneficiary's death applies to the beneficiary's family members as well as to the beneficiary's spouse.[117]

¶ 413 Charitable Contributions

Individuals who itemize deductions may deduct charitable contributions of cash or property to a qualified charity.[118] The maximum amount that can be deducted as a charitable contribution in one tax year is 50% of an individual donor's contribution base. Generally, the deduction for gifts of property is measured by the fair market value of the property on the date of the contribution. Fair market value

---

[112] Code Sec. 530(b)(1).
[113] Code Sec. 530(b)(1)(A)(iii).
[114] Code Sec. 530(c)(1).
[115] Code Sec. 530(b)(1)(E).
[116] Code Secs. 220(f) and 530(d)(7).
[117] Code Sec. 530(d)(7).
[118] Code Sec. 170(a) and (c); Reg. § 1.170A-1.

is defined as the price at which property would change hands between a willing buyer and a willing seller, neither being under any compulsion to buy or sell, and both having reasonable knowledge of the relevant facts.[119]

For contributions made after June 3, 2004, the amount that may be deducted in relation to a contribution of a patent or other intellectual property (other than certain copyrights or inventory) to a charitable organization is limited to the lesser of: (1) the taxpayer's basis in the property; or (2) the fair market value of the property.[120]

For property valued at more than $500, the taxpayer must include with its return for the tax year in which the contribution is made a written description of the donated property and such other required information as the IRS may prescribe by regulation.[121]

For property valued at more than $5,000, the taxpayer must include with its return for the tax year in which the contribution is made whatever information about the property and about the qualified appraisal of that property that the IRS prescribes by regulations.[122] If the contributions are valued at $500,000 or more, then the qualified appraisal must be attached to the return when filed.[123] Appraisal fees incurred by an individual in determining the fair market value of donated property are not treated as part of the charitable contribution, but they may be claimed as a miscellaneous deduction on Schedule A of Form 1040.[124]

Penalties may also be imposed for substantial or gross valuation overstatements that reach a certain threshold if the taxpayer, while obtaining the qualified appraisal, fails to make a good faith investigation of the value of the contributed property.[125]

If the donor is a partnership or S corporation, it must provide a copy of the appraisal summary to each partner or shareholder who receives an allocation of the charitable contribution deduction for the property described in the summary. Each such partner or shareholder must attach a copy of the summary to the tax return on which the charitable contribution is first claimed.[126]

A donor will not be allowed to deduct a charitable contribution of $250 or more unless the gift is acknowledged by the charitable donee in writing.[127] This acknowledgment must include: (1) the amount of cash and a description of property other than cash contributed; (2) any goods or services exchanged for the contribution provided by the donee organization; and (3) a description of the goods and services and a good faith estimate of their value (other than intangible religious benefits) provided to the taxpayer in exchange for the contribution. If the goods and services provided in exchange for the contribution include religious benefits, the written statement from the donee should include a remark to that effect.[128]

---

[119] Reg. § 1.170A-1(c)(2).
[120] Code Sec. 170(e)(1)(B).
[121] Code Sec. 170(f)(11).
[122] Code Sec. 170(f)(11)(C).
[123] Code Sec. 170(f)(11)(D).
[124] Rev. Rul. 67-461, 1967-2 CB 125.
[125] Code Secs. 6662(h) and 6664(c)(2)(B). *See also W.N. Kellahan, Jr.,* 77 TCM 2329, CCH Dec. 53,433(M), TC Memo. 1999-210.
[126] Reg. § 1.170A-13(c)(4)(iv)(F) and (G).
[127] Code Sec. 170(f)(8); Reg. § 1.170A-13(f).
[128] Reg. § 1.170A-13(f)(2).

As of 2005, taxpayers contributing a qualified vehicle valued at over $500 to a charity have met more stringent substantiation requirements. The taxpayer must obtain from the charity a contemporaneous written statement identifying the taxpayer, containing their social security number and the vehicle's identification number. If the vehicle is sold, the gross proceeds are the taxpayer's charitable contribution for the vehicle. If the charity retains the vehicle for its use or to make a substantial improvement, the statement must state this fact with the timeframe within which the charity will use the vehicle. The taxpayer will then be allowed to claim the fair market value of the qualified vehicle as a charitable donation.[129] Qualified vehicles are defined as motor vehicles manufactured for use on public roads and highways, boats and aircraft.[130]

The two-part test adopted by the U.S. Supreme Court in *American Bar Endowment*[131] for determining deductibility under Code Sec. 170(a) of a payment that is partly in consideration for goods and services was incorporated into the regulations. Accordingly, a deduction is allowed for a payment to charity in consideration for goods or services only to the extent that the amount of the payment exceeds the fair market value of the goods or services, and the donor intended to make a payment in excess of the fair market value of the goods or services.[132]

A charitable organization is deemed to provide goods or services in consideration for a taxpayer's contribution if, at the time of payment, the taxpayer receives or expects to receive goods or services in return. When a contribution is made in response to an express promise of a benefit, the donor will generally be deemed to have an expectation of a quid pro quo. Even in the absence of an express promise, a donor may be found to have an expectation of a quid pro quo if the donor makes the contribution knowing that the charitable donee has conferred benefits on other donors making comparable contributions. Such an expectation may exist even when the donor is not aware of the exact nature of the quid pro quo.

Any reasonable methodology may be used in making a good-faith estimate of the value of goods or services provided by the charitable donee in consideration for the donor's payment to the donee, provided the methodology is applied in good faith.

A donor who has properly rejected a benefit offered by a charitable organization may claim a deduction for the full amount of the payment to the charitable organization, and the contemporaneous written acknowledgment need not reflect the value of the rejected benefit.

.01 Split-Dollar Insurance Transactions

A charitable contribution deduction is not allowed in cases where the charitable organization pays any premium on any personal benefit contract (also known as a split-dollar insurance agreement) for the benefit of the transferor of the contribution, effective for transfers after February 8, 1999.[133] In this type of transaction, a

---

[129] Code Sec. 170(f)(12).
[130] Code Sec. 170(f)(12)(E).
[131] *American Bar Endowment,* SCt, 86-1 USTC ¶ 9482, 477 US 105, 106 SCt 2426.
[132] Reg. § 1.170A-1(h)(2).
[133] Code Sec. 170(f)(10).

taxpayer gives a "gift" of cash to a charitable organization and claims a charitable contribution deduction. The charity then uses the funds to pay premiums on a cash value insurance policy on the taxpayer's life. The taxpayer's family members and the charity are named as beneficiaries of the policy. In a variation, the taxpayer (or a related person) forms an irrevocable life insurance trust, and either the charity or the trust purchases the insurance policy. In this case, the policy's designated beneficiaries are both the charity and the trust, and the taxpayer's family members are the beneficiaries of the trust.

¶413.01

Chapter 5

Fiduciary Income Tax Return

¶ 501 Overview
¶ 502 Term of an Estate or Trust
¶ 503 Qualified Revocable Trusts Election Sec. 645
¶ 504 Taxation of Estates and Trusts
¶ 505 Income Test for Filing
¶ 506 Due Date for Return
¶ 507 When Tax Is to Be Paid
¶ 508 Filing Extensions
¶ 509 Duties of Ancillary Representatives
¶ 510 Separate Return for Each Trust

¶ 501 Overview

Although estates of decedents and trusts are taxed under the same rules, these two types of entities originate in quite different ways. An estate is a legal entity that is set up to handle the financial affairs of a person who has died and is usually set up under the laws of the state in which the decedent resided. A trust, on the other hand, is a legal arrangement whereby an individual (the settlor or grantor) transfers property to another person (the trustee) so the property can be held and administered for the benefit of a third party (the beneficiary). Note, however, both estates and trusts exist as a result of state laws, and are taxed under the federal income tax laws. *Morgan v. Commissioner* provided: "State law creates legal interests and rights. The Federal Revenue Act designates what interests or rights, so created, shall be taxed."[1]

An estate is often subject to the supervision and direction of a special state court, usually a probate court. An estate's affairs are administered by an executor or other personal representative. If the decedent failed to name an executor or personal representative in his or her will, the state court will appoint one.

Trusts can be created either during the life of the settlor (an *inter vivos* trust or living trust) or upon the settlor's death (a testamentary trust). However, they must satisfy the legal requirements for establishing a trust under state law. Generally, a trust requires:

---

[1] *Morgan v. Commissioner,* 309 US 78, 40-1 USTC ¶ 9,210; *see also* Abbin, *Income Taxation of Fiduciaries and Beneficiaries,* ¶ 102 (2013).

- an intent to create a trust;
- a designated trustee and beneficiaries;
- sufficiently identifiable property; and
- transfer of title to the trustee.[2]

The intent of the settlor determines when a trust is to terminate, subject to the rule against perpetuities (see ¶ 502).

Internal Revenue Code Secs. 641 through 692 (Subchapter J) govern the income taxation of estates and trusts. With the exception of grantor trusts (see ¶ 901 et seq.), the Code provides that an estate or trust is a separate taxable entity from the settlor or beneficiaries and must pay tax on taxable income received and retained by it and not distributed or deemed distributed to beneficiaries. However, for income distributed or deemed to be distributed to beneficiaries, the estate or trust is deemed a conduit and does not pay tax on such amounts.

Subchapter J covers most estates and trusts, such as decedents' estates, simple trusts, complex trusts, and grantor trusts. A decedent's estate comes into existence on the death of an individual, and income earned from the decedent's death until distribution is subject to Subchapter J treatment. Under Code Sec. 651, a simple trust is a trust that (1) provides that all of its income is required to be distributed currently and (2) does not pay, permanently set aside, or use any amounts for charitable purposes. A complex trust is any trust that is not a simple trust and, therefore, may accumulate income, distribute corpus, or make charitable contributions. Grantor trusts are trusts in which the grantor has not relinquished complete control or dominion over trust assets, and, as a result, the income is taxed to the grantor. Grantor trust status may also arise when persons referred to as "substantial owners" are given powers which, if retained by the settlor, would cause the trust to be taxed as a grantor trust.

Other estates and trusts, such as bankruptcy estates and business trusts are not governed by Subchapter J and receive either individual, partnership, or corporate tax treatment. Bankruptcy estates, under Chapter 11 and Chapter 13 of Title 11, United States Code, must file Form 1041 as a transmittal form, but are taxed as individuals. Business trusts (trusts created for a business purpose) do not file a Form 1041 and are taxed as a partnership or a corporation, depending upon whether the trust has more corporate characteristics or more noncorporate characteristics.

An electing small business trust (ESBT) that holds stock in an S corporation is subject to income taxation (see ¶ 1201 et seq.). The portion of the trust that consists of stock in one or more S corporations is treated as a separate trust for purposes of computing the income tax attributable to the S corporation stock held by the trust.[3] This portion of trust income is taxed at the highest rate imposed on

---

[2] *Hanover Bank,* 40 TC 532, CCH Dec. 26,180 (Acq.), appeal dism'd, CA-2 (January 7, 1964). It is common for a trust agreement to reference "[t]he Grantor transfers to the trustee the property described on the attached Schedule A, which shall constitute the initial principal of the trust," and then include a statement on an attached schedule listing property contributed as "Ten Dollars ($10.00) cash" to expressly satisfy the funding, or transfer of title to the trust.

[3] Code Sec. 641(c)(1)(A); *see also* Reg. § 1.641(c)-1.

¶501

trusts.[4] The taxable income attributable to this portion is computed based on (1) the items of income, loss, or deduction allocated to the trust as an S corporation shareholder under the rules of Subchapter S; (2) gain or loss from the sale of the S corporation stock; (3) any state or local income taxes and administrative expenses of the trust properly allocable to the S corporation stock; and (4) for tax years beginning after December 31, 2006, any interest expense paid or accrued on debt it incurred to acquire S corporation stock.[5] Otherwise allowable capital losses are allowed only to the extent of capital gains.[6]

¶ 502 Term of an Estate or Trust

.01 Estate Administration

At the death of the decedent, a new entity comes into being—the decedent's estate. The income of an estate of a deceased person is that which is received during the period of administration or settlement. The period of administration or settlement for an estate is that period actually required by the administrator or executor to perform the ordinary duties of administration, such as the collection of assets and the payment of debts, taxes, legacies, and bequests, whether the period required is longer or shorter than the period specified under the applicable local law for the settlement of estates.

> **Example 1:** An executor who is also named as trustee under the same will, fails to obtain a discharge as executor. The period of estate administration continues only until the executor's duties of administering the estate as executor are complete and he actually assumes his duties as trustee, whether or not a court order to that effect is issued.

The period of administration of an estate, however, may not be unduly prolonged.[7] In such cases, the estate is considered terminated for federal income tax purposes after the expiration of a reasonable period for the executor to perform all duties of administration. Further, an estate will be considered terminated when all the assets have been distributed, except for a reasonable amount that is set aside in good faith for the payment of unascertained or contingent liabilities and expenses (not including a claim by a beneficiary in the capacity of beneficiary).

The IRS will not provide an advance ruling of whether the estate administration is unduly prolonged.[8] Whether there is undue delay in winding up an estate is a question of fact in every case.[9] The Fifth Circuit has held that, as a matter of law, the continuing payments of federal income taxes and of legacies were insufficient reasons to prolong the administration of an estate for federal income tax purposes, given the facts of the case.[10] All papers necessary to probate the will were filed and approved, the inheritance taxes and the federal estate tax returns were filed, all debts and expenses of the estate were paid, and all assets were located and

---

[4] Code Sec. 641(c)(2)(A).
[5] Code Sec. 641(c)(2)(C)(iv), as added by P.L. 110-28.
[6] Code Sec. 641(c)(2)(C).
[7] Reg. § 1.641(b)-3(a).
[8] For a list of areas in which the IRS will not issue letter rulings, see the third Revenue Procedure issued for the year in question. For example, for tax year 201#, see Rev. Proc. 201#-3.
[9] J. Stewart, CA-5, 52-1 USTC ¶ 9315, 196 F2d 397.
[10] E.A. Brown Jr. Est., CA-5, 90-1 USTC ¶ 50,026, 890 F2d 1329.

collected. Moreover, there were no outstanding claims, will contests, or property title disputes, no litigation was pending regarding claims to the assets or claims by the estates, and no federal income tax disputes or litigation were pending. In another case, a district court ruled that an estate was not closed for federal income tax purposes when the personal representatives were involved in serious litigation concerning claims made against the assets of the estate from the date of the decedent's death to the date of the instant proceeding.[11] The Tax Court has held that there is no justification for prolonging estate administration until completion of various ancillary proceedings when the principal administration proceedings and ordinary duties of administration have been completed.[12] However, the Eighth Circuit held that it was reasonable for an estate to remain open for 11 years until litigation in which it was involved was settled. Continuation thereafter was unreasonable.[13] The IRS has also weighed in on this issue, ruling that, when the estate's sole beneficiary was the executor, the date of approval of a bond conditioned upon payment of all claims, debts, and legacies marked the close of the period of administration, and thereafter the income from the estate was taxable to the beneficiary.[14] Otherwise, when the executor is not the sole beneficiary, final distribution to the beneficiaries usually marks the closing of administration of the estate.[15]

An estate may be deemed to have been constructively terminated if the period of administration is unduly prolonged.[16]

.02 Trust Creation

A trust comes into being when all elements for a valid trust are fulfilled under state law (see ¶ 501). However, it might not become effective until the occurrence of a specified event. For example, a testamentary trust does not become effective until the settlor's death. A question may arise, however, as to whether a testamentary trust may begin to function as a separate and independent tax entity without regard to a prior settlement of the estate. This appears not to be possible according to a decision of the U.S. Court of Appeals for the Third Circuit.[17] Until distribution is properly made, a decedent's property is presumably part of the general estate.

Generally, the termination of a testamentary trust depends upon whether the property held in trust has been distributed to the persons entitled to succeed to the property upon the trust's termination rather than upon the technicality of whether the trustee has rendered a final accounting. A trust does not automatically terminate upon the happening of the event by which the duration of the trust is measured. A reasonable time is permitted after such event for the trustee to perform the duties necessary to complete the administration of the trust. During this period between the event which causes a trust to terminate and the time when the trust is considered to terminate, the provisions of Reg. § 1.651(a)-2 determine

---

[11] *C.H. Wylie, Exr.*, DC Tex., 68-1 USTC ¶ 9287, 281 FSupp 180.

[12] *J.F. Hargis Est.*, 19 TC 842, CCH Dec. 19,457 (Nonacq.); *A.T. Miller*, 39 TC 940, CCH Dec. 26,016, aff'd, CA-8, 64-2 USTC ¶ 9579, 333 F2d 400.

[13] *A.T. Miller*, CA-8, 64-2 USTC ¶ 9579, 333 F2d 400.

[14] Rev. Rul. 73-397, 1973-2 CB 211.

[15] *Id.*

[16] *Old Virginia Brick Co.*, CA-4, 66-2 USTC ¶ 9708, 367 F2d 276.

[17] *E.F. Britten, Jr.*, CA-3, 47-1 USTC ¶ 9273, 161 F2d 921.

whether the income and the net capital gains of the trust are amounts required to be currently distributed to the ultimate distributee.[18]

Example 2: Under the terms of a trust's governing instrument, the trust is to terminate upon the death of the life beneficiary, and the corpus is to be distributed to the remainderman. The trust continues after the death of the life beneficiary for a period reasonably necessary for a proper winding up of the affairs of the trust.

The winding up of a testamentary trust, however, cannot be unduly postponed and, if the distribution of the trust corpus is unreasonably delayed, the trust is considered constructively terminated for federal income tax purposes after the expiration of a reasonable period for the trustee to complete the administration of the trust. Further, a trust will be considered terminated when all the assets have been distributed, except for a reasonable amount that is set aside in good faith for the payment of unascertained or contingent liabilities and expenses (not including a beneficiary's claim in the capacity of beneficiary).[19]

.03 Rule Against Perpetuities

Trusts are also limited in time by the "rule against perpetuities," under which a trust must terminate within a time span determined with reference to a life in being at the time of creation of the trust plus 21 years or 90 years, if using the Uniform Rule Against Perpetuities. Otherwise, many states have established a set period of time for the existence of a trust, such as 500 years from the date of creation, while others allow perpetual trusts.[20]

If a trust or the administration or settlement of an estate is considered terminated for federal income tax purposes, the gross income, deductions, and credits of the trust or estate are, after the termination, considered the gross income, deductions, and credits of the person or persons succeeding to the property of the trust of estate.[21]

¶ 503 Qualified Revocable Trusts Election Sec. 645

Revocable trusts are often used as an estate planning tool for reasons that include the avoidance of probate, privacy concerns or the management of assets in the case of incapacity. A qualified revocable trust may be treated as part of a decedent's estate for income tax purposes so long as a valid election is made.[22] The election period begins on the date of the decedent's death and terminates on the earlier of (1) the day on which the electing trust and related estate have distributed all of their assets, or (2) the day before the applicable date.[23]

The "applicable date" is defined as two years after the date of the decedent's death if no federal estate tax return is required to be filed. In cases where a federal estate tax return is required to be filed, the "applicable date" is the later of (1) two

---

[18] Reg. § 1.641(b)-3(c)(1).
[19] Reg. § 1.641(b)-3(b).
[20] *See* "The Rule against Perpetuities: A Survey of State (and D.C.) Law," http://www.actec.org/assets/1/6/Zarit-sky_RAP_Survey.pdf, for a survey of the rules in the various states and the District of Columbia.
[21] Reg. § 1.641(b)-3(d).
[22] Code Sec. 645.
[23] Reg. § 1.645-1(f)(1).

years after the date of the decedent's death, or (2) six months after the date of the final determination of estate tax liability.[24]

The date of final determination of liability for election purposes is the earliest of the following: (a) the date that is six months after the issuance by the IRS of an estate tax closing letter, unless a claim for refund with respect to the estate tax is filed within 12 months after the issuance of the letter; (b) the date of a final disposition of a claim for refund that resolves the liability for the estate tax, unless suit is instituted within six months after a final disposition of the claim; (c) the date of execution of a settlement agreement with the IRS that determines the liability for the estate tax; (d) the date of issuance of a decision, judgment, decree, or other order by a court of competent jurisdiction resolving the liability for the estate tax unless a notice of appeal or a petition for certiorari is filed within 90 days after the issuance of a decision, judgment, decree, or other order of a court; or (e) the date of expiration of the period of limitations for assessment of the estate tax.[25]

> ***Example 3:*** Alice dies on September 1, Year 1. The executor of her estate and the trustee of her Trust make an election to treat the trust as part of the related estate. A Form 706 is not required to be filed by Alice's estate. The applicable date is September 1, Year 3, the day that is two years after Alice's date of death. The last day of the election period is August 31, Year 3. Beginning on September 1, Year 3, Trust will no longer be treated and taxed as part of Alice's estate.[26]

The election is irrevocable and must be made by both the trustee of the revocable trust and the executor of the decedent's estate (if applicable) by the due date for filing the estate's income tax return for its first tax year. The election is made by filing Form 8855, Election to Treat a Qualified Revocable Trust as Part of an Estate.[27]

If an election is made, the electing trust is treated during the election period as part of the related estate for all federal income tax purposes. Thus, the executor files one annual income tax return under the name and the taxpayer identification number of the estate for the combined electing trust and estate.[28]

¶ 504 Taxation of Estates and Trusts

Estates and trusts are taxed as separate entities, with the exception of bankruptcy estates, grantor trusts, business trusts, and qualified revocable trusts that elect to be treated as part of a decedent's estate (see ¶ 503). In general, the entire income of an estate or trust must be reported on Form 1041 (U.S. Income Tax Return for Estates and Trusts) by the fiduciary. The estate or trust, however, is allowed a deduction for the income included in its gross income that is currently distributable to the beneficiaries or is properly paid or credited to them (see ¶ 708 specifically and ¶ 701 et seq. generally).

---

[24] Code Sec. 645(b)(2); Reg. § 1.645-1(f)(2)(ii).
[25] Reg. § 1.645-1(f)(2)(ii).
[26] Reg. § 1.645-1(f)(2)(iv).
[27] For estates and trusts of decedents dying on or after December 24, 2002.
[28] Reg. § 1.645-1(e)(2).

The income currently distributed to a beneficiary and deducted by an estate or trust is taxable to the beneficiary in the year of allocation. The income retains the same character in the beneficiary's hands as it had in the hands of the estate or trust. In effect, the estate or trust is a conduit for income that is taxed to a beneficiary. The estate or trust is taxed on the balance only.

An estate or trust is taxed in much the same way as an individual. However, a special tax rate schedule is used. The estate or trust may use any method of accounting that an individual is permitted to use. However, both existing and newly created trusts (except trusts exempt from tax under Code Sec. 501(a) and charitable trusts) must adopt the calendar year as their tax year, although estates may select or retain any tax year.[29] Grantor trusts are not required to adopt the calendar year as their tax year.[30]

.01 Multiple Trusts

Two or more trusts are treated as if they are one trust if they have substantially the same grantor or grantors and substantially the same primary beneficiary or beneficiaries, and if their principal purpose is tax avoidance. In these cases, a married couple is treated as one person.[31]

.02 Tax Computation

The fiduciary's tax computations for an estate or trust differ from those of an individual as follows:

1. Neither an estate nor a trust is allowed an exemption for dependents.
2. An estate or trust is not concerned with the concept of "adjusted gross income" (except for minimum tax purposes) or with limitations on charitable deductions or medical expense deductions.
3. Under Code Sec. 642(c), estates and complex trusts are allowed unlimited charitable deductions for gross income paid or permanently set aside, under the decedent's will or trust instrument, for charitable purposes (see ¶ 1101 et seq.).
4. The tax on self-employment income is not imposed on an estate or trust.
5. A personal exemption is allowed under Code Sec. 642(b) (see ¶ 505).
6. The standard deduction is expressly denied to estates and trusts under Code Sec. 63(c)(6)(D).

.03 Personal Exemptions and Tax Rates

Estates and trusts are entitled to claim personal exemptions in determining the amount of taxable income. For an estate, the personal exemption is $600. For a simple trust, the exemption is $300. For all other trusts, the exemption is $100.[32] However, no personal exemption deduction is allowed for a qualified funeral trust (see ¶ 911.02).[33] A "qualified disability trust" (generally, a trust that qualifies as a disability trust under section 1917(c)(2)(B)(iv) of the Social Security Act), whether

---

[29] Code Sec. 644.
[30] Rev. Rul. 90-55, 1990-2 CB 161.
[31] Code Sec. 643(f).
[32] Code Sec. 642(b); Reg. § 1.642(b)-1.
[33] Code Sec. 685(a)(2).

taxed as a simple or complex trust, can claim, in lieu of the $100 or $300 exemption, an exemption in the amount that a single individual taxpayer can claim, subject to the phaseout rules.[34] An estate or trust is entitled to the full exemption even if the return is for a fractional part of the year. But an exemption may not be claimed for the year when the trust or estate terminates and distributes its assets to the beneficiaries.

An estate or nongrantor trust computes its tax liability according to the rates set forth in a Revenue Procedure typically issued at the end of each year. Beginning in 2013, Rev. Proc. 2013-15 set forth the rates as adopted under the American Taxpayer Relief Act, applicable after December 31, 2012.

.04 Code Sec. 1411 Medicare Tax

The "Medicare tax" applies to estates and trusts. In 2010, Code Sec. 1402(a)(1) of the Health Care and Education Reconciliation Act of 2010 added new Code Sec. 1411 to the Code effective for taxable years beginning after December 31, 2012. The proposed regulations under Code Sec. 1411 affect individuals, estates, and trusts. Code Sec. 1411 imposes a 3.8% tax on certain individuals, estates, and trusts. Estates and trusts will be subject to the net investment income tax if they have undistributed net investment income and also have adjusted gross income over the dollar amount at which the highest tax bracket for an estate or trust begins for the applicable taxable year.[35] It should be noted that Congress's recent effort in 2017 to repeal or replace parts or all of the Affordable Care Act could have a direct impact on Code Sec. 1411, and practitioners should track the status of the tax in relation to the activity involving the Affordable Care Act.

Generally, net investment income includes, but is not limited to: interest, dividends, capital gains, royalties and rents, non-qualified annuities, income from businesses involved in trading of financial instruments or commodities, and businesses that are passive activities (under Code Sec. 469) to the taxpayer. Net investment income is reduced by certain expenses allocable to the income. Some properly allocable deductions include investment interest expense, investment advisory and brokerage fees, expenses related to rental and royalty income, and state and local income taxes properly allocated to items included in net investment income. The net investment income tax is subject to the estimated tax provisions.

Proposed Reg. § 1.1411–3 provides special rules for applying Code Sec. 1411 to estates and trusts, including an estate or trust with a short taxable year resulting from the formation or termination of the estate or trust or a change in accounting period.[36] There are special computational rules for certain unique types of trusts, such as electing small business trusts, charitable remainder trusts, or trusts that are exempt from taxation under subtitle A, which can be found in the proposed regulations.[37] For ESBTs, the two separate trusts are combined to determine the AGI threshold and the calculation is outlined in the proposed Regulations. For

---

[34] Code Sec. 642(b)(2)(C).
[35] For 2017, the threshold amount is $12,500.
[36] Federal Register, Vol. 77, No. 234, December 5, 2012/Proposed Rules, pp. 72612-72652.
[37] Prop. Reg. §§ 1.1411-3(c)(1), 1.1411-3(c)(2), and 1.1411-3(b)(1), respectively.

charitable remainder trusts, annuity and unitrust distributions (not the trust itself) may be net investment income to a non-charitable beneficiary as outlined in the proposed Regulations. Grantor trusts are not subject to the Code Sec. 1411 tax.[38] Generally, under the proposed Regulations, foreign estates and trusts should not be subject to Code Sec. 1411 tax unless the income is earned or accumulated for U.S. beneficiaries.[39]

The IRS Notice of Proposed Rulemaking issued on December 5, 2012, provides for coordination of rules for estates, trusts and their beneficiaries with the computation of net investment income and any related increase or decrease to AGI in conjunction with calculation of distributable net income and other rules related to Subchapter J and Proposed Regulation § 1.1411-3. The Notice requested comments on accomplishing the coordination.

The basic rates for estates and trusts apply at lower taxable income levels than they do for individuals who are the beneficiaries of the trust or estate. These lower estate and trust income levels at the individual beneficiary level are designed to curtail the use of estates or trusts as income-shifting devices.

.05 Alternative Minimum Tax Rules

Tax law gives special treatment to certain types of income and allows special deductions for certain types of expenses, and it also requires an alternative method of computing tax—the alternative minimum tax (AMT)—to ensure that all taxpayers pay a minimum amount of tax. Estates and trusts, like individuals, are subject to the AMT. Although, under the 2017 Tax Cuts and Jobs Act,[40] the corporate AMT has been eliminated and the individual AMT exemption has been increased, the exemption for trusts and estates has remained unchanged at $22,500 as explained below, although indexed for inflation ($24,600 for 2018).[41]

The AMT is payable to the extent that it exceeds the regular tax. Thus, even if a taxpayer has no tax preference items, the taxpayer may be liable for the AMT if his or her credits, which are generally taken into account for purposes of computing the AMT, reduce the amount of regular tax liability below the amount of gross alternative minimum tax. For estates and trusts, the AMT is determined by finding the excess of a taxpayer's tentative minimum tax for a year over the regular tax for the year. The term "regular tax" has a special meaning for minimum tax calculation purposes.

A graduated, two-tiered AMT rate schedule applies to noncorporate taxpayers. A lower rate applies below the exemption amount and a higher rate applies over the exemption amount. The exemption amount is phased out at certain income levels and is adjusted for inflation. The 26% rate applies to the first $175,000 of alternative minimum taxable income (AMTI) in excess of the exemption amount (inflation adjusted to $191,500 for 2018), and a 28% rate applies to AMTI of more than $175,000 (indexed for inflation) in excess of the exemption amount.[42] Trusts and estates are entitled to a $22,500 exemption ($24,600 for 2018) in determining the

---

[38] Prop. Reg. § 1.1411-3(b)(5).
[39] Prop. Reg. § 1.1411-4(e).
[40] P.L. 115-97.
[41] Code Sec. 55(d)(1)(D).
[42] Code Secs. 55(b)(1)(A)(i), 55(d)(1)(D), 55(d)(3)(C).

amount of income subject to the AMT.[43] The exemption amount is phased out when AMTI exceeds $75,000 indexed for inflation ($82,050 for 2018).[44] However, the top regular tax rate applies to estates and trusts once taxable income exceeds a relatively low threshold reflecting the compressed nature of trust and estate tax rates and diminishing the possibility that an estate or trust will be subject to the AMT rules.[45]

AMTI is a taxpayer's taxable income computed by means of special adjustments found in Code Secs. 56 and 58 and increased by the amount of tax preference items for a tax year under Code Sec. 57.[46] Miscellaneous itemized deductions are tax preference items for AMT purposes. The definition of miscellaneous itemized deductions does not include the deduction for estate tax in the case of income in respect of a decedent under Code Sec. 691(c).

The AMTI for an estate or trust and its beneficiaries is determined by computing distributable net income under the rules for income taxation of estates and trusts and their beneficiaries under Code Secs. 641 through 685, taking into account any adjustments provided for in the minimum tax rules.[47] Estates and trusts compute the AMT on Schedule I (Alternative Minimum Tax) of Form 1041.

¶ 505 Income Test for Filing

Form 1041 (U.S. Income Tax Return for Estates and Trusts) must be filed for a domestic estate that has (1) gross income for the tax year of at least $600, (2) a beneficiary who is a nonresident alien, or (3) aggregate gross income of at least $600 from an electing qualified revocable trust and the related estate (see ¶ 503).[48]

The fiduciary of a foreign estate must file Form 1040NR (U.S. Nonresident Alien Income Tax Return). An estate is a foreign estate if its income from sources outside the United States that is not effectively connected with the conduct of a U.S. trade or business is not includible in gross income.[49]

Form 1041 must be filed for a domestic trust (taxable under Code Sec. 641) that has (1) any taxable income for the tax year, (2) gross income of $600 or more (regardless of taxable income), (3) a beneficiary who is a nonresident alien, or (4) aggregate gross income of at least $600 from an electing qualified revocable trust and the related estate (see ¶ 503).[50]

A trust will qualify as a domestic trust ("United States person") if two requirements are met: (1) a U.S. court is able to exercise primary supervision over the administration of the trust (the "court test"), and (2) one or more U.S. persons are authorized to control all substantial decisions of the trust (the "control test").[51]

The return is filed by the fiduciary, that is, the executor, administrator, trustee, etc., of the estate or trust for which he or she acts.[52] Where a will contest had prevented an administrator's appointment, a bank holding an estate's money and

---

[43] Code Sec. 55(d)(1)(D).
[44] Code Sec. 55(d)(3)(C).
[45] $12,500 in 2017 and indexed for inflation.
[46] Code Sec. 55(b)(2).
[47] Code Sec. 59(c).
[48] Reg. § 1.6012-3(a)(1).
[49] Code Sec. 7701(a)(31)(A).
[50] Reg. § 1.6012-3(a)(1).
[51] Code Sec. 7701(a)(30)(E); Reg. § 301.7701-7.
[52] Reg. § 1.641(b)-2.

paying more than $600 in interest on it, but performing no administrative duties for the estate, was not required to file Form 1041.[53]

Estates and trusts (other than certain grantor trusts) must report their income on Form 1041. Form 1041 may also be used to file an amended return for an estate or trust.

In the case of joint fiduciaries, the return must be executed by one of them. The fiduciary executing the returns must declare (1) that he or she has sufficient knowledge of the affairs of the estate or trust to enable him or her to make the return, and (2) that the return is to the best of his or her knowledge and belief true and correct.[54]

Irrespective of whether or not an income tax return must be filed for an estate, Form 1099-DIV (Dividends and Distributions) must be filed if interest or dividends are received as a nominee for another person, and payments totaling $10 or more are made to that person during the calendar year.

.01 Nonresident Aliens

Fiduciaries of nonresident alien estates or trusts with U.S. source income must file a Form 1040NR (U.S. Nonresident Alien Income Tax Return).[55] Fiduciaries of a nonresident alien estate or trust must change the form to reflect the provisions of Subchapter J of the Internal Revenue Code. In doing so, it may be helpful to refer to Form 1041 and its instructions.

A nonresident alien who was a resident of Guam or the Commonwealth of the Northern Mariana Islands (CNMI) for the entire tax year will, for this purpose, file the return and pay any tax due to Guam or the CNMI, and report all income, including income from U.S. sources, on the return. It is not necessary to file a separate U.S. income tax return. A nonresident alien who was a resident of American Samoa or Puerto Rico for the entire tax year will be taxed the same as resident aliens. Thus, they should file Form 1040 and report all income from sources both in and outside the United States.[56]

Nonresident alien estates or trusts that have an office in the United States must file the return by the 15th day of the fourth month after the tax year ends. However, nonresident alien estates or trusts that do not have an office in the United States have until the 15th day of the sixth month after the tax year ends.[57]

.02 Domestic Estates and Trusts with Nonresident Alien Beneficiaries

If one or more of the beneficiaries of a domestic estate are nonresident alien individuals, the fiduciary must file a Form 1041 even if the gross income of the estate is less than $600. In addition to filing the Form 1041, the domestic or resident fiduciary must file the return and pay the tax that may be due from a nonresident

---

[53] Rev. Rul. 82-177, 1982-2 CB 365, modified in part by Rev. Rul. 92-51, 1992-2 CB 102.

[54] Code Sec. 6012(b)(5); Reg. § 1.6012-3(c).

[55] Reg. § 1.6012-3(b)(2); IRS Publication No. 559, Survivors, Executors, and Administrators, p. 15.

[56] IRS Publication No. 519, U.S. Tax Guide for Aliens (2006), pp. 30 and 40.

[57] Reg. § 1.6072-1(c); Instructions for Form 1040NR, U.S. Nonresident Alien Income Tax Return (2006), p. 4.

alien beneficiary. This may entail, depending on a number of factors, the filing of a Form 1040NR.

Fiduciaries are not required to file the nonresident alien's return or pay the tax if that beneficiary has appointed an agent in the United States to file a federal income tax return. However, the fiduciary must attach a copy of the document appointing the beneficiary's agent to the estate's Form 1041.[58] In addition, a Form 1042 (Annual Withholding Tax Return for U.S. Source Income of Foreign Persons) must be filed in connection with income tax to be paid at the source on certain payments to nonresident aliens.

.03 Fiduciary Capacity of Guardian

A fiduciary acting as guardian for a minor or mentally disabled person is required to file the regular income tax return (Form 1040) for such person in any case where such individual is subject to the requirement for filing a return unless, in the case of a minor, the minor makes the return or causes it to be made.[59] A parent or guardian may file a return for a minor if age or other disability prevents the minor from doing so him- or herself. In such a case, the parent should sign the child's name in the proper place on the return followed by the words "By (signature) Parent (or guardian) for minor child."[60] For the tax year during which an incompetent is declared competent and the fiduciary is discharged, the former incompetent will file his or her own return.

The parent of a child who is under age 19 (or under 24 and a full time student) at the end of the tax year and who has income only from interest or dividends (including capital gain distributions and Alaska Permanent Fund dividends) may elect to report the child's income on the parent's return and the child will not have to file a return. This election, made by filing Form 8814, Parents' Election To Report Child's Interest and Dividends, with the parent's Form 1040, is available only if the child's income is less than a certain amount as adjusted by inflation,[61] the child made no estimated tax payments, the child has no tax overpayment to be applied to the return, the child had no income tax withheld from income for the year, and the child did not file a joint return for the tax year.

¶ 506 Due Date for Return

Returns by a fiduciary on behalf of the estate or trust for which he or she acts are due on or before the 15th day of the fourth month following the close of the tax year of the estate or trust.[62] For those using a calendar-year tax year, this date falls on April 15th. If a decedent was treated as the owner of a trust under the grantor trusts rules (see Chapter 9), the trust may have been filing a Form 1041 during the life of the decedent. In this case, the due date for Form 1041 that is required to be filed for the tax year ending with the decedent's death is the same as the due date for the decedent's final return (i.e., the 15th day of the fourth month following the

---

[58] Reg. § 1.6012-3(b) (2) (i) (c).
[59] Code Sec. 6012(b) (2); Reg. § 1.6012-3(b) (3).
[60] Rev. Rul. 82-206, 1982-2 CB 356.
[61] $10,500 in 2017.
[62] Code Sec. 6072(a); Reg. § 1.6072-1(a) (1).

close of the 12-month period that began with the first day of the decedent's last tax year).[63]

The estate or trust return is to be filed with the IRS Service Center covering the area (as indicated in the instructions to Form 1041) in which the fiduciary is located. Fiduciaries located outside the United States should file their returns with the IRS Service Center in Ogden, Utah.[64]

¶ 507 When Tax Is to Be Paid

.01 Calendar Year or Fiscal Year

Currently, income from an estate, like that of an individual, can be reported on either a calendar-year or fiscal-year basis.[65] Estates are permitted to select tax years in order to defer income tax because (1) estates generally do not last as long as trusts, and (2) estate fiduciaries need to select an accounting period to coincide with the administration of the estate. Trusts, however, generally must use a calendar year.[66] Tax-exempt trusts and wholly charitable trusts are excepted from this calendar-year requirement.[67]

However, the executor of an estate and the trustee of a qualified revocable trust can elect to treat a qualified revocable trust as part of an estate.[68] If elected, the qualified revocable trust will not be treated as a separate trust; instead the trust will be treated as part of the decedent's estate for federal income tax purposes. Thus, the executor files one annual income tax return under the name and taxpayer identification number of the estate for the combined electing trust and estate.[69] See ¶ 503 for further details.

The fiduciary of an estate must pay the estate's tax liability when its return is due. The fiduciary of a trust must pay any income tax due in full when the return is filed. The filing due date is the 15th day of the fourth month following the close of the tax year.

The tax may be paid by check or money order drawn to the order of "United States Treasury." Employer identification numbers should be written on checks or money orders.

.02 Estimated Tax

Estates and trusts, like individuals, must pay estimated income tax. However, estimated tax payments from an estate are not required for any tax year ending before the second anniversary of the decedent's death. Also in the case of a trust that was treated as owned by the decedent and that will receive the residue of the decedent's estate under the will (or, if no will is admitted to probate, that will be primarily responsible for paying debts, taxes, and administration expenses), estimated tax payments are not required for any tax year ending before the second anniversary of the decedent's death.[70]

---

[63] Reg. § 1.6072-1(a)(2).
[64] IRS Publication No. 559, Survivors, Executors, and Administrators (2006), p. 20.
[65] Code Sec. 441(e).
[66] Code Sec. 644(a).
[67] Code Sec. 644(b).
[68] Code Sec. 645(a).
[69] Reg. § 1.645-1(e)(2).
[70] Code Sec. 6654(l)(2); Instructions for Form 1041, U.S. Income Tax Return for Estates and Trusts, p. 8.

Payments of estimated tax for estates and trusts are made in the same manner as those for individuals. First-time filers must file Form 1041-ES (Estimated Income Tax for Estates and Trusts), which includes vouchers to be included with quarterly payments. After the first payment, the IRS will provide pre-printed vouchers.[71] The due dates of the installments for each tax year are April 15, June 15, September 15, and January 15 of the following year, as adjusted if the 15th day falls on a weekend.

Generally, a fiduciary of an estate or trust must pay estimated tax for the tax year if the estate or trust is expected to owe, after subtracting its withholding and credits, at least $1,000 in tax,[72] and the withholding and credits are expected to be less than the smaller of (1) 90% of the tax shown on the tax return for the tax year, or (2) 100% of the tax shown on the tax return for the previous tax year (assuming the return covered all 12 months).[73] If the estate or trust has adjusted gross income of more than $150,000, and less than two-thirds of gross income for the tax year or the preceding tax year is from farming or fishing, the threshold amount is 110% of the preceding year's tax.[74]

No estimated tax payments are required by a fiduciary of a domestic decedent's estate or domestic trust if there was no tax liability on the estate or trust for the 12 months preceding the tax year.[75]

In the case of a trust for any tax year or in the case of an estate for the estate's final year, the fiduciary (or executor) may elect to treat any portion of estimated tax payments for the tax year as payments made by a beneficiary (and not as payments made by the trust or estate). Such an amount is treated as payment of the estimated tax made by the beneficiary that would otherwise be due January 15 of the following tax year. The fiduciary must make the election on Form 1041-T (Allocation of Estimated Tax Payments to Beneficiaries). The election must be filed on or before the 65th day after the close of the tax year of the trust or estate.[76] Once made, the election is irrevocable.[77]

¶ 508 Filing Extensions

An estate or trust that files Form 1041 may request an automatic six-month extension of time to file by submitting Form 7004 (Application for Automatic 6-Month Extension of Time To File Certain Business Income Tax, Information, and Other Returns). Previously, a trust was allowed an automatic extension of three months by filing form 8736, and could apply for an additional three-month extension if necessary. Estates could apply for a three-month extension of time by filing Form 2758 (Application for Extension of Time To File Certain Excise, Income, Information, and Other Returns) and showing that, despite reasonable efforts, professional help cannot be obtained in time or if a return preparer, for reasons beyond his or her control, cannot complete the return on time. However, the IRS has simplified both procedures by providing for automatic extension periods of six

---

[71] Form 1041-ES, Estimated Income Tax for Estates and Trusts, p. 1.
[72] Code Sec. 6654(e)(1).
[73] Code Sec. 6654(d)(1)(B).
[74] Code Sec. 6654(d)(1)(C)(i).
[75] Code Sec. 6654(e)(2)(B).
[76] Code Sec. 643(g).
[77] Reg. § 301.9100-8(a)(4)(i).

months for both trusts and estates.[78] Form 7004 must be filed by the regular due date of the Form 1041 for which an extension is requested and show the full amount estimated as tax due for the year.[79] Taxpayers need not sign the Form 7004 or provide an explanation for their request in order to receive the automatic six-month extension of time to file.[80]

The extension of time to file the return generally does not extend the time to pay any tax due with the return, unless the extension states otherwise. Although automatic extension requests do not require payment of tax due, the balance of any tax due must be paid at the time an additional extension is requested.[81] The fiduciary may request an extension of time to pay taxes due by filing Form 1127 (Application for Extension of Time for Payment of Tax). Such extensions must be filed before the date payment is due and require a showing of undue hardship.[82]

The IRS may postpone the deadlines for filing or paying fiduciary income taxes for up to one year for taxpayers affected by a presidentially declared disaster, or a terrorist or military action, effective for disasters or actions occurring on or after September 11, 2001.[83] For example, in September 2005, Congress enacted legislation that postponed deadlines for taxpayers affected by Hurricane Katrina.[84] In December 2005, the Gulf Opportunity Zone was created and additional provisions and extensions of time were provided for those affected by Hurricanes Katrina, Rita and Wilma.[85] Also, military personnel serving or injured while serving in a presidentially designated combat zone may receive postponements for the length of their combat service and any continuous hospitalization for injuries suffered providing that service, plus an additional 180 days.[86]

.01 Interest

Interest is payable on tax not paid by the due date for payment, and extensions are disregarded in determining such regular due date.

.02 Penalties

There are penalties for late payment or late filing. Even if a return is filed late and no extension was requested, a penalty can be avoided under Code Sec. 6651(a)(1) if reasonable cause can be shown for the delay. For purposes of showing reasonable cause, a full explanation should be attached to the tardy return. An automatic extension of time to file a trust return does not extend the time for filing a beneficiary's income tax return.[87]

¶ 509 Duties of Ancillary Representatives

If a decedent leaves property in a state or country other than that of his or her domicile (usually where he or she lives), the foreign state or country may allow

---

[78] T.D. 9229, 2005-2 CB 1051.

[79] Temp. Reg. § 1.6081-6T(b)(3).

[80] Form 7004, Application for Automatic 6-Month Extension of Time To File Certain Business Income Tax, Information, and Other Returns (2006).

[81] Form 7004, Application for Automatic 6-Month Extension of Time To File Certain Business Income Tax, Information, and Other Returns (2006), p. 2.

[82] Reg. § 1.6161-1(b) and (c).

[83] Code Sec. 7508A(a).

[84] The Katrina Emergency Tax Relief Act of 2005 (P.L. 109-73).

[85] Gulf Opportunity Zone Act of 2005 (P.L. 109-135).

[86] Code Sec. 7508(a)(1); Reg. § 301.7508-1.

[87] Temp. Reg. § 1.6081-6T(c).

another to collect the assets and pay the debts there, and bring what remains into the general administration of the estate. This is referred to as "ancillary" administration.

An ancillary representative who collects income of a decedent from property located outside the state of the decedent's domicile is required to file a return on Form 1041 showing (1) the name and address of the domiciliary representative, (2) the gross income received by the ancillary representative, and (3) the deductions claimed against that income, including any income properly paid or credited by the ancillary representative to a beneficiary. However, the domiciliary representative files the principal return (Form 1041) for the estate, showing all the income and deductions of the estate, including that reported by the ancillary representative.[88] Therefore, any tax to be paid on the estate income would be reported on the domiciliary representative's return.

Where the estate of a nonresident alien has a nonresident alien domiciliary representative and an ancillary representative who is a citizen or a resident of the United States, the ancillary representative must file the Form 1041 that would otherwise be required of the domiciliary representative.

The return of the ancillary representative of the estate is required to be filed with the IRS Service Center in which the ancillary representative is located.

¶ 510 Separate Return for Each Trust

If the IRS so requests, a fiduciary must file (1) a copy of the will or trust instrument (including amendments), (2) a written declaration under the penalties of perjury that the instrument is a true and complete copy, and (3) a statement indicating which provisions, in the fiduciary's opinion, determine the extent of taxable income to the estate or trust, the beneficiaries, or the grantor.[89]

A trustee of two or more trusts must make a *separate* return for each trust even though the trusts were created by the same grantor for the same beneficiary or beneficiaries.[90] However, the further question of what constitutes a separate trust assumes a special significance because of the relationship between graduated income tax rates and the aggregate tax that is paid on the undistributed income of the trusts.

Code Sec. 643(f) requires that two or more trusts that are created after March 1, 1984, are to be treated as one trust, if they have substantially the same grantor(s) and substantially the same primary beneficiary or beneficiaries, and if a principal purpose for the use of separate trusts is tax avoidance. However, multiple trusts will not be treated as one trust if there is a substantial independent reason for the creation of the trusts and they were not formed for purposes of tax avoidance.

A grantor or testator may create several trusts for different beneficiaries by one instrument. In such case the income is taxed separately as to each trust. Each receives the $100 or $300 personal exemption (see ¶ 505) and is treated as a separate entity for all tax purposes. The U.S. Supreme Court and the U.S. Tax Court

---

[88] Reg. § 1.6012-3(a)(3).
[89] Reg. § 1.6012-3(a)(2).
[90] Reg. § 1.6012-3(a)(4).

have held that it is not necessary to have a physical division of the corpus of each trust if the intent to create more than one trust is apparent.[91]

The fact that the trusts are carved out of one fund does not necessarily defeat an otherwise clear intention to create separate trusts because an undivided interest in property may constitute the corpus of each of several trusts.[92] If there are separate trusts, the beneficiary may not offset a net loss of one trust against the distributable income of the other even though there was one grantor, one trustee, and one beneficiary for all the trusts.[93]

The U.S. Court of Appeals for the Eighth Circuit, affirming the Tax Court, has held that a retroactive reformation of a trust instrument by decree of a local court to create several trusts instead of one is not retroactive for federal tax purposes.[94] This is true even though the reformation decree may reflect the original intent of the grantor and even though the decree results from an adversary proceeding.

---

[91] *W.B. McIlvaine,* SCt, 36-1 USTC ¶ 9041, 296 US 488; *J.L. Dickinson Testamentary Trust,* 65 TC 1946, CCH Dec. 48,872.

[92] *United States Trust Co. of New York,* SCt, 36-1 USTC ¶ 9040, 296 US 481.

[93] *F.W. Smith,* 25 TC 143, CCH Dec. 21,302.

[94] *M.T. Straight Trust,* CA-8, 57-2 USTC ¶ 9727, 245 F2d 327, aff'g 24 TC 69, CCH Dec. 20,974.

¶510

Chapter 6

Fiduciary Income Tax Return Fundamentals

¶ 601   General Types of Income to Be Reported
¶ 602   U.S. Saving Bond Interest Reported by an Estate
¶ 603   Types of Estate Income in Respect of a Decedent
¶ 604   Gain or Loss When Legacy Satisfied in Property
¶ 605   Capital Gains and Losses
¶ 606   Basis of Estate or Trust Property
¶ 607   Deductions and Credits
¶ 608   Miscellaneous Itemized Deductions and Section 67
¶ 609   Deductibility of Litigation Expenses
¶ 610   Deductions in Respect of a Decedent
¶ 611   Deductibility of Interest
¶ 612   Deduction of Taxes by an Estate or Trust
¶ 613   Double Deductions for Certain Items Not Allowed
¶ 614   Depreciation Deduction Is to Be Apportioned
¶ 615   Treatment of Depletion Deduction
¶ 616   Deductible Losses of an Estate or Trust
¶ 617   Net Operating Loss Deduction Allowed
¶ 618   Unused Loss Carryovers
¶ 619   Excess Deductions on Termination
¶ 620   Allocation in Year of Termination
¶ 621   Alimony and Separate Maintenance Payments

¶ 601 General Types of Income to Be Reported

The gross income of an estate or trust is determined in the same manner as that of an individual.[1] For instance, interest and rents earned and accrued after a decedent's death are includible in the gross income of an estate or trust to the same extent that they would be if received by an individual. The income of a trust will usually arise from amounts earned during the period of administration (i.e., after the transfer of assets to the testamentary or inter vivos trust) and from gain or loss on the sale of assets by the trust. The income of an estate will usually arise from (1)

---

[1] Reg. § 1.641(a)-2.

income earned by the decedent prior to death but received by the estate (income in respect of a decedent);[2] (2) income earned during the period of administration; and (3) gain on the sale of assets during the period of administration.

The law specifically provides that *taxable* income of an estate or trust includes:

1. Income accumulated in trust for the benefit of unborn or unascertained persons or persons with contingent interests;
2. Income accumulated or held for *future* distribution under the terms of the will or trust;
3. Income that is to be distributed currently by the fiduciary to the beneficiaries, and income collected by a guardian of an infant that is to be held or distributed as the court may direct;
4. Income received by estates of deceased persons during the period of administration or settlement of the estate; and
5. Income which, in the discretion of the fiduciary, may be either distributed to the beneficiaries or accumulated.[3]

Some of the items listed above, however, may be taxed to the beneficiary in whole or in part instead of to the estate or trust. All of the income accumulated (specified in (1) and (2)) is taxed to the estate or trust; all of the income distributed currently (specified in (3)) is deductible by the fiduciary and is taxed to the beneficiary, *whether or not it is distributed*; and the income received by a decedent's estate or subject to the discretion of the fiduciary (specified in (4) and (5)) may be taxed to the fiduciary or to the beneficiary, depending upon the amounts that are properly paid or credited to the beneficiary (see ¶ 505 et seq.).

¶ 602 U.S. Saving Bond Interest Reported by an Estate

.01 Section 454 Election

Because savings bonds are issued at a discount and increase in value each year until maturity, the "incremental" increase in value is taxable as interest.[4] For a cash basis taxpayer, however, there is an option to report the increase each year on either a current basis or upon the ultimate redemption of the bonds. Code Sec. 454(c) provides that a cash basis owner of savings bonds who has not made the election under Code Sec. 454(a) to report the interest income on the bonds each year, should include the increase in redemption value in excess of the amount paid for such bonds in gross income in the first taxable year in which the bonds are disposed of, redeemed, or reach final maturity. The incremental accrued interest in value of Series E, Series EE, or Series I savings bonds is income to the date of his or her death and becomes income in respect of a decedent under Code Sec. 691.

.02 Individual Beneficiary Receiving Bonds from Estate

A cash basis individual beneficiary who acquires savings bonds also has the option of either reporting the incremental accrual of interest up to when he or she

---

[2] Code Sec. 691.
[3] Code Sec. 641(a).
[4] As to when and how interest on U.S. savings bonds is to be reflected in income for a decedent, *see* the discussion at ¶ 402.

acquires the bonds or holding the bonds until maturity or redemption and then reporting the unreported incremental interest as income. However, the IRS has ruled that if a "recipient" acquiring savings bonds from a decedent makes an election to report the increment, the recipient must include in gross income all of the unreported increment in value of all Series E bonds that he or she holds and not just the increment attributable to the decedent's bonds. Thereafter, the recipient should report in each tax year the increment in value actually accruing within such tax year.

.03 Estate Holding the Bonds

The administrator of a cash basis estate may elect to report on its income tax return all the unreported interest on all of the decedent's bonds from the dates of their purchase to the year of the election. An election by the estate will not preclude the person who ultimately receives the bonds from electing to defer and report the increment as income when the bonds are redeemed or finally mature. The IRS ruled that a testamentary trust that acquired a decedent's savings bonds was not bound by the executor's election and could report any remaining accrued increment upon the bonds' maturity or redemption, even though the executor was also the trustee.[5]

¶ 603 Types of Estate Income in Respect of a Decedent

Generally, a decedent's earnings that are not income taxable in the last return are income taxable to the estate or others when actually received. There are exceptions, however, that are discussed with the topics that follow.

The following items have resulted in realization of income by the estate that received them:

1. Back alimony (prior to 2019);[6]
2. Amounts received on notes that had a zero value on the date of death;[7]
3. Profits from a sale of pledged and unpledged securities to satisfy a debt of the decedent;[8]
4. Transfer of securities in discharge of an obligation;[9]
5. Amounts realized from a claim for patent infringement damages that was in process of litigation at the date of death;[10] and
6. A debt of the decedent that became void after death under state law because the creditor failed to file a claim against the estate.[11] (Such debts would not be deductible for estate tax purposes.)

---

[5] Rev. Rul. 64-104, 1964-1 CB (Part 1) 223, as distinguished by Rev. Rul. 68-145, 1968-1 CB 203.

[6] *S.L. Narischkine Est.*, CA-2, 51-1 USTC ¶ 9313, 189 F2d 257; Rev. Rul. 55-457, 1955-2 CB 527. Note that for payments required under a divorce or separation instrument that is executed after December 31, 2018, the new 2017 TCJA eliminates the deduction for alimony payments, thus the payor will no longer receive a deduction, and the recipient will no longer include the alimony in taxable income.

[7] *J. Roth*, CA-2, 40-2 USTC ¶ 9738, 115 F2d 239.

[8] *First Trust & Deposit Co., Exr.*, DC N.Y., 44-2 USTC ¶ 9478, 58 FSupp 162.

[9] *Id.*

[10] Rev. Rul. 55-463, 1955-2 CB 277.

[11] *E. Bankhead Est.*, 60 TC 535, CCH Dec. 32,042.

In items (1) and (2), ordinary income was realized for the full amount; items (3) and (4) were the equivalent of sales or exchanges resulting in gain or loss; item (5) was ordinary income (compensation for lost income); and item (6) was taxable as ordinary income under the discharge of indebtedness rule of Code Sec. 61(a)(12).

What has been said above in relation to income taxable to a decedent's estate is also true for income of a trust. For example, assume that, at the date of a decedent's death, the decedent held a claim to $50,000. If the "right" to the claim, assuming it constitutes income in respect of a decedent, passed to a trust as legatee or beneficiary, the trust would be taxable on the claim if it subsequently received the proceeds of collection.

For decedents dying before and after 2010, the basis of property passing from or acquired from a decedent is generally the fair market value at the time of death (see ¶ 606), and, thus, it is the subsequent increase or decrease in the value of the property reflected in a sale or other disposition that is recognized as the measure of gain or loss. The unrealized appreciation to date of death is not subject to income tax.

The same is true as to property passing under an instrument that is treated as though it were a will. An example of this is where an *inter vivos* trust makes disposition of property upon the death of the grantor. This would be true even though the grantor in his or her lifetime had the power to revoke the trust. This nonrecognition of gain from disposition of property follows through to a distribution of trust property to the beneficiaries.

.01 Interest Income Received

Unless interest is tax exempt, all interest that is received by an estate or trust is taxable income. Sources of tax-exempt interest are state or local government obligations. Tax-exempt interest accrued during the tax year must be reported as an item of information on the tax return filed for an estate or trust (Form 1041, p. 2 (other information)). Although required to be reported, this interest will not be taxed. However, a proportional amount of expenses will have to be allocated to tax-exempt interest.[12]

.02 Income from Real Property

State law controls the determination of whether income from real estate during the period of administration is taxable to the decedent's estate or to the heirs or devisees. Accordingly, the IRS has formulated the following rules for determining whether income from real estate is taxable to the estate or to the beneficiaries:

1. Where state law provides that real property is subject to administration, income derived from the property will be taxed to the estate while the estate is under administration even though legal title may pass directly to the heirs or devisees under local law.[13]

---

[12] Reg. § 1.642(a)(1)-1.

[13] Rev. Rul. 57-133, 1957-1 CB 200; *B.B. Cohen Est.*, 8 TC 784, CCH Dec. 15,709.

2. If the estate fiduciary is not entitled to possession or control of real property, the income from the property will be taxed to the heirs and devisees and not to the estate.[14]
3. Even if the property is not subject to the fiduciary's control, all or part of the gain realized from a property's sale will be taxed to the estate to the extent that the property was sold under state law to raise funds for the administration of the estate. If part of the remaining gain arises from a partition sale of the property, this gain will be taxed to the heirs or devisees.[15]
4. Income derived from real estate that is subject to a dower interest will be taxed to the estate until the property is distributed to the surviving spouse if the property is subject to administration under state law. After the property is transferred to the surviving spouse, the income will be taxed to him or her.[16]

The basis of real estate in the hands of an estate or beneficiary is the fair market value as of the date of the decedent's death or the alternate valuation date.[17] However, the fair market value "new basis" provisions do not apply with respect to property that is sold, exchanged, or otherwise disposed of before the decedent's death by the person who acquired the property from the decedent.[18]

Generally, no problems arise where the real estate is part of the corpus of a *trust*. The trustee takes full legal title to real estate for tax purposes as if it were received and held by any other tax entity. Sales by trustees are usually made pursuant to powers granted in the trust instrument for investment and reinvestment of the trust corpus, or for making an equitable distribution of the trust property upon termination. Upon any such sale, gain or loss is attributable to the trust.

.03 Income from Personal Property

Income of all types from personal property, including gain from the sale or exchange of such property, is taxable to the estate. This is because title to personal property vests in the representative immediately upon his or her appointment. Title to personal property does not pass to the legatees until the estate is fully administered and distribution is ordered or approved by the court. Upon distribution, however, title to personal property is regarded as reverting to the legatees as of the date of the decedent's death.[19] The *basis* of the property distributed also relates back to the date of the decedent's death. In other words, the interim title vests as a matter of convenience and necessity only, but income from personal property nevertheless is taxable to the person or entity then holding title.

Where a decedent's will calls for the transfer of personal property to a trust, the income from the personal property prior to the transfer is taxable to the estate because the trust cannot come into existence as to specific property until after probate administration. Thereafter the trust will have to report the income. Income

---

[14] Rev. Rul. 59-375, 1959-2 CB 161; *Guaranty Trust Co. of N.Y.*, 30 BTA 314, CCH Dec. 8499; *G.L. Craig*, 7 BTA 504, CCH Dec. 2580.

[15] Rev. Rul. 59-375, 1959-2 CB 161.

[16] Rev. Rul. 75-61, 1975-1 CB 180.

[17] Code Sec. 1014(a) and (b).

[18] Reg. § 1.1014-1(a).

[19] *E.F. Brewster*, SCt, 2 USTC ¶ 451, 280 US 327.

from personal property in the hands of an *inter vivos* trust is taxable to the trust except where it is considered to be that of the grantor under the special provisions discussed beginning at ¶ 901.

In the absence of specific testamentary or judicial directions to carry on a decedent's business, it would seem that an estate does not hold assets for use in a "business" or for sale in the course of trade, so sales would ordinarily result in capital gains or losses.

An executor's liquidation of a decedent's inventory of goods that had been held by the decedent for sale to customers in the ordinary course of business can result in capital gain (or loss) from sale of a capital asset if the estate (through the executor) did not actively engage in the decedent's trade or business, but sold the inventory on hand as expeditiously as possible in order to close the estate. Thus, the Tax Court (with the IRS acquiescing) has held that an executor realized capital gain from the sale of a large quantity of pelts and some fur garments, both in bulk and at auction sales, after it had sold a deceased furrier's retail fur business, and the pelts and garments represented articles that the purchaser of the business did not want.[20] If the executor had purchased more pelts or garments, in addition to what was on hand at the time of the decedent's death, the estate might have been regarded as having been engaged in a trade or business.

.04 Farm Loss Property and Farm Land

Under Code Sec. 1252, gain from the sale of farm land held for less than ten years will be taxed as ordinary income to the extent the deductions previously allowed for soil and water conservation expenditures and land clearing expenditures are recaptured. These statutory recapture provisions do not apply to farm property that passes at the owner's death to his or her estate or beneficiary.

They do apply, however, where the sale of the farm property was completed by the owner before death and the sale proceeds constitute income in respect of a decedent in the hands of the estate or beneficiary. Further, they apply to the extent that any Code Sec. 1252 gain is attributable to the property while owned and operated for farming purposes by the estate or beneficiary.[21]

.05 Sales of Crops

Where crops are sold after the death of a farmer, the gain on the sale is income to the estate or to the heirs. If the farmer had contracted for the sale of the crops before death, the sale proceeds would be income in respect of a decedent under Code Sec. 691 (see ¶ 304), which would have the same character as they would have had in the hands of the decedent, that is, ordinary income.

> **Example 1:** Farmer owned and operated an apple orchard. During his lifetime, Farmer sold and delivered 1,000 bushels of apples to Factory 1, a canning factory, but did not receive payment before his death. Farmer also entered into negotiations to sell 3,000 bushels of apples to Factory 2, also a canning factory, but did not complete the sale before his death. After Farmer's death, the executor received payment from Factory 1. He also completed the

---

[20] *J. Ferber Est.*, 22 TC 261, CCH Dec. 20,321 (Acq.).   [21] Reg. § 1.1252-2(b).

sale to Factory 2 and transferred to Factory 2 1,200 bushels of apples on hand at Farmer's death and harvested and transferred an additional 1,800 bushels. The gain from the sale of apples by Farmer to Factory 1 constitutes income in respect of a decedent when received. On the other hand, the gain from the sale of apples by the executor to Factory 2 does not.[22]

If the crops are sold in liquidation of the estate, they would be capital assets in the hands of the estate. However, if the executor continues to operate the farm, as a custodian for the ultimate heir or legatee, sales undoubtedly would be considered to have been made in the ordinary course of business, thereby resulting in ordinary income. In addition, a sale of crops pending sale of the farm would seem to be in liquidation of the assets of the estate. If the crops are sold by the executor along with the land, they would be assets subject to a taxable gain.

Rent received by a cash-method farmer in the form of crop shares or livestock and still held by the farmer at the time of death is income in respect of a decedent in the year in which the crop shares or livestock are sold.[23]

Where there is a specific devise of real estate or of a "farm," growing crops ordinarily would be included, because the crops are considered to be a part of the real estate. On a sale of the crops by an heir or devisee, it would apparently be more difficult for the heir or devisee than for an executor to prove that he or she was not in the business of farming. A sale of crops, either harvested or unharvested, does not seem comparable to a liquidation of a real estate inheritance. Thus, in regard to a farm passing from a decedent, the heir or devisee would realize income to the extent that the sale proceeds exceed the value assigned to the growing crops for estate tax purposes. Growing crops (and other property) that represent a surviving spouse's one-half share of what had been community property qualify for a stepped up or stepped down new basis as property passing from a decedent, provided that at least one-half of such property was includible in the decedent's gross estate.[24]

The tax consequences that result when a farmer has delivered crops to a cooperative for sale, but dies before the sale is effected or the proceeds are distributed, are not clear. In one case,[25] the U.S. Court of Appeals for the Ninth Circuit held that:

1. The net proceeds of sales made by a cooperative before the farmer's death were income in respect of a decedent, taxable as such when received by the estate and distributed to the beneficiary (the Tax Court had held that this involved a nontaxable collection of a claim, which became and was distributed as corpus of the estate); and

2. The net proceeds of sales made after the farmer's death, and after the estate was closed, were taxable on their receipt by the beneficiary as income in respect of a decedent (the Tax Court had held that these would not be income in respect of a decedent because the sales were not made until after the farmer's death).

---

[22] Reg. § 1.691(a)-2, Example 5.
[23] Rev. Rul. 64-289, 1964-2 CB 173; *H. Davison Est.*, CtCls, 61-2 USTC ¶ 9584, 292 F2d 937, cert. denied, 368 US 939.
[24] Reg. § 1.1014-2(a)(5).
[25] *R.J. Linde*, CA-9, 54-1 USTC ¶ 9384, 213 F2d 1, cert. denied, 348 US 871.

At the same time, the court affirmed a holding by the Tax Court that the estate tax valuation of the beneficiary's interest in crops not sold by the cooperative before the farmer's death became their basis to the beneficiary, and that the difference between this basis and the amount realized on their sale by the cooperative was capital gain or loss. No attempt was made by the court to fit this holding to the above holdings that the proceeds were income in respect of a decedent or to the fact that the proceeds would have been ordinary income to the decedent.

If an amount is taxable as income in respect of a decedent, it is taxable in full, but the tax is offset to some extent by a deduction allowed for the estate tax paid on the right to receive the income (see ¶ 314). If it is capital gain from sale of a capital asset that passed from a decedent, the amount received is reduced by the "basis" of the asset, the basis being the estate tax value.

¶ 604 Gain or Loss When Legacy Satisfied in Property

Generally, no taxable gain or loss results from a transfer of property to the beneficiary under a specific bequest, whether its value at the time of transfer is greater or less than that at the date of acquisition by the estate or trust. However, gain or loss is realized when property is used to satisfy a cash bequest.[26]

> *Example 2:* The trustees of a testamentary trust were required to pay $50,000 to the testator's child when the child reached 25 years of age, and payment was made in stock worth that amount. The excess of $50,000 over the basis (value at death) of the stock in the hands of the trust represents taxable gain to the trust from a "sale or other disposition."

However, if a stated percentage of the corpus is to be distributed to the beneficiary before the trust's termination, the situation is different. When property is distributed in compliance with such a provision, there is not a satisfaction of an obligation of the trust for a definite amount of cash or equivalent value in property, but rather a partial distribution of a share of the trust principal. The trustee will not realize taxable income from the distribution.[27]

Also, when the will provides for the distribution of the entire net estate between beneficiaries "share and share alike," with no provision for any equal division of the specific property, and no conversion of the assets to cash is made for that purpose, it would seem that a distribution to such beneficiaries in accordance with their agreement (that they will each receive certain specific property in satisfaction of their equal claims under the will) should not be regarded as resulting in a "sale or exchange" even though one or more of them has gained an advantage by reason of a disproportionate enhancement of the value of their shares since the date of the testator's death. The agreement should not be a taxable transaction involving liability to the estate.[28] However, where a will provided for an equalizing

---

[26] *S.P. Suisman,* DC Conn., 36-2 USTC ¶ 9443, 15 FSupp 113, aff'd per curiam, CA-2, 83 F2d 1019, cert. denied, 299 US 573.

[27] Rev. Rul. 55-117, 1955-1 CB 233.

[28] *M.L. Long,* 35 BTA 95, CCH Dec. 9525.

distribution to compensate for lifetime transfers, the IRS ruled that such a distribution was equivalent to a distribution in satisfaction of a right to receive a specific dollar amount and that, under the specific facts, the estate realized a gain.[29]

If a marital deduction trust comprises a fraction or percentage of the "adjusted gross estate" of a decedent, the marital trust fund is considered to have been provided for in a fixed and definite "dollar amount." Therefore, if, on the date of distribution to the marital trust, the legacy is satisfied in property the value of which is greater or smaller than that used for federal estate tax purposes, gain or loss is realized by the estate upon the distribution of the property to the trust.[30] Although for decedents dying after 1981 the federal estate tax marital deduction is unlimited and formulas are not required to assure its maximum utilization, wills executed or trusts created before September 12, 1981, must be specifically amended to change the "prior law" effect of a marital deduction formula.[31] Note also that, under Code Sec. 2056(b)(10), the term "specific portion" refers only to a portion that is determined on a fractional or percentage basis.

¶ 605 Capital Gains and Losses

Capital gains and losses are generally taken into account in computing taxable income just as if the estate or trust were an individual. In computing gross income, no distinction is made between capital gains and losses allocable to income and those allocable to corpus, although for trust accounting purposes a distinction is made.

The gain realized by an estate upon the sale of its capital assets is taxable even though the sale is for the purpose of liquidation to pay creditors or to make distributions of shares to heirs or beneficiaries and regardless of the fact that the tax will diminish the amount they receive. This rule also applies to a trust.

Whether gain or loss is ordinary income or capital gain depends on the character of the property in the hands of the estate or trust—that is, whether held for investment purposes, for sale to customers, or for use in a trade or business.

It is possible for the character of the income to change in the hands of the executor of an estate. For example, subdivision lots held by a real estate dealer became capital assets in the hands of the executor who held them for liquidation only and not for sale to customers in the ordinary course of business.[32] (See also ¶ 603 paragraphs .01 and .05.)

Property passing from a decedent is presumed to have been held by an estate or heirs for a sufficient period to qualify for long-term capital gain treatment.[33]

In reporting the income from the sale of capital assets, estates and trusts, like individuals, may avail themselves of the net capital gain provisions of the Code. Estates and trusts are also entitled to the benefits of Code Sec. 1231, relating to gain that is recognized on sales or exchanges of property used in a trade or

---

[29] Rev. Rul. 82-4, 1982-1 CB 99.

[30] *W.R. Kenan, Jr.*, CA-2, 40-2 USTC ¶ 9635, 114 F2d 217; Rev. Rul. 56-270, 1956-1 CB 325, as clarified by Rev. Rul. 60-87, 1960-1 CB 286.

[31] Reg. § 20.2056(a)-1(c)(3); Rev. Rul. 80-148, 1980-1 CB 207.

[32] *W.D. Haden Est.*, 12 TCM 825, CCH Dec. 19,813(M).

[33] Code Sec. 1223(10).

business or on compulsory or involuntary conversions. An estate that is a shareholder of a regulated investment company must report its share of both the distributed and undistributed capital gain income of such a company.

If a part of corpus is sold at a loss, the beneficiary may conceivably suffer to the extent that the sources of future income from the trust or estate will be less than before. The trust or estate, however, is the legal owner of the assets, and any losses from the sale thereof are available only to the estate or trust. They are not available to the beneficiary except to the extent that there may be an unused capital loss carryover or an unused net operating loss carryover upon termination of the estate or trust (see ¶ 618).[34]

The fact that a statutory stock option is exercised by an employee's estate instead of by the employee will not convert such an exercise into a taxable event.[35] Nor are holding period requirements generally applicable for statutory stock-option treatment applicable to subsequent dispositions by an estate or beneficiary. However, such dispositions—and this includes distributions—may result in capital gain (see ¶ 404).

.01 Capital Gains Tax Rates

Different rates of tax apply to gain depending on whether the gain is "ordinary" or "capital" in nature. Gain or loss from the sale or exchange of a capital asset is classified as either short-term or long-term depending on how long the asset is held. Short-term capital gain or loss is defined as the sale or exchange of a capital asset held for not more than one year. Gain or loss is long-term if the asset's holding period is more than a year. Although short-term capital gain is taxed at ordinary income tax rates, long-term capital gains of noncorporate taxpayers are generally taxed at lower rates.

Since 2013, the long-term capital gains rate of 20% applies to taxpayers who fall within the 37% tax bracket.[36] Also since 2013, capital gain income will be subject to an additional 3.8% Medicare tax for taxpayers with income at or above a certain threshold.[37]

Trusts, like estates, partnerships, and other pass-through entities, may pass through capital gains to their beneficiaries. The pass-through entity must make the determination of when a long-term capital gain is taken into account on its books. Taxpayers are permitted to exclude 50% of any gain on the sale or exchange of qualified business stock that is held for a period of more than five years.[38]

The beneficiaries of an estate or a complex trust are taxed on (1) the income of the estate or trust required to be distributed to them currently, whether or not actually distributed (this includes an amount required to be paid out of income or corpus, such as an annuity, to the extent that there is income not paid, credited or

---

[34] Code Sec. 642(h).
[35] Reg. § 1.421-2(c).
[36] Code Sec. 1(h)(1)(B).
[37] In tax years ending prior to May 6, 2003, there were up to six different rates that could apply to long-term capital gains, and from May 6 through December 31, 2010, up to four different rates could apply. For 2011-2012, 28% for collectible gain; 25% for unrecaptured Code Sec. 1250 gain; 0% for other long-term gain if in the 10% to 15% tax bracket, and 15% if over the 15% tax bracket; and 18% for qualified five-year gain.
[38] Code Sec. 1202.

required to be distributed to other beneficiaries for the tax year), and (2) "other" amounts properly paid, credited or required to be distributed to him for the tax year.[39]

Upon termination of the estate or trust, a capital loss carryover is the same in the hands of a beneficiary as it was in the hands of the estate or trust, except that the carryover is a short-term capital loss in the hands of a corporate beneficiary regardless of whether it would have been a long-term or short-term capital loss in the hands of the estate or trust.[40] The amount of the carryover is determined under Code Sec. 1212. Therefore, the carryover is determined at the fiduciary level rather than at the beneficiary level where long-term capital losses are involved and the capital gains reduction applies. The beneficiary may claim the capital loss carryover in her first tax year in which the estate or trust terminates.

.02 Depreciable Real Estate

Unrecaptured Code Sec. 1250 gain is subject to a maximum 25% rate.[41] Unrecaptured Code Sec. 1250 gain is the excess of (1) the amount of long-term capital gain (not otherwise treated as ordinary income) that would be treated as ordinary income if Code Sec. 1250(b)(1) included all depreciation, and the applicable percentage that applied under Code Sec. 1250(a) were 100%, and only gain from property held more than 12 months (18 months if applicable) were taken into account *over* (2) the excess of 28% rate loss *over* 28% gain.[42] Code Sec. 1250 will continue to treat some prior claimed depreciation as ordinary income.

.03 Collectibles

Generally, collectibles are taxed at a maximum rate of 28% even if held for more than 12 months.[43]

.04 Netting of Gains and Losses

If a taxpayer has a net capital gain for the tax year, the gain must be separated into rate groups (or rate group "baskets") to determine the portion of the net capital gain subject to each tax rate. The rate groups are (1) the 28% rate group, (2) the 25% rate group, and (3) the 20% rate group. Gains and losses are netted within each of the five rate group baskets to arrive at a net gain or loss. After the basic process is completed, the following netting and ordering rules must be applied:

- **Short-term capital gains and losses.** Short-term capital losses are applied first to reduce short-term capital gains that would otherwise be taxable at ordinary income rates. A net short-term loss is used first to reduce any net long-term capital gain from the 28% group. Any remaining short-term loss is used to reduce gain from the 25% group and then the 20% group.
- **Long-term capital gains and losses.** A net loss from the 28% group is used first to reduce gain from the 25% group, then to reduce net gain from the 20% group. A net loss from the 20% group is used first to reduce net gain from the 28% group, then to reduce gain from the 25% group, then to reduce gain from the 20% group.

---

[39] Code Sec. 662(a).
[40] Reg. § 1.642(h)-1.
[41] Code Sec. 1(h)(1)(D).
[42] Code Sec. 1(h)(6).
[43] Code Sec. 1(h)(4) and (5).

Any resulting net capital gain that is attributable to a particular rate group is taxed at that group's marginal tax rate.[44]

¶ 606 Basis of Estate or Trust Property

Prior to and after 2010, the basis of property received by a decedent's estate, under Code Sec. 1014(b)(1), is (1) the fair market value of the property at the decedent's death, (2) its fair market value at the alternate valuation date under Code Sec. 2032, if elected, (3) in the case of a special use valuation election under Code Sec. 2032A, its value under that Code section, or (4) to the extent of the applicability of the exclusion described in Code Sec. 2031(c), the basis in the hands of the decedent. However, for property acquired from a decedent dying after December 31, 2009, the basis is the lesser of the adjusted basis of the property in the hands of the decedent, or the fair market value of the property on the date of the decedent's death.[45]

> *Example 3:* Frank Thomas purchased a residence in 1972 for $100,000. When he died in 2012, the value of the residence was $500,000. In addition, its alternate valuation date value was $510,000. If the estate elects to value Thomas's estate on the alternate valuation date, the estate's basis in the residence is $510,000.

Land subject to a permanent conservation easement. An executor may elect to exclude from the taxable estate up to 40% of the value of certain land that is subject to a qualified conservation easement.[46] To the extent that the value of the land is excluded from the taxable estate, the basis of the land acquired at death is carried over from the decedent. To the extent of the exclusion, the basis of the property is not stepped up or stepped down to its fair market value at death.[47]

When a grantor creates an *inter vivos* trust, the transfer of property to the trust as trust principal or corpus usually constitutes a gift. Accordingly, for purposes of determining gain, depreciation, or depletion, the trust's basis will usually be the same as the basis of the property to the grantor, increased by any gift tax paid with respect to the gift. For purposes of determining loss, the basis will be either the grantor's basis (increased by any gift tax paid with respect to the gift) or the value of the property at the time it was transferred to the trust, whichever is lower.

If the property was acquired by the trust by bequest or devise, the basis must be determined under the rules applicable to bequests and devises—that is, generally, the property's fair market value at date of death or as of the alternate valuation date.

In the case of a sale of property by the grantor to the trust, the basis of the property to the trust will be the same as the basis to the grantor, increased by the amount of any gain or decreased by the amount of any loss recognized to the grantor on the transfer to the trust.

---

[44] Code Sec. 1(h)(1).
[45] Code Secs. 1014(f) and 1022(a).
[46] Code Sec. 2031(c).
[47] Code Sec. 1014(a)(4).

If a transfer is part gift and part sale, the basis of the property is the greater of (1) the amount paid or (2) the transferor's basis, to which is added the amount of gift tax paid on the transfer. However, for purposes of determining loss, the unadjusted basis of the property in the hands of the transferee may not exceed the property's fair market value at the time of the transfer.[48]

When property, which in the hands of the trustee has the same basis as in the hands of the grantor, is transferred by the trustee to a beneficiary who is a donee, the basis to such donee will be the same as the basis to the trustee and to the grantor of the trust.

If a trust acquires property by purchase or exchange (other than from the grantor), the same general rules applicable to an individual will apply in determining the trust's basis for the property, as distinguished from the special rules described above. In other words, if property is acquired by a straight purchase from a third party, the basis of the property will be its cost.

.01 Adjustments to Basis

A special rule is provided for computing an increase in basis as a result of a gift tax attributable to a gift made after 1976. The increase is an amount (not in excess of the tax paid) that bears the same ratio to the amount of tax paid as the net appreciation in the value of the gift bears to the amount of the gift. For this purpose, net appreciation is the amount by which the fair market value of the gift exceeds the donor's adjusted basis immediately before the gift.[49]

When property is acquired from a decedent, its basis is generally the same in the hands of every person having possession or enjoyment of the property under the will or trust instrument or under the laws of descent and distribution. This principle of uniform basis means that the basis of the property will be the same, or uniform, whether the property is possessed or used for the benefit of the estate, the heir, the legatee or devisee, or the trustee or beneficiary of a trust created by a will or an *inter vivos* trust. Therefore, since the basis is uniform for all persons having an interest in the property, adjustments to the basis will also follow the same principle. Thus, for example, when depreciation or depletion deductions are allowed or allowable to a legal life tenant, as if he or she were the absolute owner of the property, the deductions will constitute an adjustment to the basis of the property not only in the hands of the life tenant but also in the hands of the remainderman. Similarly, depreciation or depletion deductions in the case of trust property constitute an adjustment to the basis of the property in the hands of the trustee and also in the hands of the trust beneficiaries.

Generally, depreciation is allowable to an estate, devisee, or legatee from the date of the decedent's death, the basis for which would be the value of the property on the date of death or on the alternate valuation date. Thus, when an executor elects to have the estate's assets valued for estate tax purposes at a date six months later than the decedent's death (alternate valuation date), such value will be the basis for depreciation, but depreciation will nevertheless be allowable to the

---

[48] Reg. § 1.1015-4.   [49] Code Sec. 1015(d)(6).

decedent's successor (the estate or distributee, as the case may be) from the date of death since that is the date on which title passed from the decedent.[50]

Every person to whom a uniform basis of property acquired from a decedent is applicable must maintain records showing in detail all deductions, distributions, or other instances in which adjustment to basis is required for depreciation, depletion, or charges to a capital account under Code Sec. 1016, or for discharge of indebtedness under Code Sec. 1017.[51]

¶ 607 Deductions and Credits

In general, an estate or trust is entitled to the same deductions for expenses incurred in carrying on a trade or business or in the production of income as an individual.[52] This would include such deductions as trade and business expenses, interest, and taxes. However, there are many exceptions to the general rule. For example, trusts and estates have no standard deduction or deduction for medical expenses. Estates and trusts are also expressly prohibited from electing to expense certain otherwise depreciable expenses under Code Sec. 179.[53]

There are certain deductions, however, that trusts and estates can take that are not available to individuals. Most importantly, estates and trusts may deduct income distributed or distributable to beneficiaries. They can also deduct administration expenses, such as legal fees. Moreover, special rules govern certain deductions, such as those for depreciation and depletion, the personal exemption, the charitable deduction, and the deduction for casualty losses. Certain deductions are also prohibited if they were deducted on the estate's estate tax return (see ¶ 618).

.01 Credits

Estates and trusts may also claim most of the major credits that individuals are entitled to claim, except for those credits that would apply specifically to individuals, such as the dependent care credit.

.02 Expenses of Administration

Reasonable amounts paid or incurred by the fiduciary of an estate or trust on account of administration expenses, including fiduciaries' fees and expenses of litigation, that are ordinary and necessary in connection with the performance of the duties of administration are deductible as nonbusiness expenses under Code Sec. 212, generally applicable to expenses for production of income. However, to the extent such expenses are allocable to the production or collection of tax-exempt income, they are not deductible. Also, such expenses are deductible for income tax purposes only if they are not claimed as deductions for estate tax purposes (see ¶ 613).[54]

¶ 608 Miscellaneous Itemized Deductions and Section 67

In general, an estate or trust is subject to the 2% of adjusted-gross-income floor on miscellaneous itemized deductions (just like an individual). The adjusted gross

---

[50] Reg. § 1.1014-4.
[51] Reg. § 1.1014-4(c).
[52] Reg. § 1.641(b)-1.
[53] Code Sec. 179(d)(4).
[54] Reg. § 1.212-1(i).

income of an estate or trust is computed in the same manner as it is for an individual, except that the following deductions are allowed under Code Sec. 67(e) in arriving at adjusted gross income: (1) deductions for expenses paid or incurred in connection with the administration of the estate or trust that would not have been incurred had the property not been so held, (2) the Code Sec. 642(b) deduction relating to the personal exemption of an estate or trust, and (3) the distribution deductions allowed under Code Secs. 651 and 661.[55]

The exception for trusts and estates under Code Sec. 67(e) only applies to deductions that could not have been incurred if the property were held by an individual.[56] If the exception under Code Sec. 67(e) does not apply, then the general rule under Code Sec. 67(a) applies, and the deduction was historically limited to the 2% of adjusted-gross-income floor. However, the 2017 Tax Cuts and Jobs Act ("TCJA")[57] added new Code Sec. 67(g), titled "Suspension for taxable years 2018 through 2025," which provides "Notwithstanding subsection (a), no miscellaneous itemized deduction shall be allowed for any taxable year beginning after December 31, 2017, and before January 1, 2026." Thus, to what extent and to which deductions the Code Sec. 67(e) applies have become more important to practitioners—if Code Sec. 67(e) does not apply, and Code Sec. 67(a) applies, the deduction is not available.

This narrow interpretation of the exception was reflected in proposed, and now final, regulations.[58] The regulations also provide a non-exclusive list of services for which the cost is either exempt from or subject to the 2% floor.[59] Deductions under Code Sec. 642(c) (relating to deduction for amounts paid or permanently set aside for a charitable purpose) are not subject to the 2% floor.[60] The IRS has the regulatory authority to apply the 2% floor at the beneficiary level, rather than at the entity level, with respect to simple trusts.[61]

The question of whether a trust's investment-advice fees and related trust administrative and management costs fall under exception (1), above, to the 2% floor caused a split between the Sixth Circuit (a decision where the IRS nonacquiesced) and the Second Circuit.[62] Trust-related investment fees were deemed fully deductible by the Sixth Circuit, since trustees were viewed as incurring them to perform their fiduciary duties. Although individual investors routinely incur these costs, they have no potential liability if they act negligently. The IRS disagreed with this result and would not follow the rule in other cases that arose outside of the Sixth Circuit.[63] The Federal Circuit rejected the Sixth Circuit's reasoning, holding that these costs would be incurred routinely even if the trust did not hold the funds. Therefore the costs did not fall under the exception to the

---

[55] Code Sec. 67(e).

[56] *William L. Rudkin Testamentary Trust*, CA-2, 2006-2 USTC ¶ 50,569.

[57] P.L 115-97.

[58] Reg. § 1.67-4, issued May 9, 2014 (effective date January 1, 2015). Internal Revenue Bulletin 2007-36, issued September 4, 2007 (REG-128224-06).

[59] Reg. § 1.67-4.

[60] Code Sec. 67(b)(4).

[61] House Committee Report to the Technical and Miscellaneous Revenue Act of 1988 (P.L. 100-647).

[62] *W.J. O'Neill, Jr., Irrevocable Trust*, CA-6, 93-1 USTC ¶ 50,332, 994 F2d 302 (Nonacq.); *Mellon Bank, NA*, CA-FC, 2001-2 USTC ¶ 50,621; *J.H. Scott*, CA-4, 2003-1 USTC ¶ 50,428.

[63] *W.J. O'Neill, Jr., Irrevocable Trust*, CA-6, 93-1 USTC ¶ 50,332, 994 F2d 302 (Nonacq.); *Mellon Bank, NA*, CA-FC, 2001-2 USTC ¶ 50,621; *J.H. Scott*, CA-4, 2003-1 USTC ¶ 50,428.

general rule and were subject to the 2% floor for miscellaneous deductions.[64] The Fourth Circuit sided with the Federal Circuit.[65]

The U.S. Supreme Court may have settled the matter.[66] The Court held that "Investment advisory fees generally are subject to the 2% floor when incurred by a trust" ... except that when the relevant cost is "paid or incurred in connection with the administration of the ... trust" and "would not have been incurred if the property were not held in such trust," the cost may be deducted without regard to the floor, Code Sec. 67(e)(1). Shortly before the decision, the IRS issued proposed regulations,[67] which were extended several times. In a Notice issued in 2011, the IRS extended the reprieve that taxpayers will not be required to determine the portion of a "bundled fiduciary fee" that is subject to the 2% floor under Code Sec. 67 for any taxable year beginning before the date that final regulations are published in the Federal Register. In the interim, taxpayers were allowed to deduct the full amount of such fees without regard to the 2% floor.[68] Payments by the fiduciary to third parties for expenses subject to the 2% floor are readily identifiable and must be treated separately from the otherwise bundled fiduciary fee.

A bundled fiduciary fee is likely most commonly utilized by a corporate fiduciary where multiple services are combined or bundled into one fiduciary fee, which might include some fees subject to the 2% floor, such as investment advisory, and others that are clearly not, such as trustee fees. The final regulations defines the class of deductions allowed in computing the AGI of trust or estate, as opposed to being potentially classified as "miscellaneous itemized deductions" subject to 2% of AGI under Code Sec. 67. The regulations provide that if a "bundled" fee is attributable both to costs that are subject to the 2% floor and costs that are not, the fee must be allocated between the two. However, if the bundled fee is not computed on an hourly basis, only the investment management component of fee is subject to the 2% floor. To allocate a bundled fee between costs subject to the 2% floor and costs that are not, "any reasonable method" may be used, including determining the portion of a bundled fee allocable to investment advice.

¶ 609 Deductibility of Litigation Expenses

Litigation expenses incurred by a trust or estate may be deducted as administration expenses, provided the fiduciary and not the beneficiary paid the expenses.[69] These include the cost of contesting an income tax deficiency[70] and the cost of prosecuting a suit to have a residuary trust declared void with the trust property paid back into the estate.[71]

Expenses incurred in defending or protecting the estate's or trust's title to property, or recovering such property, are not deductible. Instead, they are treated

---

[64] *Mellon Bank, NA,* CA-FC, 2001-2 USTC ¶ 50,621.
[65] *J.H. Scott,* CA-4, 2003-1 USTC ¶ 50,428.
[66] *Knight v. Commissioner,* 552 US 181 (2008).
[67] Internal Revenue Bulletin 2007-36, issued September 4, 2007 (REG-128224-06).
[68] IRS Notice 2011-37, 2011-20 IRB 785.
[69] *C.P. Erdman,* 37 TC 1119, CCH Dec. 25,408, aff'd, CA-7, 63-1 USTC ¶ 9391, 315 F2d 762; *C.S. Davis,* 35 BTA 1001, CCH Dec. 9639; *H.A. Moore Trust,* 49 TC 430, CCH Dec. 28,828.
[70] *Trust of M.L. Bingham,* SCt, 45-2 USTC ¶ 9327, 325 US 365, 65 SCt 1232.
[71] *F.S. Loyd,* CtCls, 57-2 USTC ¶ 9837, 153 FSupp 416, 139 CtCls 626.

as capital expenditures.[72] Similarly, expenditures incurred in protecting or asserting the trust's rights to property of a decedent as legatee under a testamentary trust are nondeductible capital expenditures. An item that is nondeductible is not rendered deductible by the fact that the property held by the estate or trust will be sold to satisfy a claim and would otherwise be held for the production of income.

It is immaterial whether the expenses, if deductible, are paid from the corpus or from income of the estate or trust.[73] They derive their character not from the fund from which they are paid, but from the purposes for which they are incurred. Fire insurance premiums carried on a house owned by the estate and on which it is entitled to receive rent from a tenant are deductible. However, premiums on an insurance policy on the life of a debtor to secure payment of his or her indebtedness to the estate are not deductible.[74]

If the estate is engaged in winding up the decedent's business, it is entitled to deduct ordinary and necessary expenses that occur.

¶ 610 Deductions in Respect of a Decedent

The business expenses, nonbusiness expenses, interest, and taxes for which the decedent was liable, that were not properly deductible in the decedent's last tax year or any prior tax year, are deductible by the estate when it pays them. If the estate was not liable to pay those obligations, they are deductible when paid by the person who, by bequest, devise, or inheritance from the decedent or by reason of the death of the decedent, acquires an interest in the property of the decedent subject to the obligation (for details, see ¶ 310).[75]

No medical deduction is allowable for an estate or trust because a trust cannot incur such expenses on its own behalf and has no dependents as that term is defined in the law. However, medical expenses for a decedent's care, paid by an estate within one year after the decedent's death, are treated as having been paid by the decedent when incurred and, accordingly, may be deducted on the decedent's return for the year incurred (usually the decedent's last return) if not deducted for estate tax purposes (see ¶ 312).[76]

¶ 611 Deductibility of Interest

An estate or trust is generally entitled to a deduction for interest paid (whether out of income or corpus) or accrued on its obligations. Several applications of this deduction are peculiar to estates. For example, interest paid by the estate on overdue legacies where imposed by local law is deductible by the estate under Code Sec. 163, when the legacies are deferred by the executors for administration purposes.[77] No income tax (or estate tax) deduction is allowed for the interest paid on estate taxes deferred under Code Sec. 6166.[78]

---

[72] *Manufacturers Hanover Trust Co.*, CtCls, 63-1 USTC ¶ 9250, 312 F2d 785, *cert. denied*, 375 US 880.

[73] *O. Hubert Est.*, SCt, 97-1 USTC ¶ 60,261, 520 US 93, 117 SCt 1124.

[74] *J.S. Mellinger, Exr.*, CA-5, 56-1 USTC ¶ 9183, 228 F2d 688.

[75] Code Sec. 691(b).

[76] Code Sec. 213(c)(1); Reg. § 1.213-1(d)(1).

[77] Rev. Rul. 73-322, 1973-2 CB 44. *But see M. Schwan*, DC S.D., 2003-1 USTC ¶ 50,362.

[78] Code Secs. 163(k) and 2053(c)(1)(D).

Although income is computed under the cash-basis method, prepaid interest must be deducted over the term of a loan to the extent that the interest represents the cost of the use of the borrowed funds. Home mortgage points are currently deductible to the extent that such points are generally charged in the area in which the loan is made.[79] Interest is not deductible on indebtedness incurred or continued to purchase or carry obligations, such as municipal bonds, on which the interest is wholly exempt from federal income tax.

An estate or trust, like an individual, is also governed by Code Sec. 163(d), which places a limit on the deduction of interest on investment indebtedness. Interest can be deducted up to the amount of net investment income during the year only. Net investment income is defined as the excess of the investment income *over* the investment expenses.[80] Interest that is disallowed because of these rules may be carried forward to future years to the extent of net investment income in that year.

¶ 612 Deduction of Taxes by an Estate or Trust

An estate or trust is generally entitled to the same deductions for taxes as an individual.[81] Federal income or estate taxes, state inheritance, estate, legacy, or succession taxes, and gift taxes are not allowable as deductions on any income tax return.[82] Further, such taxes generally are not allowable as deductions "in respect of a decedent" as explained at ¶ 610, although federal estate taxes may be deducted under the conditions outlined at ¶ 314.

Federal import duties and federal excise taxes may be deducted as business expenses where incurred in a business or income-producing activity. Transfer taxes on a deed conveying title to estate property and assessments against local benefits that tend to increase the value of the property assessed are not deductible. State and local real and personal property taxes, state and local income taxes (except that portion that is allocable to exempt income other than exempt interest income),[83] and the generation-skipping transfer tax imposed on income distributions are deductible as taxes. So too are foreign real property and foreign income taxes. Other state, local, and foreign taxes may be deducted as taxes when they are of a business nature or for the production of income. Also, state and local sales taxes are not deductible.

Deductibility as a tax (Code Sec. 164(a)) rather than as an expense for the production of income (Code Sec. 212) can make a difference when the tax is imposed on property that generates tax-exempt income. The IRS has recognized the distinction and permitted a beneficiary of a trust to deduct Irish wealth taxes attributable to tax-exempt state and local government obligations.[84]

The IRS has followed the rule that liability for property taxes attaches on the assessment date even though the amount is not ascertainable on that date, and, therefore, the taxes accrue as of that date. However, it has accepted a Tax Court

---

[79] Code Sec. 461(g); Rev. Proc. 94-27, 1994-1 CB 613.
[80] Code Sec. 163(d)(4).
[81] Code Secs. 164(a) and 641(b).
[82] Code Sec. 275.
[83] Rev. Rul. 61-86, 1961-1 CB 41.
[84] Rev. Rul. 78-81, 1978-1 CB 57.

decision to the effect that Delaware real estate taxes accrue on the lien date and not on the earlier assessment date.[85] The U.S. Supreme Court has held that, where the liability for taxes is contested, there can be no accrual until liability is established even though the contested taxes have been paid.[86]

Property taxes on real estate sold must be apportioned between the seller and the buyer according to the number of days in the real property tax year that each holds the property. Proration is required whether or not the seller and purchaser actually apportion the tax, and whether they are on the cash or the accrual basis.[87]

Example 4: An estate sells real estate to Georgia Johnson on August 1, Year 1. Both the estate and Johnson use the cash basis of accounting. Taxes for the real property tax year April 1, Year 1, through March 31, Year 2, become due and payable on May 15, Year 3. Johnson pays the real estate taxes when they fall due. Regardless of any agreement between the parties, for federal income tax purposes, 122/365 of the real estate taxes are treated as imposed upon the estate and are deductible by it.

Under the provisions of Code Sec. 266, taxes and carrying charges, otherwise deductible that are, under sound accounting principles, chargeable to a capital account may be capitalized at the election of the taxpayer. By reason of this provision, one court permitted an estate to capitalize real estate taxes and mortgage interest on rental property while it was being rented when the executor held the property for sale and liquidation and did not deduct the expenses from the incidental rental income during the period the property was being held for sale.[88] The executor contended that rental of the property was incidental to the primary purpose of holding it for an advantageous sale, and that this was the proper treatment for fiduciary accounting purposes. It is to a taxpayer's advantage to exercise an election to capitalize taxes and carrying charges and add them to the basis of the property when a deduction would not result in a tax benefit.

¶ 613 Double Deductions for Certain Items Not Allowed

For estate tax purposes, the Internal Revenue Code allows certain deductions from the gross estate in computing the taxable estate.[89] Of these, administration expenses and losses during administration might include items that would also be deductible from gross income for income tax purposes.

To prevent duplication of the deductions, the law provides that amounts that qualify for estate tax purposes under Code Sec. 2053 or 2054 may not be used in computing the taxable income of the estate (or any other person) for income tax purposes unless the deduction for estate tax purposes is waived.[90] A similar rule applies concerning the generation-skipping transfer tax. Accordingly, items that are otherwise allowable in computing a decedent's taxable estate are not deductible on the estate's income tax return unless the executor or administrator files a statement

---

[85] *Keil Properties, Inc.*, 24 TC 1113, CCH Dec. 21,245 (Acq.); Rev. Rul. 56-145, 1956-1 CB 612. *See also* Rev. Rul. 73-64, 1973-1 CB 70, and Rev. Rul. 72-409, 1972-2 CB 99.

[86] *Consolidated Edison Co. of N.Y.*, SCt, 61-1 USTC ¶ 9462, 366 US 380.

[87] Code Sec. 164(d).

[88] *J.A. Sullivan, Exr.*, CA-9, 55-2 USTC ¶ 9735, 227 F2d 12.

[89] Code Sec. 2051.

[90] Code Sec. 642(g); Reg. § 1.642(g)-1.

(in duplicate) that the items have not been claimed as federal estate deductions. In disallowing an income tax deduction for a charitable contribution where the estate had already claimed an estate tax deduction for the same contribution, the Fifth Circuit noted that Congress's intention was to provide a benefit for charitable transfers in the nature of either an offset against the estate's gross value or an offset against income, and to allow a double deduction would go beyond the conduit framework established in the Code.[91] A trust is not allowed a charitable deduction under Code Sec. 642(c) and is not allowed a distribution deduction under Code Sec. 661(a)(2) with respect to a contribution of trust principal to a charity that meets the requirements of a qualified conservation contribution under Code Sec. 170(h).[92]

An estate's administration expenses can be deducted either from the gross estate in figuring the federal estate tax on Form 706 or from the estate's gross income in figuring the estate's income tax on Form 1041.[93] To prevent a double deduction, amounts otherwise allowable in calculating the decedent's taxable estate for federal estate tax purposes will not be allowed as a deduction in figuring the income tax of the estate or of any other person unless the personal representative files a statement, in duplicate, indicating that the items of expense listed in the statement were not claimed as deductions for federal estate tax purposes and that all rights to claim such deductions are waived. This statement can be filed at any time before the statute of limitations applicable to the tax year for which the deduction is sought expires.[94]

The rule against double deductions does not apply to deductions for taxes, interest, business expenses, or other items accrued at the date of the decedent's death. Consequently, such items are deductible from the gross estate as claims against the estate and also from gross income as "deductions in respect of a decedent" for income tax purposes.[95]

> *Example 5:* On July 1, Herman, a cash-basis taxpayer borrows $5,000 against the equity in his home (thereby making the interest on this loan fully deductible) and agrees to pay 5% interest on the succeeding July 1. On December 31, Herman dies. Herman's estate may deduct $125 of interest for both income and estate tax purposes because that much interest had accrued at the date of death as a claim against the estate.

Items not accrued at the date of death, so that they are allowable for estate tax purposes as administration expenses only, are not deductible in computing the taxable income of the estate unless a statement is filed waiving the deduction for estate tax purposes.[96] Where income tax deductions were claimed for interest payable on deferred estate tax, the statute of limitations had run out for some of the tax years in issue, and no waiver had been filed under Code Sec. 642(g), the IRS has ruled that the doctrine of equitable recoupment prevents an estate from

---

[91] *United States Trust Co.*, CA-5, 86-2 USTC ¶ 9777, 803 F2d 1363, rev'g and remanding DC Miss., 85-2 USTC ¶ 9741, 617 FSupp 575.

[92] Rev. Rul. 2003-123, 2003-2 CB 1200.

[93] IRS Publication No. 559, Survivors, Executors, and Administrators, p. 17.

[94] Reg. § 1.642(g)-1.

[95] Reg. § 1.642(g)-2.

[96] Id.

realizing a double deduction by claiming an estate tax refund based on treatment of the deferred interest as an expense of the estate.[97]

As long as deductions are not duplicated, administration expenses may be the basis of an estate tax deduction in one year and an income tax deduction the next.[98] Statutory fees for regular probate services and fees for preparation of estate and income tax returns, if they are ordinary and necessary expenses of the estate, are, to the extent not attributable to tax-exempt income, deductible either on the estate tax return or on the income tax return filed by the estate, but not on both. In making the administration expense election, the possible conflicts that may result between beneficiaries—because of the shifting of burdens and benefits that may be brought about—should be taken into consideration. For example, if the executor claims the administration expenses as deductions on the estate's income tax return, a life beneficiary may be enriched at the expense of a remainderman, and the remainderman may seek some sort of reimbursement under state law.

The allocation of indirect expenses to exempt and nonexempt income is to be made on the basis of all of the facts in the case. The amount disallowed as a deduction for income tax purposes may be allowed as a deduction for estate tax purposes.[99]

The Code Sec. 642(g) disallowance of double deductions has no bearing on items such as funeral expenses that qualify for estate tax deductions but are not applicable in determining taxable income.[100]

¶ 614 Depreciation Deduction Is to Be Apportioned

Depreciation is deductible by an estate or trust, but only to the extent the deduction is not apportioned to the beneficiaries.[101] For the purpose of allocating the depreciation deduction, the term "beneficiaries" includes charitable beneficiaries. This is so even though the income is retained in the trust and permanently set aside for charity.[102]

.01 Trusts—Depreciation Deduction

For property held in trust, the deduction is apportioned between the income beneficiaries and the trustee in accordance with the pertinent provisions of the instrument creating the trust. In the absence of such provisions, the deduction is apportioned on the basis of the trust income allocable to each, unless the trust instrument or local law requires or permits the trustee to maintain a reserve for depreciation. This means that if the trustee does charge depreciation (crediting an equivalent amount to corpus, in order to preserve the trust principal), the depreciation allowable for income tax purposes will first be allocated to the trustee, up to the amount actually set aside for this purpose. Any excess deduction allowable for income tax purposes will then be allocated between the trustee and beneficiary in proportion to their shares in the trust income. However, if, under the trust instru-

---

[97] Rev. Rul. 81-287, 1981-2 CB 183. Note that no income or estate tax deduction is currently allowed for interest on deferred estate tax (see ¶ 611 and Code Sec. 6166).

[98] Rev. Rul. 70-361, 1970-2 CB 133.

[99] Rev. Rul. 63-27, 1963-1 CB 57, clarifying Rev. Rul. 59-32, 1959-1 CB 245.

[100] *O.F. Yetter Est.*, 35 TC 737, CCH Dec. 24,654.

[101] Code Sec. 642(e); Reg. § 1.642(e)-1.

[102] Reg. § 1.642(e)-1.

ment or local law, the income of the trust computed without regard to depreciation is to be distributed to a named beneficiary, then the beneficiary is entitled to the deduction to the exclusion of the trustee. IRS regulations state that no effect will be given to any allocation of the depreciation deduction that gives any beneficiary or the trustee a share of such deduction greater than his or her pro rata share of the trust income, irrespective of any provisions in the trust instrument, except when the trust instrument or local law requires or permits the trustee to maintain a reserve for depreciation.[103]

A life tenant is entitled to the entire amount of allowable depreciation. In other words, the deduction is computed as if the life tenant were the absolute owner of the property without any apportionment between the life tenant and the remainderman.[104]

It has been held that where, under the terms of the trust instrument, no provision was made for the deduction of depreciation by the trust, the beneficiary who was entitled to all of the trust income could deduct depreciation suffered by the trust property although, in the particular year, there was no income from the property available for distribution.[105]

Where a testamentary trust established a reserve for depreciation and directed that "net income before taxes" be paid to named beneficiaries, the trust was entitled to deduct the entire amount of the depreciation on the trust corpus.[106]

.02 Estates—Depreciation Deduction

There is a single rule for estates. Depreciation is apportioned among the estate and the heirs, legatees, and devisees on the basis of the estate income allocated to each.[107]

Estates and trusts are not eligible to elect under Code Sec. 179 to expense any part of the cost of otherwise qualifying recovery property.[108]

¶ 615 Treatment of Depletion Deduction

Life tenants (but not remaindermen), trusts, and beneficiaries (including charitable beneficiaries) are all entitled to their respective shares of the depletion allowance. For trust property, the same general rules used for depreciation apply for depletion. The allowable deduction for depletion is to be apportioned between the income beneficiaries and the trustee on the basis of the trust income allocable to each.[109] The U.S. Court of Appeals for the Fifth Circuit has held that such apportionment is mandatory when the trust instrument is silent on the matter.[110] The Code and regulations include a similar provision.[111] However, if the trust instrument or local law requires or permits the trustee to maintain a reserve for depletion in any amount, the deduction is first allocated to the trustee to the extent

---

[103] Code Sec. 167(d); Reg. § 1.167(h)-1(b).
[104] Code Sec. 167(d).
[105] *S. Carol*, 30 BTA 443, CCH Dec. 8520 (Acq.).
[106] *C.L.F. McIntosh*, DC Vt., 64-2 USTC ¶ 9716.
[107] Code Sec. 167(d); Reg. § 1.167(h)-1(c).

[108] Code Sec. 179(d)(4).
[109] Code Sec. 611(b)(3); Reg. § 1.611-1(c)(4).
[110] *W. Fleming, Trustee*, CA-5, 41-2 USTC ¶ 9590, 121 F2d 7.
[111] Code Sec. 611(b)(3); Reg. § 1.611-1(c)(4).

that income is set aside for a depletion reserve.[112] Any part of the deduction in excess of the income set aside for the reserve is then apportioned between the income beneficiaries and the trust on the basis of the trust income (in excess of the income set aside for the reserve) allocable to each. If, under the trust instrument or local law, the income of the trust computed without regard to depletion is to be distributed to a named beneficiary, the beneficiary is entitled to the deduction to the exclusion of the trustee. Reg. §1.611-1(c)(4) also states that no effect is to be given to any allocation of the depletion deduction that gives any beneficiary or the trustee a share of such deduction greater than his or her pro rata share of the trust income, irrespective of any provisions in the trust instrument, except when the trust instrument or local law requires or permits the trustee to maintain a reserve for depletion.[113]

For an estate, the depletion deduction is to be apportioned among the estate and the heirs, legatees, and devisees on the basis of income of the estate that is allocable to each heir, legatee, and devisee.[114] This rule applies regardless of whether any such person also receives the property from which the income is derived.

¶ 616 Deductible Losses of an Estate or Trust

Deductions for losses are allowed to an estate or trust to the same extent as they are for an individual. That is, losses sustained during the tax year, not compensated for by insurance or otherwise, and either from a trade or business, from a transaction entered into for profit but not connected with a trade or business, or from a casualty or theft are deductible under Code Sec. 165.

.01 Casualty Losses

Casualty and theft losses are allowed only if, at the time the return is filed, the loss has not been claimed as a deduction from the gross estate of the decedent in a federal *estate* tax return (see ¶ 613).[115] However, in determining the amount of casualty or theft loss, estates and trusts are allowed to deduct the costs paid or incurred in connection with an estate or trust in arriving at adjusted gross income.[116] The $100 limitation under Code Sec. 165(h)(1) and the 10% rule under Code Sec. 165(h)(2) apply to estates and trusts as well as to individuals.

> **Example 6:** An estate having interest income of $20,000 and administration expenses of $4,000 incurs a casualty loss of $5,000. After the casualty loss is reduced by $100, it is compared to 10% of the estate's adjusted gross income, $1,600 ($20,000 − $4,000 administration expenses × 10%). The $5,000 loss reduced by $100 ($4,900) exceeds $1,600 by $3,300. Therefore, $3,300 is deductible by the estate or trust. (If the administration expenses were not taken into consideration, the deductible loss would have been $2,900 ($20,000 × 10% = $2,000, $4,900 exceeds $2,000 by $2,900)).

---

[112] Reg. § 1.611-1(c)(4); Rev. Rul. 60-47, 1960-1 CB 250.
[113] Code Secs. 611(b) and 642(e); Reg. §§ 1.611-1(c) and 1.642(e)-1.
[114] Code Sec. 611(b)(4); Reg. § 1.611-1(c)(5).
[115] Code Sec. 165(h)(4)(D).
[116] Code Sec. 165(h)(4)(C).

.02 Capital Losses

Capital losses from the sale of trust or estate corpus, title to which is in the trust or estate, are deductible only by the fiduciary. Therefore, if a trust or estate sells part of its corpus at a loss (even though the beneficiary may conceivably suffer to the extent that the trust or estate sources of future income will be fewer than before), only the trust or estate, as legal owner of the capital assets, may utilize the losses resulting from such sales.[117] However, if, under local law, legal title to real estate is considered to be in the residuary legatee from the moment of the decedent's death, a loss on the sale of the property may be deductible by the residuary legatee, the sale being considered as made by the estate or trust as an agent.[118]

Capital loss carryovers are allowed to the beneficiaries of an estate or trust on termination (see ¶ 618).

Trusts, other than grantor trusts, and estates are subject to the passive activity loss limitations (see ¶ 316).[119] When a trustee manages an investment, it is usually in an administrative (i.e., passive) capacity in which direct material participation in the business behind the investment does not take place. As such, losses realized by the trust are usually limited by the passive activity loss rules. However, a federal district court ruled that the material participation of a testamentary trust in a ranching business could not be decided by evaluating only the activities of the trustee, but had to be determined by addressing the activities of the trust through its fiduciaries, employees, and agents. Because the collective activities of those persons were regular, continuous, and substantial, the material participation requirement was satisfied and the trust's ranching losses were improperly disallowed by the IRS as passive activity losses.[120]

On the other hand, where trustees hired to operate the business had only limited power under the contract, the limited number of hours the trustees spent on the management and operations of the business did not constitute a regular, continuous and substantial involvement in the business. Thus, the trust did not satisfy the material participation requirement.[121]

.03 Losses Sustained by Decedent or Estate

A distinction must be made between losses sustained by the decedent and those sustained by the decedent's estate. A loss sustained by the decedent during the last tax year before death is deductible only by the decedent on the return filed on his or her behalf.[122] If the event determining worthlessness of a debt or security occurred after the decedent's death, the loss can be claimed only by the estate while those assets are in its possession. Apportionment of losses between the decedent and the estate would only be possible in the case of a business bad debt,

---

[117] *W.W. Abell*, CA-4, 1 USTC ¶ 355, 30 F2d 54, cert. denied, 279 US 849; *T.R. Beatty*, 28 BTA 1286, CCH Dec. 8221; *F.D. Bisbee*, DC Fla., 49-1 USTC ¶ 9139, 80 FSupp 929; *M.S. Wilson, Exr.*, SCt, 3 USTC ¶ 1066, 289 US 20.

[118] *L.R. Arrott*, CA-3, 37-2 USTC ¶ 9491, 92 F2d 773.

[119] Code Sec. 469(a)(2)(A); Temp. Reg. § 1.469-1T(b)(2).

[120] *Mattie K. Carter Trust*, DC Tex., 2003-1 USTC ¶ 50,418, 256 FSupp2d 536.

[121] IRS Technical Advice Memorandum 200733023, August 17, 2006.

[122] *J.S. Hoffman Est.*, 36 BTA 972, CCH Dec. 9820 (Acq.).

where partial loss is taken by the decedent, and the balance of the debt became worthless after death. Deduction for partial worthlessness of a nonbusiness bad debt is not permitted under Code Sec. 166(d). Therefore, a loss from the worthlessness of a nonbusiness bad debt is to be claimed by either the decedent or the decedent's estate and cannot be allocated between them on the basis of partial worthlessness. Also, a nonbusiness bad debt is subject to the capital loss limitations.

An estate or trust may not deduct losses related to income in respect of a decedent or losses that may result from the sale or other transfer of income in respect of a decedent under Code Sec. 691(a)(2). Beneficiaries (including trusts) who receive no distribution from an estate during a year when the allowable deductions of an estate exceed the gross income thereof are not entitled to offset against income from other sources their share of such a loss of the estate.[123] As to unused loss carryovers and excess deductions on termination of an estate or trust, see ¶ 618.

A taxpayer who has a life estate in the income of a trust may not deduct amounts representing shrinkage (by whatever name called) in the value of such interest due to the lapse of time.[124] The life tenant, however, must use a zero basis for his or her interest, and the entire amount he or she receives for the interest is taxable.

.04 Related Parties

Code Sec. 267 specifically provides that losses from sales and exchanges of property between certain related parties, including those listed below, are not deductible. These related parties include:

- A grantor and a fiduciary of any trust;
- A fiduciary of a trust and a fiduciary of another trust, if the same person is a grantor of both trusts;
- A fiduciary of a trust and a beneficiary of such trust;
- A fiduciary of a trust and a beneficiary of another trust, if the same person is a grantor of both trusts;
- A fiduciary of a trust and a corporation when more than 50% of the outstanding stock's value is owned, directly or indirectly, by or for the trust or by or for a person who is a grantor of the trust; and
- An executor of an estate and a beneficiary of the estate, except in the case of a sale or exchange in satisfaction of a pecuniary bequest.[125]

The good faith of the parties in the transaction has no bearing on the application of the above provision, which is strictly construed, and, even if a transaction is not between any of the statutorily enumerated parties, the IRS still insists that it be a bona fide transaction.[126] However, a Tax Court decision allowed trusts with a common trustee, a common income beneficiary, and closely related

---

[123] *G.M. Studebaker*, 2 BTA 1020, CCH Dec. 902.
[124] Code Sec. 273; Reg. § 1.273-1.
[125] Code Sec. 267(b).
[126] Reg. § 1.267(a)-1(c).

¶616.04

successor beneficiaries and remaindermen to establish losses by selling each other stock.[127]

The IRS has ruled that where stock owned by an estate was sold at a loss by the executor to a trust, which had been created by the decedent-husband for his wife before his death, the loss was a capital loss, which was deductible from the estate's gross income to the extent provided in Code Sec. 1211(b). The loss was not disallowed by Code Sec. 267.[128]

¶ 617 Net Operating Loss Deduction Allowed

The net operating loss deduction under Code Sec. 172 is allowed to estates and trusts. However, the following exceptions and limitations apply:

1. In computing gross income and deductions for Code Sec. 172, a trust is to exclude that portion of the income and deductions attributable to the grantor or another person under the grantor trust rules of Code Secs. 671 through 678 (see ¶ 901).
2. An estate or trust is not, for Code Sec. 172, to avail itself of the charitable contributions deduction under Code Sec. 642(c) and the deduction for distributions under Code Secs. 651 and 661.[129]

Beneficiaries succeeding to the property of an estate or trust on termination are allowed to claim the benefits of any unused net operating loss carryover as explained at ¶ 618.

.01 At-Risk Limitations

There are limits on the extent to which losses from investments that are financed through nonrecourse loans or that are otherwise protected from economic risk (for example, by stop loss agreements, guarantees, or insurance) are deductible. In general, the at-risk rules limit a taxpayer's loss to the amount that the taxpayer has at risk and could actually lose from an activity.[130] These rules are designed to discourage tax shelter investors who had sheltered other taxable income with losses from investments in activities that were financed to a large extent through nonrecourse loans for which they are not liable. Without loss deduction limitations, these tax losses would usually exceed the amount of the taxpayer's economic risk.

The at-risk rules generally apply to all activities other than certain equipment leasing by closely held corporations. Activities that are part of a trade or business, or that are engaged in for the production of income, are also subject to the at-risk rules.

For purposes of the at-risk loss limitation rule, a loss is the excess of allowable deductions, including losses from prior years that were disallowed as deductions in prior years because of these at-risk limitations, *over* the amount of income received or accrued by a taxpayer from one of those activities. Form 6198 (At-Risk Limitations) is used to compute the lesser of the amount of loss or the amount at risk.

---

[127] *J.E. Widener,* 80 TC 304, CCH Dec. 39,858 (Acq.).
[128] Rev. Rul. 56-222, 1956-1 CB 155.
[129] Code Sec. 642(d); Reg. § 1.642(d)-1.
[130] Code Sec. 465.

¶ 618 Unused Loss Carryovers

An unused capital loss carryover under Code Sec. 1212 or an unused net operating loss carryover under Code Sec. 172 remaining on termination of an estate or trust is allowed to the beneficiaries succeeding to the property of the estate or trust.[131] The carryovers are the same in the hands of the beneficiaries as in the hands of the estate or trust and are deductible from gross income in computing adjusted gross income.

The first tax year of the beneficiary to which the net operating loss or capital loss is to be carried is the tax year of the beneficiary in which or with which the estate or trust terminates.

> ***Example 7:*** A trust distributes all of its assets to the sole remainderman, and terminates on December 31, Year 1, when it has a capital loss carryover of $10,000. The remainderman, who reports on the calendar-year basis, otherwise has ordinary income of $12,000 and capital gains of $4,000 for Year 1. The remainderman would offset his capital gains of $4,000 against the capital loss of the trust and, in addition, offset the capital loss against $3,000 of his taxable income for Year 1, as provided by Code Sec. 1211(b). The $3,000 balance of the capital loss carryover will then be carried over to Year 2 and later years until it is used up.[132]

When an estate or trust sustains a net operating loss (NOL) in the year of its termination, the NOL would become an unused NOL carryover, which, under the provisions of Code Sec. 642(h)(1), is allowable to the beneficiary.[133] The NOL carryforward period (for NOLs other than eligible farming losses[134]) is unlimited—the 20-year limitation was eliminated by the 2017 TCJA, giving the taxpayer the ability to carry forward losses indefinitely. However, NOL carryforward arising after January 1, 2018 will now be limited to 80% of taxable income.[135]

The carryback period for farming loss is two years.[136]

An NOL in the year of termination is available *only* to the beneficiary. See Example 9 below. A beneficiary was never able to carry back any part of an NOL made available to the beneficiary through the provisions of Code Sec. 642(h)(1), even if the estate or trust had *no* preceding tax years eligible for a carryback.

When the last tax year of an estate or trust is the last year to which a loss can be carried (e.g., the carryover period expires during the estate's or trust's last tax year), the loss is allowed to the beneficiary as an "excess deduction" (discussed below) to the extent that it is not absorbed in the tax year by the estate or trust.

---

[131] Code Sec. 642(h)(1); Reg. § 1.642(h)-1.

[132] Reg. § 1.642(h)-1(c), Example 1.

[133] The 2017 TCJA denies any carryback for noncorporate taxpayers, and rather any excess business loss in the year of termination is treated as part of the beneficiary's net operating loss (NOL) and carried forward to subsequent tax years pursuant to Code Sec. 172.

[134] Under the 2017 TCJA, the farming loss limitation of Section 461(j) will not apply for tax years beginning after December 31, 2017 and before January 1, 2026.

[135] Code Sec. 172(b)(1)(A). The rules for existing pre-2018 NOLs remain the same. These losses can be carried back two years and forward 20 years. There is no taxable income limit to usage of pre-2018 losses.

[136] Code Sec. 172(b)(1)(G) as modified under the 2017 TCJA. Prior to 2018, in some tax years, the two-year carryback period was extended to five years. Code Sec. 172(b)(1)(H).

Prior to 2018, a net operating loss carryback had the effect of reducing the distributable net income of an estate or trust for the prior tax year to which the net operating loss is carried, and, therefore, the beneficiaries would be eligible to recompute their tax liability for such prior year.[137]

¶ 619 Excess Deductions on Termination

Historically, if the deductions (other than the personal exemption (prior to 2018) and charitable contributions) of an estate or trust for its last tax year exceed gross income, the excess was allowed as a deduction to the beneficiaries succeeding to the property for the tax year of the beneficiaries in which or with which the estate or trust terminates.[138] The deduction could not be carried over, and, because it was allowable only from adjusted gross income, it did not benefit taxpayers who did not itemize deductions.[139]

.01 Limitation on the Deductibility of Excess Deductions on Termination

The 2017 TCJA limits the deductibility of excess deductions on terminations. The Regulations under Code Sec. 642 provide that "the deduction is allowed only in computing taxable income and must be taken into account in computing the items of tax preference of the beneficiary; it is not allowed in computing adjusted gross income."[140] Since the deduction is not specifically mentioned under Code Sec. 67(b) as an exception to Code Sec. 67(a), excess deductions on terminations are a miscellaneous itemized deduction. Under new Code Sec. 67(g) added by the 2017 TCJA, a beneficiary is not allowed a final-year estate or trust excess deduction (for tax years 2018 through 2025). Additionally, the Joint Explanatory Statement noted "[e]xcess deductions (including administrative expenses) allowed a beneficiary on termination of an estate or trust" as one of the "above listed items" that cannot be claimed as a deduction under Code Sec. 67(g).

An argument that charitable contributions can serve as a floor in computing excess deductions, even though not themselves allowable as a deduction to beneficiaries, has been rejected by the Tax Court.[141]

> **Example 8:** An estate's final income tax return lists gross income of $100,000, charitable contributions of $60,000, and other deductions of $110,000. The excess allowable to beneficiaries is $10,000 (other deductions less gross income), not $70,000 (the excess of all the deductions over the estate's gross income.)

In determining excess deductions, any item of income or deduction that is considered in computing the net operating loss or capital loss carryover for the last tax year may not be utilized in determining excess deductions.

---

[137] Rev. Rul. 61-20, 1961-1 CB 248.
[138] Code Sec. 642(h)(2).
[139] Code Sec. 642(h)(2); Reg. §1.642(h)-2; Rev. Rul. 57-31, 1957-1 CB 201.
[140] Treas. Reg. §1.642(h)-2.
[141] *F.M. O'Bryan*, 75 TC 304, CCH Dec. 37,423.

Example 9: A decedent died in January Year 1, leaving a will that provided for distribution of her estate to Beneficiary. The period of administration terminated on December 31, Year 1, at which time all of the property was distributed to Beneficiary, who reports on the calendar-year basis. The estate had the following income and deductions:

Business income	$3,000
Plus: Nonbusiness income	2,500
Gross income	$5,500
Business expenses	$5,000
Plus: Administration expenses and corpus commissions	9,800
	$14,800

The estate has a net operating loss of $2,000 ($5,500 gross income reduced by $5,000 of business expenses and $2,500 of nonbusiness expenses, the deduction for nonbusiness expenses being limited to nonbusiness income). Beneficiary may deduct this net operating loss in Year 1 and carry forward any balance indefinitely. The excess deductions are $7,300, the amount of administrative expenses and corpus commissions not considered in determining the net operating loss ($9,800 − $2,500 that was offset against nonbusiness income in computing the net operating loss). The excess deductions will be deemed to be miscellaneous itemized deductions, limited, or not deductible, pursuant to Code Sec. 67(g).

Under Code Sec. 175, farmers may elect to deduct soil and water conservation expenditures rather than to capitalize them. Such deduction is limited to 25% of the taxpayer's gross income from farming for a tax year. Expenditures in excess of the 25% limitation may be carried over and applied in future years, subject to the 25% annual limitation. If, upon termination, a trust or estate has excess deductions that include conservation expenditures, the beneficiaries may deduct such expenditures to the extent that they do not exceed 25% of the gross income of the estate or trust from farming for its last tax year. Any expenditures in excess of this 25% limitation are lost.[142]

¶ 620 Allocation in Year of Termination

The carryovers (and excess deductions prior to 2018) described above are allocated among the beneficiaries succeeding to the property of an estate or trust proportionately according to the share of each in the burden of the loss or deductions. A person who qualified as a beneficiary succeeding to the property of an estate or trust with respect to one amount and who does not qualify with respect

---

[142] Rev. Rul. 58-191, 1958-1 CB 149.

to another amount is a beneficiary succeeding to the property of the estate or trust as to the amount with respect to which he or she qualifies.

> ***Example 10:*** Tom Rogers' will leaves $100,000 to Ann Clark and the residue of his estate equally to Bud White and Cary Smith. His estate is sufficient to pay only $90,000 to Clark and nothing to White and Smith. There is an excess of deductions over gross income for the last tax year of the estate of $5,000 and a capital loss carryover of $15,000. Clark is a beneficiary succeeding to the property of the estate to the extent of $10,000, and since the total of the excess of deductions and the loss carryover is $20,000, Clark is entitled to the benefit of one-half of each item. The remaining half is divided equally between White and Smith.[143]

¶ 621 Alimony and Separate Maintenance Payments

Payments to surviving spouses by an estate as dower or other statutory allowances are deductible by the estate to the extent of distributable net income (as explained at ¶ 707 thru ¶ 709) if paid pursuant to a court order or decree or pursuant to applicable state law. According to the applicable regulations,[144] this is the case regardless of whether the payment is made out of corpus or income. The Tax Court agrees but concedes that the governing provisions may be inconsistent with the general Code Sec. 102(a) rule that gifts, inheritances, and bequests are not included in gross income.[145] Thus, under IRS regulations, as upheld by the Tax Court, such statutory allowances are includible in the recipient's income to the extent of his or her share of the distributing estate's distributable net income.[146]

A dower interest will not cause property that is still subject to administration under state law but not yet distributed to the spouse to be taxable to the spouse rather than to the estate. Nor will passage of legal title to beneficiaries when a trustee remains responsible for protecting and conserving the property cause income from the property to be taxable to beneficiaries.[147]

---

[143] Reg. § 1.642(h)-4.
[144] Reg. § 1.661(a)-2(e).
[145] *M.H. Schaefer,* 46 TCM 986, CCH Dec. 40,338(M), TC Memo. 1983-465. Specifically emphasized was Code Sec. 102(b)(2), under which amounts included in a beneficiary's gross income under Code Secs. 641 through 692 shall, for purposes of Code Sec. 102(b)(2), be treated as a gift, bequest, devise, or inheritance of income from property.
[146] Reg. §§ 1.662(a)-2(c) and 1.662(a)-3(b).
[147] Rev. Rul. 75-61, 1975-1 CB 180.

Chapter 7

Fiduciary Accounting Income and Distributable Net Income

¶ 701 Conduit Nature of Fiduciary Income Taxation
¶ 702 Fiduciary Accounting Income (FAI)
¶ 703 Total Return Legislation
¶ 704 Distributable Net Income (DNI)
¶ 705 Distributing Capital Gains in Distributable Net Income
¶ 706 Distinction between Simple and Complex Trusts
¶ 707 How to Determine Distributable Net Income
¶ 708 Simple Trust's Deduction for Distributions to Beneficiaries
¶ 709 Estate's and Complex Trust's Deduction for Distributions to Beneficiaries
¶ 710 Illustration of an Estate and Complex Trust Deduction Computation
¶ 711 Distributions in Kind
¶ 712 65-Day Election Rule Under Section 663(b)

¶ 701 Conduit Nature of Fiduciary Income Taxation

One of the main objectives of fiduciary income taxation is to determine where the income is taxed and whether it is taxed to the beneficiary or the fiduciary (i.e., the trust or estate). In order to avoid double taxation by both the entity and a beneficiary, the trust is allowed a distribution deduction for distributions to beneficiaries. Ultimately, the distribution deduction identifies the amount of income taxed to the beneficiary, and the distribution deduction is determined after calculating the amount of income *available* for distribution: distributable net income ("DNI"). Thus, in many ways, the process of determining DNI is at the center of understanding fiduciary income tax.

One way to understand the role of DNI is to ask the question: how should the fiduciary account for and thereby tax the income earned on property of a trust or estate as that property is either accumulated by the trust or estate or distributed by an trust or estate to the beneficiary? The nature of this question is the essence of the "conduit" nature of fiduciary income taxation—the concept that income of a trust or estate is only taxed once, by either the entity or the beneficiary, but not both.[1]

There are some fundamentals of fiduciary income tax regarding distributions that are important to understand at the outset:

1. The taxation of trusts and estates generally follows the rules for individual taxpayers.
2. The primary authority governing estates and trusts is either the estate planning document (i.e., trust agreement for a trust) or local law establishing the rules.
3. Taxes are paid at the final destination by the recipient beneficiaries (whether those are individuals, other trusts, entities, etc.) absent an accumulation of income.
4. Except for the year of termination, gains and losses are generally retained by the trust, and not distributed to the beneficiaries.
5. If the distribution is the satisfaction of a pecuniary bequest in a general form (e.g., $5,000 to my daughter Taylor) with appreciated property, no income is carried out, and the difference between the basis in the property and fair market value is treated as a sale or exchange and taxed to the fiduciary.

¶ 702 Fiduciary Accounting Income (FAI)

Fiduciary accounting income ("FAI") (sometimes referred to as trust accounting income or "TAI," the two terms are interchangeable) is the amount of income generally available for distribution to the income beneficiaries of a trust or estate as determined by the governing instrument and/or applicable local law. It is not "taxable income," "gross income," or "distributable net income," which are tax concepts. Fiduciary accounting income is determined by the governing instrument, or if not stated in the governing instrument, by local law.

Fiduciary accounting income allocates receipts and disbursements between income and principal of the estate or trust for a fiscal year. The governing instrument may direct how income is calculated, determining how much income is to be distributed to an income beneficiary or held for the benefit of other beneficiaries. The Uniform Principal and Income Act is the basis for the rules used in most states, but many of those states have made their own modifications to the Act, some of which are quite significant.

If the state law default does not provide guidance, the trustee must determine what is "fair and reasonable" to all of the beneficiaries, not just the income beneficiaries. Under the 1997 version of the Uniform Prudent Investor Act, trustees investing as a prudent investor were authorized to make "adjustments" between income and principal as necessary to provide the income beneficiary with an appropriate degree of beneficial enjoyment where the income component of the

---

[1] Code Secs. 651(a) and 661(a).

trust portfolio's total return is too small or too large because of investment decisions under the prudent investor rule.

In fiduciary accounting, the term "income" usually means the amounts for which a fiduciary would be required to account in rendering an accounting to the court having jurisdiction of the estate or trust.[2] Items of gross income constituting extraordinary dividends or taxable stock dividends that the fiduciary, acting in good faith, allocates to corpus are not considered income.[3] As a general rule, if it is not clear whether an item is principal or income, it is allocated to principal.

¶ 703 Total Return Legislation

In an attempt to catch up to the changes being made to state laws regarding fiduciary investment standards and the definitions of principal and income, the IRS adopted final regulations that revised the definition of "income" under Code Sec. 643.[4] The changes in state statutes resulted from investment strategies that seek total positive return on trust assets. The statutes are designed to ensure that, when a trust invests in assets that may generate little traditional income (including dividends, rents and interest), the income and remainder beneficiaries are allocated reasonable amounts of the total return of the trust so that both classes of beneficiaries are treated impartially. Some statutes permit the trustee to pay to the person entitled to the income a unitrust amount based on a fixed percentage of the fair market value of the trust assets. Other statutes permit the trustee the discretion to make adjustments between income and principal to treat the beneficiaries impartially.

Under the regulations, trust provisions that depart fundamentally from traditional concepts of income and principal (such as allocating ordinary income to income and capital gains to principal or allocating all tax-exempt income to distributions to noncharitable beneficiaries) continue to be disregarded as they had been in the past.

For example, a typical ordering provision in a charitable lead trust requires the source of funds payable to charities as directed minimize income tax consequences to the trust by exhausting higher tax rate income before using nontaxable sources, such as principal or tax-exempt interest. The IRS has consistently taken the position that such ordering rules have no "economic effect independent of their tax consequences" because the amount paid to the charity is not dependent upon the type of income it is allocated, and therefore, such ordering rules will be disregarded for federal tax purposes. The final regulations, effective April 16, 2012, clarify this stance.[5]

However, amounts allocated between income and principal pursuant to applicable state law will be respected if state law provides for a reasonable apportionment between the income and remainder beneficiaries of the total return of the trust for the year, taking into account ordinary income, capital gains, and, in some situations, unrealized appreciation. Items such as dividends, interest and rents are generally

---

[2] Reg. § 1.643(b)-1.
[3] Reg. § 1.643(b)-2.
[4] T.D. 9102, 2004-1 CB 366.
[5] T.D. 9582, 2012-18 IRB 868.

allocated to income and proceeds from the sale or exchange of trust assets are generally allocated to principal.[6]

Which state's law governs a fiduciary's allocation of accounting principal and income? For an estate, it will be the primary state where the will is probated, generally where the decedent was domiciled on date of death. In a trust, the governing instrument should identify the governing law. But if it does not, there will likely be some confusion as to which state's law applies. For example, if a grantor establishes and funds a trust in one state and moves to another state, which state's law applies? This question has not been fully addressed.

¶ 704 Distributable Net Income (DNI)

Once fiduciary accounting income is determined under the governing instrument or state law, the trustee will distribute that amount to the beneficiaries. The question then becomes how much of the distribution is taxable to the beneficiaries and what is the character of that income.

Distributable net income is generally the largest amount of income to be taxed to trust beneficiaries who receive distributions from the trust or estate and the amount that will be deductible by the trust. It is generally beneficial to pass as much income to the beneficiary due to the highly compressed tax rates for estates and trusts and to the 3.8% Medicare tax on passive income for trusts.

Once the tentative taxable estate is calculated as described in Chapter 6 titled "Fiduciary Income Tax Return Fundamentals," the trust's distributable net income is computed as described in this chapter. The trust's distribution deduction equals the distributable net income as modified to *exclude* the items of income not included in the trust's gross income, such as tax-exempt interest as adjusted for commissions and any charitable contributions. The character of the income is determined as described in Chapter 8 titled "Beneficiary's Tax Liability."

All of the fiduciary accounting income, limited to DNI, passes automatically to the beneficiary of a simple trust whether or not it is actually distributed, except for capital gains that are typically allocated to principal. Furthermore, trusts and estates receive no deduction for net tax-exempt income due to the tax-exempt nature (i.e., not included in taxable income, so no distribution from taxable income).

For complex trusts, there are typically two levels or tiers of beneficiaries: those to whom net income is to be distributed and those to whom discretionary income may be distributed. The net income distributable to the first level of beneficiary is limited up to the amount of DNI, and the remainder is distributed to the second level of beneficiary to the extent of any actual distributions to them. DNI is not allocated to distributions to satisfy specific gifts or bequests of money or property payable in no more than three installments. The distribution deduction combines the income allocable to both levels of beneficiaries.

---

[6] Reg. § 1.643(b)-1.

¶ 705 Distributing Capital Gains in Distributable Net Income[7]

The general rule for fiduciary income tax purposes is that gains from sale or exchange of capital assets are excluded from distributable net income to the extent that such gains are allocated to principal. The regulations under Regulation Section 1.643(a)-3(a) provide that capital gains are ordinarily excluded from distributable net income. However, the regulations under Regulation Section 1.643(a)-3(b) specifically acknowledge that capital gains may be allocated to distributable net income under: (1) a state unitrust statute, (2) when allocated to corpus but treated consistently by the fiduciary on the trust's books, records, and tax returns as part of a distribution to a beneficiary, or (3) when allocated to corpus but actually distributed to the beneficiary or utilized by the fiduciary in determining the amount that is distributed or required to be distributed to a beneficiary. An allocation of capital gains to income will generally be respected if the allocation is made either pursuant to the terms of the governing instrument and applicable local law or pursuant to a reasonable and impartial exercise of a discretionary power granted to the fiduciary by applicable local law or by the governing instrument, if not prohibited by applicable local law. This is a trend among certain states that have amended local law, including North Carolina[8] and Alaska and those that are considering such changes, for example, Arizona and New York.

¶ 706 Distinction between Simple and Complex Trusts

In determining the deduction for distributions to beneficiaries, different rules may apply depending upon whether the trust is a simple trust or a complex trust. A simple trust is one that is required to distribute all of its income currently, regardless of whether the trustee actually does so, and has no provision in the trust instrument for charitable contributions.[9]

.01 Simple Trust: All Income Distributed

A trust is not a simple trust if the terms of the trust instrument require that none of the income be distributed until after the year of its receipt by the trust. However, if the fiduciary is under a duty to distribute the income currently but as a matter of practical necessity the income is not distributed until after the close of the trust's tax year, treatment as a simple trust will still be proper.[10]

> **Example 1:** Under the terms of a trust instrument, all of the income is currently distributable to Betty. The trust reports on a calendar-year basis and as a matter of practical necessity makes a distribution to Betty of each quarter's income on the 15th day of the month following the close of the

---

[7] The author would like to recognize the contribution of Gregory V. Gadarian of Gadarian & Cacy, PLLC, for input on distributing gains in DNI and the application to trusts.

[8] For example, see North Carolina General Statute § 36C-8-816(16) regarding specific powers of trustee. "Without limiting the authority conferred by G.S. 36C-8-815, a trustee may: . . . (16) Exercise elections with respect to federal, state, and local taxes including, but not limited to, considering discretionary distributions to a beneficiary as being made from capital gains realized during the year"; Alaska Statute § 13.36.109(29): "Except as otherwise provided by this chapter, in addition to the powers conferred by the terms of the trust, a trustee may perform all actions necessary to accomplish the proper management, investment, and distribution of the trust property, including the power . . . (29) to consider discretionary distributions to a beneficiary as being made from capital gains realized during the year."

[9] Reg. § 1.651(a)-1.

[10] Reg. § 1.651(a)-2(a).

quarter. The distribution made by the trust on January 15, Year 2, of the income for the fourth quarter of Year 1 does not disqualify the trust for treatment as a simple trust.

In determining whether all the income is required to be distributed currently, it is not necessary that the amount of income for each beneficiary be specified in the instrument.[11]

> **Example 2:** A fiduciary is required to distribute all of the income of a trust currently, but she has discretion to sprinkle the income among a class of beneficiaries or among named beneficiaries in such amounts as she may see fit. All of the income is required to be distributed currently even though the amount distributable to a particular beneficiary is unknown until the fiduciary has exercised her discretion.

.02 Complex Trust: Any Principal Distributed

In the year in which a trust distributes corpus, it loses its classification as a simple trust. Thus, a trust can never be a simple trust in the year of its termination or in a year of partial liquidation.[12]

A trust may otherwise qualify as a simple trust because the trustee makes discretionary distributions of *only* all the income in a given year (no principal). But, if the trustee makes a discretionary distribution of principal in any year, or if the trust is required under the trust instrument to make a distribution of principal upon the happening of a specified event, it will be treated as a complex trust for the tax year in which an actual distribution of principal is made.[13]

> **Example 3:** Under the terms of a trust that is required to distribute all of its income currently, half of the corpus is to be distributed to beneficiary Tyler when he becomes 30 years old. The trust reports on the calendar-year basis. On December 28, Year 1, Tyler becomes 30 years old and the trustee distributes half of the trust corpus to him on January 3, Year 2. The trust will be disqualified for treatment as a simple trust only for the tax year, Year 2, the year in which an actual distribution of corpus is made.

.03 Complex Trust: Income Accumulated

If a trust's income for one tax year is required or permitted to be accumulated, and in another tax year its income for the year is required to be distributed currently (and no other amounts are distributed), the trust is a simple trust for the latter year.[14]

> **Example 4:** The terms of a trust provide that income may be accumulated until a beneficiary is 21 years old but thereafter must be distributed currently. The trust is a simple trust for tax years beginning after the beneficiary reaches the age of 21 years, assuming that no accumulated income or other "noncurrent" amounts are distributed.

---

[11] Reg. § 1.651(a)-2(b).
[12] Reg. § 1.651(a)-3(a).
[13] Reg. § 1.651(a)-3(b).
[14] Reg. § 1.651(a)-2(c).

.04 Distributions in Kind

If a trust distributes property in kind as part of its requirement to distribute currently all the income, the trust shall be treated as having sold the property for its fair market value on the date of distribution (subject to the rules discussed at ¶ 711).[15] If no amount in excess of the amount of income is distributed by the trust during the year, the trust will qualify as a simple trust even though property in kind was distributed as part of a distribution of all such income.[16]

.05 Decedent's Estate—Complex Trust Treatment

A decedent's estate is treated for income tax purposes in the same manner as a complex trust.[17] For both simple and complex trusts, the deduction for distributions to beneficiaries is determined by reference to "distributable net income," which is defined and discussed at ¶ 704.

¶ 707 How to Determine Distributable Net Income

An estate or trust is generally a taxpaying entity. However, if income is distributed to a beneficiary, the estate or trust is considered a conduit. The amount of income distributed is allowed as a deduction to the estate or trust[18] and is taxed to the beneficiary.[19] (See Chapter 8 for the taxation of amounts distributed to beneficiaries.)

Before the amount of the deduction for distributions to beneficiaries may be determined, it is necessary to compute what is termed the "distributable net income" of the estate or trust. This must be done because "distributable net income" limits the amount deductible by the estate or trust for distributions and the amount of the distributions taxable to the beneficiaries. It is also used to determine the character of the distributions (dividend income, interest income, etc.) to the beneficiaries. Thus, the computation of distributable net income is essential in understanding the taxation of trusts, estates, and beneficiaries.

According to the regulations, distributable net income for any tax year is the taxable income of the estate or trust, with the following modifications:[20]

1. The deduction for distributions to beneficiaries is disallowed.
2. The deduction for a personal exemption is disallowed.
3. Capital gains are ordinarily excluded unless they are (a) allocated to income under the terms of the governing instrument or local law, (b) allocated to corpus, but actually distributed *as capital gains* to beneficiaries during the tax year, or (c) used in determining the amount that is distributed or required to be distributed.

The IRS has specifically ruled that a simple trust that does not distribute capital gains because, under local law or the trust instrument, they are allocable to corpus may not include such gains in the formula for allocating indirect expenses to

---

[15] This rule applies for taxable years of trusts ending after January 2, 2004.
[16] Reg. § 1.651(a)-2(d).
[17] Reg. § 1.661(a)-1.
[18] Code Secs. 651 and 661.
[19] Code Secs. 652 and 662.
[20] Code Sec. 643; Reg. §§ 1.643(a)-1 through 1.643(a)-7.

tax-exempt income.[21] However, if capital gains are paid, permanently set aside, or to be used for charitable purposes so that a charitable contribution deduction is allowed in respect of the capital gains, they must be included in the computation of distributable net income. However, Code Sec. 643(a)(3) provides that gain from the sale of qualified small business stock that is excluded under Code Sec. 1202(a) is not taken into account in computing the exclusion of capital gains in determining distributable net income.

Example 5: A trust is created to pay its income to Susan for life, with a discretionary power in the trustee to invade principal for Susan's benefit. During the tax year, $10,000 is realized from the sale of securities at a profit, and $10,000 in excess of income (note that this corresponds to the $10,000 of capital gain but legally is identifiable only as $10,000 of corpus) is distributed to Susan. The capital gain is not allocable to Susan by the trustee. During the tax year, the trustee received and paid out $5,000 of dividends. No other cash was received or on hand during the tax year. The capital gain will not ordinarily be included in distributable net income.[22] However, if the trustee follows a regular practice of distributing the exact net proceeds of the sale of trust property, capital gains will be included in distributable net income.[23]

1. Capital losses are to be excluded except to the extent that they enter into the determination of any capital gains that are paid, credited, or required to be distributed to any beneficiary during the tax year. But see ¶ 618 as to capital loss carryovers in the year of termination of an estate or trust.

2. In the case of a simple trust only, extraordinary dividends (whether paid in cash or in kind) or taxable stock dividends that are not distributed or credited to a beneficiary are excluded if the fiduciary in good faith determines that under the terms of the governing instrument and local law such dividends are allocable to corpus. Taxable dividends of this sort would be included in distributable net income of a complex trust.

3. Tax-exempt interest, reduced by nondeductible expenses attributable to such amount, is to be included. If the estate or trust is allowed a charitable contribution deduction under Code Sec. 642(c), the amount of tax-exempt interest included in the computation of distributable net income must be reduced to the extent that the amount of income that is paid, permanently set aside, or to be used for charitable purposes consists of tax-exempt interest. If the governing instrument specifically provides for the source out of which amounts are paid, permanently set aside, or to be used for such charitable purposes, the specific provisions will control. Otherwise, the contribution will be deemed to consist of the same proportion of the tax-exempt interest as the interest bears to the total of all income.

Example 6: A trust has income of $130,000, including $20,000 of tax-exempt interest. The trustee contributed $27,950 to charity, there being no designation of the source of the payment. In such case, the charitable contribu-

---

[21] Rev. Rul. 77-355, 1977-2 CB 82.
[22] Reg. § 1.643(a)-3(a).
[23] Reg. § 1.643(a)-3(b).

tion would reduce distributable net income. It would also reduce the tax-exempt interest includible in distributable net income to the extent that such interest is allocable to the charitable contribution. The amount of tax-exempt interest includible in the charitable contribution is $4,300 (($20,000 ÷ $130,000) × $27,950). Therefore, the amount of tax-exempt interest includible in distributable net income is $15,700 ($20,000 − $4,300). The charitable contribution deduction is $23,650 ($27,950 − $4,300).

Example 7, below, illustrates the computation of distributable net income as described in the above provisions.

Example 7: A trust has the income and expenses listed below. Capital gains are allocable to corpus. During the tax year, the trust distributed $27,950 to a charity and the balance of its income to other beneficiaries, Beryl and Meg. The trust instrument was silent on depreciation, and no reserve was required or allowed under local law (so all depreciation is allocable to the beneficiaries).

Income

Rents	$50,000
Dividends from domestic corporations	50,000
Tax-exempt interest on municipal bonds	20,000
Taxable interest	10,000
Net capital gains	20,000

Deductions

Depreciation on buildings	$10,000
Expenses allocable to rents	15,000
* Expenses directly allocable to tax-exempt interest	400
* Trustee's commissions allocable to tax-exempt interest	600
* Trustee's commissions allocable to other income	2,200
* Trustee's commissions allocable to corpus	1,100

---

* Note that the trustee's commissions and other overall expenses are broken down into three groups, identified as those allocable to exempt income, taxable income, and corpus. No statutory formula is provided for making this allocation, but the examples in the IRS regulations indicate, by making such identification in every instance, that it is a prerequisite to this and other computations for which statutory rules are provided. Presumably, expenses would be allocated directly, if possible, and then by ratio of related income classes. For example, $600 would be allocated to the exempt income, $20,000 ÷ $130,000 of the $3,900 in commissions (including exempt income).

Distributable net income consists of the above items with the following adjustments: (1) amounts distributed to beneficiaries are not deducted; (2) the charitable contribution allowable under Code Sec. 642(c) must be reduced by the portion of tax-exempt interest included in the contribution, that is, by $20,000 ÷ $130,000 of $27,950, or $4,300; (3) the capital gains are excluded; (4) the $20,000 of tax-exempt interest is counted in, but is first reduced by the $1,000 expenses allocable thereto and by the $4,300 included in the charitable

¶707

contribution; (5) the dividends are included in full; and (6) depreciation is allocated in full to the beneficiaries. Distributable net income, therefore, is:

Income items

Rental	$50,000	
Dividends	50,000	
Taxable interest	10,000	
Tax-exempt interest (as adjusted for expenses and charitable contribution)	14,700	$124,700

Less: Deductions

Rental expenses	$15,000	
Trustee's commissions	3,300	
Charitable deduction	23,650	$41,950
Distributable net income		$82,750

Where corporate distributions to a trust represent a return of capital that reduces the basis of stock rather than the payment of a dividend, distributions cannot be reflected in computing distributable net income and, therefore, cannot be reflected in allocating the trust's expenses to its tax-exempt income.[24]

¶ 708 Simple Trust's Deduction for Distributions to Beneficiaries

A simple trust may deduct the amount of income that is required under the terms of the trust instrument to be distributed currently. If the amount of income required to be distributed currently exceeds the distributable net income, the deduction is limited to the amount of the distributable net income. For this purpose, distributable net income is to be computed without regard to items of trust income (and deductions allocable thereto) that are not included in the gross income of the trust. Therefore, the modifications specified in Example 6 at ¶ 707 (tax-exempt interest) are not to be considered in computing distributable net income.[25]

Example 8: A trust that is required to distribute all of its income currently has the following income and deductions:

Rent		$25,000
Dividends		50,000
Tax-exempt interest	$25,000	
Less: Allocable expense	975	24,025
Total income		$99,025
Less: Deductions (less $975 allocable to exempt interest)		7,925

---

[24] Rev. Rul. 80-165, 1980-1 CB 134.   [25] Code Sec. 651(b); Reg. § 1.651(b)-1.

Distributable net income (without distribution adjustments)		$91,100
Adjustments for limitation on deduction for distributions—		
Tax-exempt interest less allocable expenses	$24,025	24,025
Deduction for distributions		$67,075

Electing Alaska Native Settlement Trusts (see ¶ 912) are not allowed a deduction for distributions under Code Sec. 651.[26]

¶ 709 Estate's and Complex Trust's Deduction for Distributions to Beneficiaries

Estates and complex trusts are allowed to deduct (1) the amount of income for the tax year that is required to be distributed currently and (2) any other amounts properly paid or credited or required to be distributed for the tax year.

The deduction cannot exceed the distributable net income.[27] A further limitation, as explained below, may also apply.

Income that is required to be distributed currently includes any amount required to be distributed that may be paid out of income or corpus, such as an annuity, to the extent that it is paid out of income for the tax year.[28]

"Other amounts" for which a deduction is allowed (item (2) above) include all amounts properly paid, credited, or required to be distributed during the tax year other than income required to be distributed currently. The term would include such things as:

- amounts distributed in the discretion of the fiduciary,
- payment of an annuity to the extent that it is not paid out of income for the tax year, and
- a distribution of property in kind (subject to the rules discussed at ¶ 711).[29]

Surviving spouse allowances and dependent support allowances that are paid under a court order or decree or under local law also qualify as "income required to be distributed currently" or as an "other" amount depending upon how the fiduciary pays the allowance.[30] If there is a standing court order requiring monthly payments of a surviving spouse's allowance it would probably qualify as an "amount required to be distributed currently." If the fiduciary every so often secures a court order for payment of a surviving spouse's allowance, it would probably qualify as an "other" amount (see also ¶ 621). The above rule also applies to amounts used to satisfy any person's legal obligation (but not alimony payments), such as a parent's legal obligation to support a minor child. Where a surviving spouse's right to maintenance of property that he or she occupied was derived from a leasing

---

[26] Code Sec. 646(g).
[27] Code Sec. 661(a).
[28] Reg. § 1.661(a)-2(b).
[29] Reg. § 1.661(a)-2(c) and (f).
[30] Reg. § 1.661(a)-2(e).

arrangement predating the decedent's death, a testamentary trust could not deduct expenditures for maintaining the property.[31]

Electing Alaska Native Settlement Trusts (see ¶ 912) are not allowed a deduction for distributions under Code Sec. 661 unless the election to be treated as such a trust is terminated by disqualification.[32]

.01 Character of Amounts Distributed

The deduction for distributions is to be treated as consisting of the same proportion of each class of items entering into the computation of distributable net income as the total that each bears to the total distributable net income. However, if the trust instrument or local law requires a different method of allocation, the items will be allocated accordingly.[33] Thus, if one-quarter of the distributable net income consists of tax-exempt interest, one-quarter of the beneficiary's distribution will constitute tax-exempt interest, in the absence of a contrary trust provision or local law. No deduction will be allowed to the estate or trust for that part of a beneficiary's distribution that consists of tax-exempt income.

In determining the items that make up the distributions deduction, all deductions entering into the computation of distributable net income (including charitable contributions) are to be allocated among the different types of income that make up such distributable net income according to the three principles set forth below. Where a charitable contribution is involved, however, the amounts paid, permanently set aside, or to be used for charitable purposes are *first* ratably apportioned among each class of items of income that enter into the computation of the distributable net income as explained at ¶ 1101 et seq.[34]

1. Deductions directly attributable to one class of income are allocated thereto. For instance, repairs to, taxes on, and other expenses directly attributable to the maintenance of rental property or the collection of rental income are allocated to rental income. Similarly, all expenses directly attributable to a business are allocated to the income from such business.

2. Deductions that are not directly attributable to a specific class of income may be allocated to any item of income (including capital gains) included in computing distributable net income. But a portion of such deductions must be allocated to nontaxable income. For example, if trust income is $30,000 (after direct expenses), consisting equally of $10,000 of dividends, tax-exempt interest, and rents, and income commissions amount to $3,000, one-third ($1,000) of such commissions should be allocated to tax-exempt interest, but the balance of $2,000 may be allocated to the rents or dividends in such proportions as the trustee may elect.

Allocation of indirect expenses to taxable and nontaxable income on the basis that each bears to the total of the taxable and nontaxable income is not mandatory. Allocation is to be based on all the facts and circumstances in each case.[35]

---

[31] *A.I. DuPont Testamentary Trust*, CA-5, 78-2 USTC ¶ 9515, 574 F2d 1332.
[32] Code Sec. 646(g).
[33] Code Sec. 661(b); Reg. § 1.661(b)-1.
[34] Reg. §§ 1.661(b)-1 and 1.661(b)-2.
[35] Rev. Rul. 63-27, 1963-1 CB 57, clarifying Rev. Rul. 59-32, 1959-1 CB 245.

The fact that the governing instrument or local law treats certain deductions as attributable to corpus or income not included in distributable net income will not affect this allocation. Examples of expenses that are considered as not directly attributable to a specific class of income are trustee's commissions, the rental of safe-deposit boxes, and state income and personal property taxes.

Where a trust instrument allocates capital gains to corpus, thus making the capital gains nondistributable, none of the deductions that are not directly attributable to such capital gains can be allocated to the capital gains.[36] Similarly, if legal fees incurred by a trust to determine who is entitled to the trust property are chargeable to the trust principal, such fees do not reduce the trust income distributed to the beneficiaries.[37]

3. To the extent that any deductions that are directly attributable to a class of income exceed that class of income, they may be allocated to any other class of income (including capital gains) in the manner provided in (2) above. However, the amount allocated to any one item of income may not exceed the amount of that item of income. If there is an excess, the excess must be reallocated to another item of income. Moreover, any excess deduction attributable to tax-exempt income may not be offset against any other class of income. Thus, if the trust has rents, taxable interest, dividends, and tax-exempt interest, and the deductions directly attributable to the rents exceed the rental income, the excess may be allocated to the taxable interest or dividends in such proportions as the fiduciary may elect. However, if the excess deductions are attributable to the tax-exempt interest, they may not be allocated to the rents, taxable interest, or dividends.[38]

.02 Limitation of Distribution Deduction

As stated previously, the distribution deduction may not exceed the distributable net income of the estate or trust. Also, the distribution deduction may not consist of any amount that is treated as consisting of an item of distributable net income that is not included in the gross income of the estate or trust.[39]

Example 9: A trust has distributable net income of $20,000, which is deemed to consist of $10,000 of dividends and $10,000 of tax-exempt interest. It distributes $10,000 to the trust beneficiary. The deduction, without the special limitation noted above, would be $10,000, consisting of $5,000 of dividends and $5,000 of tax-exempt interest.

¶ 710 Illustration of an Estate and Complex Trust Deduction Computation

The provisions discussed above on how to compute an estate's or complex trust's distribution deduction are illustrated in the Example below.

---

[36] *M.B. Tucker,* CA-2, 63-2 USTC ¶ 9654, 322 F2d 86; *Manufacturers Hanover Trust Co.,* CtCls, 63-1 USTC ¶ 9250, 312 F2d 785.

[37] *C.P. Erdman,* CA-7, 63-1 USTC ¶ 9391, 315 F2d 762.
[38] Reg. § 1.652(b)-3.
[39] Code Sec. 661(c); Reg. § 1.661(c)-1.

Example 10: Under the terms of a trust, which reports on the calendar-year basis, $10,000 a year is required to be paid out of income to a designated charity. The balance of the income may, in the trustee's discretion, be accumulated or distributed to its beneficiary, Pierce. Expenses are allocable against income and the trust instrument requires a reserve for depreciation. During the tax year, the trustee contributes $10,000 to charity and in his discretion distributes $15,000 of income to Pierce. The trust has the following items of income and expense for the tax year:

Dividends	$10,000
Taxable interest	10,000
Tax-exempt interest	10,000
Rents	20,000
Rental expenses	2,000
Depreciation of rental property	3,000
Trustee's commissions	5,000

.01 Income—FAI

The income of the trust for fiduciary accounting purposes is $40,000, computed as follows:

Dividends		$10,000
Taxable interest		10,000
Tax-exempt interest		10,000
Rents		20,000
Total		$50,000
Less: Rental expenses	$2,000	
Depreciation	3,000	
Trustee's commissions	5,000	10,000
Income for accounting purposes		$40,000

.02 Distributable Net Income

The distributable net income of the trust is $30,000, determined as follows:

Rents			$20,000
Dividends			10,000
Taxable interest			10,000
Tax-exempt interest		$10,000	
Less: Interest expenses (($10,000 ÷ $50,000) × $5,000)	$1,000		
Charitable contributions (($10,000 ÷ $50,000) × $10,000)	2,000	3,000	7,000
Total			$47,000

¶710.01

Deductions:
Rental expenses	$2,000
Depreciation of rental property	3,000
Trustee's commissions ($5,000 – $1,000 allocated to tax-exempt interest)	4,000
Charitable contributions ($10,000 – $2,000 allocated to tax-exempt interest)	8,000 17,000
Distributable net income	$30,000

.03 Character of Distribution

The character of the amounts distributed, determined in accordance with the rules described above, is shown by the following table (for the purpose of this allocation, it is assumed that the trustee elected to allocate the trustee's commissions to rental income except for the amount required to be allocated to tax-exempt interest):

	Rental Income	Taxable Dividends	Taxable Interest	Tax-exempt Interest	Total
Trust income	$20,000	$10,000	$10,000	$10,000	$50,000
Less:					
Charitable contributions....	4,000	2,000	2,000	2,000	10,000
Rental expenses .	2,000	—	—	—	2,000
Depreciation	3,000	—	—	—	3,000
Trustee's commissions	4,000	—	—	1,000	5,000
Total deductions.....	$13,000	$2,000	$2,000	$3,000	$20,000
Distributable net income	$7,000	$8,000	$8,000	$7,000	$30,000
Amounts distributed under Code Sec. 661(a) before applying the limitation of Code Sec. 661(c)	$3,500	$4,000	$4,000	$3,500	$15,000

In the absence of specific provisions in the trust instrument for the allocation of different classes of income, the charitable contribution is deemed to consist of a pro rata portion of the gross amount of each item of income of the trust, and the trust is deemed to have distributed to Pierce a pro rata portion (one-half) of each item of income included in distributable net income.

.04 Taxable Income

The taxable income of the trust is $11,400, computed as follows:

Rental income		$20,000
Dividends		10,000
Taxable interest		10,000
Gross income		$40,000
Less: Deductions		
Rental expenses	$2,000	
Depreciation of rental property	3,000	
Trustee's commissions	4,000	
Charitable contributions	8,000	
Distributions to Pierce	11,500	
Personal exemption	100	$28,600
Taxable income		$11,400

In computing the taxable income of the trust, no deduction is allowable for the portions of the charitable contributions deduction ($2,000) and trustee's commissions ($1,000) that are treated as attributable to the tax-exempt interest excludable from gross income.

¶ 711 Distributions in Kind

Distributions of property in kind are distributions of property other than cash. A trust that makes an in-kind distribution is classified as a complex trust because the distribution is of an amount other than income.[40] Accordingly, the rules that apply to in-kind distributions are applicable to complex trusts and estates only.[41]

In-kind distributions present three issues:

1. Whether gain or loss is recognized by the trust as a result of the distribution.
2. The amount of the beneficiary's basis in the property distributed.
3. The amount of the distribution for purposes of the trust's distribution deduction and the amount includible in the beneficiary's gross income.

If the in-kind distribution is made to satisfy a gift or bequest of a specific sum of money or of specific property, the distribution will not be deductible by the trust or includible in the beneficiary's gross income.[42]

.01 Gain or Loss

Trust or estate does not recognize gain or loss when it distributes property in kind to beneficiary unless distribution satisfies right to receive property other than that distributed. Generally, no gain or loss is realized by a trust (or its beneficiaries) as a result of an in-kind distribution unless the distribution is in satisfaction of a right to receive a distribution of a specific dollar amount or of specific property other than the distribution itself.[43] The basis of the property received by the

---

[40] Reg. § 1.662(a)-3(b).
[41] Rev. Rul. 67-74, 1967-1 CB 194.
[42] Code Sec. 663(a)(1).
[43] Reg. § 1.661(a)-2(f).

beneficiary is the basis that the property had in the hands of the trust immediately before the distribution.[44]

The amount of the distribution for purposes of the distribution deduction and the amount includible in the beneficiary's gross income is the lesser of the beneficiary's basis in the property or the fair market value of the property (see ¶ 809).[45]

1041 ★
Prob.

.02 Election to Recognize Gain

A trustee may elect to recognize gain or loss on a distribution.[46] The amount of gain or loss to the trust is calculated as if the trust sold the property to the beneficiary at its fair market value (i.e., the difference between the trust's basis in the property and the fair market value of the property).[47] No gain will be recognized by the beneficiary.

It is important to note that the recognition of a loss will not benefit the trust because a loss deduction is disallowed under the rules that disallow losses between related taxpayers.[48] If a loss is recognized by the trust and the property is later sold or exchanged at a gain by the beneficiary, the beneficiary will recognize gain only to the extent that the gain exceeds the amount of the loss previously disallowed.[49]

The basis of the property in the hands of the beneficiary is the trust's basis in the property immediately prior to distribution, adjusted for the amount of gain or loss recognized.[50] The amount of the distribution for purposes of determining the distribution deduction and the amount includible in the beneficiary's gross income is the fair market value of the property.[51]

The election is not available where the in-kind distribution is made to satisfy a gift or bequest of a specific sum of money or of specific property.[52] Once made, an election to recognize gain or loss applies to all distributions made by the trust for the tax year and may be revoked only with the permission of the IRS.[53]

.03 Mandatory Recognition of Gain or Loss

A trust must recognize gain or loss if the in-kind distribution is in satisfaction of a beneficiary's right to receive a distribution in a specific dollar amount or in specific property other than that distributed.[54] Such distributions are not treated as inheritances or gifts, but are treated as sales or exchanges (i.e., the trust is considered to have sold the property to the beneficiary at its fair market value).[55] Again, it should be noted that under the related taxpayer rules, a trust will not be allowed to deduct the loss.[56] The amount of gain or loss is measured by the difference between the amount of the bequest satisfied and the trust's basis in the property distributed.[57]

---

[44] Code Sec. 643(e)(1) for distributions made after December 31, 1983.
[45] Code Sec. 643(e)(2).
[46] Code Sec. 643(e)(3).
[47] Code Sec. 643(e)(3)(A)(ii).
[48] Code Sec. 267.
[49] Code Sec. 267(b) and (d).
[50] Code Sec. 643(e)(1)(B).
[51] Code Sec. 643(e)(3)(A)(iii).
[52] Code Sec. 643(e)(4).
[53] Code Sec. 643(e)(3)(B).
[54] Reg. § 1.661(a)-2(f).
[55] Reg. § 1.1014-4(a)(3).
[56] Code Sec. 267.
[57] *S.P. Suisman*, CA-2, 83 F2d 1019, aff'g DC Conn., 36-2 USTC ¶ 9443, 15 FSupp 113, cert. denied, 299 US 573;

.04 Holding Period

The holding period for distributions will depend on whether or not the estate elects to recognize gain or loss on the distribution pursuant to Code Sec. 643(e)(3). If no election is made, the tacking provisions of Code Sec. 1223(2) will apply, and the period for which the estate held the property will be added to the beneficiary's holding period. If the election is made, the beneficiary will assume a new holding period beginning the day after the distribution.

The beneficiary's basis in the property distributed is the fair market value of the asset (cost basis).[58]

¶ 712 65-Day Election Rule Under Section 663(b)

The fiduciary of a complex trust or the executor of an estate may elect to treat any distribution or any portion of any distribution to a beneficiary within the first 65 days following the end of a tax year as an amount that was paid or credited on the last day of the tax year.[59]

Generally, the amount to which the election applies cannot exceed the greater of (1) the amount of the trust's or estate's income or (2) the amount of the trust's or estate's distributable net income for the tax year. This amount is reduced by any amounts paid, credited, or required to be distributed (other than the amounts covered by the election) to arrive at the maximum amount subject to the election.

The election is irrevocable for the tax year and is effective for the year of election only.[60] A fiduciary who makes the election must deduct the amounts covered in the election in the tax year of the election.

> **Example 11:** A trust has income of $1,000 and distributable net income of $800 for Year 2. The trust properly pays $550 to Smith on January 15, Year 2. The trustee elects to treat the $550 payment as paid on December 31, Year 1. The trust also properly pays Smith $600 on July 19, Year 2, and $450 on January 17, Year 3. For Year 2, the maximum amount that may be treated as properly paid, credited, or required to be distributed on the last day of Year 2 is $400 ($1,000 − $600). The $550 payment on January 15, Year 2, does not reduce the maximum amount to which the election may apply because the amount is treated as properly paid on December 31, Year 1.

(Footnote Continued)

and *W.R. Kenan, Jr., Trustee,* CA-2, 40-2 USTC ¶ 9635, 114 F2d 217.

[58] Code Sec. 1012; Rev. Rul. 67-74, 1967-1 CB 194.

[59] Code Sec. 663(b).

[60] Reg. §§ 1.663(b)-1 and 1.663(b)-2.

Chapter 8

Beneficiary's Tax Liability

SIMPLE TRUSTS
¶ 801   Amounts Included in Beneficiary's Gross Income
¶ 802   Tax Years of Beneficiaries and Trusts

ESTATES AND COMPLEX TRUSTS
¶ 803   Income Taxed on a "Tier" Basis
¶ 804   Comprehensive Example
¶ 805   Interest Paid on Deferred Legacies
¶ 806   Elective Shares
¶ 807   Separate Shares Treated as Separate Trusts
¶ 808   Calendar-Year Requirement; Complex Trust
¶ 809   Gifts and Bequests May Be Exempt
¶ 810   Charitable Contributions Not Allowed as Part of Distribution Deduction
¶ 811   Double Deductions Are Denied
¶ 812   Treatment of Gain from Sale of Life Interest
¶ 813   Assignment of Trust Interest vs. Trust Income
¶ 814   Throwback Rules—In General
¶ 815   Accumulation Distributions
¶ 816   Undistributed Net Income
¶ 817   How the Throwback Rule Operates
¶ 818   Computation of Beneficiary's Tax

The premise of beneficiary liability is based on the function of distributable net income (DNI) discussed in Chapter 7. Under the 1939 Code, a distribution was deductible by the estate or trust and taxable to the beneficiaries only if it could be traced to the income of the estate or trust for the current year. The 1986 Code eliminated the need to identify the source of the distribution. Beneficiary liability is based on the concept of DNI—a limit on the amount deductible by the estate or trust and taxable to the beneficiary. DNI serves a qualitative function to preserve "the same proportion of each class of items entering into the computation of distributable net income as the total of each class bears to the total distributable net income of the estate or trust . . . ."[1]

SIMPLE TRUSTS

¶ 801 Amounts Included in Beneficiary's Gross Income

A simple trust is defined as a trust that is required to distribute all its income currently, makes no charitable contributions, and does not distribute trust corpus during the year.[2] Trusts that are not simple trusts are complex trusts. The determination of whether a trust is a simple trust or a complex trust is made on an annual basis. Thus, a trust may be considered a simple trust in one year and a complex trust (because, for example, a distribution from corpus is made) in another year.

.01 Income Required to Be Distributed

The beneficiaries of a simple trust must include in their gross income for the tax year the amounts of income required to be distributed currently to them for such year, whether or not the income was distributed. If the amount of the income required to be distributed currently to beneficiaries exceeds the trust's distributable net income, each beneficiary includes in gross income an amount equal to the beneficiary's proportionate share of the distributable net income.[3] Whether trust income is required to be distributed currently depends upon the terms of the trust instrument and not on any action by the trustee.[4] Thus, if a beneficiary, under the terms of a trust instrument, may demand the entire net income of a trust, the income is taxable even though the beneficiary does not make the demand and the income is accumulated primarily for the beneficiary's benefit.[5] In *Mallinckrodt*, the Eighth Circuit held that a beneficiary was liable for taxes on trust income where, as co-trustee, he had (1) broad powers of management over the trust, (2) the right to terminate the trust at any time and receive the entire corpus, and (3) the power to receive trust income upon request.[6] In *Bunting*, the Sixth Circuit held that a co-beneficiary was liable for taxes on trust income where he had the authority to (1) modify the trust, (2) change the beneficiaries, (3) appoint himself as a beneficiary, (4) withdraw property from the trust, and (5) revoke the trust instrument.[7]

.02 Character of Income and Allocation of Expenses

Each of the trust's income items has the same character in the beneficiary's hands that it had in the fiduciary's hands.[8] In other words, dividends distributed to the beneficiary are dividends in the beneficiary's hands. Tax-exempt interest that is distributed would also be tax exempt in the beneficiary's hands. Capital gains that

---

[1] Code Sec. 662(b).

[2] Reg. § 1.651(a)-1.

[3] Code Sec. 652(a); Reg. § 1.652(a)-1.

[4] Rev. Rul. 62-147, 1962-2 CB 151; Rev. Rul. 85-116, 1985-2 CB 174.

[5] *E.J. Mallinckrodt, Jr.*, CA-8, 45-1 USTC ¶ 9134, 146 F2d 1, cert. denied, 324 US 871; *A.I. Grant*, CA-5, 49-1 USTC ¶ 9297, 174 F2d 891. However, the U.S. Court of Appeals for the Third Circuit has held to the contrary where the beneficiary's demand right was exercisable within 30 days after the close of the trust's fiscal year (*B.N. Hallowell*, CA-3, 47-1 USTC ¶ 9185).

[6] *E.J. Mallinckrodt, Jr.*, CA-8, 45-1 USTC ¶ 9134, 146 F2d 1, cert. denied, 324 US 871.

[7] *C.E. Bunting*, CA-6, 47-2 USTC ¶ 9391, 164 F2d 443, cert. denied, 333 US 856. See also *F. Flato*, CA-5, 52-1 USTC ¶ 9282, 195 F2d 580.

[8] Code Sec. 652(b); Reg. § 1.652(b)-1.

are distributed would be capital gains to the beneficiary. This is commonly known as the "conduit" rule (see ¶ 501).

A trust's deductions that enter into the computation of distributable net income (which, as indicated above, limits the income taxable to the beneficiaries) are to be allocated among the items of income in accordance with the rules set forth at ¶ 708.[9] Example 1 illustrates the allocation of such expenses and the effect on the amount and character of income taxable to the beneficiaries.

> **Example 1:** A simple trust is required to distribute all income currently to two beneficiaries in equal amounts. During the tax year, it had the following income: rents, $25,000; dividends, $50,000; and tax-exempt interest, $25,000. Rental expenses were $5,000, depreciation was $5,000 (no provision in the trust instrument having been made for depreciation), and trustee's commissions were $3,900. The allocation of expenses and the character of the income received by the beneficiaries are as follows (assuming that the trustee allocates to rents all expenses not directly attributable to any other item of income and not allocable to tax-exempt interest):

Tax-exempt interest		$25,000
Less: Trustee's commissions allocable to tax-exempt interest (($25,000 ÷ $100,000) × $3,900)		975
Net tax-exempt interest		$24,025

> Each beneficiary is therefore deemed to have received $12,012.50 of the tax-exempt interest.

Rents		$25,000
Less: Expenses allocable		
Rental expenses	$5,000	
Trustee's commissions ($3,900 − $975 allocable to tax-exempt interest)	2,925	7,925
Net rents		$17,075

> Each beneficiary is therefore deemed to have received $8,537.50 of the rents.
>
> No expenses were allocated to the $50,000 of dividends, and each beneficiary is therefore deemed to have received $25,000 of the dividends. Also, each beneficiary is allowed a deduction of $2,500 for depreciation of rental property attributable to the one-half of rental income distributed to her.

According to the IRS, commissions payable under state law to trustees upon a trust's termination were partially allocable to tax-exempt income even though the trust had sold all of its taxable bonds and had realized no tax-exempt income in the year of termination. Under the particular circumstances, allocating commissions on the basis of the ratio of tax-exempt income realized during the life of the trust to the

---

[9] Code Sec. 652(b); Reg. § 1.652(b)-3.

total of ordinary income (tax-exempt income included) plus the excess of capital gains realized over capital losses sustained over the life of the trust plus any net unrealized capital appreciation of the assets distributed would have been reasonable and appropriate.[10]

If the income of the trust that is required to be distributed currently exceeds the distributable net income, each beneficiary is considered to have received only a proportionate share of the distributable net income. The amount taxable to each beneficiary in such case is the same fractional part of distributable net income as the amount of trust income required to be distributed currently to such beneficiary bears to the trust income required to be distributed to all beneficiaries. Only a proportionate part of each item of gross income (and its related deduction) is allocated to each beneficiary. That is, a beneficiary is considered to have received the same proportion of each class of income, such as dividends, rent, interest, etc., as the total of each class bears to the total distributable net income, unless the trust instrument specifically allocates different classes of income to different beneficiaries.[11]

>*Example 2:* Under a trust instrument, Beneficiary 1 is to receive 40% of the trust income and Beneficiary 2 is to receive 60%. The trust instrument provides that in no event shall Beneficiary 1's annuity be less than $4,000, or Beneficiary 2's annuity less than $6,000. During the tax year, the distributable net income of the trust is $3,000, all from dividends. There are no deductions to be allocated. Beneficiary 1 will be considered to have received $1,200 (($4,000 ÷ $10,000) × $3,000); and Beneficiary 2 will be considered to have received $1,800 (($6,000 ÷ $10,000) × $3,000). These amounts will retain their character as dividend income in the hands of the beneficiaries.

If the trust instrument specifically allocates different classes of income to different beneficiaries, or if local law requires such an allocation, each beneficiary is considered to have received the items of income specifically allocated to that beneficiary. A trust instrument will be considered to specifically allocate different classes of income to different beneficiaries only to the extent that the specific allocation has an economic effect independent of the income tax consequences of the allocation. The IRS regulations exemplify this latter statement with the following examples:[12]

>*Example 3:* Allocation pursuant to a provision in a trust instrument granting the trustee discretion to allocate different classes of income to different beneficiaries is not a specific allocation by the terms of the trust; rather such power is a discretionary exercise by the trustee.

>*Example 4:* Allocation pursuant to a provision directing the trustee to pay all of the income to Beneficiary 1 (in Example 2 above), or $10,000 to Beneficiary 1, and the balance of the income to Beneficiary 2, but directing the trustee first to allocate a specific class of income to Beneficiary 1's share (to

---

[10] Rev. Rul. 77-466, 1977-2 CB 83.
[11] Code Sec. 652(a); Reg. § 1.652(a)-2.
[12] Reg. § 1.652(b)-2(b).

the extent there is income of that class and to the extent it does not exceed Beneficiary 1's share) is not a specific allocation by the terms of the trust.

Example 5: Allocation pursuant to the provision directing the trustee to pay half of one class of income (whatever it may be) to Beneficiary 1 (in Example 2 above), and the balance of the income to Beneficiary 2, is a specific allocation by the terms of the trust.

¶ 802 Tax Years of Beneficiaries and Trusts

Although estates may select or retain any tax year, both existing and newly created trusts must adopt the calendar year as their tax year (except for trusts exempt from tax under Code Sec. 501(a) and charitable trusts).[13] Note also that if both the executor of an estate and the trustee of a qualified revocable trust elect, the qualified revocable trust may be treated as part of the decedent's estate for federal income tax purposes and not as a separate trust (see ¶ 503).[14]

If a trust is required to distribute all of its income currently and the trust and the beneficiary have different tax years, the amount includible in the beneficiary's gross income is based on the trust's income for the tax year or years ending with or within the beneficiary's tax year. This rule applies to short tax years of the trust as well as to tax years of normal duration. The trust's income is determined by its accounting method, without regard to the accounting method of the beneficiary.[15]

.01 Death of a Simple Trust Beneficiary

When a beneficiary dies, the above rule does not apply. The gross income for the last tax year of a beneficiary on the cash basis includes only income actually distributed to the beneficiary before death. Income required to be distributed, but in fact distributed to the estate, is included in the estate's gross income as income in respect of a decedent under Code Sec. 691.[16]

If the existence of a beneficiary that is not an individual terminates, the amount to be included in its gross income for its last tax year is computed as if the beneficiary were a deceased individual, except that income required to be distributed before the termination but actually distributed to the beneficiary's successor in interest is included in the terminated beneficiary's income for its last tax year.[17]

ESTATES AND COMPLEX TRUSTS

¶ 803 Income Taxed on a "Tier" Basis

A beneficiary of an estate or complex trust is taxed on

1. The income of the estate or trust required to be distributed to the beneficiary currently, *whether or not actually distributed*, and
2. All "other" amounts properly paid, credited, or required to be distributed to the beneficiary for the tax year.[18]

---

[13] Code Sec. 644.
[14] Code Sec. 645(a).
[15] Code Sec. 652(c); Reg. § 1.652(c)-1.
[16] Reg. § 1.652(c)-2.
[17] Reg. § 1.652(c)-3.
[18] Code Sec. 662(a); Reg. § 1.662(a)-1.

The phrase "income required to be distributed currently" includes any amount required to be paid out of income or corpus, such as an annuity, to the extent that there is income not paid, credited, or required to be distributed to other beneficiaries for the tax year. What may constitute "other" amounts is discussed at ¶ 711. In general, an "other" amount would include current income distributable in the discretion of the fiduciary, payments out of corpus, and distributions out of accumulated income.[19]

.01 Tier 1: Income Required to be Distributed

The fiduciary income tax classification of distributions of income into groups (1) and (2) provides a "tier" system of taxing beneficiaries. The maximum amount that can be taxed to a beneficiary is limited, as in the case of a simple trust, by the distributable net income of the estate or trust (see ¶ 704).

If the amount of income required to be distributed currently, that is, the income in tier (1), is less than the distributable net income of the estate or trust (computed without the deduction for charitable contributions), the entire amount of such income is taxable to the beneficiaries. However, if the amount of income required to be distributed currently to all beneficiaries exceeds the distributable net income (computed without the deduction for charitable contributions), then there is included in each beneficiary's gross income an amount that bears the same ratio to distributable net income (as so computed) as the income amount (required to be distributed currently to the beneficiary) *over* the amount required to be distributed currently to all beneficiaries.[20]

> **Example 6:** A trust instrument requires all of the net income to be distributed, 40% to Beneficiary 1 and 60% to Beneficiary 2. Net income for the year is $15,000; distributable net income is $10,000. Beneficiary 1's share of the net income is $6,000; his proportionate share of the distributable net income is $4,000 (($6,000 ÷ $15,000) × $10,000). He is therefore taxed on $4,000 of the distribution. In similar fashion, Beneficiary 2's share of the net income is $9,000; his proportionate share of the distributable net income is $6,000. He is therefore taxed on $6,000 of the distribution. If distributable net income had been $15,000, both Beneficiaries would be taxed on their full shares of the income required to be distributed currently.

.02 Tier 2: Other Amounts Properly Paid, Credited, or Required to be Distributed

Distributions that fall into tier (2), that is, amounts "other" than income required to be distributed currently, are taxed to the beneficiaries only if the distributable net income exceeds distributions that fall into tier (1). If more than one beneficiary is involved, each beneficiary is taxed on a proportionate share of such excess. The proportionate share will be an amount that bears the same ratio to the excess of distributable net income *over* the amount required to be distributed

---

[19] Reg. § 1.662(a)-2(c). [20] Reg. § 1.662(a)-2(b).

currently as the "other" amounts distributed to the beneficiary *over* the "other" amounts distributed to all beneficiaries.[21]

Example 7: A trust instrument requires payments of $5,000 annually to Ina, payable out of net income only, and $3,000 per year to Remy, payable out of income or corpus. The trust has $5,000 of net income for the tax year, all of which is distributed to Ina. The trust also has $5,000 of distributable net income. The $3,000 payment to Remy is made out of corpus. Ina is taxed on the full amount of her distribution. There is no tax on the distribution to Remy because the distributable net income after reduction by the amount required to be distributed currently is zero.

Example 8: The terms of a trust require an annual income distribution of $10,000 to Ann. If any income remains, it may be accumulated or distributed to Bea, Cece, and Dee in an amount under the trustee's discretion. The trustee may also invade corpus for the benefit of Ann, Bea, Cece, or Dee. In the tax year, the trust has $20,000 of income after the deduction of all expenses. Distributable net income is $20,000. The trustee distributes $10,000 of income to Ann. Of the remaining $10,000 of income, he distributes $3,000 each to Bea, Cece and Dee, and also distributes an additional $5,000 to Ann. Ann includes $10,000 in income. The $14,000 of "other amounts distributed" is includible in the income of the recipients to the extent of $10,000, distributable net income *less* the income currently distributable to Ann. Ann will include an additional $3,571 (($5,000 ÷ $14,000) × $10,000) in income, and Bea, Cece and Dee will each include $2,143 (($3,000 ÷ $14,000) × $10,000) in income.

The amounts taxed to beneficiaries of estates and complex trusts retain the same character (rents, dividends, etc.) as they had in the hands of the estate or trust. In allocating the various types of income to the beneficiaries, the amount of a particular item reflected in distributable net income is first charged with directly related expenses and a proportionate share of other expenses (see ¶ 708). Then each beneficiary's share of income is multiplied by fractions for each class of income, in which the numerator is the amount of such income includible in distributable net income, and the denominator is the distributable net income. However, if the governing instrument specifies or local law requires a different allocation, such allocation is to be followed.[22]

¶ 804 Comprehensive Example

The following example illustrates the provisions dealing with the taxation of estates and complex trusts and their beneficiaries.

Example 9: Under the terms of a testamentary trust, one-half of the trust income is to be distributed currently to the decedent's wife, during her lifetime. The remaining trust income may, in the trustee's discretion, be paid to the decedent's daughter, to designated charities, or be accumulated (note, this would not qualify for the marital deduction, so this is not a marital trust). The trust is to terminate at the death of the surviving spouse, and the principal will

---

[21] Reg. § 1.662(a)-3(c).

[22] Code Sec. 662(b); Reg. §§ 1.662(b)-1 and 1.662(b)-2.

then be payable to the decedent's daughter. No provision is made in the trust instrument for depreciation of rental property. Capital gains are allocable to the principal account under the applicable local law. The trust and both beneficiaries file returns on a calendar-year basis. The records of the fiduciary show the following items of income and deduction for the tax year:

Rents	$50,000
Dividends of domestic corporations	50,000
Tax-exempt interest	20,000
Taxable interest	10,000
Capital gains	20,000
Depreciation of rental property	10,000
Expenses attributable to rental income	15,400
Trustee's commissions allocable to income account	2,800
Trustee's commissions allocable to principal account	1,100

.01 Trust Accounting Income

The income for trust accounting purposes is $111,800, and the trustee distributes one-half ($55,900) to the surviving spouse, and in his discretion he makes a contribution of one-quarter ($27,950) to the designated charity and distributes the remaining one-quarter ($27,950) to the decedent's daughter. The total of the distributions to beneficiaries is $83,850, consisting of (1) income of $55,900 required to be distributed currently to the surviving spouse and (2) other amounts properly paid or credited to the decedent's daughter of $27,950. The income for trust-accounting purposes of $111,800 is determined as follows:

Rents		$50,000
Dividends		50,000
Tax-exempt interest		20,000
Taxable interest		10,000
Total trust income		$130,000
Less: Rental expenses	$15,400	
Trustee's commissions allocable to income account	2,800	18,200
Income for trust accounting purposes		$111,800

.02 Distributable Net Income

The distributable net income of the trust is $82,750, determined as follows:

Rents		$50,000
Dividends		50,000
Taxable interest		10,000
Tax-exempt interest	$20,000	

Less: Trustee's commissions allocable thereto (($20,000 ÷ $130,000) × $3,900)	$600		
Charitable contributions allocable thereto (($20,000 ÷ $130,000) × $27,950)	4,300	4,900	15,100
Total			$125,100
Less: Deductions			
Rental expenses		$15,400	
Trustee's commissions ($3,900 − $600 allocated to tax-exempt interest)		3,300	
Charitable deduction ($27,950 − $4,300 attributable to tax-exempt interest)		23,650	42,350
Distributable net income			$82,750

In computing the distributable net income of $82,750, the trust's taxable income was computed with the following modifications: (1) no deductions were allowed for distributions to beneficiaries and for personal exemption of the trust; (2) capital gains were excluded; and (3) the tax-exempt interest (as adjusted for expenses and charitable contributions) was included.

.03 Distribution Deduction

Since the distributable net income of $82,750 is less than the sum of the amounts distributed to the surviving spouse and the decedent's daughter of $83,850, the trust's distribution deduction equals the distributable net income as modified to exclude the items of income not included in the trust's gross income:

Distributable net income	$82,750
Less: Tax-exempt interest (as adjusted for commissions and the charitable contribution)	15,100
Distribution deduction	$67,650

.04 Character of Income

To determine the character of the amounts included in the charitable contribution deduction and distribution deduction, the trustee elected to offset the trustee's commissions (other than the portion required to be allocated to tax-exempt interest) against the rental income. The following table shows the determination of the character of the amounts deemed distributed to beneficiaries and contributed to charity:

	Rents	Taxable Dividends	Tax-exempt Interest	Taxable Interest	Total
Trust income	$50,000	$50,000	$20,000	$10,000	$130,000
Less: Charitable contribution	10,750	10,750	4,300	2,150	27,950
Rental expenses	15,400	—	—	—	15,400
Trustee's commissions	3,300	—	600	—	3,900
Total deductions	$29,450	$10,750	$ 4,900	$ 2,150	$ 47,250
Amounts distributable to beneficiaries	$20,550	$39,250	$15,100	$ 7,850	$ 82,750

The character of the charitable contribution is determined by multiplying the total charitable contribution ($27,950) by a fraction consisting of each item of trust income, respectively, *over* the total trust income. For example, the charitable contribution is deemed to consist of rents of $10,750 (($50,000 ÷ $130,000) × $27,950).

.05 Taxable Income

The taxable income of the trust is $19,900, determined as follows:

Rental income		$50,000
Dividends		50,000
Taxable interest		10,000
Capital gains		20,000
Gross income		$130,000
Less: Deductions		
Rental expenses	$15,400	
Trustee's commissions	3,300	
Charitable contributions	23,650	
Distributions to beneficiaries	67,650	
Personal exemption	100	$110,100
Taxable income		$19,900

.06 Tier 1: Income Required to be Distributed

In computing the amount includible in the surviving spouse's gross income, the $55,900 distribution to her is deemed to be composed of the following proportions of any item of income deemed to have been distributed to the trust's beneficiaries (see paragraph *.04 Character of Income* of this section):

¶804.05

Rents (($20,550 ÷ $82,750) × $55,900)	$13,882
Dividends (($39,250 ÷ $82,750) × $55,900)	26,515
Taxable interest (($7,850 ÷ $82,750) × $55,900)	5,303
Tax-exempt interest (($15,100 ÷ $82,750) × $55,900)	10,200
Total distribution	$55,900

Accordingly, the surviving spouse will exclude $10,200 of tax-exempt interest from gross income. In addition, she may deduct a share of the depreciation deduction proportionate to the trust income allocable to her; that is, one-half of the total depreciation deduction, or $5,000.

.07 Tier 2: Other Amounts Required to Be Distributed

Since the sum of the amount of income required to be distributed currently to the surviving spouse ($55,900) and the other amounts properly paid, credited, or required to be distributed to the decedent's daughter ($27,950) exceeds the trust's distributable net income ($82,750), the decedent's daughter is deemed to have received $26,850 ($82,750 - $55,900) for income tax purposes. The character of the amounts deemed distributed to her is determined as follows:

Rents (($20,550 ÷ $82,750) × $26,850)	$ 6,668
Dividends (($39,250 ÷ $82,750) × $26,850)	12,735
Taxable interest (($7,850 ÷ $82,750) × $26,850)	2,547
Tax-exempt interest (($15,100 ÷ $82,750) × $26,850)	4,900
Total	$26,850

Accordingly, the decedent's daughter will exclude $4,900 of tax-exempt interest from gross income. In addition, she may deduct a share of the depreciation deduction proportionate to the trust income allocable to her; that is, one-fourth of the total depreciation deduction, or $2,500.

.08 Depreciation

The remaining $2,500 of the depreciation deduction is allocated to the amount distributed to the designated charity and is hence nondeductible by the trust, the surviving spouse, or the decedent's daughter.[23]

¶ 805 Interest Paid on Deferred Legacies

Interest on specific legacies that were paid under state law because the legacy payment was deferred until one year after the date of death is taxable income to the beneficiary whether paid out of the estate's corpus or income. These payments are also deductible by the estate as interest paid.[24]

¶ 806 Elective Shares

Most non-community property states have some form of elective share statute that generally gives the surviving spouse the right to claim a share of the deceased

---

[23] Reg. § 1.662(c)-4.   [24] Rev. Rul. 73-322, 1973-2 CB 44.

spouse's estate if the surviving spouse is dissatisfied with what the spouse would have received under the will or otherwise. In most states, the elective share consists of a percentage of the decedent's estate. Elective share statutes vary as to when the share vests and whether the share includes a portion of the estate income, as well as whether the share participates in the appreciation or depreciation of the estate's assets.

The First Circuit Court of Appeals determined that income distributed to a surviving spouse pursuant to her statutory claim to a one-third share of the estate was taxable to her under Code Sec. 662 as gross income.[25] The spouse was not deemed to be a mere "elector" of a statutory right since any person who gratuitously receives estate assets is a "beneficiary" within the meaning of Code Sec. 662. Furthermore, the appellate court found that the elective share was not a state law interest that was exempt from the income distribution provisions of Code Secs. 661 and 662 because, by definition, the elective share is a "portion of the estate."

The Tax Court, however, held that payments to a surviving spouse in satisfaction of her elective share under Florida law were not distributions of income or amounts properly paid or credited or required to be distributed to beneficiaries within the meaning of Code Secs. 661 and 662.[26] The spouse was not entitled to any income from the estate and did not participate in appreciation or depreciation of the estate assets.

Regulations have been issued in response to concern over the proper treatment of payments in satisfaction of a surviving spouse's elective share.[27] These regulations provide that the surviving spouse's elective share constitutes a separate share of the estate for the sole purpose of determining the amount of distributable net income. Thus, only the income that is (1) allocable to the surviving spouse's separate share (see ¶ 807) for a tax year and (2) distributed to the surviving spouse in satisfaction of the elective share will be treated as a distribution subject to Code Secs. 661 and 662. This approach results in the surviving spouse being taxed on the estate's income earned during administration only to the extent of that surviving spouse's right to share in the estate's income under state law.

¶ 807 Separate Shares Treated as Separate Trusts

When a trust has two or more beneficiaries and is to be administered in well-defined and separate shares, such shares must be treated as separate trusts for purposes of determining the amount of distributable net income allocable to the beneficiaries. The purpose of this rule is to limit the beneficiary's tax liability on income that is accumulated for another beneficiary's benefit.[28]

> ***Example 10:*** Trust income is accumulated for Lauren, but a distribution is made to Taylor of both income and corpus in an amount exceeding the share of income that would be distributable to Taylor had there been separate trusts. In the absence of a separate share rule, Taylor would be taxed on income that is accumulated for Lauren. The division of distributable net income into separate shares will limit the tax liability of Taylor.

---

[25] *P.L. Brigham, Jr., Exr.,* CA-1, 98-2 USTC ¶ 50,871.
[26] *R. Deutsch,* Dec. 52,307(M), TC Memo. 1997-470, 74 TCM 935.
[27] Reg. §§ 1.663(c)-1 through 1.663(c)-6.
[28] Code Sec. 663(c).

Ordinarily, a separate share exists if the economic interests of the beneficiary or class of beneficiaries neither affect nor are affected by the economic interests accruing to another beneficiary or class of beneficiaries.[29] Therefore, a separate share must include both corpus and the income attributable to that corpus. Also the income earned on the assets of that share, together with the appreciation and/or depreciation in value of that share's assets, must have no effect on any other share.

Example 11: Under the decedent's will and applicable state law, all the shares of decedent's closely held corporation, are to go to his daughter, Emily. In addition, all of the dividends paid to the estate from the closely held corporation stock are to be paid only to Emily, and the payment of those dividends does not affect any other amounts that Emily is entitled to receive under the will. The separate share rule would apply in this instance.

The separate share treatment is mandatory and not elective. A trustee or fiduciary may be required to apply it even though separate and independent accounts are not maintained for each share and even though there is no physical segregation of assets. The separate share rule does not apply to successive interests (such as when a trust provides for a life estate to A and a remainder to B). It also does not affect situations in which a single trust instrument creates not one but several separate trusts, as opposed to separate shares in the same trust.[30]

The IRS has privately ruled that a widow's exercise of discretion in withdrawing funds from her deceased husband's individual retirement accounts (IRAs), paying the proceeds to his estate, using the proceeds to satisfy testamentary bequests to their children, and rolling over a portion of the IRA monies from the estate to her IRA was a reasonable interpretation of the separate share rules.[31]

Separate share treatment applies only for determining distributable net income in computing the distribution deduction allowable to the trust or estate and the amount includible in the income of the beneficiary. It cannot be applied to split the income of the trust or estate into several shares to be taxed at lower-bracket rates. Example 12 illustrates the operation of the separate share rule.

Example 12: Decedent passed away and is survived by a spouse and two children. The decedent's will contains a fractional formula bequest dividing the residuary estate between the surviving spouse and a trust for the benefit of the children. Under the fractional formula, the marital bequest constitutes 60% of the estate and the children's trust constitutes 40% of the estate. During the year, the executor makes a partial proportionate distribution of $1,000,000 ($600,000 to the surviving spouse and $400,000 to the children's trust) and makes no other distributions. The estate receives dividend income of $20,000, and pays expenses of $8,000 that are deductible on the estate's federal income tax return.

The fractional formula bequests are separate shares. Because the decedent's will provides for fractional formula residuary bequests, the income and any appreciation in the value of the estate assets are proportionately allocated

---

[29] Reg. § 1.663(c)-4(a).
[30] Reg. § 1.663(c)-1(a).
[31] IRS Letter Ruling 200210002, August 6, 2001.

between the marital share and the trust's share. So, in determining the distributable net income of each share, the income and expenses must be allocated 60% to the marital share and 40% to the trust's share. The distributable net income is $7,200 (60% of income *less* 60% of expenses) for the marital share and $4,800 (40% of income *less* 40% of expenses) for the trust's share. Because the amount distributed in partial satisfaction of each bequest exceeds the distributable net income of each share, the estate's distribution deduction is limited to the sum of the distributable net income for both shares. The estate is allowed a distribution deduction of $12,000 ($7,200 + $4,800). As a result, the estate has a zero taxable income ($20,000 income *less* $8,000 expenses and $12,000 distribution deduction). The surviving spouse and the trust must include in gross income $7,200 and $4,800, respectively.

¶ 808 Calendar-Year Requirement; Complex Trust

Trusts are generally required under Code Sec. 644 to adopt the calendar year as their tax year. An exception to this general rule applies to charitable trusts and trusts exempt from tax under Code Sec. 501. Note also that if both the executor of an estate and the trustee of a qualified revocable trust elect, the qualified revocable trust may be treated as part of the decedent's estate for federal income tax purposes and not as a separate trust (see ¶ 503).[32]

If a beneficiary's tax year is different from that of a complex trust or a decedent's estate, the amount includible in the beneficiary's gross income is based on the distributable net income of the trust or estate and the amounts required to be distributed (or properly paid or credited) to the beneficiary for any tax year or years of the estate or trust ending with or within the beneficiary's tax year.[33]

When a beneficiary dies and an amount is paid, credited, or required to be distributed by an estate or a complex trust for a tax year that does not end with or within the last tax year of the beneficiary, the amount to be included in the beneficiary's gross income for the last tax year or in the estate's gross income is determined by the computations under Code Sec. 662 for the tax year of the estate or trust in which the beneficiary's last tax year ends. The gross income for the last tax year of a beneficiary on the cash basis includes only income actually distributed to the beneficiary before death. Income required to be distributed, but in fact distributed to the estate, is included in the estate's gross income as income in respect of a decedent under Code Sec. 691.[34]

If a nonindividual beneficiary terminates, the amount to be included in its gross income for the last tax year is computed as if the beneficiary were a deceased individual. However, income required to be distributed prior to the termination but actually distributed to the beneficiary's successor in interest is included in the terminated beneficiary's income for its last tax year.[35]

---

[32] Code Sec. 645(a).
[33] Code Sec. 662(c); Reg. § 1.662(c)-1.
[34] Reg. § 1.662(c)-2.
[35] Reg. § 1.662(c)-3.

¶ 809 Gifts and Bequests May Be Exempt

Gifts or bequests of specific sums of money or of specific property are not allowed as deductions to a complex trust or to an estate, and they are not includible in the beneficiary's taxable income.[36] The gift or bequest must be required by the specific terms of the will or trust instrument, and it must be paid or credited all at once or in not more than three installments in order to come within this special exclusion rule.

To qualify as a gift or bequest of a specific sum of money or of specific property, the amount of money or the identity of the specific property must be ascertainable under the terms of the testator's will as of the date of death, or under the terms of an *inter vivos* trust instrument as of the date of the inception of the trust.

The following amounts are *not* gifts or bequests of a sum of money or of specific property:

- an amount that can be paid or credited only from the income of an estate or trust, whether from current or accumulated income;
- an annuity, or periodic gifts of specific property instead of (or having the effect of) an annuity;
- a residuary estate;
- the corpus of a trust; and
- a gift or bequest paid in a lump sum or in not more than three installments, if the gift or bequest is required to be paid in *more* than three installments under the governing instrument's terms.[37]

For example, gross income portions of individual retirement account proceeds distributed to a decedent's children would be included in the estate's distributive net income and would be deductible by the estate under Code Sec. 661. The bequest to the children is not a specific sum of money under Code Sec. 663(a)(1) because it is in the form of a pecuniary formula bequest and the amount cannot be ascertained as of the date of the decedent's death.[38]

Example 13: Black's will directs that a bequest of $30,000 be paid to White and that the residue of the estate be held in trust for the benefit of White's children. After taxes, the sole asset left in the estate is an apartment building worth $200,000. In order that the executor-trustee not be required to sell the apartment building, White voluntarily allows the executor-trustee to pay the bequest out of rent over several years. The net rentals are $10,000, which the executor-trustee pays to the taxpayer in three annual installments. The rent when received by the estate is subject to income tax to the estate, but the three payments to satisfy the bequest are not taxable upon receipt by White, because of Code Sec. 663(a)(1).

---

[36] Code Sec. 663(a)(1).
[37] Reg. § 1.663(a)-1(b).
[38] IRS Letter Ruling 200210002, August 6, 2001.

Example 14: Under the terms of a will, a legacy of $5,000 was left to Ann, 1,000 shares of stock was left to Ellen, and the estate's balance was to be divided equally between other beneficiaries. No provision was made in the will for the disposition of the estate's income during the period of administration. The estate had income of $25,000 during the tax year, which was accumulated and added to corpus for estate-accounting purposes. During the tax year, the executor paid the legacy of $5,000 in a lump sum to Ann and transferred the stock to Ellen. No other distributions to beneficiaries were made during the tax year. The distributions to Ann and Ellen qualify for exclusion, and thus, are not taxable to them.

Example 15: Under the terms of a will, the decedent's estate was to be divided equally between two beneficiaries. No provision was made in the will for the disposition of the estate's income during the period of administration. The estate had income of $50,000 for the tax year. The beneficiaries agreed to distribute part of the estate's assets in kind to the beneficiaries, and stock was distributed to one of the beneficiaries during the tax year. The stock's fair market value was $40,000 on the date of distribution. No other distribution was made during the year. The distribution does not qualify as an exclusion from the beneficiary's gross income because it is not a specific gift to the beneficiary required under the terms of the will. Therefore, the property's fair market value ($40,000) represents a distribution to be considered in determining the estate's distribution deduction, and it would be includible as such in the beneficiary's gross income.

Example 16: Under the terms of a testamentary trust instrument, Ann and Bea are each to receive $75,000 in three equal installments of $25,000, each installment to be paid in alternate years. A total of six payments are to be spread over six years, but not more than three payments to a single beneficiary. Therefore, the bequests for Ann and Bea qualify for the exclusion. This is because the gifts to each beneficiary are to be treated separately and independently for purposes of Code Sec. 663(a)(1).

In determining whether a gift or a bequest of a specific sum of money or of a specific property is required to be paid or credited to a particular beneficiary in more than three installments, gifts or bequests of articles for personal use (such as personal and household effects, automobiles, and the like) are disregarded.

Also, specifically devised real property, the title to which passes directly from the decedent to the devisee under local law, is not taken into account. All gifts and bequests under a decedent's will (other than gifts of personal effects and real property passing under local law, discussed above) for which no time of payment or crediting is specified, and which are to be paid or credited in the ordinary course of administration of the decedent's estate, are considered as required to be paid or credited in a single installment. Also, all gifts and bequests that are not disregarded and that are payable at any one specified time under the terms of the governing instrument are taken into account as a single installment. For purposes of determining the number of installments paid or credited to a particular beneficiary, a decedent's estate and a testamentary trust shall each be treated as a separate entity.[39]

---

[39] Reg. § 1.663(a)-1(c).

¶ 810 Charitable Contributions Not Allowed as Part of Distribution Deduction

The charitable contributions of an estate or trust are deducted from taxable income under Code Sec. 642(c) only (see ¶ 1101). For that reason, charitable contributions are specifically disallowed as a deduction under Code Sec. 661, that is, as part of the distribution deduction. Also, such charitable contributions are not to be treated as amounts distributed for purposes of determining the amounts includible in the income of the beneficiaries under Code Sec. 662.[40]

Further, effective April 16, 2012, final regulations were issued regarding the ordering rules for determining the sources of funds that are to be paid, permanently set aside or used for a charitable purpose from trusts and estates under Code Sec. 642(c).[41] The final regulations override ordering provisions in a governing instrument or under local law that do not have "independent economic effect" aside from income tax purposes. The final regulations focus mainly on instances where the charity is to be the "lead" beneficiary and noncharitable beneficiaries are to receive the remainder. A typical ordering provision in a trust requires the source of funds payable to charities as directed minimize income tax consequences to the trust or the estate by exhausting higher tax rate income before using nontaxable sources, such as principal. The IRS has clarified its position that these ordering rules have no economic effect, particularly for CLTs, and therefore will not be respected for federal tax.

¶ 811 Double Deductions Are Denied

Double deductions of certain payments or credits to beneficiaries are specifically denied. An amount that is paid, credited, or distributed in the tax year of an estate or trust will not be deductible by it under Code Sec. 661, nor will it be treated as an amount distributed to beneficiaries under Code Sec. 662 if Code Sec. 651 or 661 (deductions of "simple" trusts distributing current income only) applied to such amount for a prior tax year.[42]

> ***Example 17:*** All of a trust's income is required to be distributed currently to beneficiary, and both the trust and beneficiary report on a calendar-year basis. For administrative convenience, the trustee distributes in January and February, Year 2 a portion of the trust income required to be distributed in Year 1. The portion of the income for Year 1 that was distributed in Year 2 may not be claimed as a deduction by the trust for Year 2 because it is deductible by the trust and includible in the beneficiary's gross income for Year 1.

¶ 812 Treatment of Gain from Sale of Life Interest

The consideration received by life beneficiaries of trusts for the transfer of their life interests in the trust to the remainderman is capital gain proceeds and not

---

[40] Code Sec. 663(a)(2); Reg. § 1.663(a)-2.
[41] T.D. 9582, 2012-18 IRB 868.
[42] Code Sec. 663(a)(3); Reg. § 1.663(a)-3.

ordinary income.[43] The owner of a life estate or an estate for a term of years in a trust, which interest was acquired by gift, bequest, inheritance, or by a transfer in trust, must use a zero basis in determining gain or loss from the sale of the interest pursuant to Code Sec. 1001(e) and Reg. § 1.1001-1(f). An exception to this rule applies when the life tenant and the remainderman simultaneously sell the entire fee interest in a single transaction.

The purchaser of a life estate (except when a single entire interest in property is acquired) is allowed to amortize the basis (purchase price) of the life interest and is able to offset the basis against the income received from the life interest.

¶ 813 Assignment of Trust Interest vs. Trust Income

The U.S. Supreme Court has held that a life beneficiary of a testamentary trust who made an absolute assignment to his children of portions of the trust's interest is not taxable upon income later distributed under the assignment.[44] However, an assignment of a sum of money payable out of the trust's income is not the same as an assignment of a share of income without retention of any control over the interest assigned. Accordingly, when the life beneficiary of a testamentary trust assigned income from the trust for the succeeding year, the Supreme Court held that such income was taxable to the assignor.[45]

The validity of assignments of trust income is largely governed by the laws and court decisions of the state in which the trust is administered. For example, if state law permits an income beneficiary of a spendthrift trust to release or disclaim a right to income from the trust in favor of one or more of the beneficiary's descendants, the disclaimer, if irrevocable, will be recognized as an effective divestment of the trust interest. Presumably, if the disclaimer is revocable, it will not be recognized as an effective divestment.[46]

The IRS has ruled that where a lifetime income beneficiary of a testamentary trust gives written consent from time to time (pursuant to the will's terms) to pay a certain portion of the trust income to another individual, the amounts so paid will be taxable as income to the beneficiary insomuch as the beneficiary, in substance, has parted with no substantial interest in property other than the specified payments of income.[47]

A purchaser of an interest in a testamentary trust was not regarded as a beneficiary and, accordingly, was denied a deduction for excess deductions upon the trust's termination.[48]

¶ 814 Throwback Rules—In General

The Taxpayer Relief Act of 1997 (P.L. 105-34) repealed the "throwback rules" with respect to distributions made from most domestic trusts. These rules now apply only to a limited number of trusts. The throwback rules were designed to

---

[43] Rev. Rul. 72-243, 1972-1 CB 233; *B.E. McAllister,* CA-2, 46-2 USTC ¶ 9337, 157 F2d 235, cert. denied, 330 US 826; *First National Bank & Trust Co. in Macon,* CA-5, 46-2 USTC ¶ 9367, 157 F2d 592, cert. denied, 330 US 828; *F.S. Bell Est.,* CA-8, 43-2 USTC ¶ 9565, 137 F2d 454.

[44] *E. Blair,* SCt, 37-1 USTC ¶ 9083, 300 US 5.

[45] *S.H. Schaffner,* SCt, 41-1 USTC ¶ 9355, 312 US 579.

[46] Rev. Rul. 64-62, 1964-1 CB 221.

[47] Rev. Rul. 55-38, 1955-1 CB 389.

[48] *A. Nemser,* 66 TC 780, CCH Dec. 33,943, aff'd, CA-2, 77-1 USTC ¶ 9406, cert. denied, 434 US 855.

prevent abuse of the tax laws that arose when complex trusts would accumulate income for distribution to beneficiaries in low-income years. The rules continue to apply to (1) foreign trusts; (2) trusts created before March 1, 1984, that would be treated as multiple trusts under Code Sec. 643(f); and (3) domestic trusts that were once treated as foreign trusts (except as provided in regulations).[49]

When they apply, the throwback rules treat accumulation distributions (see ¶ 815) made by complex trusts as if they had been distributed to the beneficiary in the years when the trust income was accumulated. An accumulation distribution is thrown back first to the earliest preceding tax year in which there is undistributed net income (see ¶ 816).

Although the beneficiary is taxed on the income in the year he or she receives the distribution, the beneficiary's tax liability is computed under special rules. To prevent double taxation of the accumulated income, the beneficiary is entitled to a credit against the tax already paid by the trust.

¶ 815 Accumulation Distributions

When the throwback rules apply it is necessary to determine whether the trust has made an accumulation distribution in the relevant tax year. An accumulation distribution is the amount by which other amounts properly paid, credited, or required to be distributed for the tax year (other than income required to be distributed) exceed distributable net income reduced (but not below zero) by income required to be distributed currently.[50]

Note that distributions of income accumulated by a domestic trust before a beneficiary's birth or while the beneficiary is under 21 years of age do not constitute accumulation distributions.[51] Accordingly, such distributions are not subject to the throwback rules, unless a special multiple trust rule applies.

¶ 816 Undistributed Net Income

The throwback rules apply to undistributed net income and, thus, the amount thrown back to any one preceding tax year is the amount of the trust's undistributed net income for that year. Income that is currently distributable is not subject to the throwback rules. If the accumulation distribution exceeds the undistributed net income for the trust's earliest preceding tax year, the distribution is thrown back beginning with the next earliest tax year to any of the preceding years of the trust and so on, to the extent of the accumulation distribution.

The undistributed net income of a trust for any tax year is the excess of distributable net income *over* the sum of (1) the taxes imposed on the trust with respect to the distributable net income and (2) required and other distributions.[52] Taxes imposed on the trust are the federal income taxes, before allowance of any income tax credits, which are allocable to the accumulation distribution.[53] This has the effect of passing these credits on to the beneficiary who receives an accumulation distribution, although these credits are not readily identifiable amounts, but,

---

[49] Code Sec. 665(c)(2).
[50] Code Sec. 665(b).
[51] Id.
[52] Code Sec. 665(a).
[53] Code Sec. 665(d)(1).

instead, comprise a portion of the federal tax that is used as an offset against the partial tax created by the accumulation distribution. Note also that, if the trust has been subject to estate or generation-skipping transfer tax and then makes a distribution to a beneficiary, the partial tax on the distribution is reduced by the amount of the estate or generation-skipping transfer tax attributable to the accumulated income.[54]

Income taxes imposed on a trust in the throwback years are considered to be an additional distribution in the accumulation distribution year. For purposes of computing the additional distribution, the term "income taxes" includes the amount of federal income taxes before the allowance of income tax credits. The term, however, does not include taxes imposed under the alternative minimum tax provisions.[55]

¶ 817 How the Throwback Rule Operates

The throwback rules treat an accumulation distribution as though it had been distributed to a beneficiary in the year in which the trust income was earned. These deemed distributions, and the taxes paid by the trust on the distributed accumulated income, are taxed to the beneficiary in the year the distribution is made.

The beneficiary's tax liability in the accumulation distribution year is the sum of:

1. a partial tax on taxable income for the year, computed at the normal rate and in the usual manner, but excluding the accumulation distribution, and
2. a partial tax on the accumulation distribution.

If the trust has no accumulated income, or if the distribution is greater than the income accumulations, then, to this extent, the transaction will be treated as a distribution of corpus and no additional tax will be imposed.[56] The base period for computing the tax on an accumulation distribution consists of the beneficiary's five tax years preceding the year of distribution. However, the years with the highest and lowest taxable income are disregarded and, thus, the partial tax is computed on a three-year base period.[57]

For purposes of computing the partial tax, the total amount of the accumulation distribution (including taxes considered distributed) is divided by the number of throwback years to which the trust distribution relates, and the result is added to the beneficiary's taxable income for each of the three base years. The partial tax paid by the beneficiary is the excess of (1) the average increase in taxes multiplied by the number of years to which the distribution relates *over* (2) the amount of trust taxes distributed to the beneficiary.

¶ 818 Computation of Beneficiary's Tax

A beneficiary's tax liability for the year in which he or she receives an accumulation distribution is the sum of (1) the partial tax imposed on the accumula-

---

[54] Code Sec. 667(b)(6).
[55] Code Sec. 666(b).
[56] Reg. § 1.665(a)-0A.
[57] Code Sec. 667(b)(1).

tion distribution and (2) a partial tax computed in the normal manner on the other income he or she received during the year.[58]

.01 Multiple Trust Distributions

Beneficiaries receiving accumulation distributions from three or more trusts in the same tax year are subject to a special rule. It denies an offset or credit for the taxes paid by a trust that are attributable to a third trust and any additional trust. However, this does not apply to a distribution that is less than $1,000.[59]

.02 Foreign Trusts

Separate rules apply to distributions made by foreign trusts to domestic beneficiaries. In the case of foreign trusts, "taxes imposed on the trust" include foreign taxes (income, war profits, and excess profits) paid or accrued by the trust and allocable to the accumulation distribution. Such taxes are deemed distributed as part of the distribution.[60]

As in the case of domestic trusts, a partial tax is computed on the basis of three computation years (arrived at by taking the five immediately preceding tax years and excluding the high-income year and the low-income year), but, subject to foreign tax credit limitations, the distributed foreign taxes deemed included in income in a computation year may be credited against the tax increase only in the computation year. They may not be carried over or back to the other two computation years.[61]

Beneficiaries who elected the foreign tax credit on their computation year return must credit the foreign taxes deemed distributed in computing the year's tax increase. Beneficiaries who did not elect the foreign tax credit on their computation-year return may treat the foreign tax imposed either as a deduction or as a credit in determining that year's increase in tax.[62]

Under a recapture rule,[63] when the beneficiary has sustained an overall foreign loss in a predistribution year, the portion of an accumulation distribution that is out of foreign source income is treated as U.S. source income in computing the credit in the computation year. This rule does not apply to the extent that losses have been recaptured in intervening tax years.[64]

When the income of a foreign trust is not taxed to the grantor under the grantor trust rules, an interest charge is imposed on the beneficiaries receiving taxable accumulation distributions from a foreign trust. This additional, nondeductible interest is computed as compound interest under the rules applicable to general underpayments of income tax.[65] The generally applicable underpayment rate is the federal short-term interest rate plus three percentage points.[66] The period for which interest is charged is determined as a weighted average. For each year in which there is undistributed net income, the undistributed net income for

---

[58] Code Sec. 667(a).
[59] Code Sec. 667(c).
[60] Code Sec. 665(d).
[61] Code Sec. 667(d).
[62] Code Sec. 667(d)(1)(B).
[63] Code Sec. 904(f)(4).
[64] Reg. § 1.904(f)-4(b).
[65] Code Sec. 668(a)(1).
[66] Code Sec. 6621(a)(2).

the year is multiplied by the number of tax years between the undistributed net income year and the year of distribution (including the undistributed net income year, but excluding the year of distribution). The sum of these products is divided by aggregate undistributed net income to arrive at the period for which the interest rate is applied.[67] However, the total interest charge, when added to the partial tax computed, cannot exceed the amount of the distribution.[68]

---

[67] Code Sec. 668(a)(3).

[68] Code Sec. 668(b).

¶818.02

Chapter 9

Grantor Trusts

¶ 901 History of the Grantor Trust Rules
¶ 902 Overview of the Grantor Trust Rules and the Use of Grantor Trusts
¶ 903 Adverse and Nonadverse Parties—Code Sec. 672
¶ 904 Reversionary Interests in Grantor Trusts—Code Sec. 673
¶ 905 Power to Control Beneficial Enjoyment—Code Sec. 674
¶ 906 Exercise of Administrative Powers—Code Sec. 675
¶ 907 Power of Substitution—Code Sec. 675(4)
¶ 908 Power to Revoke Grantor Trusts—Code Sec. 676
¶ 909 Income for Benefit of Grantor—Code Sec. 677
¶ 910 Income Taxable to Person Other than Grantor—Code Sec. 678
¶ 911 Certain Types of Trusts—Code Secs. 679 and 685
¶ 912 Specialty Non-Grantor Trusts—Alaska, Divorce Settlement, Cemetery
¶ 913 Overview of Grantor Trust Tax Reporting
¶ 914 The Grantor Trust Reporting Regulations
¶ 915 Alternative Filing Methods for Grantor Trusts
¶ 916 First Alternative Method of Reporting—All by Grantor Directly on Form 1040
¶ 917 Second Alternative Method of Reporting—All on Form 1099 with a Statement
¶ 918 Traditional Method of Reporting—Blank Form 1041 with Grantor Tax Letter
¶ 919 Changing Methods of Reporting
¶ 920 Grantor Trusts that Cannot Report Under an Alternative Method
¶ 921 Tax Identification Numbers: Must the Trustee Obtain a Separate Number
¶ 922 Tax Reporting for Grantor Trusts and Disregarded Entities
¶ 923 Coordinating Other Disregarded Entities with Grantor Trusts

¶ 901 History of the Grantor Trust Rules

The grantor trust rules can be found under Subpart E of Subchapter J of the Internal Revenue Code. Those code sections remain substantially the same today as when they were enacted in 1954.¹ The rules were initially codified to prevent high-bracket taxpayers from shifting income to lower-bracket taxpayers during their lifetimes, with those grantors still enjoying dominion and control over the income and principal of the property transferred.² At the time, the rules were necessary because of the disparity between the income taxation of individuals and trusts.³

When the federal income tax was enacted in 1913, the grantor of a trust was not taxed on the income generated by a trust. In 1924, revocable trusts, and trusts where the grantor "held or accumulated for future distribution" the income, became taxable to the grantor.⁴ Thereafter, between 1924 and 1954, a number of cases tested the grantor trust planning techniques to shift income to lower-bracket taxpayers.⁵

In 1942, for example, under the progressive rate structure, the first $2,000 was taxed at 19%, and 19 brackets later, at 88% on incomes of $200,000 and above.⁶ Thus, prior to 1954 and the enactment of the grantor trust rules, taxpayers could avoid the progressive rate structure of the federal income tax by simply creating and funding grantor trusts.

With the enactment of the grantor trust rules, grantors were forced to relinquish control, or pay tax on the income of a grantor trust where they retained dominion and control. Commentators refer to this as safeguarding the progressive nature of the federal income tax⁷—or ensuring that grantors remain liable for tax over property they essentially control.⁸ In *Lucas v. Earl*, Justice Holmes famously summed up this premise when he said "the fruits [must not be] attributed to a different tree from that on which they grew."⁹

.01 Helvering v. Clifford

In 1940, *Helvering v. Clifford*,¹⁰ a significant case reached the Supreme Court. This decision had a long-term impact on grantor trusts. In *Clifford*, the grantor created an irrevocable trust for a five-year term for the benefit of his wife. Clifford, the grantor, retained for himself a reversionary interest in the principal after five years. Clifford was also trustee, and retained the discretion to make distributions to his wife. The Court noted the short duration of the trust and the control Clifford maintained over the trust in ruling against the taxpayer.¹¹ The Supreme Court found the trust income taxable to Clifford as the grantor, but the decision had the

---

¹ Code Secs. 671-678.

² *See* S. Rep. No. 83-1622, at 86–87, 364–72 (1954), reprinted in 1954 U.S.C.C.A.N. 4621, 4718–19, 5005–13; H.R. Rep.. No. 83-1337, at 63–64, app. at 211–17 (1954), reprinted in 1954 U.S.C.C.A.N. 4017, 4089–90, 4350–57.

³ Early on, trusts and estates were subject to zero or low bracket taxation.

⁴ Revenue Act of 1924, § 219(h), 43 Stat. at 277, the precursor to Code Sec. 677; *see Burnett v. Wells*, 289 US 670 (1933).

⁵ *Corliss v. Bowers*, 281 US 376 (1930); *Lucas v. Earl*, 281 US 111 (1930); *Helvering v. Horst*, SCt, 40-2 USTC ¶ 9787, 311 US 112; *Blair v. Commissioner*, SCt, 37-1 USTC ¶ 9083, 300 US 5. *See also* Siegel, Grantor Trust Answer Book (2014).

⁶ Personal Exemptions and Individual Income Tax Rates, 1913-2002, Data Release (http://www.irs.gov/pub/irs-soi/02inpetr.pdf).

⁷ Soled, *Reforming the Grantor Trust Rules*, 76 Notre Dame L. Rev. 375 (2001).

⁸ Ascher, *The Grantor Trust Rules Should Be Repealed*, 96 Iowa L. Rev., 885 at 888 (2011).

⁹ *Lucas v. Earl*, 281 US 111, 115 (1930).

¹⁰ *Helvering v. Clifford*, 309 US 331, 338 (1940).

¹¹ Siegel, Grantor Trust Answer Book Q 1.7 (2014).

¶ 901.01

effect of providing a blueprint to other taxpayers, and increasing the planning of those taxpayers to shift income.[12]

.02 Clifford Trusts

A byproduct of the *Clifford* case was the "Clifford Trust" which was a permitted exception to the Court's holding in *Clifford*. A Clifford Trust is an irrevocable trust with income payable to someone other than the grantor for ten years, with the principal reverting back to the grantor after ten years. Clifford Trusts remained an effective wealth transfer technique until Code Sec. 673(a) was amended in 1986 to provide that if trust property or income can revert back to the grantor or the grantor's spouse, the trust would be taxable to the grantor.[13]

.03 The Clifford Regulations

Notwithstanding the Clifford Trust technique, the *Clifford* case is credited as a significant contributor to the grantor trust rules. In 1946, a little over five years after the case was decided, the IRS issued regulations, referred to as the "Clifford Regulations" called so because those regulations were drafted to curb the perceived abuses highlighted in *Clifford*.[14] The Clifford Regulations provided three key provisions that, if violated, created grantor trust status: (1) a reversionary interest following a trust term of less than ten years,[15] (2) if either the settlor or a nonadverse party had a power to control the beneficial enjoyment of either the income or principal,[16] and (3) possession of administrative powers exercisable for the taxpayer or her own benefit.[17]

.04 Contemporary Planning and Rate Compression

Modern legislation, however, has caused a shift in the application of the grantor trust rules. The earlier compression of income tax rates (noted above) is still applicable to trusts and estate, where the 39.6% rate in the highest bracket applies to trusts and estates with income over $12,300 (in 2015), while a single individual reaches the 39.6% rate in the highest bracket at income in excess of $400,000. Therefore, commentators note that the grantor trust rules no longer safeguard the progressive nature of the federal income tax that they were originally intended to provide.[18]

Nevertheless, today, grantor trusts are commonly used as a component of wealth transfer planning. Prior to 1986, the taxpayers sought to avoid any possibility that subpart E would apply. Now, gift, trust and wealth planning strategies routinely fail (and are subject to) the grantor trust rules to enable the grantors to benefit the trust beneficiaries by paying the tax attributed to the trust—in fact, the grantor is required to pay the tax.[19] It may seem ironic that the same grantor trust rules that

---

[12] The Supreme Court in *Clifford* essentially found that the taxpayer retained "the substance of full enjoyment of all the rights which previously he had in the property" without any quantification as to what "full enjoyment" was or, for that matter, how to qualify for "less enjoyment." 309 US at p. 336, 60 SCt at p. 557.

[13] Thus, since 1986, and the amendment to Code Sec. 673(a), Clifford Trusts are no longer used in practice.

[14] T.D. 5488, 1946-1 CB 19.

[15] The predecessor to Code Sec. 673 (which is why the Clifford Trusts were drafted to revert after ten years).

[16] The predecessor to Code Sec. 674.

[17] The predecessor to Code Sec. 675.

[18] Ascher, *The Grantor Trust Rules Should Be Repealed*, 96 Iowa L. Rev. 885 (2011).

[19] Rev. Rul. 2004-64, 2004-27 IRB 7 (July 6, 2004).

were initially utilized to ensure that wealthy taxpayers were not avoiding paying income tax, are frequently used to facilitate gift and estate tax minimization strategies. This is the case because of the flexibility of taxpayers to make irrevocable gifts for gift and estate tax purposes, but neutral as to the income tax effect by application of the grantor trust rules.

¶ 902 Overview of the Grantor Trust Rules and the Use of Grantor Trusts

As noted above, intrafamily transfers of income-producing property cannot be used to reduce income tax liability by shifting income from the parents' high marginal rate to their child's generally lower tax bracket if the child is under age 19 or under age 24 and a full time student. Instead, if the child's net unearned income exceeds the sum of (1) the "kiddie" standard deduction and (2) the greater of the kiddie standard deduction *or* the itemized deductions directly related to the production of that unearned income, the child's net unearned income is taxed at the parents' top marginal rate.[20]

The grantor trust rules, explained throughout this chapter, prevent a taxpayer from escaping tax on a property's income when he or she, in effect, remains the property owner because of his or her control retained over the trust. Although a grantor trust is a valid trust under state law, it is not treated as a separate entity under the tax code. This is because the grantor retains too much dominion and control over the property placed in the grantor trust. Even part of a trust, rather than the entire trust, can be treated as a grantor trust.

Taxing income to the grantor instead of to the trust was often undesirable when fiduciary income tax rates were often lower than those for individuals. Now, however, the taxable income of a trust or estate is subject to tax rates that are less favorable than those for individuals.

Grantor trusts are broadly used in estate planning. For example, the donor's individual income tax payments on trust income can be viewed as a means of transferring more property to the trust beneficiary without paying additional gift taxes. In addition, grantor trusts are useful in eliminating the costs associated with court-supervised estate administration.

A revocable living trust is a good example of a grantor trust. Revocable trusts typically allow the grantor wide discretion to influence both who will receive trust distributions and when such distributions are to be made. Also, as the name suggests, a grantor can revoke a revocable living trust while the grantor is alive and then reacquire the trust property.

In general, the grantor trust rules (Code Secs. 671–679) provide that a grantor is taxed on the income from a trust (or a portion of the trust) over which the grantor retains substantial dominion and control. Several circumstances must be present to cause the grantor to be treated as the owner of the trust. These include:

---

[20] Code Sec. 1(g).

- The grantor's retention of a reversionary interest in the trust exceeding 5% of the trust's value (see ¶ 904).[21]
- The grantor's power to affect beneficial enjoyment of trust income or corpus without the approval or consent of an adverse party (see ¶ 905).[22]
- The trust's administrative powers benefit the grantor (see ¶ 906).[23]
- The trust's administrative power to substitute assets (see ¶ 907).[24]
- The grantor's power or a nonadverse party's power to revoke the trust or return the corpus to the grantor (see ¶ 908).[25]
- The grantor's power or a nonadverse party's power to distribute income to or for the benefit of the grantor or grantor's spouse (see ¶ 909).[26]

A grantor will be treated as holding any power or interest of the grantor's spouse at the time the power or interest was created. If the grantor was not married at the time the power or interest was created, the rule applies to any subsequent period during which the grantor is married.[27] A grantor is not considered married if legally separated under a decree of divorce or separate maintenance.[28] A person other than the trust's grantor is treated as the trust's owner if he or she has the sole power to vest corpus or income in him- or herself unless the grantor is treated as the trust's owner.[29]

A grantor who retains too much control over a trust computes his or her taxable income using all of the trust's income, deductions, and credits that are attributable to or included in a portion of the trust in which the grantor is treated as the owner. These items are treated as if they had been directly received by the grantor.[30]

Generally, a grantor includes any person to the extent such person either creates a trust, or directly or indirectly makes a gratuitous transfer of property (including cash) to a trust. However, a person who either creates a trust, or funds a trust with an amount that is directly repaid to such person within a reasonable period of time, but who makes no other transfers to the trust that constitute gratuitous transfers, will not be treated as an owner of any portion of the trust under the grantor trust rules.[31] In addition, if a trust makes a gratuitous transfer of property to another trust, the grantor of the transferor trust generally is treated as the grantor of the transferee trust. However, if a person with a general power of appointment over the transferor trust exercises that power in favor of another trust, such person is treated as the grantor of the transferee trust, even if the grantor of the transferor trust is treated as the owner of the transferor trust under the grantor trust rules.[32]

---

[21] Code Sec. 673; Reg. § 1.671-1(a)(1).
[22] Code Sec. 674; Reg. § 1.671-1(a)(2).
[23] Code Sec. 675; Reg. § 1.671-1(a)(3).
[24] Code Sec. 675(4).
[25] Code Sec. 676; Reg. § 1.671-1(a)(4).
[26] Code Sec. 677; Reg. § 1.671-1(a)(5).
[27] Code Sec. 672(e)(1).
[28] Code Sec. 672(e)(2).
[29] Code Sec. 678.
[30] Code Sec. 671; Reg. § 1.671-2(a) and (c).
[31] Reg. § 1.671-2(e)(1).
[32] Reg. § 1.671-2(e)(5).

.01 Returns

Generally, items of income, deduction, or credit that are treated as belonging to a trust grantor (or another person) are not reported by the trust on Form 1041. Instead, those items are reflected on the income tax return of the grantor (Form 1040) or other person who is taxed on the trust income. A separate statement is attached to Form 1041 that states the name, taxpayer identification number, and address of the person to whom the income is taxable and his or her income deductions and credits.[33] When the grantor is a trustee and is treated as the owner of the trust's assets, Form 1041 should not be filed. Instead, the trust's income, deductions, and credits are to be listed on the grantor's Form 1040.

¶ 903 Adverse and Nonadverse Parties—Code Sec. 672

A grantor may be treated as a trust's owner if the grantor or a "nonadverse party" can exercise a power over the trust without the consent of an "adverse party."

.01 Adverse Parties

An adverse party is a person who (1) has a substantial beneficial interest in the trust and (2) would be adversely affected by the exercise or nonexercise of the power possessed.[34] To be treated as an adverse party, a person must have more than a beneficial interest, and the interest must be substantial. An interest is substantial if its value in relation to the total value of the property subject to the power is not insignificant.[35] An individual with a substantial beneficial interest in a trust is an adverse party only if the exercise or nonexercise of powers would be adverse to the interest of another in the trust.[36]

The interest of a trust's ordinary income beneficiary may or may not be adverse to the exercise of a power over corpus. Thus, the following trust beneficiaries have been deemed to hold adverse interests:

- A current income beneficiary who has the power to appoint the trust corpus to a grantor before or after death has an adverse interest in the return of a corpus before death.[37]
- The interest of a contingent income beneficiary is adverse to a return of corpus only before the beneficiary's interest is terminated.
- A remainderman who has interest is adverse to the exercise of any power over the trust's corpus but not to the exercise of a power over any income interest preceding the remainder.[38]

.02 Nonadverse Parties

Code Sec. 672 defines a nonadverse party as "any person who is not an adverse party".[39] This is a facts and circumstances test that can have interesting results. In

---

[33] Reg. § 1.671-4(a).
[34] Code Sec. 672(a).
[35] Reg. § 1.672(a)-1(a).
[36] This would include members of the grantor's family and close friends if the interest was substantial and the exercise would be adverse to an interest held by the grantor. See Savage v. Commissioner, CA-3, 82 F2d 92.
[37] Reg. § 1.672(a)-1(c).
[38] Reg. § 1.672(a)-1(d).
[39] Code Sec. 672(b); Reg. § 1.672(b)-1.

Haeri, the court found no adverse party existed where all of the trustees were friends and business associates of the beneficiaries, even though they were unrelated pursuant to Code Sec. 672(c).[40]

A trustee is not an adverse party merely because of his or her interest as trustee.[41] His or her moral duty to act in accordance with the best interests of the beneficiaries or his or her interest in earning trustee's fees is not treated as an adverse interest.[42] However, a trustee with the power to distribute income or corpus to himself or herself is an adverse party.[43] The interest of a trustee who is not a beneficiary is not adverse merely because he or she might inherit the corpus of the trust if no trust beneficiary survives the grantor.[44]

.03 Related or Subordinate Under Code Sec. 672(c)

The term "related or subordinate" under Code Sec. 672(c) generally means subservient. The Code Section lists the grantor's spouse, the grantor's mother or father, children, and siblings.[45] Also included are employees of the grantor, including employees of a corporation in which the grantor holds voting control of the stock and employees subordinate to an executive of the grantor.[46] Individuals who are not subordinate include corporate directors,[47] and partners of the grantor. Accountants and attorneys are viewed as independent contractors.[48] Distribution Committees of family owned Private Trust Companies exercising discretion over distributions from trusts where the trust company is serving as trustee generally are not subordinate to the grantor as identified in a number of private letter rulings.[49]

¶ 904 Reversionary Interests in Grantor Trusts—Code Sec. 673

A grantor is considered to be the owner of any portion of a trust in which he or she has a reversionary interest in either the trust's income or corpus. The value of the reversionary interest must exceed 5% of the value of the trust (or portion of the trust) at the time property is transferred to it.[50]

Presumably, the method used to value the reversionary interest is the same method used to value property passing into a decedent's estate in cases where the decedent has retained a reversionary interest in the transferred property.[51] Taxation of the grantor on trust income and inclusion of the transferred property's value in the gross estate both depend upon the reversionary interest exceeding 5%.

---

[40] *F. Haeri*, 56 TCM 1061, CCH Dec. 45,423(M), TC Memo. 1989-20.

[41] Reg. 1.672(a)-1(a).

[42] *M.G. Reinecke v. Smith*, SCt, 3 USTC ¶ 1089, 289 US 172, 53 SCt 570; *S.G. Carkhuff*, CA-6, 36-1 USTC ¶ 9271, 83 F2d 626, cert. denied, 299 US 568; *S. Morton*, 38 BTA 1283, CCH Dec. 10,518, aff'd, CA-7, 40-1 USTC ¶ 9178, 109 F2d 47; *M.S. Witherbee*, 28 BTA 256, CCH Dec. 8091, aff'd, CA-2, 4 USTC ¶ 1279, 70 F2d 696, cert. denied, 293 US 582.

[43] *F.G. Paxton Est.*, 44 TCM 771, CCH Dec. 39,262(M), TC Memo. 1982-464, appeal dism'd, CA-9 (1984).

[44] *O.A. Ewald*, 2 TC 384, CCH Dec. 13,347, aff'd, CA-6, 44-1 USTC ¶ 9266, 141 F2d 750; *J. Sapirstein*, 47 BTA 903, CCH Dec. 12,860.

[45] *See also* Rev. Rul 58-19, 1958-1 CB 251.

[46] Code Sec. 672(c); Reg. § 672(c)-1.

[47] Rev. Rul. 66-160, 1966-1 CB 164.

[48] *Goodwyn Estate v. Commissioner*, 35 TCM 1026 (1926).

[49] Notice 2008-63, 2008-2 CB 261; IRS Letter Ruling 200637025 (June 5, 2006); IRS Letter Ruling 200546052 (Aug. 2, 2005).

[50] Code Sec. 673(a).

[51] Code Sec. 2037.

If the value of the reversionary interest cannot be determined with actuarial certainty (i.e., the interest does not revert to the grantor after a fixed period or upon the death of an individual), a special rule is provided for determining the interest's value. Under this rule, it is assumed that any discretionary powers are exercised in a manner that would maximize the reversionary interest's value.[52]

The date that a reversionary interest is to revert to the grantor may be postponed, for example, by the extension of the trust's term. The postponement is considered a new transfer in trust, commencing on the date that the postponement becomes effective and terminating on the date prescribed by the postponement. The postponement will not cause the grantor to be taxed on the trust's income unless the grantor would be taxed absent the postponement.[53]

A grantor will not be treated as the trust's owner if the reversionary interest takes effect only upon the death of a minor lineal descendent. In order for this exception to apply, the beneficiary must hold the entire present interest, as defined by Code Sec. 2503(c), in the trust (or trust portion).[54]

A grantor who has a reversionary interest in a trust's corpus that does not fall within the 5% rule may still be treated as the owner of the trust's corpus under Code Sec. 677 (relating to income for benefit of the grantor, discussed at ¶ 909). This is because income allocable to corpus may be accumulated for future distributions to the grantor. Items allocable to corpus, such as capital gains, are used to compute the grantor's taxable income.[55]

¶ 905 Power to Control Beneficial Enjoyment—Code Sec. 674

The power of a grantor or a nonadverse party to affect the beneficial enjoyment of the trust income or corpus without the consent of an adverse party will cause the grantor to be treated as the trust's owner.[56] The power to affect the beneficial enjoyment of the trust may be a fiduciary power, a power of appointment, or any other power.[57]

A grantor or nonadverse party has the power to dispose of the beneficial enjoyment of the trust if that person has the power to "spray" or "sprinkle" income or corpus of the trust unevenly among the beneficiaries. This power allows the grantor or other nonadverse party to control the beneficial enjoyment of the trust.[58]

.01 Independent Trustees

The power of an independent trustee to sprinkle income or corpus of a trust, however, will not cause the grantor to be treated as the trust's owner.[59] An independent trustee is a trustee who is not related or subordinate to the grantor or the grantor's spouse. If there is more than one trustee, no more than half of them may be related or subordinate to the grantor or the grantor's spouse.[60]

---

[52] Code Sec. 673(c).
[53] Code Sec. 673(d).
[54] Code Sec. 673(b).
[55] Reg. § 1.671-3(b)(2).
[56] Code Sec. 674(a).
[57] Reg. § 1.674(a)-1.
[58] Reg. § 1.674(a)-1(b)(3).
[59] Code Sec. 674(c).
[60] Code Secs. 672(c) and 674(c); Reg. § 1.674(c)-1.

In order for the above exception to apply, the independent trustee must be able to exercise the power without the approval or consent of another person. Additionally, the exception will not apply if any person has the power to add beneficiaries designated to receive income or corpus unless the addition is to account for subsequently born or adopted children.[61]

A trustee who is not an independent trustee, and who is not the grantor or the grantor's spouse, may sprinkle income among the trust's beneficiaries if his or her power is limited by a reasonably definite external standard set forth in the trust instrument.[62] The exception is subject to the same limitations that apply to independent trustees.

.02 Permissible Powers

The following powers held by any person will *not* cause a grantor to be treated as a trust's owner:[63]

- Power to apply income to a dependent's support (other than the grantor's spouse)
- Power to affect the beneficial enjoyment of a trust after the occurrence of an event, such that the grantor would not be treated as the owner under Code Sec. 673, applicable to reversionary interests (see ¶ 904) if the power were a reversionary interest (for transfers in trust made after March 1, 1986)
- Power exercisable by will only
- Power to allocate among charitable beneficiaries
- Power, subject to a reasonably definite standard, to invade corpus for a beneficiary
- Power to temporarily withhold income
- Power to withhold income during the disability of a beneficiary
- Power to allocate receipts and disbursements between income and corpus

With the exception of a power to apply income to support the grantor's dependents, it is immaterial whether these powers are exercisable in the holder's capacity as trustee.[64]

¶ 906 Exercise of Administrative Powers—Code Sec. 675

If a grantor retains certain administrative powers, the income from a trust will be taxed to the grantor.

A grantor will be treated as the owner of any portion of a trust in which any of the following occur:

- The grantor and/or a nonadverse party have the power to deal with the trust property for less than adequate consideration without the consent of an adverse party.[65]

---

[61] Code Sec. 674(c); Reg. § 1.674(c)-1.
[62] Code Sec. 674(d); Reg. §§ 1.674(b)-1(b)(5) and 1.674(d)-1.
[63] Code Sec. 674(b).
[64] Reg. § 1.674(b)-1(a).
[65] Code Sec. 675(1).

- The grantor and/or a nonadverse party have the power to borrow directly or indirectly from the trust without adequate interest or security.[66]
- The grantor either directly or indirectly borrows from the trust and does not repay the loan before the beginning of the tax year (but see "Actual Borrowing from the Trust" below for an exception for loans with adequate interest and security).[67]
- A person in a nonfiduciary capacity can exercise general powers of administration over the trust without the consent of a person in a fiduciary capacity.[68]

The terms of the trust instrument or the actual operation of the trust are used to determine whether these administrative controls exist.[69] The power to amend a trust so that the prohibited administrative powers can be exercised will cause the grantor to be treated as the owner of the trust (or trust portion) from the trust's inception.[70]

The power of the grantor and/or a nonadverse party to directly or indirectly loan income or corpus to the grantor without adequate interest or security will cause the grantor to be treated as the owner of the trust (or trust portion).

.01 Power to Make Loans

The regulations provide an exception when a nongrantor trustee is authorized to make loans without adequate interest or security.[71] This exception will not apply, however, if the evidence indicates that the same favorable loan treatment accorded to the grantor would have been accorded to a disinterested third party.[72]

The power of a sole grantor/trustee to make loans to anyone and to determine what constitutes adequate interest or security does not necessarily mean the grantor has the power to receive favorable loans from the trust.[73]

.02 Actual Borrowing from the Trust

It is possible for a grantor to actually borrow trust income or corpus without being treated as the owner of a trust if

- the loan is made by a nongrantor-trustee who is not a related or a subordinate trustee who is subservient to the grantor,
- adequate interest is to be paid on the loan, and
- the loan is adequately secured.

Loans that do not meet these qualifications will cause the grantor to be treated as the trust's owner if the loan, plus interest, is not repaid before the beginning of the tax year.[74]

A grantor whose borrowing is inadequately secured will be treated as the owner of a trust (or trust portion) and will be taxed in the year that the loan is

---

[66] Code Sec. 675(2).
[67] Code Sec. 675(3).
[68] Code Sec. 675; Reg. § 1.675-1(b)(1)-(4).
[69] Reg. § 1.675-1(a).
[70] Id.
[71] Reg. § 1.675-1(b)(2).
[72] L.W. Benson, 76 TC 1040, CCH Dec. 37,990.
[73] Reg. § 1.675-1(b)(2).
[74] Code Sec. 675(3); Reg. § 1.675-1(b)(3).

made. The grantor will also be taxed in any succeeding year if the loan, plus interest, is not repaid before the beginning of that year.[75] Repayment of the loan in the year that the loan is made will not prevent the grantor from being taxed in that year.[76]

.03 Other Powers

If the grantor or trustee has significant voting power through the stock or securities held in a corporation, the powers of administration include the power to vote or direct the voting of stock or securities and the power to control investment of the trust funds that consist of the stock or securities.

¶ 907 Power of Substitution—Code Sec. 675(4)

A power of administration under Code Sec. 675(4) includes the power to reacquire the trust corpus by substituting other property of an equivalent value. This is perhaps the most common power included in a trust agreement to cause the trust to be treated as a grantor trust for income tax purposes.

> *Example 1:* "I may (acting in a non-fiduciary capacity) reacquire all or any part of the property of a trust hereunder by substituting other property of equivalent value."

Powers that are exercisable by trustees are presumed to be exercised in a fiduciary capacity, unless the presumption is rebutted by clear and convincing evidence. The terms of the trust instrument and the circumstances surrounding the creation and administration of the trust will determine whether a nontrustee is operating in a fiduciary or nonfiduciary capacity.[77]

¶ 908 Power to Revoke Grantor Trusts—Code Sec. 676

If a grantor or a nonadverse party has a power, which is exercisable at any time, to revest title to trust property in the grantor (i.e., to revoke the trust), the grantor is treated as the owner of the corresponding portion of the trust.[78] Accordingly, all of the income received will be taxed to the grantor.

A grantor has the power to revest title if a trust instrument expressly provides that the trust is revocable. Any issue as to the trust's revocability is determined under state law. A final decree by a state court on a trust's revocability is binding on the Tax Court.[79]

There are other powers, besides an express power to revoke a trust, that are the equivalent of revesting title in a grantor. For example, a grantor's power to terminate, alter, or amend a trust so that a trust can be revoked, or to appoint another person to revoke the trust, will revest title in the grantor.

.01 Postponement of Beneficial Enjoyment

If the power to revest title in a grantor is exercisable only upon the occurrence of an event, rather than at any time, the grantor is treated as a trust's owner only if

---

[75] *L.W. Benson,* 76 TC 1040, CCH Dec. 37,990.
[76] Rev. Rul. 86-82, 1986-1 CB 253.
[77] Reg. § 1.675-1(b)(4).
[78] Code Sec. 676(a).
[79] *W. Flitcroft,* CA-9, 64-1 USTC ¶ 9294, 328 F2d 449.

the grantor would be treated as the trust's owner under the reversionary interest rules discussed at ¶ 904.[80]

Generally, for transfers in trust made after March 1, 1986, a grantor is not treated as the owner of a trust under the reversionary interest rules unless the value of the reversionary interest exceeds 5% of the value of the trust (or portion of the trust) at the time the property is transferred to the trust.[81] The trust's grantor will, however, be treated as the trust's owner after the event occurs, unless the grantor relinquishes the power.[82]

Generally, for transfers in trust made before March 2, 1986, a grantor is treated as the trust's owner under the reversionary interest rules if it can reasonably be expected that the interest will revert to the grantor within ten years.[83]

¶ 909 Income for Benefit of Grantor—Code Sec. 677

Income from a trust is taxable to the grantor when the income is or may be, in the discretion of the grantor and/or a nonadverse party (see ¶ 903),

- distributed to the grantor or the grantor's spouse,[84]
- held or accumulated for future distribution to the grantor or the grantor's spouse,[85] or
- applied to premiums of life insurance covering the grantor or the grantor's spouse, except policies irrevocably payable to charities.[86]

Additionally, trust income is taxable to the grantor if the income is used to discharge the grantor's legal obligation to support an individual other than his or her spouse.[87]

.01 Constructive Distributions

Current distributions of trust income to a grantor or a grantor's spouse without an adverse party's consent will cause the grantor to be taxed on the trust income. The distributions may be either actual or constructive. Constructive distributions are made by the trust to third parties at the grantor's direction.[88] For example, a trust makes a constructive distribution to the grantor when it is required to pay the grantor's legal obligations.[89] Constructive distributions also include the payment of premiums for policies on the life of the grantor and the grantor's spouse.[90]

.02 Uses of Trust Income

Trust income that is used, or may be used, at the discretion of a nonadverse party to discharge a grantor's debts (other than legal support obligations) is treated as a distribution of income to the grantor, regardless of whether the income is used for that purpose.[91]

---

[80] Code Sec. 676(b); Reg. § 1.676(b)-1.
[81] Code Sec. 673(a).
[82] Code Sec. 676(b).
[83] Code Sec. 673(a), prior to amendment by P.L. 99-514 and P.L. 100-647.
[84] Code Sec. 677(a)(1).
[85] Code Sec. 677(a)(2).
[86] Code Sec. 677(a)(3).
[87] Code Sec. 677(b).
[88] Reg. § 1.677(a)-1(c).
[89] *C.R. Sheaffer,* CA-8, 63-1 USTC ¶ 9272, 313 F2d 738.
[90] Reg. § 1.677(a)-1(c).
[91] Reg. §§ 1.677(a)-1(d) and 1.677(b)-1(d).

If a grantor transfers mortgaged property into a grantor trust and instructs or authorizes the trustee to use trust income to make the mortgage's principal and interest payments, the grantor will be taxed on the trust income, at least to the extent that the payments are made and the grantor is primarily liable for the payment of the mortgage.[92]

.03 Payment of Gift Tax and Net Gift

The payment of gift taxes is the primary legal obligation of the donor, or grantor in the case of transfers in trust.[93] Payment of the grantor's gift tax liability by the trust may cause the grantor to be liable for tax. "Net gifts" are gifts made on the condition that the donee pay the gift tax liability resulting from the transfer. The net gift technique commonly has been used when the donor is unable or unwilling to pay the gift tax and it is not practical or desirable to sell a portion of the property to pay the gift tax liability. Typically, the trust would obtain a loan, using the property as security, and then use the loan proceeds to pay the tax. Note that the U.S. Supreme Court has held that when a "net gift" of appreciated property is made, the donor realizes taxable income to the extent that the gift taxes paid by the donee exceed the donor's adjusted basis in the property.[94] In that case, income was taxable to the grantor under Code Sec. 61, rather than the grantor trust provisions, as the discharge of indebtedness through a part-gift and part-sale of the property. Nevertheless, so long as the gift tax does not exceed the donor's basis, the technique will be successful. Although the amount of gift tax that will be paid on the transfer is part of the property that passes from the donor to the donee, it is not considered as property taxable for gift tax purposes since the donee is obligated to pay that amount and the donor is receiving consideration.[95] Under Revenue Ruling 75-72, "[g]ift tax paid by the donee may be deducted from the value of transferred property where it is expressly shown or implied that payment of tax by the donee or from the property itself is a condition of the transfer."[96] Note that a net gift technique does not result in any overall transfer tax savings. The "Net, Net Gift" technique involves adding a second payment obligation by the donee (in addition to the gift tax liability) if estate tax is assessed on the donor's estate under Section 2035(b) and the donee also agrees to pay the additional estate tax on the Section 2035 inclusion.[97]

.04 Payment of Income Taxes and Revenue Ruling 2004-64

Because a grantor is liable for the income tax attributable to a grantor trust, a grantor's payment of income taxes attributable to the inclusion of the trust's income in the grantor's taxable income *is not considered* a gift of the amount of tax to the trust's beneficiaries. In addition, the trust's reimbursement of the grantor for the amount of income tax liability attributable to the trust income is not a gift from the beneficiaries to the grantor.[98] Note, however, the power of having the grantor pay

---

[92] Rev. Rul. 54-516, 1954-2 CB 54; *L.J. Jenn,* DC Ind., 70-1 USTC ¶ 9264.
[93] Code Sec. 2502(c).
[94] *V.P. Diedrich,* SCt, 82-1 USTC ¶ 9419, 457 US 191.
[95] Code Sec. 2512(b); Reg. §§ 25.2511-1(g)(1), 25.2512-8; *Commissioner v. Wemyss,* 324 US 303, 306–307 (1945); *Harrison v. Commissioner,* 17 TC 1350, 1357 (1952).
[96] Rev. Rul. 75-72, 1975-1 CB 310.
[97] *Steinberg v. Commissioner,* 145 TC 184 (2015).
[98] Rev. Rul. 2004-64, 2004-2 CB 7.

the income tax for the trust—essentially amounts to an indirect gift to the trust without being subject to gift tax, because the trust is not reduced by the amount of the tax paid by the grantor.

.05 Private Annuity

The transfer of property to a trust by a grantor in exchange for private annuity payments from the trust may cause the grantor to be treated as the owner of the trust, if, rather than being characterized as a sale, the transaction is characterized as a reservation by the grantor of a lifetime income interest in the trust—this of course is not the intended result.

In *Lazarus*, what was purported to be a transfer to a trust for a private annuity was found to be a retention of a life estate by the grantor with the grantor being taxed on the trust's income.[99] The grantor transferred stock to a trust in exchange for an annuity. Almost immediately, the trust sold the stock in exchange for a note that was then the only asset in the trust and that produced a yield that matched the annuity payment. The nonnegotiable note was the sole source of the payment of the annuity, which could not be paid out of corpus.[100] In another case, the Ninth Circuit upheld a private annuity transaction where it determined that there was no connection between the amount of the trust's income and the amount of the annuity and where the annuity could be, and to a limited extent was, paid out of corpus.[101] However, recent decisions have clarified how to successfully execute a private annuity transaction.[102]

.06 Reversionary Interests in Excess of 5%

A grantor may retain a reversionary interest in a trust up to 5%, and will not be taxed on the ordinary income of the trust if the value of the reversionary interest does not exceed 5% of the value of the trust (or trust portion) at the time the property is transferred to the trust (see ¶ 904).[103] The grantor, however, is treated as the owner of any reversionary interest in the trust's corpus. Any income attributable to the trust's corpus in which the grantor has a reversionary interest, such as capital gains, is income accumulated for future distribution to the grantor, and it is taxed to the grantor in the year that it is earned.[104]

If the power to affect a grantor's beneficial enjoyment of trust income is exercisable only upon the occurrence of an event, rather than at any time, the grantor is treated as the trust's owner only if the grantor would be treated as the owner under the reversionary interest rules discussed at ¶ 904.[105] This rule does not apply when income is to be accumulated for future distribution to the grantor, even if the period of time is such that the grantor would not be taxed as the owner of the trust's ordinary income under the reversionary interest rules.[106]

---

[99] *S.M. Lazarus*, 75-1 USTC ¶ 9387, 513 F2d 824.
[100] *S.M. Lazarus*, 75-1 USTC ¶ 9387, 513 F2d 824.
[101] *E. LaFargue*, 82-2 USTC ¶ 9622, 689 F2d 845.
[102] *Estate of Kite v. Commissioner*, TC Memo. 2013-43.

[103] Code Sec. 673(a).
[104] Reg. § 1.673(a)-1(a); *W. Scheft*, 59 TC 428, CCH Dec. 31,634.
[105] Code Sec. 677(a).
[106] Reg. § 1.677(a)-1(f).

.07 Discharge of Legal Obligation

A discretionary power (whether exercised or not) to pay income to a grantor generally will cause the grantor to be treated as the trust's owner. This includes a discretionary power to use trust income to discharge the grantor's legal obligations.[107] However, a discretionary power to use the trust's income to discharge the grantor's legal obligation to support an individual other than a spouse will not cause the grantor to be treated as the trust's owner. The grantor is treated as the trust's owner only to the extent that the income is actually used to discharge the obligation.[108] For the rule to apply, the power can be held by

- any individual other than the grantor,
- the trustee, or
- the grantor acting as trustee or co-trustee.[109]

This rule will not apply if trust income is required to be used to discharge a support obligation.[110] The existence of a legal obligation of support is determined under state law.[111]

Amounts other than ordinary income can be used to discharge a support obligation. If a trust uses either corpus or accumulated income to discharge a support obligation, the grantor is taxed as a beneficiary of the trust. Accordingly, the grantor may be subject to the throwback rules for distributions of accumulated income (see ¶ 1304.05).[112]

¶ 910 Income Taxable to Person Other than Grantor—Code Sec. 678

A person other than a trust's grantor may be taxed on income if such person has a power, exercisable solely by himself or herself, to vest the corpus or income of the trust in himself or herself.[113] These rules apply, for example, in the case of a trust established by a grantor for the benefit of his or her children but under which the grantor's spouse may at any time take the trust property. The spouse is then treated as the owner and, thus, is taxable on the income. These rules do not apply if the power is renounced or disclaimed within a reasonable period of time.[114]

There is an exception where the general rule under Code Sec. 678(a) does not apply to a power over income if the grantor of the trust is treated as the owner of the trust under Code Sec. 673 through 677.[115] For example, if the grantor holds a power of administration under Code Sec. 675(4) such as the power to reacquire the trust corpus by substituting other property of an equivalent value, then the trust is a grantor trust in its entirety to the grantor, and the power over income to another person is not a Code Sec. 678(a) inclusionary power.[116]

---

[107] Code Sec. 677(a); Reg. § 1.677(b)-1(d).
[108] Code Sec. 677(b); Reg. § 1.677(b)-1.
[109] Code Sec. 677(b); Reg. § 1.677(b)-1(e).
[110] Reg. § 1.677(b)-1(f).
[111] Rev. Rul. 74-94, 1974-1 CB 26.
[112] Reg. § 1.677(b)-1(c).
[113] Code Sec. 678(a); Reg. § 1.678(a)-1.
[114] Reg. § 1.678(d)-1.
[115] Code Sec. 678(b).
[116] Code Sec. 678(b).

.01 Crummey Powers and Code Sec. 678

Crummey powers in a trust grant the right to a beneficiary to demand a withdrawal of funds from the trust for some reasonable period of time, which usually is 30 to 60 days.[117] When additions to the trust are made, the trustee informs the beneficiary in writing of this withdrawal right. Then the beneficiary either declines to exercise the right by notifying the trustee in writing or by failing to respond to the trustee's letter within the prescribed time. Crummey withdrawal rights are not typically limited to income, and therefore apply to corpus. Thus, if a beneficiary can vest the corpus or income of the trust in himself or herself, Code Sec. 678(a) would apply, and that portion of the trust would be grantor type to the beneficiary. However, where Code Sec. 678(b) applies because the trust is a grantor trust in its entirety to the grantor, Code Sec. 678(b) not cause the Crummey power to apply the grantor trust rules.[118]

¶ 911 Certain Types of Trusts—Code Secs. 679 and 685

.01 Foreign Grantor Trusts—Code Sec. 679

To prevent foreign trusts from being used for tax-avoidance purposes, foreign trusts are treated as taxable entities and U.S. beneficiaries are subject to tax on trust distributions. These inbound and outbound trust rules are discussed in detail in Chapter 13.

.02 Pre-need Funeral Trusts

A funeral trust is an arrangement whereby an individual purchases funeral services or merchandise from a funeral home (or cemetery) before death. The payment amount is held in trust and paid to the seller upon the individual's death. The only allowable beneficiaries of such a trust are the individuals to whom such property or services are to be provided at their death.[119]

Such trusts are generally treated as grantor trusts, and any income earned by the trust is taxed to the grantor/purchaser. However, special treatment is afforded to qualified pre-need funeral trusts under Code Sec. 685. If a trustee elects special tax treatment, a qualified pre-need funeral trust will not be treated as a grantor trust, and the tax on the annual earnings of the trust will be payable by the trustee. If this election is made, the Code Sec. 1(e) income tax rate schedule (generally applicable to estates and trusts) will be applied to the trust by treating each beneficiary's interest as a separate trust.[120] However, the trust is not entitled to a Code Sec. 642(b) personal exemption in calculating the tax.[121] The trustee's election must be made separately for each purchaser's trust. No gain or loss is recognized to a purchaser of a pre-need funeral trust contract if any payment from the trust to him or her is for the contract's cancellation.[122]

A trust is a qualified funeral trust and, thus, may avoid treatment as a grantor trust if all of the following requirements are met:

---

[117] *Crummey v. Commissioner*, 68-2 USTC ¶ 12,541, 397 F2d 82.
[118] IRS Letter Ruling 201235006, September 5, 2012.
[119] Code Sec. 685.
[120] Code Sec. 685(d).
[121] Code Sec. 685(a)(2).
[122] Code Sec. 685(e).

- The trust arises from a contract with a person engaged in the trade or business of providing funeral or burial services, or property necessary to provide such services.
- The sole purpose of the trust is to hold, invest, and reinvest the trust funds and to use the funds solely to make payments for such services or property for the trust's beneficiaries.
- The only trust beneficiaries are the individuals for whom such services or property are to be provided under the contract at their deaths.
- The only trust contributions are by or for the benefit of the trust's beneficiaries.
- The trustee makes the qualified funeral trust (QFT) election.
- The trust would, but for this election, be treated as owned (under the grantor trust provisions) by the contract's purchasers.[123]

There is a funding limitation on the aggregate contributions by or for the benefit of any one individual.[124] For purposes of the funding limitation, all trusts having trustees that are related persons are treated as one trust.[125]

These provisions apply to contracts purchased by one individual to have funeral and burial services or merchandise provided for another individual upon that individual's death, to the extent that such trust would otherwise be treated as a grantor trust.

A qualified pre-need funeral trust will continue to qualify for the special tax treatment during the 60-day period beginning on the grantor's death.[126] But for this rule, a trust would lose its qualified funeral trust (QFT) status upon the death of the grantor because it would not qualify as a grantor trust. Because the actual distributions of the trust assets to the seller of the merchandise or service usually do not occur immediately upon the death of the decedent, a QFT retains its QFT status for the period of time between the decedent's death and the actual distribution of the trust assets to the seller (not to exceed the 60-day period).

The qualified funeral trust (QFT) election is made by filing Form 1041-QFT (U.S. Income Tax Return for Qualified Funeral Trusts).[127] The filing must take place no later than the due date (including extensions) for filing Form 1041 for the year at issue. If no election is made for the first eligible year, a QFT election may still be made for subsequent tax years. Once made, the QFT election cannot be revoked without the consent of the IRS.

The IRS has simplified the reporting requirements for trustees of multiple QFTs by allowing a trustee to file a single, composite Form 1041-QFT (including short-period QFTs) covering all the QFTs managed by the trustee.[128] A trustee of multiple QFTs has until April 15 of the year following the close of the calendar year, to file a composite Form 1041-QFT even when the return includes QFTs that terminate during the calendar year.

---

[123] Code Sec. 685(b).
[124] Code Sec. 685(c).
[125] Code Sec. 685(c)(2).
[126] Code Sec. 685(b).
[127] Notice 98-6, 1998-1 CB 337.
[128] Notice 98-66, 1998-2 CB 810.

.03 Trusts Holding S Corporation Stock

A grantor trust may hold S corporation stock during the grantor's lifetime and for as long as two years from the date of the grantor's death.[129] Similarly, the post-death holding period during which a trust may hold S corporation stock because of a testamentary transfer is two years from the date the stock is transferred into the trust.

¶ 912 Specialty Non-Grantor Trusts—Alaska, Divorce Settlement, Cemetery

.01 Alaska Native Settlement Trusts

The Alaska Native Claims Settlement Act allows the creation of Settlement Trusts by Alaska Native Corporations ("ANCs") to "promote the health, education and welfare of its beneficiaries and preserve the heritage and culture of the natives."[130] A Settlement Trust permits the separation of portfolio assets from the business assets of an ANC and allows these portfolio assets to be invested to provide income to Alaska Natives and their future generations free of the business risks of the ANCs.

Effective for tax years beginning before January 1, 2011, and to contributions made to an electing Settlement Trust for such year or subsequent year, an electing trust will pay tax on its income, other than net capital gain, at the lowest rate provided in Code Sec. 1(c) on the ordinary income of single individuals. Net capital gain is taxed at the rate that would apply to the gain if the taxpayer were subject to a tax on its other taxable income at only the lowest tax rate for single individuals.[131]

The earnings and profits of the sponsoring ANC are not reduced on account of any contribution to the Settlement Trust and no amount is included in the gross income of a beneficiary by reason of contribution to the trust. However, the ANC earnings and profits are reduced when distributions are made by the trust and taxed to beneficiaries.[132]

Election. To obtain favorable tax treatment under Code Sec. 646, a Settlement Trust must make a one-time election. The election must be made by a trustee of the trust for its first tax year ending after June 7, 2001. A Settlement Trust that elects tax treatment under Code Sec. 646 may not revoke that election after it is made.[133] The fiduciary makes the election by signing Form 1041-N (U.S. Income Tax Return for Electing Alaska Native Settlement Trusts).[134]

A fiduciary of an electing Settlement Trust is required to provide the IRS with Form 1041-N, as well as an additional statement containing (1) the amount of distributions made to each beneficiary during the tax year; (2) the tax treatment to the beneficiary of such distributions, including any amount that is excludable from gross income under Code Sec. 646; and (3) the amount of any distribution during the tax year that is deemed made by the Alaska Native Corporation (ANC).[135] The

---

[129] Code Sec. 1361(c)(2)(A).

[130] 43 USC § 1601 *et seq.*

[131] Code Sec. 646(b); *see also* IRS Letter Ruling 200329018 (April 4, 2003).

[132] Code Sec. 646(d).

[133] Code Sec. 646(c).

[134] Form 1041-N (December 2013), p. 1.

[135] Code Sec. 6039H(a) and (c).

electing trust is also required to furnish this information to the ANC. If the distribution is treated as made by the ANC, the ANC must report such amounts to the beneficiaries and indicate whether the distribution is a dividend or not, in accordance with the earnings and profits of the ANC.[136] Form 1041-N is used for these information reporting requirements.[137]

Loss Disallowance Rule. A special loss disallowance rule reduces any loss that would otherwise be recognized by a shareholder upon the disposition of stock of a sponsoring ANC by a per-share loss adjustment factor that reflects the aggregate of all contributions to an electing trust sponsored by an ANC made on or after the first day the trust is treated as an electing trust, expressed on a per-share basis and determined as of the day of each contribution.[138]

Limitation on Transfer of Beneficial Interest. The tax treatment of a Settlement Trust may be terminated if the beneficial interests in the Settlement Trust may be disposed of to a person other than an Alaska Native. Upon termination, the special provisions of Code Sec. 646, including the favorable ordinary income tax rate and the corresponding lower capital gains tax rate, cease to apply as of the beginning of that tax year and all subsequent tax years.[139]

In addition, the distributable net income (see ¶ 709) of the trust is increased by the current accumulated earnings and profits of the ANC as of the close of the tax year with adjustments made for all distributions made by the ANC during the tax year. In no event may the increase exceed the fair market value of the trust's assets as of the date that the first beneficial interest becomes disposable. The earnings and profits of the trust are to be adjusted as of the last day of the tax year by the amount of earnings and profits included in the trust's distributable net income.[140]

If the electing Settlement Trust's Code Sec. 646 treatment is terminated, the trust and its beneficiaries will generally be subject to the rules of Subchapter J and the applicable trust income tax rates.

.02 Alimony and Separate Maintenance Payments

In computing its net income, a trust or estate is entitled to a deduction for amounts paid for alimony and separate maintenance payments (including those paid under a private separation agreement) that are required to be included in the recipient's income. This deduction is limited to the extent that such amounts are paid, credited, or required to be distributed out of income of the estate or trust for its tax year. For divorce or separation instruments executed before 1985, the recipient is taxed on such payments whether made out of income or corpus.[141]

.03 Cemetery Perpetual Care Funds

Perpetual care fund trusts (established for the care and maintenance of gravesites) can deduct amounts actually expended for the care and maintenance of gravesites that they are obligated to maintain up to $5 per gravesite.[142] The $5-per-

---

[136] Code Sec. 6039H.
[137] Form 1041-N (December 2013), p. 4.
[138] Code Sec. 646(i).
[139] Code Sec. 646(f).
[140] Code Sec. 646(f)(1).
[141] Code Secs. 71 and 682; Temp. Reg. § 1.71-1T(e).
[142] Code Sec. 642(i).

unit ceiling applies to the number of gravesites purchased prior to the fund's tax year from a taxable cemetery corporation created under local law. Amounts are deductible solely for purposes of Code Secs. 651 and 661, limiting deductions to a trust's net distributable income.

In filing a Form 1041 for a perpetual care fund, the words "Section 642(i) trust" should be entered in parentheses following the name of the cemetery perpetual care fund trust in the name block at the top of Form 1041. The number of gravesites should also be entered to the right of the line for income distribution deductions.[143]

¶ 913 Overview of Grantor Trust Tax Reporting

Generally, all fiduciaries or trustees of trusts are required to file Form 1041 "U.S. Income Tax Return for Estates and Trusts" if the trust has (i) any taxable income for the tax year, (ii) gross income of $600 or more (regardless of taxable income), or (iii) has a beneficiary who is a nonresident alien.[144] However, where the grantor trust rules apply, the general rule is that the items of income, deduction, and credits are reported on the grantor's personal income tax return and the numeric information is not reported on a Form 1041.[145]

An important element in determining where the numeric information is reported is whether the grantor (or another person) is treated as the owner of the trust. Where the grantor is determined to be the owner of the trust, reporting items of income, deduction, and credits on a Form 1041 is not required, and that numeric information is alternatively reported on a separate grantor tax letter statement attached to an informational Form 1041.[146] This option, to report numeric information on an attachment rather than completing Form 1041, and, under what circumstances these alternative methods of trust tax reporting for grantor trusts is available are discussed below.

¶ 914 The Grantor Trust Reporting Regulations

These income tax reporting rules for grantor trusts can be found in Treasury Regulation 1.671-4(b).[147] The current Regulations were finalized in December of 1995 and provide alternative methods of reporting for trusts that are treated as owned by grantors under Subpart E of Subchapter J of the Internal Revenue Code (the "Grantor Trust Rules"). In the preamble to the final regulations, the Treasury noted that the rules were intended to (i) make filing income tax less burdensome on grantors and trustees, (ii) reduce duplicate filings, and (iii) provide more meaningful information to the IRS.[148] These Regulations that were effective January 1, 1996 are applicable to grantors and trustees of trusts that are treated as owned by a grantor as well as persons required to file information returns for grantor trusts.[149]

---

[143] Instructions for Form 1041, U.S. Income Tax Return for Estates and Trusts (2006), p. 19.

[144] Code Sec. 6012(a)(4). *See also* ¶ 505, *supra*.

[145] Reg. § 1.671-4(a). These items are either reported directly on the personal income tax return, or shown separately on a separate grantor tax letter statement.

[146] Reg. § 1.671-4(a).

[147] T.D. 8633, 60 Fed. Reg. 66085.

[148] T.D. 8633, 60 Fed. Reg. 66085.

[149] *See* S. Rep. No. 83-1622, at 86–87, 364–72 (1954), *reprinted in* 1954 U.S.C.C.A.N. 4621, 4718–19, 5005–13; H.R. Rep.. No. 83-1337, at 63–64, app. at 211–17 (1954), *reprinted in* 1954 U.S.C.C.A.N. 4017, 4089–90, 4350–57.

¶ 915 Alternative Filing Methods for Grantor Trusts

The Treasury Regulations provide the general filing rule, commonly referred to as the "traditional" method, for grantor trusts under 1.671-4(a), and two filing alternatives provided under 1.671-4(b).[150] As discussed in greater detail below, but by way of summary for the chart: (i) method 1 would be to report directly on the grantor's Form 1040, essentially no filings, (ii) method 2 involves limited filings on a Form 1099 but not on a Form 1041, and (iii) the traditional method would include a blank Form 1041 with a grantor tax letter attached showing detail. The following table provides a summary overview of these filing alternatives:

Grantor Trust Alternatives Filing Methods

	Method #1	Method #2	Traditional Method
Tax ID # Used	Grantor's SS# on W-9	Trust Tax ID#	Trust Tax ID#
Form Filed	No Form Filed[151]	Form 1099[152]	Form 1041 with Grantor Letter
Ownership	Single owner Husband and Wife	Single or multiple owners	Multiple owners are OK
Required Info	No additional statement required	Trustee provides grantor with a Tax Letter Statement[153]	
Flow Through of 1099's and K-1's	All Form 1099's and Form K-1's flow through	Report Form 1099 income only. Form K-1's flow through	Report Form 1099 and Form K-1
Due Dates and Extension	Form 1040 due 4/15 Can be extended to 10/15	Form 1099 due 2/28, can be extended to 3/31 Form 1096 due 3/31 Tax Letter due 4/15[154] Form 1040 can be extended to 10/15	Tax Letter due 4/15 Form 1041 due 4/15, can be extended to 9/30[155]

¶ 916 First Alternative Method of Reporting—All by Grantor Directly on Form 1040

The first alternative is available where there is only one grantor, and the grantor is also a trustee or the only trustee. The benefit of this method is that all income, deductions and credits generated by assets owned by the trust are reported directly

---

[150] See Ivan Taback and Scott Bowman, *"Frequently Asked Questions on Grantor Trust Tax Reporting"* Estate Planning, Vol. 39 No. 8, August 2012, for a thorough discussion of the trust tax reporting rules and a review of the Regulations.

[151] Reg. § 1.671-4(b)(2)(ii)(B).

[152] See Marvin D. Hills, *"Alternatives to Form 1041 for Grantor Trusts,"* The Tax Advisor, September 2013, for practice pointers on alternative filing options.

[153] Reg. § 1.671-4(b)(2)(ii).

[154] Code Sec. 6034A(a).

[155] P.L. 114-41, The Surface Transportation and Veterans Health Care Choice Improvement Act of 2015 (H.R. 3236).

on the grantor's personal income tax return. There is no separate tax filing or reporting required.[156] Additionally, no separate tax identification number is required for the trust—the grantor's social security number is used.

For many taxpayers and tax preparers, this may be the preferred choice, because of the simplicity and lack of filings. However, for some attorneys and advisors, the lack of filings and related annual documentation supporting the ownership of the assets by the trust can prove concerning. There is no annual clear paper trail that the assets are owned by the trust. Practitioners will rightly point out that using this alternative method of reporting does not change the fact that the assets are in fact owned by the trust. As a best practice, some practitioners do not just give the grantor's name to the payor; rather, the asset can be titled: "John Smith, grantor of the Smith Dynasty Trust dated 3/17/2017."[157]

¶ 917 Second Alternative Method of Reporting—All on Form 1099 with a Statement

The second alternative method requires more reporting than the first alternative method, in that a Form 1099 is produced by the trustee for the trust.[158] However, there is less reporting than with the traditional method because no blank Form 1041 is required.[159] Unless the grantor is also the trustee, the trustee must provide the grantor with a grantor tax letter statement (in addition to filing the Form 1099s).

The level of additional reporting depends on the activity of the trust. The trustee has the same obligation for filing the "appropriate" Form 1099 as would a payor making reportable payments (i.e., a brokerage institution), except that the trustee must report each type of income in the aggregate, and each item of gross proceeds separately.[160] This means that if a trust has only interest income, only one Form 1099–INT is appropriate to be filed. However, if the trust has interest, dividends, and gross proceeds from the sale of securities, the trustee would be required to file, by February 28 of the following year, Form 1099–INT, Form 1099–DIV, Form 1099–B, as well as the grantor tax letter by April 15 of the following year.[161] Some practitioners find that preparing multiple Forms 1099 to report the trust income is nearly as tedious as producing a Form 1041 with a grantor tax letter statement under the traditional method.

The amounts that must be included on any Forms 1099 required to be filed by the trustee under method 2 above do not include any amounts that are reported on a Form K-1.[162] The Regulations provide an example that if a trust owned an interest in a partnership, the trust's distributive share of the income and gain from the partnership would not be includible on any Forms 1099 filed by the trustee if the distributive partnership share was reportable by the partnership on Schedule K-1.[163]

---

[156] Reg. § 1.671-4(b)(2)(ii)(B).
[157] *See* Marvin D. Hills, *"Alternatives to Form 1041 for Grantor Trusts,"* The Tax Advisor, September 2013, for practice pointers on alternative filing options.
[158] Reg. § 1.671-4(b)(2)(iii).
[159] Reg. § 1.671-4(b)(2)(ii)(B).
[160] Reg. § 1.671-4(b)(2)(iii).
[161] Reg. § 1.671-4(b)(2)(iv), Example 2.
[162] Reg. § 1.671-4(b)(5)(i).
[163] *Id.*

¶ 918 Traditional Method of Reporting—Blank Form 1041 with Grantor Tax Letter

The traditional method of reporting for grantor trusts, the items of income, deduction, and credits are reported to the grantor through a grantor tax letter statement for inclusion on the grantor's personal income tax return.[164] A Form 1041 is filed, although the numeric information is not reported on the Form 1041. Rather, on the front of the return, the informational boxes are completed and the front page will include the following statement:

> "Under the terms of the trust instrument, this is a grantor trust. All income is taxed to the grantor under IRC § 671-678. A statement of income, deductions and credits is attached."

¶ 919 Changing Methods of Reporting

.01 Changing from Filing Form 1041 to Methods 1 (Grantor) or 2 (Form 1099)

If the trustee has previously filed a Form 1041 for a trust and is changing to one of the alternative methods, the trustee should file a final Form 1041 for the taxable year which immediately precedes the first taxable year for the alternative method and indicate the following on the front of the Form 1041: "Pursuant to § 1.671-4(g), this is the final Form 1041 for this grantor trust."[165]

.02 Changing from Method 1 (Grantor) to Filing Form 1041 (Traditional)

If the trustee reported under alternative method 1 and is changing to filing a Form 1041, and previously reported under the name and social security number of the grantor to all payors, the trustee must furnish the name, tax identification number, and address of the trust to all payors for such subsequent taxable years.[166]

.03 Changing from Method 2 (Form 1099) to Filing Form 1041 (Traditional)

If the trustee reported under alternative method 2 and is changing to filing a Form 1041, the trustee must indicate on each Form 1096, "Annual Summary and Transmittal of U.S. Information Returns," that it files (or appropriately on magnetic media) for the final taxable year for which the trustee so reports that it is the final return of the trust.[167]

.04 Changing From Method 1 (Grantor) to Method 2 (Form 1099)

If the trustee is changing from furnishing the social security number of the grantor to the tax identification number of the trust, the trustee should furnish the name and tax identification number of the trust to all payors for subsequent taxable years.[168]

---

[164] Reg. § 1.671-4(a).
[165] Reg. § 1.671-4(g)(1).
[166] Id.
[167] Reg. § 1.671-4(g)(2).
[168] Reg. § 1.671-4(g)(3)(i).

.05 Changing From Method 2 (Form 1099) to Method 1 (Grantor)

If the trustee is changing from furnishing the tax identification number of the trust to providing the social security number of the grantor, the trustee must indicate on each Form 1096, "Annual Summary and Transmittal of U.S. Information Returns," that it files (or appropriately on magnetic media) for the final taxable year for which the trustee reports that it is the final return of the trust.[169]

¶ 920 Grantor Trusts that Cannot Report Under an Alternative Method

There are a number of situations where a grantor trust may not elect to report under an alternative method, and a Form 1041 must be filed.[170] Perhaps the most common is a trust treated as a Section 1361(d)(3) qualified subchapter S trust ("QSST")— a QSST may not report under an alternative method.[171] Additionally, trusts that have non-U.S. connections do not qualify, including a trust that has its situs or any of its assets located outside the United States and a trust owned by one, two or more grantors, who are not U.S. persons. Finally, if the grantor is taxed on a fiscal year, or the trust is a Section 584 common trust fund, the Regulations provide that the alternative methods are not available.

¶ 921 Tax Identification Numbers: Must the Trustee Obtain a Separate Number

As discussed above, an initial threshold question when considering grantor trust reporting is whether the trustee is required to obtain or should obtain a taxpayer identification number for a grantor trust. For many grantor trusts, especially those used in wealth transfer strategies, the taxpayer and only the taxpayer is treated as owning the trust. Where the grantor is also the trustee, the traditional method and both alternative methods are available.

The Regulations under Section 301.6109-1 titled "Identifying Numbers" provides that a trust that is treated as owned by one or more persons pursuant to Sections 671 through 678 (i.e., a grantor trust) must obtain a taxpayer identification number, unless the exception applies.[172] The exception provides that a trust treated as owned by *one grantor* or *one other person* under the grantor trust rules need not obtain a taxpayer identification number, provided the trust reports under alternative method 1.[173]

The trustee must obtain a taxpayer identification number for the first taxable year that the trust is no longer owned by one grantor or one other person or for the first taxable year that the trust does not report pursuant to method 1.[174]

---

[169] Reg. § 1.671-4(g)(3)(ii).
[170] Reg. § 1.671-4(b)(6).
[171] *See* Chapter 12, S Corporation and Fiduciary Income Tax, ¶ 1203, *infra*.
[172] Reg. § 301.6109-1(a)(2)(i)(A).
[173] Reg. § 301.6109-1(a)(2)(i)(B), referencing method 1 under Reg. § 1.671-4(b)(2)(i)(A).
[174] Reg. § 301.6109-1(a)(2)(i)(B).

¶ 922 Tax Reporting for Grantor Trusts and Disregarded Entities

As discussed above, where the trust is treated as owned by the grantor, the trustee need not obtain a separate taxpayer identification number for the trust until the trust is no longer owned by the grantor.[175] The following are circumstances where the grantor trustee may choose to use the grantor's social security number or may have to apply for a tax identification number.

.01 Irrevocable Life Insurance Trust

Irrevocable life insurance trusts typically do not hold income producing assets, and therefore the necessity for obtaining a separate tax identification number is diminished because there may be no reporting obligation.

.02 Term Trusts: GRAT and QPRT

Grantor retained annuity trusts ("GRATs"), qualified personal residence trusts ("QPRTs") are trusts for a term or period of time. During the term period, the trusts are treated as grantor trusts, and they could qualify under method 1.

.03 Husband and Wife who File a Joint Return—One Grantor

A husband and wife who file a single return jointly for income taxes (joint return) are treated as one grantor for purposes of the alternative filing methods discussed, so long as all of the trust is treated as owned by the husband and wife, and the husband and wife file their income tax return jointly for that tax year.[176]

.04 Revocable Joint Trust Grantor Trust Tax Reporting

A trust jointly owned by a husband and wife, such as a revocable joint trust, and where the husband and wife file a joint return is considered to be owned by one grantor, and therefore is not required to obtain a separate tax identification number.[177] This should be distinguished from the general rule where trusts owned by two or more grantors require the trustee to file Form 1099 and obtain a separate tax identification number.[178] Since the husband and wife are considered one grantor, either social security number can be attached to the trust. Upon the predeceasing spouse's death, the surviving spouse's tax identification number should be used.

.05 Revocable Trust but Grantor Not a Trustee

Grantor trust status can apply to either irrevocable transfers, or revocable transfers. Revocable transfers are commonly referred to as revocable trusts, or living trusts. With a revocable trust, the grantor is typically the trustee, and although it is likely not much analysis is involved, the typical revocable trust utilizes alternative method 1 where the grantor reports all the items of income, deduction and credit, no Form 1041 is involved, and no separate tax identification number is considered.

There are circumstances where the grantor may not be a trustee, such as with a child who has attained majority age to create a trust, but where additional supervision may be desired. A revocable trust where the grantor is not a trustee

---

[175] Reg. § 301.6109-1.
[176] Code Sec. 6013.
[177] Reg. § 1.671-4(b)(8).
[178] Reg. § 1.671-4(b)(3)(ii).

does not qualify under alternative method 1, and therefore a grantor tax letter statement under alternative method 2 or the traditional filing may be used, which would require the trustee to obtain a separate tax identification number if the traditional method were used.

¶ 923 Coordinating Other Disregarded Entities with Grantor Trusts

Grantor trusts are typically coordinated with other wealth transfer strategies frequently involving a gift or sale (a transfer) of property. Depending on the other entities, it is not uncommon for those other entities to be treated as disregarded entities. The IRS has ruled that if an eligible entity has two owners under local law, but one of the owners is, for federal tax purposes, disregarded as an entity separate from the other owner of the eligible entity, then the eligible entity cannot be classified as a partnership and is either disregarded as an entity separate from its owner or an association taxable as a corporation. Thus, the eligible entity is treated as having only one member, and can be treated as a disregarded entity. Thus, the entity cannot be a partnership for tax purposes; it must be classified either as a disregarded entity or as an association taxable as a corporation.[179]

---

[179] Rev. Rul. 2004-77, 2004-31 IRB 119.

Chapter 10

Death of a Partnership Member

¶ 1001   Income on Deceased Partner's Final Return
¶ 1002   Electing Large Partnerships
¶ 1003   Partnership Representative
¶ 1004   Partnership Accounting Periods
¶ 1005   Transfer of Decedent's Entire Partnership Interest to Spouse
¶ 1006   Payments to Deceased Partner's Successor in Interest
¶ 1007   Allocation of Payments
¶ 1008   Partner Receiving Income in Respect of a Decedent
¶ 1009   Partnership Goodwill
¶ 1010   The 754 Election
¶ 1011   Mandatory Basis Adjustment Rules

¶ 1001 Income on Deceased Partner's Final Return

For federal income tax purposes, the death of a partner does not, in itself, terminate the partnership. Nor does it generally close the partnership's tax year.[1] However, the tax year of a partnership will close *with respect to a partner* whose entire interest in the partnership terminates by death or otherwise.[2] Accordingly, a partner's death will require a computation of his or her share of partnership income, actual or estimated, up to the time of death, as is required when a partner sells his or her interest or retires during the year. Such a computation may already be necessary for estate or inheritance tax purposes to value the partnership interest.

.01 Death of a 50% Partner

Even if there are only two partners and one of them dies, the partnership is not considered to be terminated if the deceased partner's estate (or other successor in interest) continues to share in the partnership's profits or losses.[3] This is true even while the partnership business is being liquidated, as long as the payments to the estate (or other successor in interest) are being made.[4] In short, as long as the

---

[1] Code Secs. 706(c)(1) and 708(b)(1). A partnership is considered as terminated only if (1) no part of any business, financial operation, or venture of the partnership continues to be carried on by any of its partners in a partnership, or (2) within a 12-month period there is a sale or exchange of 50% or more of the total interest in partnership capital and profits (Code Sec. 708(b)(1)). Note that individual state laws should be consulted for the effect of the death of a partner on a partnership.

[2] Code Sec. 706(c)(2)(A).

[3] Reg. § 1.708-1(b)(1)(i).

[4] Reg. § 1.736-1(a)(6).

deceased partner's successors in interest are receiving payments from the partnership, they are taxed as partners.

.02 Final 1040 Reporting

The last return of a decedent partner includes only the partner's share of partnership taxable income, deductions, and credits for the partnership tax year or years ending within or with his or her last tax year, that is, the short tax year ending with the date of death. The distributive share of partnership taxable income, etc. for the partnership tax year ending after the decedent's last tax year will be included in the return of the estate or other successor in interest. This is the case even if some distributions of such income were made before the decedent's death. If the deceased partner's estate (or other successor in interest) continues to share in the profits and losses of the partnership business, the distributive share of such profits and losses must be included in income in the tax year of the estate (or other successor in interest) within or with which the tax year of the partnership ends. Where the deceased partner's estate or other successor in interest receives distributions, any gain or loss on such distributions is includible in the partner's gross income for its tax year in which the distribution is made.[5]

.03 Treatment of Self-Employment Tax in Final Year

An exception to the above rules applies in the case of the self-employment tax. If a general partner dies within the partnership tax year, the general partner's self-employment income will include his or her distributive share of the income earned by the partnership through the end of the month in which death occurs. This is so even though the estate or heir succeeds to the general partner's rights in the partnership. For self-employment tax purposes, the partnership income for the year is considered to be earned ratably each month.[6]

>*Example 1:* Partner's distributive share of profits for the partnership year ending June 30, Year 1, is $2,000. Partner, who filed her return on a calendar-year basis, died on August 28, Year 1. For the partnership year ending June 30, Year 2, assume that the distributive share of Partner and her estate is $3,000. The amount of self-employment income that must be shown on Partner's Year 1 return will be $2,500 ($2,000 of Year 1 profits) + (($3,000 ÷ 12) × 2 = $500 of Year 2 profits).

To the extent that any part of a distributive share of partnership income of the deceased partner's estate (or other successor in interest) is attributable to the decedent for the period ending with the date of death, such part of the distributive share must be treated as income in respect of a decedent under Code Sec. 691. This treatment is applicable even though, before death, the partner withdrew all or a portion of his or her share of the current year's earnings.[7]

>*Example 2:* Decedent has a calendar tax year ending December 31 is a member of the ABC partnership. The partnership's tax year ends on June 30 (see ¶ 1004 for partnership tax years). Decedent dies on October 17, Year 1.

---

[5] Code Sec. 706(a) and (d); Reg. § 1.706-1(c)(3)(ii).
[6] Code Sec. 1402(f); Reg. § 1.1402(f)-1.
[7] Reg. §§ 1.706-1(c)(3)(v) and 1.753-1(b).

Her estate (which may adopt any fiscal or calendar tax year) adopts a tax year ending September 30. The final return, (for the period January 1 to October 17, Year 1), will include only her distributive share of taxable income of the partnership for its tax year ending June 30, Year 1. The distributive share of taxable income of the partnership for its tax year ending June 30, Year 2, arising from the interest of Decedent while she was alive (July 1, Year 1 through October 17, Year 1), will be includible in the return of the estate for its tax year ending September 30, Year 2 because the partnership's Year 2 tax year ran from July 1, Year 1 through June 30, Year 2. That part of the distributive share attributable to Decedent for the period ending with the date of her death (July 1 through October 17, Year 1) is income in respect of a decedent.[8]

¶ 1002 Electing Large Partnerships

Simplification rules for electing large partnerships and their members have implications for the final return of decedents who were partners of such partnerships.[9] Large partnerships (excluding certain service and commodity-trading partnerships) with at least 100 members in the preceding tax year may elect this special treatment to significantly reduce the number of items that must be separately reported to their numerous partners.

In determining the taxable income of a partner of an electing large partnership, each partner in the large partnership takes into account separately his or her distributive share of a number of designated items, as determined at the partnership level.

The character of any item separately stated to the partners is based on its character to the partnership. Thus, the items are treated as incurred by the partnership.[10]

However, the following provisions will be applied at the *partner* level:

- Code Sec. 68 overall limitation on itemized deductions
- Code Sec. 49 and Code Sec. 465 at-risk limitations
- Code Sec. 469 limitation on passive activity losses and credits
- Any other provisions specified in regulations.[11]

¶ 1003 Partnership Representative

Under TEFRA[12] and the unified audit proceedings, the tax matters partner (TMP) was designated to participate in the audit proceedings, not the individual partners. Under the new audit rules released November 2015 under the BBA,[13] Code Sec. 6223 provides that the role of the TMP is replaced by a partnership representative who is authorized to participate in the audit proceedings on behalf of the partnership. This authority includes the ability to bind the partnership and the

---

[8] Reg. § 1.706-1(c)(3)(vi), *Example 1*.
[9] Code Secs. 771–777.
[10] Code Sec. 772(c)(1).
[11] Code Sec. 773(a)(3)(B).
[12] Tax Equity and Fiscal Responsibility Tax Act of 1982.
[13] Bipartisan Budget Act of 2015.

partners in audits and other proceedings, including settlement authority and decisions on procedural issues such as whether to proceed to litigation. Unlike a TMP, the partnership representative does not need to be a partner of the partnership. Under TEFRA, smaller partnerships with less than ten partners could opt out of the TEFRA audit proceeding rules. The BBA rules preserve and expand the exemption from partnership level audit proceedings for small partnerships, increasing the limitation on the number of partners from ten to 100, and adding S corporations to the type of eligible partners.

¶ 1004 Partnership Accounting Periods

Generally, a partnership's tax year is determined as though the partnership were a taxpayer. A partnership is required to adopt the "majority interest tax year" as its own tax year, unless it can demonstrate to the IRS a business purpose for adopting a different tax year. The "majority interest tax year" is the tax year that on each testing date constituted the tax year of one or more partners having (on such date) an aggregate interest in partnership profits and capital of more than 50%. If the partnership does not have a majority interest tax year, it must use the tax year of all of its principal partners. If the partnership does not have a majority interest tax year and all of its principal partners do not have the same tax year, the partnership must use the tax year that results in the least aggregate deferral of income to its partners.[14]

Example 3: Partnership P is on a fiscal year ending June 30. Partner A reports income on the fiscal year ending June 30 and Partner B reports income on the fiscal year ending July 31. A and B each have a 50% interest in partnership profits. For its tax year beginning July 1, Year 1, the partnership will be required to retain its tax year since the fiscal year ending June 30 results in the least aggregate deferral of income to the partners. This determination is made as follows:

Test 6/30	Year End	Interest in Partnership Profits	Months for Deferral for 6/30 Year End	Interest × Deferral
Partner A	6/30	.5	0	0
Partner B	7/31	.5	1	.5
Aggregate deferral				.5

Test 7/31	Year End	Interest in Partnership Profits	Months for Deferral for 7/31 Year End	Interest × Deferral
Partner A	6/30	.5	11	5.5
Partner B	7/31	.5	0	0
Aggregate deferral				5.5

---

[14] Code Sec. 706(b); Reg. § 1.706-1(b).

A partnership may have a tax year other than its required tax year if it makes an election to use a 52-53-week tax year that ends with reference to its required tax year or a permitted tax year,[15] or establishes a business purpose for that tax year and obtains approval of the IRS.[16]

The partner's percentage share of partnership net income for a partnership tax year is the ratio of the partner's distributive share of partnership net income for the tax year, to the partnership's net income for the year. If a partner's percentage share of partnership net income for the tax year depends on the amount or nature of partnership income for that year, the partnership must make a reasonable estimate of the amount and nature of its income for the tax year. This estimate must be based on all facts and circumstances known to the partnership as of the first day of the current partnership tax year, and the partnership must then use this estimate in determining the partners' interests in partnership profits for the tax year.[17]

A partnership can apply for approval for a tax year other than its required tax year if it has a business purpose. A partnership may also elect to adopt or change to a tax year other than the year required by the partnership provisions under specified conditions. A partnership or partner may have its annual accounting period end on the same day of the week by adopting a tax year that varies between 52 and 53 weeks. Generally, a partnership that does not have a tax year that conforms to the required tax year rules must change its tax year to one that does conform, or the partners may change their tax years. If a partnership terminates, its tax year ends for all of its partners.

¶ 1005 Transfer of Decedent's Entire Partnership Interest to Spouse

When a partnership agreement designates a spouse of a deceased partner to succeed to the interest of the partner after the partner's death, the spouse is to be regarded as a successor in interest. Therefore, the deceased partner's and the spouse's distributive share of income for the partnership tax year ending within or with the surviving spouse's tax year may be included in a joint return.[18]

> *Example 4:* Decedent is a member of a partnership, which operates on a calendar year. Decedent and her husband file joint returns for calendar years. In the partnership agreement, Decedent designated Husband to succeed to her interest in the partnership upon her death. Decedent, who had withdrawn $10,000 from the partnership before her death, dies on October 20, Year 1. Husband's distributive share of partnership income for the tax year is $5,000. Husband may include $15,000 in income on a joint return with Decedent for Year 1. That part of the $15,000 distributive share attributable to Decedent for the period ending with the date of her death (i.e., $10,000 from January 1 through October 20) is income in respect of a decedent.

When a decedent partner's spouse (or other successor in interest) sells or exchanges his or her entire interest in the partnership, or if his or her entire

---

[15] Code Sec. 444.
[16] Reg. § 1.706-1(b)(2)(ii).
[17] Reg. § 1.706-1(b)(4)(ii)(B).
[18] Reg. § 1.706-1(c)(3)(iii).

interest is liquidated, the partnership tax year is closed on the date of such sale or exchange, or the date of completion of the liquidation, insofar as the spouse (or other successor in interest) is concerned.[19]

¶ 1006 Payments to Deceased Partner's Successor in Interest

The Internal Revenue Code contains specific rules on the treatment of payments made to the estate or other successor in interest of a deceased partner in liquidation of his or her entire partnership interest.[20] The provisions are intended to clarify the extent to which such payments should be regarded as a distribution of the deceased partner's share of the profits, and to what extent they are capital gain from the disposition of the partner's capital interest. It should be remembered that the rules discussed below have no application when the deceased partner's estate (or other successor in interest) continues as a partner in its own right under local law. In such a case, the estate (or other successor in interest) would merely continue to report its distributive share in accordance with the general partnership rules.

The law makes it clear that the gain distinction will be available only to the extent that the payments are for an interest in partnership property. Payments made to a deceased partner's successor in interest in liquidation of his or her entire interest in partnership property are treated as Code Sec. 736(b) payments. Gain or loss with respect to such a partnership distribution is recognized under Code Sec. 731 and taken into account by the recipient for the tax year in which the payments are made.[21]

The treatment of payments that are not made for an interest in the partnership depends upon whether or not they are determined by reference to the income of the partnership. If they are so determined, they are treated under Code Sec. 736(a) as a distributive share to the estate or other successor in interest of the deceased partner. If not, they are treated as guaranteed payments (i.e., payments for services or the use of capital). Thus, if the payments consist of a percentage of partnership income, they are considered to be ordinary income to the deceased partner's successor in interest and reduce the ordinary income of the remaining partners. If they are not so determined, the effect is the same, because they are deductible as business expenses in determining partnership taxable income. In either event, the payment will be treated as ordinary income in the hands of the estate or other successor in interest of the deceased partner.

Payments to the deceased partner's estate (or other successor in interest) for an interest in the partnership's assets are not deductible by the remaining partners because they represent either a distribution or a purchase of the deceased partner's capital interest by the partnership, composed of the remaining partners.

¶ 1007 Allocation of Payments

IRS regulations[22] provide rules for segregating payments that are made in exchange for the interest in partnership property, and treated as distributions

---

[19] Code Sec. 706(c)(2).
[20] Code Sec. 736.
[21] Reg. § 1.736-1(a)(5).
[22] Reg. § 1.736-1(b)(5).

under Code Sec. 736(b), from those that are regarded as a distributive share or as guaranteed payments under Code Sec. 736(a). If a fixed amount (whether or not it is supplemented by additional amounts) is to be received over a fixed number of years, the portion of each payment that is to be treated as having been made for the recipient's share in partnership property will bear the same ratio to the total fixed agreed payment for the tax year (as distinguished from the amount actually received) as the total fixed agreed payments for the interest in property bear to the total agreed payments to be received. The balance is a distributive share, if payable from profits, or a guaranteed payment, if payable without reference to profits. If the total amount received in any one year is less than the amount considered as a distribution of a share in partnership property, any unapplied portion is to be added to the portion of the payments for the following year or years that is to be treated as a distribution of the share of such property.

Example 5: The estate of Taylor, a deceased partner, is entitled to an annual payment of $6,000 for 10 years in exchange for her interest in partnership property. In Year 1, Taylor's estate received only $3,500. In Year 2, it receives $10,000. Of this amount, $8,500 may be treated as a distribution for an interest in partnership property—that is, the $6,000 annual payment for Year 2 and the $2,500 shortage carried over from Year 1. The remaining $1,500 ($10,000 - $8,500) is treated as a guaranteed payment if it is determined and paid without regard to Year 2 profits of the partnership; otherwise, it is treated as a distributive share.

If the payments are not fixed in amount, they are to be treated first as payments for an interest in partnership property to the extent of the value of that interest, and thereafter as payments of a distributive share of profits or guaranteed payments, as the case may be.

In place of the above rules, allocation may be made in any manner to which the estate or other successor in interest and the remaining partners agree, but the total amount allocated to an interest in partnership property is limited to the fair market value of that property on the date of the deceased partner's death.

¶ 1008 Partner Receiving Income in Respect of a Decedent

Payments to the deceased partner's estate (or other successor in interest) that represent a distributive share or a guaranteed payment under the rules explained at ¶ 1007 are treated as income in respect of a decedent.[23] This means that the payment will be taxable to the estate or other successor in interest when received, and the estate tax attributable to the inclusion of the right to such amount in the deceased partner's estate will be allowed as a deduction. Thus, while the deceased partner's estate (or other successor in interest) will be required to include in gross income amounts received from the partnership that are attributable to the value of the decedent's interest in unrealized fees, the recipient will at the same time receive a deduction for the estate tax paid with respect to the inclusion of such rights to income in the decedent's estate.[24]

---

[23] Code Sec. 753; Reg. § 1.753-1(a).   [24] Code Sec. 691.

The estate or other successor in interest of a deceased partner will also be treated as receiving income in respect of a decedent to the extent that amounts are paid by a third person in exchange for rights to future distributive share payments or guaranteed payments.

If a partner dies while receiving payments from the partnership in liquidation of his or her partnership interest, any remaining payments that are guaranteed payments or distributive shares are also treated as income in respect of a decedent.

As noted at ¶ 1001, when a partner dies, the entire portion of the distributive share that is attributable to the period ending with the date of death and that is taxable to the partner's estate (or other successor in interest) constitutes income in respect of a decedent. This rule applies even though that part of the distributive share for the period before death, which the decedent withdrew, is not included in the value of the decedent's partnership interest for estate tax purposes.[25]

Example 6: Survivor and Decedent were equal partners in a business having assets (other than money) worth $40,000 and an adjusted basis of $10,000. Some work of the partnership was almost completed before Decedent's death, and, after Decedent's death, but before the end of the partnership year, payment of $10,000 was made to the partnership for such work.

The partnership agreement provided that, upon the death of one of the partners, all partnership property, including unfinished work, would pass to the surviving partner, and that the surviving partner would pay the estate of the decedent the undrawn balance of his share of partnership earnings to the date of death, plus $10,000 in each of the three years after death.

Decedent's share of earnings to the date of his death was $4,000, of which he had withdrawn $3,000. Decedent's distributive share of partnership income of $4,000 to the date of his death is income in respect of a decedent (although only the $1,000 undrawn at Decedent's death will be reflected in the value of Decedent's partnership interest on the estate tax return).

Assume that the value of Decedent's interest in partnership property at the date of his death was $22,000, composed of the following items: (1) Decedent's one-half share of the assets of $40,000 and (2) $2,000, Decedent's interest in partnership cash. It should be noted that Decedent's $1,000 undrawn share of earnings to the date of his death is not a separate item but will be paid from partnership assets.

Under the partnership agreement, Survivor is to pay Decedent's estate a total of $31,000. The difference of $9,000 between the amount to be paid by Survivor ($31,000) and the value of Decedent's interest in partnership property ($22,000) is treated as a guaranteed payment and, thus, constitutes income in respect of a decedent. However, the $17,000 difference between the $5,000 basis for Decedent's share of the partnership property and its $22,000 value at the date of his death does not constitute income in respect of a decedent.

---

[25] Reg. § 1.753-1(b).

If, before the close of the partnership tax year, Survivor pays Decedent's estate $11,000, of which they agree to allocate $3,000 to the guaranteed payment, Decedent's estate will include $7,000 in its gross income (Decedent's $4,000 distributive share plus $3,000 as a guaranteed payment). The remaining $8,000 of the $11,000 represents a payment for Decedent's partnership interest, all of which is a nontaxable recovery of basis (the estate's basis for the partnership interest is $22,000, the value at the date of Decedent's death, not Decedent's basis of $5,000). In computing the estate tax deduction under Code Sec. 691(c), the $7,000 will be treated as the value for estate tax purposes of such income in respect of a decedent even though only $4,000 ($1,000 of the distributive share not withdrawn, plus $3,000, the guaranteed payment) of this amount can be identified on the estate tax return as part of the partnership interest.

Of the $10,000 collected in each of the next two years, $3,000 would be taxable to the estate as ordinary income, assuming the parties agreed that such amount should be allocated to the guaranteed payment. The remaining $7,000 would represent a payment for Decedent's partnership interest and, again, a nontaxable recovery of basis.

¶ 1009 Partnership Goodwill

Although neither the Code, the regulations, nor the Supreme Court has precisely defined "goodwill," it is often defined as the value of a trade or business that is attributable to the expectancy of continued customer patronage, whether due to the name or reputation of the trade or business or to any other factor. Partnership interests must be valued for tax purposes whenever ownership changes. In valuing a partnership interest, special attention should be given to establishing the value of goodwill, unless its value is established by a partnership agreement.

.01 Payments for Goodwill

Goodwill may be included in the property of the partnership for which the estate or other successor in interest of a decedent partner may receive payment from the partnership (which can result in capital gain instead of ordinary income) under one of two conditions: (1) if the goodwill was bought by the partnership or otherwise acquired in a transaction resulting in a monetary basis to the partnership, in which case a payment for goodwill can be regarded as a payment for partnership property, resulting in capital gain or loss instead of ordinary income or deductions to the extent of the partnership basis; or (2) the payment may be regarded as a payment for partnership property to the extent that it represents a reasonable value of goodwill, if the partnership agreement provides that, upon the death of a partner, the partner's estate or other successor in interest be paid for the partner's share of the goodwill.

The figure for goodwill may be stated in the partnership agreement, or the reasonable amount may be determined at the time of the partner's death. The latter is probably more feasible because a valuation agreed upon at the time of the partnership's formation may have decreased to zero at the time a partner dies if the partnership is unsuccessful, or conversely it may have greatly increased if the partnership is highly successful. The value may be a round sum agreed upon by all of the partners, or it may be determined by use of a formula in the partnership agreement or informally agreed upon by the parties at the time of the death of one of the partners.

It must be emphasized that payments by the partnership for goodwill cannot be treated as payments for an interest in partnership property if the partnership had no basis for goodwill, unless the partnership agreement provides for payment for goodwill to the deceased partner's estate (or other successor in interest). Such payments will be treated as a distributive share of partnership income or as a guaranteed payment only if (1) capital is not a material income-producing factor for the partnership, and (2) the deceased partner was a general partner in the partnership.[26] If these two requirements are not met, payments for goodwill will be treated as made in exchange for property and will not give rise to a deduction or its equivalent for the partnership.

Capital is not a material income-producing factor in a partnership if substantially all of the gross income of the business consists of fees, commissions, or other compensation for personal services performed by individuals. Therefore, doctors, lawyers, dentists, architects and accountants will not be treated as engaging in business in which capital is a material income-producing factor even though they may have a substantial capital investment in professional equipment or in the office where the practice is conducted, as long as such investment is merely incidental to their professional practice.[27]

What if the partnership does have a basis for goodwill acquired by it for valuable consideration? Usually, in order to have a basis, it would have to have been acquired from outside parties, because if it was transferred to the partnership as a contribution by one of the incoming partners, it would have to take as its basis the basis in the hands of the contributing partner, who would have no basis for it unless he or she had acquired it from an outsider for a valuable consideration. Or, the contributing partner may have acquired it by inheritance, having taken over, for instance, a family business. Because the contributing partner's basis for the entire business, including goodwill, would be its value at the date of death of the business's previous owner, here the contributing partner could invoke the formula in Rev. Rul. 68-609 and create a basis for it. If the goodwill had been separately valued for estate or inheritance tax purposes, that value would apply, unless it could be proved to be wrong.

> ***Example 7 :*** Upon the death of his father, Son inherited a hardware store that his father had operated as sole owner. For estate tax purposes, the business was valued at $75,000, which included $25,000 for goodwill. Son formed a partnership with another individual immediately after his father's death, and turned the hardware business over to the partnership. Son's interest in the partnership capital and profits was two-thirds; the other partner had a one-third interest. The partnership agreement stated that the entire $25,000

---

[26] Code Sec. 736(b)(3).   [27] House Committee Report to P.L. 103-66.

¶1009.01

value of goodwill on the partnership books was distributable to Son's estate in case of his death. Six years later when the basis of Son's partnership interest was $80,000, Son died and the business was sold to outside interests for $150,000, of which the estate's share was $100,000, which it received in cash upon dissolution of the partnership. Of the sale price, $45,000 was allocated to goodwill, that having been the amount agreed upon by all parties to the transaction. The $105,000 remainder of the sale price represented the book value of the tangible assets. (There were no liabilities.) Of the $100,000 payment to the estate, $70,000 (× $105,000) represented payment for its interest in tangible assets of the partnership, and $30,000 represented payment for its interest in the goodwill. However, based on the partnership's basis and also on the partnership agreement, only $25,000 of this is regarded as payment for partnership property. Therefore, the estate's $20,000 gain on sale of its interest (the difference between the $100,000 received and the $80,000 basis of its interest) represents ordinary income.

Example 8 : Assume the same facts as in Example 7, except that the partnership agreement provided that a reasonable value be placed by the surviving partner and estate or estates upon the value of goodwill in case of death of either or both of the partners. The agreement also provided that, of such value, the entire $25,000 representing the partnership's basis for the goodwill and ⅔ of any excess value over the $25,000 as determined by the parties should be allocated to Son or Son's estate. Because the reasonable value was determined to be $45,000, of which the share for Son's estate was $25,000 plus ⅔ of $20,000, or a total of $38,333.33, that amount may be regarded as received by the estate for its share of partnership property. Assuming that the estate also received $70,000 as its share of the value of the tangible assets, or a total payment of $108,333.33, it had a gain of $28,333.33, all of which represents ordinary income.

.02 Formula for Valuing Goodwill

For many years, the IRS has sanctioned a formula approach that may be used under certain circumstances to determine the fair market value of a business's intangible assets.[28] This formula approach may be used only if there is no better basis available for determining the fair market value of intangible assets. Under this formula, a percentage return on the average annual value of the tangible assets used in the business is determined by using a period of years (preferably not less than five) immediately prior to the valuation date. The amount of the percentage return on tangible assets, thus determined, is deducted from the average earnings of the business for such period, and the remainder, if any, is considered to be the amount of the average annual earnings from the intangible assets of the business for the period. This amount, capitalized at a percentage of 15% to 20%, is the value of the business's intangible assets.

---

[28] The formula was originally stated in A.R.M. 34, 2 CB 31 (1920), but it has since been updated and is currently restated in Rev. Rul. 68-609, 1968-2 CB 327.

The percentage return on the average annual value of the tangible assets used should be the percentage prevailing in the industry involved at the date of valuation.[29]

¶ 1010 The 754 Election

If a Code Sec. 754 Election is in effect with respect to the transfer of the decedent's interest to his successor, the basis of the partnership's assets will be increased or decreased under Code Sec. 743(b) with respect to the successor by the difference between:

(1) the adjusted basis of the partnership interest in the hands of the successor, and

(2) the successor's proportionate share of the basis of the partnership's assets.

The Code Sec. 754 basis adjustment rule is intended to equalize the partnership's "inside basis" in partnership property and the partners' "outside basis" in their partnership interest. These rules are necessary to alleviate distortions in the timing and character of income or loss for a new partner. Differences between "inside" and "outside" basis arise as a result of several events, including the death of an existing partner, or the purchase of an interest by a new partner.

.01 The Election

Death results in a new outside basis under Code Sec. 1014 equal to the fair market value at the date of death. There is no corresponding basis adjustment for the partnership. Upon a sale or exchange, the outside basis to a purchaser of the partnership interest is that purchaser's purchase price paid for the partnership interest. The basis to the partnership in the underlying property is not impacted by the sale or exchange. Property distributed to a partner may not retain its inside basis to the distributing partner if gain or loss might be recognized by the distributing partner.

The rules providing for a Code Sec. 754 basis adjustment are found in Code Secs. 734(b) and 743(b). The basis adjustments under these sections can be divided into two categories:

(1) Those adjustments made by the partnership,

(2) Those adjustments made by the transferee partner.

If the election is made, the partner or the partnership, depending upon the circumstances, will be able to equalize "inside" and "outside" basis. A Code Sec. 754 Election to adjust the basis of partnership property under Code Sec. 743 must be made by the partnership in a written statement setting forth the election and signed by any one of the partners – presumably, a partner who can bind the partnership in such matters under local law and/or under the partnership agreement.[30] The Regulations provide that the written statement must include the name and address of the electing partnership and a declaration that the partnership elects to apply

---

[29] Rev. Rul. 68-609, 1968-2 CB 327.

[30] Reg. § 1.754-1(b).

both Code Secs. 734(b) and 743(b).[31] The election must be filed with the partnership's return for the taxable year during which the distribution or transfer occurs. The Regulations also provide that once made, the election will apply to all subsequent sales or exchanges, transfers by reason of death, or distributions to partners unless the election is subsequently revoked, which requires the consent of the director of the district in which the partnership's returns are filed.[32]

.02 Termination of the Election

A technical termination terminates a Code Sec. 754 Election. As noted at ¶ 1001, *supra,* a partnership is considered as terminated when either (1) no part of any business, financial operation, or venture of the partnership continues to be carried on by any of its partners in a partnership, or (2) within a 12-month period there is a sale or exchange of 50% or more of the total interest in partnership capital and profits.[33] Thus, a Code Sec. 708(b) Technical Termination can be utilized to revoke a Code Sec. 754 election. This results in the creation of a new partnership that is not currently subject to a Code Sec. 754 election, but may make such election in the future.

.03 Coordination of the 754 Election and Mandatory Basis Adjustment Rules

Regardless of whether the partnership makes a Code Sec. 754 Election, mandatory Code Sec. 743(b) adjustments must be made to the basis of partnership assets if, immediately after the transfer of a partnership interest, the adjusted tax basis of all of the partnership assets exceeds the FMV of the partnership assets by more than $250,000. The mandatory basis adjustment rules and Code Sec. 743(d) are discussed in detail below at ¶ 1011. A taxpayer can avoid the application of the mandatory basis adjustment rules by selling the built-in-loss assets prior to the partner's death. However, careful consideration must be given not only as to whether a partnership should make a Code Sec. 754 election, but also as to the timing of when such an election should be made. For example, a partnership utilizing valuation discounts for its interests should not elect the Code Sec. 754 election in the year of a partner's death, but possibly in a subsequent year to avoid a Code Sec. 743 step down in basis.

¶ 1011 Mandatory Basis Adjustment Rules

Historically, no basis adjustments to partnership property would be made following the transfer of a partnership interest by sale or death of a partner unless the election provided by Code Sec. 754 (relating to optional adjustment to basis of partnership property) was in effect with respect to the partnership.

The American Jobs Creation Act of 2004 revised the rules regarding partnership loss situations. To prevent the transfer of partnership losses, the 2004 law places limits on the use of partnerships to shift or duplicate losses by restricting partnership allocations traceable to built-in loss property and by limiting opportunistic elections not to make partnership basis adjustments under Code Secs. 743 and

---

[31] *Id.*
[32] Reg. § 1.754-1(c).
[33] Code Secs. 706(c)(1) and 708(b)(1).

734 in "substantial" loss situations. There are some exceptions to these rules for investment and securitization partnerships. The specific changes in the law designed to achieve these results are that:

- built-in loss may be taken into account only by the contributing partner, and not by other partners;[34]
- allocations to non-contributing partners are made by assuming that the basis of contributed property is its fair market value at the time of contribution;[35]
- the partnership must make Code Sec. 743 basis adjustments following a transfer of a partnership interest if the partnership has a substantial built-in loss (over $250,000), whether or not a Code Sec. 754 election is in effect;
- property with a substantial built-in loss (over $250,000) is adjusted downward to its fair market value if the contributing partner's partnership interest is transferred or liquidated, whether or not a Code Sec. 754 election is in effect; and
- the partnership must make a Code Sec. 734(b) basis adjustment with respect to any distribution of partnership property with respect to which there is a substantial basis reduction (a downward adjustment of more than $250,000).[36]

The IRS has provided guidance implementing these provisions. Notice 2005-32 generally requires partners and partnerships subject to the new rules to report their required basis adjustments as though an election under Code Sec. 754 had been made. Partnerships that are required to reduce their basis in partnership property following a transfer of a partnership interest must attach an informational statement to their annual returns.[37] The transferee must provide certain information to the partnership within 30 days of the transfer (or if the transfer occurs upon the death of a partner, within one year of the death of the deceased partner).[38] The notice also provides rules implementing the partner-level loss disallowance rule that applies instead of the basis adjustment requirement for electing investment partnerships.

---

[34] Code Sec. 704(c)(1)(C)(i).
[35] Code Sec. 704(c)(1)(C)(ii).
[36] Code Sec. 734(b) and (d).
[37] Reg. § 1.743-1(k)(1).
[38] Reg. § 1.743-1(k)(2).

Chapter 11

Charitable Deduction and Split-Interest Trusts: CRTs and CLTs

¶ 1101 Overview of the Fiduciary Charitable Deduction
¶ 1102 Charitable Contribution Deduction Limited to Sums Paid Out of Gross Income
¶ 1103 Distributions Pursuant to the Terms of the Governing Instrument
¶ 1104 Charitable Deduction for Section 691 IRD Property
¶ 1105 Charitable Contribution Deduction for Distributions from Flow-Through Entities
¶ 1106 Charitable Distributions Not Allowed as Part of Distribution Deduction
¶ 1107 Charitable Contribution Substantiation Requirements *exclude*
¶ 1108 Split-Interest Charitable Trusts—Overview
¶ 1109 Funding of Split-Interest Charitable Trusts
¶ 1110 Annuity and Unitrust Interests
¶ 1111 Charitable Remainder Trusts—Distributions to Beneficiaries
¶ 1112 Charitable Lead Trusts
¶ 1113 CLT Tax Reporting
¶ 1114 CLT Distribution Income Ordering Regulations
¶ 1115 Pooled Income Trusts

¶ 1101 Overview of the Fiduciary Charitable Deduction

The tax law provides special rules regarding the deduction of charitable contributions by an estate or complex trust. Instead of the limited charitable contribution deduction under Code Sec. 170(a) for individual income tax purposes, a complex trust is allowed an *unlimited* deduction. There are other limitations, however, in that the distribution must be made from *gross income*, and the distribution must be directed "pursuant to the terms of the governing instrument."[1] The recipient must be paid for a purpose specified in Code Sec. 170(c)(2)(A). Ordinarily, distributions made to organizations for religious, charitable, scientific, literary, or educational purposes will qualify for the Code Sec. 170(c) charitable deduction. Furthermore, some trusts may be tax-exempt. For example, a split-interest trust that qualifies as a charitable remainder annuity trust or charitable remainder

---

[1] Code Sec. 642(c)(1).

unitrust (CRUT, see ¶ 1110.05) will be exempt from income tax (except with respect to unrelated business taxable income).[2] Additionally, a "pooled income fund" is essentially a common trust fund established and maintained by a charitable organization for its own ultimate benefit, and is allowed to deduct long-term gains set aside for the charitable remainder (see ¶ 1115).[3]

¶ 1102 Charitable Contribution Deduction Limited to Sums Paid Out of Gross Income

Although the deduction for charitable contributions under Code Sec. 642(c) is stated above as being "unlimited," the deduction is in reality unlimited only to the extent that it consists of items includible in the gross income of the estate or trust. In other words, if the contribution consists of items of income that do not enter into the computation of gross income for tax purposes, such as tax-exempt interest, only that portion of the contribution that represents items of gross income is deductible.[4] Thus, for example, if a taxpayer excluded 50% of the gain arising from the sale or exchange of qualified small business stock under Code Sec. 1202(a), Code Sec. 642(c)(4) would prohibit his or her estate from claiming the excluded gain as part of a charitable deduction.

In determining whether charitable contributions include items of income not included in gross income, the governing instrument will control if it specifically provides for the source of payment. In the absence of a specific provision, charitable contributions are deemed to consist of the same proportion of each class of the items of income as the total of each class bears to the total of all classes.

> ***Example 1:*** Rene Rossi transfers property to a trust. $3,000 per year is to be paid out of income to the Divine Word Church while the remainder of the income is to be accumulated for Rossi's son. During the tax year the income was $10,000, consisting of $4,000 derived from rent and $6,000 derived from exempt interest on municipal bonds. The trustee during the year paid $3,000 to the church. Since the trust instrument does not specifically provide for the source of such payment, 30% ($3,000 ÷ $10,000) of each class of the trust's income will be allocated to the charitable contribution. Thus, the charitable contribution consists of 30% of the $4,000 rental income, or $1,200, and 30% of the $6,000 tax-exempt interest, or $1,800. The deduction for the charitable contribution, therefore, is $1,200.

¶ 1103 Distributions Pursuant to the Terms of the Governing Instrument

Code Sec. 642(c) provides a deduction for any distribution of gross income that is "pursuant to the terms of the governing instrument"—the governing instrument must direct payment, and such payment must be traced to income.[5] However, the direction in a trust instrument providing for the source of payment of a charitable contribution (such as "to be paid from an IRA asset first") merely to achieve

---

[2] Code Sec. 664(c), as amended by P.L. 109-432.
[3] Code Sec. 642(c)(3).
[4] Code Sec. 642(c).
[5] *Van Buren v. Commissioner,* 89 TC 1101, 1108-9 (1997).

ordering of income most beneficial to the taxpayer is not effective because the IRS has consistently taken the position that such ordering rules have no "economic effect independent of their tax consequences" if the amount paid to the charity is not dependent upon the type of income it is allocated, and, therefore, any such ordering rules are to be disregarded for federal tax purposes (but see ¶ 1106). For example, a typical ordering provision in a charitable lead trust requires the source of funds payable to charities as directed to minimize income tax consequences to the trust by exhausting higher tax rate income before using nontaxable sources, such as principal or tax-exempt interest (see ¶ 1106). The final regulations, effective April 16, 2012, clarify this stance.[6]

¶ 1104 Charitable Deduction for Section 691 IRD Property

The term "gross income" for purposes of the charitable contributions deduction includes income in respect of a decedent under Code Sec. 691(a)(1). Accordingly, an estate or complex trust will be entitled to a charitable contribution deduction for income in respect of a decedent that is paid for charitable purposes as outlined above.[7]

The IRS has ruled that where, under applicable state law, real property is subject to administration, the income derived therefrom is includible in the gross income of the estate while the estate is under administration; and if, under the terms of the decedent's will, the net income from such property is to be used exclusively for a charitable purpose, it is deductible by the estate under the provisions of Code Sec. 642(c).[8] The deduction described above is allowed instead of, and not in addition to, the deduction for charitable contributions allowed to individuals. The U.S. Supreme Court in *Old Colony Trust Co.*, held that contributions that are discretionary with the trustee are also deductible if the discretionary payments were made "pursuant to" the terms of the trust agreement.[9] However, where the trust instrument did not authorize the trustee to make the payments in question, the Eighth Circuit found the preceding holding to be inapplicable.[10]

¶ 1105 Charitable Contribution Deduction for Distributions from Flow-Through Entities

As discussed above, distributions made directly to charity are only deductible if the governing instrument authorizes the trustee to make charitable contributions. However, the IRS provided an exception to this rule for trusts owning an interest in flow-through entities. A trust may claim a deduction for its distributive share of a charitable contribution made by a partnership from the partnership's gross income even though the trust's governing instrument does not authorize the trustee to make charitable contributions.[11] In a Field Service Advice, the IRS determined that a trust without specific authority in its governing instrument to make charitable contributions can claim a Code Sec. 642(c) charitable deduction for its distributive

---

[6] T.D. 9582, IRB 2012-18, 868.
[7] Reg. § 1.642(c)-3(a).
[8] Rev. Rul. 57-133, 1957-1 CB 200.
[9] *Old Colony Trust Co.*, 37-1 USTC ¶ 9301, 301 US 379 (1937).
[10] *J.A. Love Charitable Foundation*, 83-2 USTC ¶ 9441, 710 F2d 1316 (8th Cir. 1983).
[11] Rev. Rul. 2004-5, 2004-1 CB 295.

share of a contribution made by a flow-through entity, a partnership, in which it had an interest.[12] The FSA cited the *Lowenstein* and *Bluestein* cases, which came to a similar result for estates.[13] This treatment for a trust's distributive share of contributions made to charities by a flow-through entity has now been officially confirmed as the Service's position in a public ruling. In this case, contributions were made to a charity by a partnership that was partially owned by a trust. Even though the governing document did not make provision for trust distributions to charity, the deduction was allowed under Code Sec. 642(c), since the payment by the partnership to the charity was made out of its gross income. Thus, a trust's deduction for its distributive share of a charitable contribution made by a partnership will be allowed even if the trust's governing instrument does not authorize the trustee to make charitable contributions.

¶ 1106 Charitable Distributions Not Allowed as Part of Distribution Deduction

The charitable distributions of an estate or trust are deducted from taxable income only under Code Sec. 642(c). For that reason, charitable distributions are specifically disallowed as a deduction under Code Sec. 661, that is, as part of the distribution deduction. Also, such charitable distributions are not to be treated as amounts distributed for purposes of determining the amounts includible in the income of the beneficiaries under Code Sec. 662.[14]

Furthermore, effective April 16, 2012, Treasury issued final regulations regarding the ordering rules for determining the sources of funds that are to be paid, permanently set aside or used for a charitable purpose from trusts and estates under Code Sec. 642(c).[15] The final regulations override ordering provisions in a governing instrument or under local law that do not have "independent economic effect" aside from income tax purposes. The final regulations focus mainly on instances where the charity is to be the "lead" beneficiary and non-charitable beneficiaries are to receive the remainder. A typical ordering provision in a trust requires the source of funds payable to charities as directed to minimize income tax consequences to the trust or the estate by exhausting higher tax rate income before using nontaxable sources, such as principal. The IRS has clarified its position that these ordering rules have no economic effect, particularly for CLTs, and therefore will not be respected for federal tax. (CLTs are discussed in detail at ¶ 1112.) An example of a charitable bequest in a governing instrument that likely would have independent economic effect would state that the trustee shall distribute so much of the IRD property, not to exceed $X dollars; —thus, there is a bequest of $X dollars, but only and to the extent of specific property; if there was no IRD property, there would be no bequest.

¶ 1107 Charitable Contribution Substantiation Requirements

Charitable contributions of $250 or more must be substantiated in order to be deductible. This is done by means of a written contemporaneous acknowledgement

---

[12] FSA 200140080 (Oct. 5, 2001).
[13] *Lowenstein v. Commissioner*, 12 TC 694 (1949); *Bluestein v. Commissioner*, 15 TC 770 (1950).
[14] Code Sec. 663(a)(2); Reg. § 1.663(a)-2.
[15] T.D. 9582, IRB 2012-18, 868.

from the donee organization that states (1) the amount of cash and a description of property other than cash contributed, (2) whether the donee organization provided any goods or services in exchange for the contribution, (3) a description of such goods or services, and (4) if the donee organization provides any intangible religious benefits, a statement to that effect.[16] In addition, if the deduction for a property donation exceeds $500, a taxpayer must include with its return for the tax year in which the contribution is made a written description of the donated property[17] and such other required information as the IRS may prescribe in regulations.

Contributions of noncash property, such as land, antiques, and art objects, pose special problems. For noncash contributions to charity made after June 3, 2004, the American Jobs Creation Act of 2004 increased the reporting requirements. A charitable deduction under Code Sec. 170(a) will be denied to any individual, partnership, or corporation that fails to meet specific appraisal and documentation requirements.[18] An exception exists if the taxpayer fails to meet these requirements due to reasonable cause, and not because of willful neglect.[19] For purposes of determining the threshold values for the various reporting requirements, all similar items of noncash property, whether donated to a single donee or multiple donees, are aggregated and treated as a single property donation.[20]

For donated property valued at more than $5,000, the taxpayer must include with its return for the tax year in which the contribution is made whatever information about the property and about the qualified appraisal of that property that the IRS prescribes by regulations.[21] If the contributions are valued at $500,000 or more, then the qualified appraisal must be attached to the return when filed.[22] Please note that for property valued at $5,000 or more but less than $500,000, there is no change in the reporting requirements from those currently established under Reg. § 1.170A-13(c), but the door is left open for the IRS to amend this regulation and these reporting requirements.

A charitable contribution for the year of payment is deductible only to the extent to which it exceeds the value of goods or services received by the donor in exchange for the contribution. This is the case even when such goods or services are not available to the donor until a subsequent year. However, a donor who has properly rejected a benefit offered by a charitable organization may claim a deduction in the full amount of the charitable contribution, and the written acknowledgment need not reflect the value of the rejected benefit. A charitable organization may use any reasonable methodology to determine the fair market value of goods or services given in exchange for a charitable contribution.[23]

¶ 1108 Split-Interest Charitable Trusts—Overview

Split-Interest Charitable Trusts are exempt organizations operated exclusively for charitable and other purposes described in Code Sec. 501(c)(3) that combine

---

[16] Code Sec. 170(f)(8)(B); Reg. § 1.170A-13(f)(2).
[17] Code Sec. 170(f)(11)(B).
[18] Code Sec. 170(f)(11).
[19] Code Sec. 170(f)(11)(A)(ii)(II).
[20] Code Sec. 170(f)(11)(F).
[21] Code Sec. 170(f)(11)(C).
[22] Code Sec. 170(f)(11)(D).
[23] T.D. 8690, 1997-1 CB 68.

income, gift and estate tax efficiency with charitable giving. These "split-interest" trusts function as a conduit to fulfill an individual's charitable intentions while providing for assets to pass to the individual's beneficiaries with minimal gift tax consequences—thus, the beneficial interest is split between an individual and charity. The charitable interest must be a charity approved by the IRS and can be a family foundation or donor-advised fund.

Split-interest charitable trusts are irrevocable and may be created inter vivos (during lifetime) or testamentary (upon death). The duration is a term of years or the length of one or more lives. Depending on the individual's goals, charitable *remainder* trusts provide for initial payments to individual beneficiaries with the remainder passing to charity, and, charitable *lead* trusts provide for initial payments to charity with the remainder passing to designated beneficiaries. Payments during the term of years are typically annuities (fixed amount) or unitrust (fixed percentage) payments, but charitable remainder trusts may be income only, or a combination. Where the objective is to maximize wealth transfers to individuals, or noncharitable beneficiaries, charitable remainder trusts are typically best suited to *low* interest rate environments while charitable lead trusts are typically suited to *high* interest rate environments.

.01 Grantor v. Non-Grantor Trust Status

A charitable *remainder* trust may not be a grantor type trust. However, a charitable *lead* trust may be either a grantor or non-grantor trust. In fact, the only way for a grantor to receive a charitable deduction for establishing a charitable lead trust is to create a grantor trust.

.02 Charitable Remainder Trust (CRT)

A charitable remainder trust (CRT) is a type of split-interest trust wherein a taxpayer transfers property to the trust with the provision that the income interests of the trust are to be paid to himself or another for a specified or determinable period of time. When that period of time expires, the interests in the trust, both corpus and income, are devoted to a qualified charitable organization exempt from taxes. The transferor is entitled to a charitable contribution deduction for the value of that portion of the interest that is estimated to be given to the charity. There are two types of charitable remainder trusts under the present tax laws: the annuity trust (CRAT) and the unitrust (CRUT).

A charitable remainder annuity trust (CRAT) is a trust from which a sum certain or specified amount (which is not less than five percent of the initial net fair market value of all property placed in trust) is to be paid annually to noncharitable income beneficiaries.

A charitable remainder unitrust (CRUT) is a trust that specifies that the noncharitable income beneficiary or beneficiaries are to receive annual payments based on a fixed percentage (which is not less than five percent) of the net fair market value of the trust's assets as determined each year.

¶1108.01

.03 Charitable Lead Trust (CLT)

A charitable lead trust (CLT) is a type of split-interest trust wherein a taxpayer transfers property to the trust with the provision that the income interests of the trust are to be paid to a charity for a specified or determinable period of time. When that period of time expires, the interests in the trust, both corpus and income, either revert to the taxpayer (or his estate) or to another party. The transferor is entitled to a charitable contribution deduction for the value of that portion of the property that is given to the charity.

A charitable lead annuity trust (CLAT) is a trust in which a settlor transfers an annuity interest in the trust assets to a charity, with the remainder going to a noncharitable beneficiary, generally a child or grandchild of the transferor. The annuity interest may be for a term of years, for the life of one person, or for the joint lives of two persons. The settlor receives a charitable deduction for the present value of the annuity interest.

A charitable lead unitrust (CLUT) is a trust in which a settlor transfers a gift in trust of a unitrust interest to a charity, followed by a noncharitable remainder interest.

.04 Initial Interest: Annuity or Unitrust

The lead interest in a charitable trust is either an annuity or unitrust amount. An annuity is a fixed sum or a fixed percentage of the *initial* fair market value of the trust determined with reference to the IRS actuarial tables. A unitrust amount is a fixed percentage of the fair market value of the trust determined *annually* on the same date.

The selection of which form to use will depend on the grantor's intent. At low payout rates, the remainder interest is typically greater. At higher pay out rates, the remainder interest is typically smaller. However, many other factors will affect the selection and the value of the remainder interest, such as the term of the trust, the anticipated growth rate of the assets, income, the age of the grantor, etc.

.05 Additional Contributions to Unitrust, Not to Annuity Trust

Because an annuity amount is fixed on the date of creation, additional contributions are prohibited. With unitrusts, additional contributions are allowed because the trust is revalued each year to determine the unitrust amount.

If a charitable organization, particularly a private foundation, is an income beneficiary, there will be specific limitations on the amount of the deduction available to the grantor, either 30% or 20% of the grantor's adjusted gross income, depending on the type of property contributed.[24] In general, however, the grantor should be able to spread the excess deduction over five years.[25]

.06 Definition of Trust Income

The term "income," when not preceded by the words "taxable," "distributable," "undistributed net," or "gross," means the amount of income of the trust for the

---

[24] Code Sec. 170(b)(1)(B).   [25] Code Sec. 170(d)(1)(A).

taxable year determined under the terms of the governing instrument and applicable local law.[26] Under most states' laws, which have adopted the Uniform Income and Principal Act, "income" includes interest, dividends, rents, royalties, and the discount element of original issue discount obligations. Unless otherwise defined, income does not include capital gains. Trust provisions that depart fundamentally from local law in determining income are not recognized for federal tax purposes.[27]

For purposes of determining the unitrust amount for a net income unitrust, discussed below, state law typically provides that expenses incurred in the administration, management or preservation of trust property, and all expenses reasonably incurred by the trustee are charges against trust income. Regular trustee compensation is generally charged in equal portions against income and principal.

The typical presumption under most states' laws that capital gains are allocated to trust accounting principal may be altered by the trust agreement. By allocating realized gains to income, the grantor can generate a large amount of trust income by selling appreciated assets. This can accelerate unitrust makeup distributions to the noncharitable beneficiary, generally to the detriment of the remainder beneficiary. In 1997, the IRS changed the Regulations to limit the allocation of proceeds attributable to pre-contribution gains to trust principal in order for the trust to qualify as a charitable remainder unitrust, so that only post-contribution gains can be allocated to income.[28]

¶ 1109 Funding of Split-Interest Charitable Trusts

The creation of, or addition to, a charitable trust may entitle the donor or settlor of the trust to an estate tax deduction or an income tax deduction.

.01 Current 7520 Rate and Two Months Preceding

The applicable federal (or discount) rate and payment frequency adjustments by which remainder interest amounts are calculated is based on 120% of the Applicable Federal Mid-term Rate (Code Sec. 7520 Rate) rounded to the nearest two-tenths of 1%. The regulations provide that if any part of the property interest transferred qualifies for an income tax charitable deduction under Code Sec. 170(c), an election may be made to compute the present value of the interest transferred by use of the Code Sec. 7520 interest rate for the month during which the interest is transferred or the Code Sec. 7520 interest rate component for either of the two months preceding the month during which the interest is transferred.[29]

Mortality tables are important in computing the present value of an annuity trust or a unitrust. By statute, mortality tables must be updated every ten years. The mortality tables effective for gifts after April 30, 1989 were based on the 1980 census. Mortality rates effective for gifts after April 30, 1999 are based on the 1990 census. On April 30, 2009 the IRS released an updated mortality table for use in computing (among other things) the charitable deduction arising from a contribution to a charitable remainder trust, charitable lead trust, charitable gift annuity, or pooled-income fund where the term of the agreement is measured by one or more

---

[26] Code Sec. 643(b).
[27] Reg. § 1.643(b)-1.
[28] Reg. § 1.664-3(a)(1)(i)(b)(3).
[29] Reg. § 1.7520-2(a)(2).

lives. The new table, Table 2000CM, replaces Table 90CM and prior tables. The newer tables project a longer life expectancy for younger beneficiaries. IRS Publication 1457, "Actuarial Valuations" includes examples of how to compute the factors for annuities, life estates and remainders. IRS Publication 1458 provides factors for computing unitrust payments and related examples.

.02 Charitable Deduction Present Value

For income tax purposes, the amount that may be deductible by the taxpayer for a charitable remainder trust is the present value of the remainder interest. This amount depends on a variety of factors: the net fair market value of the contribution, whether the format is an annuity or a unitrust, whether the trust term is based on the lives of one or more individuals or a term of years, the annual annuity rate or payout rate, payment frequency, whether the payments are at the beginning or end of the payment period, the applicable federal rate, and the applicable factors from IRS tables. The higher the Code Sec. 7520 interest rate, the larger the charitable contribution deduction for a charitable remainder trust.[30] How much the remainder beneficiary will actually receive depends on growth, income and interest rates attributable to the property, and the term of the trust.

The present value of the lead interest will likely need to be reported on a taxpayer's gift tax return for the year of the gift.

For charitable remainder trusts, similar factors for annuity trusts and unitrusts generally produce different deductions. An annuity trust measured by the life of one or more individuals results in higher income tax deductions at higher annuity rates and younger ages than a unitrust with similar payout rates and ages. But as the annuity rate and unitrust payout rate near the AFR and the income recipient's gets older, the deduction for a unitrust is larger than the deduction for an annuity trust. For CRTs, the value of the lead interest will need to be reported on a taxpayer's gift tax return for the year of the gift, identifying the beneficiaries. The remainder interest will be reported for the charitable gift tax deduction.

For testamentary CRTs, the value of the assets are includible in the decedent's estate for estate tax purposes, but the executor can take a charitable deduction on the federal estate tax return.

For a charitable lead trust that is a grantor trust, the calculation of the annuity or unitrust amount that may be deductible will be similar, except that the charitable deduction will be based on the present value of lead interest, not the remainder interest. For CLTs, the value of the lead interest if the fair market value less the value of the annuity or unitrust interest. Note that for a grantor charitable lead trust, the value of the remainder interest passing to individual beneficiaries will need to be reported on a taxpayer's gift tax return for the year of the gift and, for grantor CLTs, the lead interest will be reported to take advantage of the charitable gift tax deduction.

---

[30] Code Sec. 7520(a); Regs. §§ 20.7520-2(b), 301.9100-8(a)(1).

For testamentary CLTs, the value of the assets are includible in the decedent's estate for estate tax purposes and the then present value of the lead interest may be deducted on the federal estate tax return.

¶ 1110 Annuity and Unitrust Interests

Whenever there is a noncharitable income beneficiary of a trust, gifts of remainder interests qualify for a charitable contribution deduction only if the trust is a charitable remainder annuity trust (CRAT) or a charitable remainder unitrust (CRUT).[31] Charitable contribution deductions are denied for gifts of remainder interests in all other types of trusts. However, if the donor gives all the interests in a trust to charity, it will not be a split-interest trust, and the above rules do not apply, and a deduction is allowable.

One reason CRTs are popular, apart from satisfying donative intent, is to convert low yield, appreciated assets into a payment stream to the grantor or beneficiaries named by the grantor and avoid or delay the recognition of capital gain. As long as there is no prearranged sale agreement for illiquid assets in funding the CRT, the grantor should not recognize gain on the sale.[32]

The IRS has published sample forms of CRTs. Some of the requirements for qualified CRTs include:

- The income interest must be a sum certain;
- No restrictions limiting investments so income is a reasonable amount;
- The grantor must be a single individual or entity (i.e., one donor);
- At least one income beneficiary must be a "person" for income tax purposes;
- The trustee must be able to name a qualified charity as the remainder beneficiary if a named charity no longer qualifies;
- The trust must be exclusively a CRT from inception;
- The trust agreement must include prohibitions against violating all private foundation excise tax rules;
- A CRT must not be a grantor trust;
- Valuation of unmarketable assets must be performed exclusively by an independent trustee or a qualified appraiser;
- The present value of the charitable remainder interest must be at least 10% of the net fair market value of such property transferred in trust on the date of transfer;
- A fixed annuity percentage must be no less than 5% of the fair market value of the trust on contribution and no more than 50%;
- There must be at least a 5% probability that assets will be remaining in the trust after the lead interests terminate; and
- The appraisal of unmarketable assets must be undertaken by an independent trustee.

---

[31] Code Sec. 664; Reg. §§ 1.664-1, 1.664-2, and 1.664-3. [32] IRS Letter Ruling 9452026.

.01 Sum Certain Annuity or Fixed Percentage Unitrust

A charitable remainder trust (CRT) provides for specific distributions to at least one or more persons (and may include a 170(c) organization), at least annually, of a sum certain which is not less than 5% (but no more than 50%) of the initial net fair market value of the trust property (charitable remainder annuity trust), or 5% (but no more than 50%) of the net fair market value of trust assets valued annually (charitable remainder unitrust), with the remainder passing to qualified charities at the last beneficiary's death.

The payout rate is integral to the calculation of the present value of the remainder interest, which the amount that establishes the charitable deduction for the donor. For CRTs created after July 1997, the present value must be no less than 10% of the amount transferred to the trust.[33]

An annuity trust is a trust from which a sum certain or a specified amount is to be paid to the income beneficiary.[34] The above specified amount (not less than 5% or more than 50%) of the initial net fair market value of all property placed in trust, and it must be paid at least annually to the income beneficiary. Furthermore, the value of the charitable remainder interest must be at least 10% of the initial net fair market value of all of the property placed in trust. There are several provisions designed to provide relief to trusts that do not meet the "10-percent" test. No contributions can be made to a CRAT after the initial contribution, and the governing instrument must contain a prohibition against future contributions.

A unitrust is a trust that specifies that the income beneficiary is to receive annual payments based on a fixed percentage of the net fair market value of the trust's assets as determined each year.[35] The fixed percentage cannot be less than five percent or more than 50% of the net fair market value of the trust's assets for the year. However, a qualified CRUT may provide for the distribution each year of five percent of the net fair market value of its assets or the amount of the trust income, whichever is lower. For this purpose, trust income excludes capital gains, and trust assets must be valued annually. This payment requirement may not be discretionary with the trustee. Additional contributions can be made to a unitrust. For most transfers in trust, the value of the charitable remainder interest with respect to each contribution to the unitrust must be at least 10% of the net fair market value of such contributed property as of the date the property is contributed to the trust. If an additional contribution would cause the trust to fail the "10-percent" remainder test, then the contribution will be treated as a transfer to a separate trust under regulations. Other provisions may provide relief to trusts that fail to meet the "10-percent" test.

CRATs and CRUTs cannot have noncharitable remainder interests. The remainder interests must pass to a charity upon the termination of the last income interest, and the trust instrument must contain a provision that determines how the final payment of a specified distribution is to be made. However, a charitable trust may make certain limited "qualified gratuitous" transfers of qualified employer

---

[33] Code Sec. 664(d)(1)(D) and 664(d)(2)(D).
[34] Code Sec. 664(d)(1); Reg. §§ 1.664-1 and 1.664-2.
[35] Code Sec. 664(d)(2); Reg. §§ 1.664-1 and 1.664-3.

securities to an employee stock ownership plan (ESOP) without adversely affecting the status of the charitable remainder trust.

To avoid the possible disqualification of a charitable remainder trust due to a surviving spouse's right of election against the grantor spouse's estate under state law, the IRS created a safe harbor requiring the surviving spouse to irrevocably waive the right.[36] However, until further guidance is published, the IRS will disregard the existence of a right of election without requiring a waiver, but only if the surviving spouse does not exercise the right.[37]

There may be more than one noncharitable income beneficiary, either concurrently or successively, and the income interest may be a life estate or for a term of years not in excess of 20 years. However, a contingency clause may be placed in the trust instrument providing that the noncharitable interest is to terminate and the charitable remainder interest is to be accelerated upon the happening of an event, such as the remarriage of the noncharitable beneficiary.[38] The income beneficiary can receive only a specified or fixed amount from the trust, and the trustee cannot have additional power to invade corpus or to alter, amend, or revoke the trust for the benefit of the noncharitable income beneficiary. The trustee cannot be restricted from investing in income-producing assets.[39]

A charitable remainder trust is not an eligible S corporation shareholder.[40]

.02 CRAT Payment

1. Required payment of annuity amount not less often than annually and may be paid within a reasonable time which is not after the date the trustee is required to file Form 5227, Split-Interest Trust Information Return, including extensions.[41]
2. Trust must provide for reallocation of sum certain if valuation is adjusted.
3. Permissible recipients must be named persons, at least one of which is not a 170(c) organization, who must be living at the creation of the trust. If the trust is for a term of years, the recipients may be a class of people, who must be in existence at the creation of the trust.
4. Trustee may not have the power to alter the amount payable to a named person if the power would cause the person to be the owner.
5. Trust may not be subject to a power to invade, alter, amend or revoke for the beneficial use of a person other than the 170(c) organization. The grantor may retain a power exercisable by will to revoke or terminate the interest of an individual recipient (but such power may cause inclusion in the grantor's estate).
6. Trust duration and annuity amount must be paid beginning with first year of the trust and continues for the life or lives of named individual(s) or a term of years not to exceed 20 years. The period may not last longer than the lives of the recipients in being at the creation of the trust.

---

[36] Rev. Proc. 2005-24, 2005-1 CB 909.
[37] Notice 2006-15, 2006-1 CB 501.
[38] Code Sec. 664(f).
[39] Reg. § 1.664-1(a)(3).
[40] Rev. Rul. 92-48, 1992-1 CB 301.
[41] Reg. § 1.664-2(a)(1)(i)(c).

7. At the end of the term, the entire corpus must be transferred to or for the use of one or more 170(c) organizations or retained for such use.

8. No additional contribution may be made after initial creation.

9. A gift to charitable remainder annuity trusts, where the term of the trust is measured by the life of an individual, will only qualify for income, gift and estate tax deductions if there is less than 5% probability that trust assets will be exhausted before reaching the remainder charitable beneficiary.

10. Fair market value of the remainder interest is net fair market value less present value of the annuity and the valuation date is the date assets are transferred to the trust. If the election is made to use the 7520 rate of the previous two months, the month so selected is the valuation date for purposes of determining the interest rate and mortality tables. If the CRAT is created on death, valuation date is the date of death or alternate valuation date as provided in Code Sec. 2032 and may be within the two months earlier.

.03 CRUT Payment

There are several options under Reg. § 1.664-3 for charitable remainder unitrusts (CRUTs). The standard option requires the trustee to distribute an amount equal to at least 5% of the annual value of trust assets. Trust assets must be revalued annually to determine that amount. If income is not sufficient to make up the amount, trust corpus must be used to make up the difference. The annual revaluation allows the grantor to make additional gifts to the unitrust, unlike CRATs which do not allow additional contributions.

A CRUT may include an optional provision that requires the trustee to pay the lesser of the unitrust amount and trust income.[42] If the trustee pays an amount that is less than the unitrust amount, the trustee may be granted the power to make up deficiencies from prior years by paying out excess income earned in a current year. Neither CRATs nor CLTs have this option. This type of CRUT is referred to as a NIMCRUT, or net income with makeup provision.

In a Flip-CRUT, the trust agreement may provide that a trust may start out as a NIMCRUT but later flip to a straight CRUT. This allows a grantor to fund a CRUT with a low-income unmarketable asset and allow the trustee to take time for either the asset to mature and/or be sold, at which time there will be sufficient income to pay a full unitrust amount. The triggering event, however, must be beyond the control of the trustee. Permissible triggers include a birth, death, marriage, or the sale of unmarketable assets. The sale of marketable assets is not a permissible trigger. The conversion takes place as of the beginning of the tax year following the triggering event and any makeup amount is forfeited.[43]

---

[42] Reg. § 1.664-3(a)(1)(i)(b).

[43] Reg. § 1.664-3(a)(1)(i)(c)(3).

.04 Division of Trust

The IRS has provided guidelines for dividing a CRAT or a CRUT into two or more separate and equal trusts without violating the charitable remainder trust requirements.[44]

.05 Taxation

A charitable remainder annuity trust (CRAT) or a charitable remainder unitrust (CRUT) is generally exempt from income tax.[45] However, if a CRAT or CRUT has unrelated business taxable income (UBTI), it is subject to a 100-percent excise tax on its UBTI, but will retain its tax-exempt status. The excise tax is treated as paid from corpus, and trust income that is UBTI is income of the trust for purposes of determining the character of distributions made to beneficiaries.[46] The tax is reported on Form 4720, which must be filed by the due date for Form 5227. The rule preventing the IRS from filing an additional deficiency notice once a taxpayer files a Tax Court petition challenging the deficiency also applies to this tax. In addition to the tax on UBTI, a charitable remainder trust may be subject to the income and excise taxes imposed on private foundations.

.06 Tax Reporting

A CRAT or CRUT does not file Form 1041, but instead is required to file Form 5227. In addition, the fiduciary of a CRAT or CRUT may be required to file other returns regarding the excise tax on unrelated business taxable income, and the excise taxes on private foundations that apply to charitable remainder trusts. Form 5227 must generally be filed on or before the 15th day of the fourth month following the close of the tax year of the trust.[47]

Form 1041, U.S. Fiduciary Income Tax Return, and related Schedule K-1 will be required to report the income tax consequences of distributions to the beneficiaries of the annuity or unitrust payments.

Form 1041-B, reporting of unrelated business taxable income (UBTI), is no longer required and is replaced by Form 5227 and Form 4720.

Form 5227, Split-Interest Trust Information Return. A copy of the trust instrument accompanied by a certification of its conformity to the original must be submitted with the initial Form 5227 of a CRT. All taxable split-interest trusts, which includes all qualified and grantor charitable lead trusts, are treated as private foundations under Code Sec. 4947 and the IRS requires this form to be filed for them.

Other filing requirements may include:

- Form 56, Notice Concerning Fiduciary Relationship.
- Form 8283, Noncash Charitable Contributions. The CRT trustee must acknowledge receipt of assets from the donor (greater than $500) in section of Form 8283 which is then attached to the donor's 1040 to claim the charitable

---

[44] Rev. Rul. 2008-41, 2008-2 CB 170.
[45] Code Sec. 664(c); Reg. § 1.664-1.
[46] Reg. § 1.664-1(c).
[47] Rev. Proc. 83-32, 1983-1 CB 723.

deduction. The donor is required to support the calculation of the present value of the remainder interest.

- Form 8282, Donee Information Return. If a contributed asset is sold within three years of the gift, Form 8282 must be filed to report the sale price within 125 days of the sale.
- Form 8868, Application for Extension of Time to File an Exempt Organization Return, provides a three-month automatic extension of time to file with an optional three-month extension for cause.
- Form 4720, Return of Certain Excise Taxes on Charities and Other Persons. This form is used to report the UBTI and related excise tax in any year the tax is due. Also, because a CRT is subject to private foundation rules regarding self-dealing with a disqualified person, this form is used to report the act and compute the excise tax due.
- Form 709, U.S. Gift (and Generation Skipping Transfer) Tax Return, will be required to report gifts of present interests to the beneficiaries and to claim the charitable deduction for gift tax purposes. If a noncharitable beneficiary may be a skip person, the GST tax will apply to related distributions, and therefore, this tax return can be used to allocate a portion of the grantor's GST exemption to that portion of the trust allocable to the skip person.

Finally, some states require CRTs to register as charitable trusts with the state Attorney General and the Attorney General of those states also have reporting requirements in addition to any state income tax reporting requirements.

¶ 1111 Charitable Remainder Trusts—Distributions to Beneficiaries

.01 Income Beneficiary

At least one income beneficiary must not be a 170(c) organization. A beneficiary may be a "person" as defined in Code Sec. 7701(a)(1), which includes an individual, trust, estate, association, company, or corporation.

Only an individual or an organization described in Code Sec. 170(c) may be named as the income recipient of a trust payable for the life of an individual. If an individual receives an amount for life, it must be solely for his life. In the case of an amount payable for a term of years, the length of the term must be ascertainable with certainty at the time of creation of the trust.

If the income beneficiary is an entity other than an individual, the duration of the trust is limited to 20 years. In the case of a class which includes individuals, all of the individuals must be living and ascertainable when the trust is created unless the trust is limited to a term of years rather than a measuring life.

If the charitable remainder trust is measured by a term of years, it can make distributions to a trust without restriction. If, however, the charitable remainder trust is measured by the life of an individual, payments to a trust on that individual's behalf will be allowed only when that individual is incompetent.

If a charitable organization, particularly a private foundation, is an income beneficiary, certain matters must be addressed in the trust agreement (e.g., Code Sec. 4943 relating to excess business holdings and Code Sec. 4947(b)(3) regarding jeopardizing investments).[48]

.02 Remainder Beneficiary

The remainder beneficiary may be a public charity, a private foundation or a donor advised fund, or some combination thereof. The grantor may retain the right to change the charitable remainder beneficiaries, as long as the substitutions are qualified charities.[49] On creation of the trust, there must be at least a 5% probability that assets will be available to the remainder beneficiary when the trust terminates.

.03 Trust Term

The term of the trust may be based on a measuring life or lives or a term of years. The character of the income beneficiaries will determine which term may be applicable.

Common forms of measuring terms for payments to recipients include: (1) Payments for the life or one or more individuals until the death of the last individual; (2) Payments to one or more persons must not exceed twenty years, if a term of a years is selected; (3) Payments for the longer of the life of one or more individuals and a guaranteed term of years; (4) Payments for the shorter of a term of years (no more than 20) or the life of one or more individuals; and (5) Payments for the life of one or more individuals, followed by a class of recipients measured by the shorter of their lives or a term of years (no more than 20) that begins at the death of the life recipients.

.04 Valuation of the Remainder Interest

All of the above factors are taken into account to value the remainder interest. For an annuity trust, Table S is used to compute the annuity factor and Table K is used to adjust the factor for payment frequency, if applicable. For a unitrust, Table F provides the payout rate factor based on the payment period, number of months between the valuation date and payment date and the AFR. Then Table D is used to interpolate that factor for a term certain, if applicable, or Table U is used interpolate the Table F factor for a life or lives. These Tables are contained in Reg. § 1.664-4 and are used to determine the present value of the remainder interest.

.05 Assets to Consider for Funding a CRT

Assets having a low basis, which if sold by the donor, would result in significant gain are excellent for funding CRTs, since the CRT will not incur capital gains on the sale. Cash and publicly traded securities are useful to fund CRTs. Closely held businesses or other difficult to value assets may not be advisable to fund a charitable remainder unitrust, unless a sale is anticipated shortly after funding, because trust assets must be revalued each year.

---

[48] See IRS Letter Rulings 9323039 and 200108035.

[49] Rev. Ruls. 76-7, 1976-1 CB 179, and 76-8, 1976-1 CB 179.

Funding a CRT with S corporation stock will immediately terminate the subchapter S status of the S-corporation because a CRT is not an eligible shareholder under Code Sec. 1361(c). CRTs cannot qualify as either a Qualified Subchapter S Trust (QSST) under Code Sec. 1361(d) or an Electing Small Business Trust (ESBT) under Code Sec. 1361(e).[50]

Assets that secure a debt should be avoided, as recognition of income may result from the transfer and the transfer could result in conversion to grantor trust status, which would disqualify the CRT. Great care should be used to fund a CRT with incentive stock options.

Further, a CRT should not be used to pay an existing pledge amount.[51] However, it is unclear whether a grantor who promises to create a CRT in exchange, for example, for a named endowment to a specific charity would be an acceptable method of circumventing the self-dealing prohibition of Section 4941 relating to private foundations and CRTs.

.06 Ordering Rules of Distributions

The governing instrument or local law controls the allocation of the trust accounting income rules. However, for federal income tax purposes, the ordering rules for distributions from CRTs consist of four tiers, with each tier having sub-tiers.[52] In general, the distributions are allocated pro-rata among the beneficiaries according each beneficiary's income interest, beginning with the highest rate class of tax and ending with the lowest class. Reg. § 1.664-1(d)(viii) contains numerous examples of these rules. Items within the ordinary income and capital gains categories are assigned to different subcategories based on the federal income tax rate applicable to each type of income within the category. Categories of income that are taxed at the same rate can be combined into a single class if the tax rate will not change in the future. If the tax rate is temporary, then the categories must be maintained as separate groups.[53]

> a. *Ordinary Income.* First, ordinary income is to be distributed to the extent of the sum of the trust's ordinary income for the taxable year and any undistributed ordinary income for prior years. Any ordinary loss for the current year shall be used first to reduce undistributed ordinary income for prior years, and any excess shall be carried forward indefinitely to reduce ordinary income for future years. For purposes of this section, the amount of current and prior years' income shall be computed without regard to net operating losses provided by Code Secs. 172 or 642(d).
>
> b. *Capital Gain.* Second, capital gain is to be distributed to the extent of the trust's undistributed capital gains. Undistributed capital gains of the trust are determined on a cumulative net basis without regard to the provisions of Code Sec. 1212, as follows:
>
>> 1. *Long- and short-term capital gains.* If, in any taxable year of the trust, the trust has both undistributed short-term capital gain and undistrib-

---

[50] Rev. Rul. 92-48, 1992-1 CB 301.
[51] IRS Letter Ruling 9714101.
[52] Code Sec. 664(b); Reg. §§ 1.664-1 through 1.664-4.
[53] Reg. § 1.664-1(d)(1)(i).

uted long-term capital gain, then the short-term capital gain shall be deemed distributed prior to any long-term capital gain.

2. *Long- and short-term capital gains.* If the trust has in any taxable year any capital losses in excess of capital gains, any excess of the short-term capital loss over the net long-term capital gain shall be a short-term capital loss in the succeeding taxable year and any excess of the net long-term capital loss over the net short-term capital gain for such year shall be a long-term capital loss in the succeeding taxable year.

3. *Capital gains in excess of capital losses.* If the trust has for any taxable year capital gains in excess of capital losses, any excess of the net short-term capital gain over the short-term capital loss for such year shall be, to the extent not deemed distributed, a short-term capital gain in the succeeding taxable year and any excess of the net long-term capital gain over the net short-term capital loss for such year shall be, to the extent not deemed distributed, a long-term capital gain in the succeeding taxable year.

c. *Other income.* Third, other income (including income excluded under part III, subchapter B, chapter 1, subtitle A of the Code) is to be distributed to the extent of the sum of the trust's other income for the taxable year and its undistributed other income for prior years. A loss in this category for prior years and any excess shall be carried forward indefinitely to reduce income for future years.

d. *Corpus.* Finally, corpus is distributed, where applicable. For purposes of this section, the term "corpus" means the net fair market value of the trust assets less the total undistributed income (but not loss) in each of the above categories.[54]

The characterizations of income items distributed or deemed distributed at any time during the tax year of the charitable remainder trust are determined as of the end of the tax year. Distributions are subject to the tax rate applicable to the income class from which the distribution is derived, not the tax rate applicable when the income was received by the trust.[55] Gains and losses of long-term capital gain classes are netted prior to netting short-term capital loss against any class of long-term capital gain.[56] Special transition rules also apply for classifying long-term capital gains and losses.[57] Distributions in kind are valued as the amount realized from sale or other disposition. Basis in the hands of the recipient is the fair market value at the time it was paid, credited or required to be distributed.[58]

¶ 1112 Charitable Lead Trusts

Charitable Lead Trusts (CLTs) may be created either inter vivos or at death. There are two types of CLTs, one a charitable lead annuity trust (CRAT), which can be of the grantor or non-grantor type, and the other a charitable lead unitrust

---

[54] Reg. § 1.664-1(d)(1)(i).
[55] Reg. § 1.664-1(d)(1)(ii)(a).
[56] Reg. § 1.664-1(d)(1)(iv).
[57] Reg. § 1.664-1(d)(1)(vi).
[58] Reg. § 1.664-1(e).

(CLUT). The trustee distributes the annuity or unitrust amount to the designated charities for a term of years or for a period measured by the life of an individual or individuals. The remainder beneficiaries are typically the grantor's descendants (although it is possible for the remainder to revert to the grantor). CLTs are useful to satisfy a grantor's charitable intentions and transfer assets to others at significant estate and gift tax savings.

If a grantor creates a CLT during his or her lifetime, the grantor makes a gift to charity of the present value of the right to receive distributions from the trust, which qualifies for the federal gift tax charitable deduction. The grantor must file a gift tax return for the year of the gift, not only to claim the charitable deduction, but also to report the gift to the remainder beneficiaries. Annual gift tax exclusions are not applicable since the gifts to the remainder beneficiaries are gifts of future interests. If a decedent creates a testamentary CLT, the assets are includible in the decedent's estate and the estate will receive a charitable deduction.

Unlike a CRT, a CLT is a taxable entity. If a grantor trust is used as a CLT, the income is taxed to the grantor over the term of the trust. If a non-grantor trust is used, the grantor will not receive a charitable income tax deduction either on creation of the trust or on distribution to the charity, but the grantor will have removed income producing assets from the grantor's tax base.

Unless a grantor retains some power over a CLT that makes it includable in the grantor's estate, such as a reversionary interest or the power to change beneficial interests, the gift is completed on the date of transfer and is not includible in the grantor's estate. A testamentary CLT is includible in the grantor's estate for estate tax purposes, but the estate will receive a charitable deduction for the present value of the charity's interest. As a further benefit, the assets in the CLT will receive stepped up basis.

Trusts that "qualify" as CLTs are split-interest trusts, created during a grantor's life or at death, in which charities are the lead recipients of an annuity or unitrust amount for the trust term. An inter vivos CLT may be a grantor trust or a nonqualifying non-grantor trust; neither may be created at death.

A non-qualifying CLT does not meet the payout requirements of a qualifying CLT, and typically pay income only to the charity. No income tax deduction is allowed on creation, but the trust may take a charitable deduction for its distributions to charities.

A qualified CLT must provide for distributions to charities in the form of guaranteed annuity or unitrust payments.

The IRS has published sample forms of CLTs.[59]

.01 Grantor Charitable Lead Trusts

A grantor charitable lead trust is governed by the grantor trust rules.[60] The grantor of a CLT will only receive an income tax charitable deduction for the

---

[59] Rev. Proc. 2007-45, 2007-2 CB 89 (inter vivos CLAT); Rev. Proc. 2007-46, 2007-2 CB 102 (testamentary CLAT); Rev. Proc. 2008-45, 2008-2 CB 224 (inter-vivos CLUT); Rev. Proc. 2008-46, 2008-2 CB 238 (testamentary CLUT); and Rev. Proc. 2007-39, 2007-1 CB 1446.
[60] Code Sec. 170(f)(2)(B).

present value of the charitable interest if the trust is a "grantor" trust that qualifies under Code Secs. 671-677. Because the contributions are treated as "for the use of" the charity, the deduction is limited to 30% of the grantor's contribution base, or 20% if the contributed property has long-term capital gain,[61] with the excess spread over five years. One benefit of using a grantor trust as a CLT is that the grantor can compress a term of charitable deductions into one year when it may be needed most. The grantor, however, is required to pay tax on the income each year, even the income paid out to charity.

.02 Qualified Non-Grantor Charitable Lead Trust

To be qualified, an inter vivos or testamentary CLT must provide for guaranteed annuity or unitrust payments to charitable organizations for the trust term. The income of non-grantor CLTs is taxed to the trust and the trust is treated as a complex trust (except for nonqualified CLTs that pay income only to the charity). The grantor is not allowed a charitable deduction on creation, but an inter vivos gift is complete on contribution and the assets are not includible in the grantor's estate on death.

Further, a non-grantor CLT may take charitable deductions for the annuity or unitrust distributions in the year made. If there is insufficient income to pay the annuity or unitrust amount, the difference must be paid from corpus. If there is excess income, it is taxed to the CLT. Excess income could be paid to the charity, but no charitable deduction for such distributions is allowed.

Beneficiaries. There may be one or more charitable beneficiaries and one or more remainder beneficiaries and remainder beneficiaries may be individuals, including the grantor, legal entities such as partnerships or corporations, trusts or estates. There is a requirement of at least a 15% probability that lineal descendants of the grantor will be remainder beneficiaries.[62] The charitable organization may be a public charity or a controlled charitable organization.

.03 Payments of Annuity or Unitrust Amounts

Payments to the charitable recipients must be made a least annually. There are no limitations on the minimum or maximum annuity or unitrust payment, but the present value must be less than the assets transferred to the trust.

.04 Trust Term

The term may be for a specified term of years or for the life or lives of certain individuals, living and ascertainable on the date of transfer. The measuring life must be one of the following: the grantor, the grantor's spouse, or an individual who, with respect to the remainder beneficiaries, other than charitable organizations, is either a lineal descendant or spouse of a lineal descendant of the grantor.[63] If the grantor or the grantor's spouse is the measuring life, then the remainder beneficiaries do not have to be their lineal descendants. If the term is a fixed period of time, there is no relational limitation on the identity of the noncharitable remainder beneficiaries Unlike CRTs, there is no statutory limit to a term of years.

---

[61] Reg. § 1.170A-8(a)(2).
[62] Reg. § 1.170A-6(c)(2).
[63] Reg. § 1.170A-6(c)(2).

.05 Valuation of the Remainder Interest

For a charitable lead annuity trust, Table B is used to compute the annuity factor and Table K is used to adjust the factor for payment frequency, if applicable, to determine the value of the annuity interest (the charitable deduction for a grantor trust, which is then subtracted from the fair market value to determine the remainder interest which will be actuarial value of the gift to the remainder beneficiaries. For a non-grantor charitable lead unitrust trust, Table F provides the payout rate factor based on the payment period, number of months between the valuation date and payment date and the 7520 Rate. Then Table U is used to interpolate the Table F factor for a term certain, if applicable, resulting in the present value of the remainder interest, which is then subtracted from the fair market value to determine the gift or estate tax deducted related to the charitable gift of the lead interest. These Tables are contained in Reg. § 1.664-4 and are used to determine the present value of the remainder interest.

.06 Assets to Consider for Funding a CLT

Assets that are expected to grow in value are useful to fund CLTs. Cash or assets sufficient to generate enough income to fund the guaranteed payments. If contributed property has associated debt, the grantor will recognize gain on the transfer if the indebtedness exceeds the grantor's basis.

¶ 1113 CLT Tax Reporting

Because a CLT is a taxable entity, the trustee must file Form 1041 each year and pay any applicable tax, unless the trust is a grantor trust, when only the reporting form is required. The CLT may take a charitable deduction for the gifts to the charity, but it will also report any income that passes through to the charity. Some of the filing requirements may include:

- Form 1041, U.S. Fiduciary Income Tax Return, and related Schedule K-1 will be required to report the income tax consequences of distributions to the beneficiaries of the annuity or unitrust payments.
- Form 1041-A, Trust Accumulation of Charitable Amounts, is no longer required and are replaced by Form 5227.
- Form 5227, Split-Interest Trust Information Return. A copy of the trust instrument accompanied by a certification of its conformity to the original must be submitted with the initial Form 5227 of a CLT. All taxable split-interest trusts, which includes all qualified and grantor charitable lead trusts, are treated as private foundations under Code Sec. 4947 and the IRS requires this form to be filed for them.
- Form 56, Notice Concerning Fiduciary Relationship.
- Form 8283, Noncash Charitable Contributions. The CLT trustee must acknowledge receipt of assets from the donor (greater than $500) in section of Form 8283 which is then attached to the donor's 1040 to claim the charitable deduction for a grantor CLT. The donor is required to support the calculation of the present value of the remainder interest.

- Form 8282, Donee Information Return. If a contributed asset is sold within three years of the gift, Form 8282 must be filed to report the sale price within 125 days of the sale.
- Form 8868, Application for Extension of Time to File an Exempt Organization Return.
- Form 4720, Return of Certain Excise Taxes on Charities and Other Persons. This form is used to report the UBTI and related excise tax in any year the tax is due. Also, because a charitable trusts are subject to private foundation rules regarding self-dealing with a disqualified person, this form is used to report the act and compute the excise tax due.
- Form 709, U.S. Gift (and Generation Skipping Transfer) Tax Return, will be required to report gifts of present interests to the beneficiaries and to claim the charitable deduction for gift tax purposes. If a noncharitable beneficiary may be a skip person, the GST tax will apply to related distributions, and therefore, this tax return can be used to allocate a portion of the grantor's GST exemption to that portion of the trust allocable to the skip person.

¶ 1114 CLT Distribution Income Ordering Regulations

The source of funds that are to be paid, permanently set aside or used for a charitable purpose from CLTs under Section 642(c) have been somewhat controversial. A typical CLT agreement will direct the source of funds payable to charities in a manner that will minimize income tax consequences to the trust by exhausting higher tax rate income before using nontaxable sources, such as principal. In normal circumstances, the governing instrument or local law will control the source of payments. This is no longer acceptable practice.

Effective April 16, 2012, after several years of notices and discussion, the IRS issued final regulations that provide an ordering provision in a governing instrument or imposed under local law must have economic effect independent of income tax consequences in order to be respected for federal income tax purposes.[64] These regulations are aimed specifically to CLTs. The preamble states that "Ordering provisions in CLTs will never have economic effect independent of their tax consequences because the amount paid to the charity is not dependent upon the type of income it is allocated." The distributed amount is either fixed from year to year or based on a predetermined percent of the total, so there is no independent economic effect.

As a result, if the ordering provisions do not have economic effect, the income distributed for a charitable purpose must consist of the same proportion of each class of the items of income as the total of each class bears to the total of all classes.

To the extent a payment to a charity is allocable to the unrelated business taxable income (UBTI) of the CLT, Code Sec. 681 disallows the Code Sec. 642 deduction up to 100% of the UBTI.[65] A CLT's UBTI consists of: (1) its gross income derived from an unrelated trade or business (as defined in Code Sec. 513) regularly carried on by it, less the deductions attributable to such business; and (2) a portion

---

[64] T.D. 9582, IRB 2012-18, 868.   [65] Reg. § 1.681(a)(2).

of its gross income derived from debt-financed property, less a portion of the expenses attributable to such income. Under Code Sec. 512(b)(11), the trust is permitted to deduct payments of UBI actually made to a charity subject to the percentage limitation rules applicable to individual taxpayers. Therefore, if the distributions consist of cash, the trust can deduct distributions of UBI to the extent of 50% of the trust's contribution base. If the payments are made to a private non-operating foundation, the percentage limitation is 30%.

¶ 1115 Pooled Income Trusts

A pooled income fund is formed by one or more donors to pay income to one or more noncharitable beneficiaries and the remainder to charity and is controlled by the charity. It is similar to charitable remainder trusts in many respects.

A sample trust agreement was published in Rev. Proc. 88-53. The requirements for pooled income trusts are outlined in Reg. § 1.642(c)(5) and include:

- The donor(s) must transfer property to the fund and contribute an irrevocable remainder interest to or for the use of a public charity.
- Each donor must either retain a life income interest or creating life income interests for other beneficiaries, each of whom must be living at the time of the transfer. The governing instrument must specify the life income beneficiaries and the share to which each is entitled. It is not necessary that all of the income be distributable to these beneficiaries, but any income not distributed to them must be paid to or provided for the use of the public charity within the year it is received. The donors do not receive a charitable deduction for income tax purposes for such distributions.
- The property transferred to the fund by each donor must be comingled.
- The property transferred to the fund must not include any tax-exempt securities and the fund may not invest in such securities.
- Maintenance of the fund by the designated charitable organization is required. The charitable organization should have the power to remove and replace the trustee of the fund. The charity operating the fund may also be an income beneficiary, as long as there is at least on individual who is also a beneficiary.
- The governing instrument must provide that neither the donor nor an income beneficiary may serve as trustee.
- The income beneficiary must receive the income determined by the rate of return of the fund either currently or within the first 65 following the close of the tax year in which the income is earned. The governing instrument must state that the income beneficiary's interest terminates with the last regular payment before death or be prorate to the date of death.
- On termination of a life income interest, the trustee must sever from the fund an amount equal to the value of the remainder interest in the property on which income interest is based.
- Pooled income fund investments should not include tax-exempt securities, which could disqualify the fund.

Each income interest is assigned a proportionate share of the annual income based on the fair market value of the property on the date of transfer. Each income interest or beneficiary is assigned units of participation based on dividing the fair market value of the property by the fair market value of a unit in the fund at the time of transfer.[66] Reg. § 1.642 outlines how this is administered.

The trustee must value the fund four times a year, one the determination date which is the first day of the taxable year of the trust and the first day of each quarter thereafter. A pooled income fund is taxed on a calendar year.

Table R(2) is used to obtain joint and survivor remainder factors for pooled income funds. The interest rate to be used to find the remainder factor is the yearly rate of return for the fund as defined in I.R.S. Notice 89-60. If the yearly rate of return falls between two interest rates for which the factors are given in Table R(2), a linear interpolation must be made.

Estates and complex trusts are allowed an unlimited charitable deduction for amounts paid to recognized charities out of gross income (other than unrelated business income of a trust) under the terms of the governing instrument during the tax year.[67] For example, amounts bequeathed to charity that are paid out of corpus under state law are not deductible from income as charitable contributions or as distributions to beneficiaries. However, payments in compromise of bequests to charity are deductible. Limitations on the charitable deduction for estates and trusts are discussed at ¶ 413.

The trustee or administrator may elect to treat charitable payments made during the year following the close of a tax year as having been paid in the earlier year for deduction purposes.[68] The election must be made no later than the time, including extensions, prescribed by law for filing the income tax return for the tax year in which payment is made. The election is binding for the tax year for which it is made and may not be revoked after the time for making the election has expired.

Estates may also claim an unlimited deduction for amounts of gross income permanently set aside for charitable purpose.[69] The income must be permanently set aside for a purpose specified in Code Sec. 170(c) or it must be used exclusively for: (i) religious, charitable, scientific, literary, or educational purposes; (ii) the prevention of cruelty to children or animals; or (iii) the establishment, acquisition, maintenance, or operation of a nonprofit public cemetery. For most complex trusts, the unlimited deduction for gross income that is permanently set aside for charitable purposes does not apply.

A provision in a governing instrument or local law that specifically identifies the source out of which amounts are to be paid, permanently set aside, or used for charitable purposes must have economic effect independent of income tax consequences in order to be respected for federal tax purposes.[70]

---

[66] Reg. § 1.642(c)-5(c)(1).
[67] Code Sec. 642(c).
[68] Code Sec. 642(c)(1); Reg. § 1.642(c)-1(b).
[69] Reg. § 1.642(c)-2.
[70] Reg. § 1.642(c)-3(b)(2).

Pooled income funds may claim a set-aside deduction only for gross income attributable to gain from the sale of a long-term capital asset that is permanently set aside for the benefit of the charity.[71] No deduction is allowed with respect to gross income of the fund that is (1) attributable to income other than net long-term capital gains; or (2) earned with respect to amounts transferred to the fund before August 1, 1969. The investment and accounting requirements applicable to trusts also apply to pooled income funds.

The charitable deduction is normally computed on Schedule A of Form 1041. However, pooled income funds claiming the set-aside deduction for long-term capital gain and nonexempt charitable trusts under Code Sec. 4947(a)(1) treated as private foundations must compute their deduction on a separate schedule, rather than Schedule A. Also, a nonexempt charitable trust not treated as a private foundation must file Form 990 in addition to Schedule A if its gross receipts are normally more than $50,000. However, the trust may file Form 990 or Form 990-EZ to satisfy its Form 1041 filing requirement if it has zero taxable income.

Every trust claiming a charitable deduction for amounts permanently set aside (other than nonexempt charitable trusts under Code Sec. 4947(a)(1), and split-interest trusts under Code Sec. 4947(a)(2)) is required to file an information return on Form 1041-A generally by April 15 following the close of the trust's calendar year.[72] However, Form 1041-A does not have to be filed if the trust must distribute all of its income for the tax year (i.e., a simple trust). Split-interest trusts (i.e., pooled income funds, charitable remainder trusts, and charitable lead trusts) file their information return on Form 5227.

Both the trust and the trustee can be liable for a penalty of $10 per day up to a maximum of $5,000 for failure to timely file Form 1041-A.[73] A split-interest trust that fails to file or to provide the required information on Form 5227 can be liable for a penalty of $20 per day, up to a maximum of $10,000. If the split-interest trust's gross income exceeds $250,000, the penalty is $100 per day, up to a $50,000 maximum. An additional penalty may be assessed against the person required to file the return if he or she knowingly fails to file or provide the information. Criminal penalties also apply for willful failure to file a return and filing a false or fraudulent return.[74]

---

[71] Reg. § 1.642(c)-2(c).
[72] Code Sec. 6034.
[73] Code Sec. 6652(c)(2)(A) and (C).
[74] Reg. § 1.6034-1(d).

Chapter 12

S Corporations and Fiduciary Income Tax[1]

¶ 1201   S Corporation Rules—In General
¶ 1202   Eligible S Corporation Shareholders
¶ 1203   Qualified Subchapter S Trusts—QSST
¶ 1204   Electing Small Business Trusts—ESBT
¶ 1205   QSST Election
¶ 1206   ESBT Election

¶ 1201 S Corporation Rules—In General

An S corporation is a pass-through entity that is treated very much like a partnership for federal income tax purposes. Unlike C corporations, an S corporation does not pay an entity-level tax on its income. Instead, all income and expenses are passed through to shareholders. To qualify for S status, a corporation must make an election to be treated as an S corporation. In addition, the corporation must be a small business corporation, meaning that it has no more than one class of stock and no more than 100 shareholders.[2] All shareholders must be natural persons who are U.S. citizens or resident aliens, or estates (subject to limitations), certain specified trusts, or certain tax-exempt organizations.[3]

The election of S corporation status must be made by a qualified corporation with the unanimous consent of the shareholders, on or before the 15th day of the 3rd month of its tax year in order for the election to be effective beginning with the year when made.[4] The election is made on Form 2553. The corporation must meet all of the eligibility requirements for the pre-election portion of the tax year and all persons who were shareholders during the pre-election portion also must consent to the election. If these requirements are not met during the pre-election period the election becomes effective the following year.

.01 Taxation of S Corporation Shareholders

Each shareholder of an S corporation separately accounts for his pro rata share of corporate items of income, deduction, loss, and credit in his tax year in which the

---

[1] The author would like to recognize the contribution of Kenneth A. Goldstein of Horwood Marcus & Berk, Chartered, for input on S corporations and the application to trusts and estates.

[2] Code Sec. 1361(b)(1)(A).

[3] Code Sec. 1361(b)(1)(B).

[4] Code Sec. 1362(a), (b), and (c); Reg. § 1.1362-6.

¶1201.01

corporation's tax year ends.⁵ Certain items must be separately stated whenever they could affect the shareholder's individual tax liability. A shareholder's share of each item generally is computed based on the number of shares he held on each day of the corporation's tax year.

The character of an item included in a shareholder's pro rata share of S corporation income is generally determined as if the item was realized directly from the source from which the corporation realized it or was incurred in the same manner in which the corporation incurred it, subject to exceptions.⁶ Thus, when income passes through from the S corporation to the shareholder, the character of that income passes through as well. For example, if an S corporation makes a charitable contribution to a qualifying organization, a shareholder's pro rata share of the S corporation's charitable contribution is characterized as made to a qualifying organization.

Similarly, if an S corporation has capital gain on the sale or exchange of a capital asset, a shareholder's pro rata share of that gain is also characterized as a capital gain regardless of whether the shareholder is otherwise a dealer in that type of property. However, this general rule does not apply when the S corporation is formed or availed of for a principal purpose of selling or exchanging contributed property that, in the hands of the shareholder, would not have produced capital gain if sold or exchanged by the shareholder. The same exception applies when the S corporation is formed or availed of for a principal purpose of selling or exchanging contributed property that, in the hands of a shareholder, would have produced capital loss if sold or exchanged by the shareholder. Any loss recognized by the corporation is treated as a capital loss to the extent that, immediately before the contribution, the adjusted basis of the property in the hands of the shareholder exceeded the fair market value of the property.

.02 Duty of Consistency

A shareholder of an S corporation must treat a Subchapter S item in a manner consistent with the treatment of that item on the corporate return.⁷ Any shareholder who does not treat the item consistently must file a statement identifying the inconsistency.

.03 At-Risk and Passive Activity Rules

The at-risk rules disallow losses that exceed an investor's amount at risk. Generally, the amount at risk is the amount of investment that an investor could lose. The at-risk rules apply to all taxpayers, including S corporation shareholders, and are applied at the shareholder level.⁸ The at-risk amount is determined at the close of the S corporation's tax year. Thus, an S corporation shareholder who realizes that his or her at-risk amount is low, and wishes to deduct an anticipated S corporation net loss, can make additional contributions to the entity.

---

⁵ Code Sec. 1366(a); Reg. §§ 1.1366-1(a) and 1.1377-1.
⁶ Code Sec. 1366(b); Reg. § 1.1366-1(b).
⁷ Code Sec. 6037.
⁸ Code Sec. 465.

.04 Passive Activity Loss Rules Apply[9]

Likewise, passive activity loss (PAL) rules generally are applied at the shareholder level.[10] However, several determinations that affect the application of the PAL rules must be made at the corporate level. For example, the determination of whether an activity constitutes a trade or business, as opposed to a rental activity, is made at the corporate level. The distinction between portfolio and non-portfolio income is also made at the corporate level. This information is conveyed via the Schedule K-1 that is provided to the shareholder by the corporation. The shareholder then uses the information to apply the PAL and at-risk limitations when preparing his individual tax return.

Since a QSST is treated as the shareholder when it disposes of S corporation stock, the application of the at-risk and PAL rules would normally be determined at the trust level, not the beneficiary level. To ensure that the beneficiary can take disallowed losses on the QSST's disposition of the stock, the at-risk and passive activity loss rules apply as if the beneficiary disposed of the stock.[11]

.05 Small Business Stock

Because S corporations are not entitled to ordinary loss treatment from the sale of qualified small business stock under Code Sec. 1244, and because the character of loss items passes through to shareholders, S corporation shareholders cannot claim ordinary losses incurred by the S corporation from the sale of qualified small business stock.[12] However, when the S corporation stock itself is qualified small business stock, shareholders may get an ordinary loss deduction if all the requirements are met.

¶ 1202 Eligible S Corporation Shareholders

All shareholders of an S corporation must be individuals, estates, certain specified trusts, or certain tax-exempt organizations.[13] Partnerships and C corporations are not eligible to hold stock in an S corporation. The prohibition on a partnership holding S corporation stock does not extend to an LLC with a single, individual member that is taxed as a disregarded entity. The owner of the single member LLC is treated as the owner of the S corporation stock. Single-member LLCs that "check the box" to be taxed as C corporations may not hold stock in an S corporation. Taxpayers who only hold restricted bank director stock are not considered shareholders for determining whether an S corporation has an ineligible shareholder.[14]

.01 Individuals

There is a 100 shareholder limit for shareholders of an S corporation. The family attribution rules treat married couples and their family as one shareholder.[15] For purposes of the shareholder limit, a husband and wife, their estates, and all

---

[9] *See* ¶ 105, "Passive Activity Losses and Material Participation for Fiduciaries and Beneficiaries," for updates to these rules.
[10] Code Sec. 469.
[11] Code Sec. 1361(d)(1).
[12] *V.D. Rath*, 101 TC 196, CCH Dec. 49,266 (1993).
[13] Code Sec. 1361(b)(1)(B).
[14] Code Sec. 1361(f).
[15] Code Sec. 1361(c)(1)(A).

members of a family and their estates are treated as one shareholder. The Regulations provide that members of a family include a common ancestor, any lineal descendant of the common ancestor (without any generational limit), and any spouse (or former spouse) of the common ancestor or of any lineal descendants of the common ancestor.[16]

.02 Estates

An individual S Corporation shareholder who dies is treated as the shareholder for the day of his or her death. Following the death of a shareholder, the decedent's estate can be an eligible shareholder of the S Corporation stock.[17] During the administration process, an estate may remain an eligible shareholder for a reasonable time, but may be deemed to have been constructively terminated if the period of administration is unduly prolonged.[18]

.03 Trusts

Trusts eligible to hold S corporation shares include grantor trusts (where the grantor is regarded as the shareholder) and voting trusts (where each beneficiary is treated as a shareholder).[19] Special elections are available to allow a trust to hold S corporation stock include: Qualified Subchapter S Trusts or "QSST's" discussed below in ¶ 1203 and Electing Small Business Trusts or "ESBT's" discussed below in ¶ 1204.

With one exception, an individual retirement arrangement (IRA) trust is not an eligible S corporation shareholder.[20] An IRA or a Roth IRA may hold stock in a bank S corporation if the IRA held the stock on October 22, 2004.[21] If the IRA decides to sell bank stock held on October 22, 2004, it can sell the stock to the IRA beneficiary within 120 days after the corporation made the S corporation election without violating the prohibited transaction rules.

Any testamentary trust that receives S corporation stock is an eligible S corporation shareholder unless the trust is treated as an eligible shareholder only for two years after the deemed owner's death.[22] The IRS may extend the two-year limit under an extension for estate tax payments. A charitable remainder trust is not an eligible S corporation shareholder.[23]

.04 Exempt Organizations as Shareholders

Certain tax-exempt organizations can be S corporation shareholders. These are qualified pension, profit-sharing, and stock bonus plans; charitable organizations; and Code Sec. 501(c)(3) organizations.

.05 QSSS

Even though a corporation generally cannot be an S corporation shareholder, an S corporation is permitted to own a qualified subchapter S subsidiary (QSSS or

---

[16] Reg. § 1.1361-1(e)(3).
[17] Code Sec. 1361(b)(1)(B).
[18] *Old Virginia Brick Co.*, CA-4, 66-2 USTC ¶ 9708, 367 F2d 276.
[19] Code Sec. 1361(c)(2)(A)(iv); Reg. § 1.1361-1(h)(1)(v).
[20] *Taproot Administrative Services, Inc.*, 133 TC 202 (2009), aff'd, CA-9, 2012-1 USTC ¶ 50,256; Rev. Rul. 92-73, 1992-2 CB 224.
[21] Code Sec. 1361(c)(6).
[22] Code Sec. 1361(c)(2)(A)(ii).
[23] Rev. Rul. 92-48, 1992-1 CB 301.

QSub).[24] This includes any domestic corporation that qualifies as an S corporation and is 100% owned by an S corporation parent that elects to treat it as a QSSS. A QSSS is not taxed as a separate corporation, and all its tax items are treated as belonging to the parent. Form 8869 should be used by all S corporations to elect QSub treatment for wholly owned corporate subsidiaries.

¶ 1203 Qualified Subchapter S Trusts—QSST

A trust is eligible to become a shareholder of an S corporation if the individual beneficiary of the trust elects to be treated as the owner of the trust for purposes of the Code.[25] A trust with respect to which an election is made provides that it: (1) owns stock in one or more electing S corporations, (2) distributes or is required to distribute all of its income to a citizen or resident of the United States, (3) has certain trust terms, including one requiring that there be only one income beneficiary, (4) does not distribute any portion of the trust corpus to anyone other than the current income beneficiary during the income beneficiary's lifetime, including the time at which the trust terminates, and (5) the income interest of the current income beneficiary ceases on the earlier of such beneficiary's death or the termination of the trust.

A qualified subchapter S trust (QSST) whose beneficiary chooses to be treated as owner of the S corporation stock held by the trust also may hold stock in an S corporation.[26] A QSST must own stock in at least one S corporation and must distribute all of its income to one individual who is a U.S. citizen or resident. The QSST beneficiary is taxed on all items of income, loss, deduction, and credit attributable to the S corporation stock held by the QSST. However, the QSST, not the beneficiary, is treated as the owner of the S corporation stock for purposes of determining the tax consequences of the trust's disposition of the S corporation stock. In addition, the terms of the QSST must provide:

1. during the life of the current income beneficiary there may be only one income beneficiary at any time;
2. trust corpus may be distributed only to the income beneficiary;
3. each income interest must end no later than the death of the income beneficiary or the termination of the trust; and
4. if the trust ends at any time during the life of the income beneficiary, it must distribute all of its assets to the beneficiary.

Successive income beneficiaries are permitted. The income beneficiary's election to treat the trust as a QSST may be revoked only with the consent of the IRS. The election is effective for up to two months and 15 days before the election date. A separate election must be made with respect to each corporation the stock of which is held by the trust and must be made by each successive income beneficiary. Finally, under Regulation Section 1.1361-1(j)(12), a QSST may convert to an ESBT.

---

[24] Code Sec. 1361(b)(3).
[25] Code Sec. 1361(d)(2).
[26] Code Sec. 1361(d); Reg. § 1.1361-1(j).

¶ 1204 Electing Small Business Trusts—ESBT

For tax years beginning after 1996, an electing small business trust (ESBT) may be a shareholder in an S corporation. This permits broader estate planning opportunities for S corporation shareholders by allowing trusts to be established and funded with S corporation stock to "spray" income among family members or other trust beneficiaries. To qualify, all beneficiaries of the small business trust must be individuals, estates, or charitable organizations eligible to be S corporation shareholders. Interests in qualifying trusts must be acquired by reason of gift, bequest, or other non-purchase acquisition; no interest in the trust may be acquired by "purchase" (i.e., acquired with a cost basis). Each potential current beneficiary of the trust is counted as a shareholder for purposes of the 100-shareholder limitation.[27]

An ESBT is taxed in a different manner than other trusts.[28] The portion of the ESBT that consists of stock in one or more S corporations is treated as a separate trust for purposes of computing the income tax attributable to the S corporation stock held by the trust. This portion of the trust's income is taxed at the highest rate imposed on estates and trusts, and includes:

1. the items of income, loss, deduction or credit allocated to the trust as an S corporation shareholder;
2. gain or loss from the sale of the S corporation stock;
3. any state or local income taxes and administrative expenses of the trust properly allocable to the S corporation stock; and
4. any interest expense paid or accrued on debt incurred to acquire S corporation stock.

Capital losses are allowed in computing an ESBT's income only to the extent of capital gains. Moreover, no deduction is allowed for amounts distributed to beneficiaries and, except as described above, no additional deductions or credits are allowed. Also, the ESBT's income is not included in the DNI of the trust and, therefore, is not included in the beneficiaries' income. Furthermore, no item relating to the S corporation stock is apportioned to any beneficiary. The trust's AMT exemption amount is zero. Special rules apply upon termination of all or a part of the ESBT. Finally, under Regulation Section 1.1361-1(m)(7), an electing small business trust may convert to a QSST.

¶ 1205 QSST Election

The beneficiary of the QSST trust makes the election to have QSST treatment apply to the trust.[29] The beneficiary makes the election by signing and filing a statement with the Internal Revenue Service Center where the S Corporation files its income tax return within two months and fifteen days of the effective date.[30] The trustee is not a party to the election, and need not consent to the election. The election is only revocable with the Commissioner's consent.[31]

---

[27] Code Sec. 1361(b)(1)(A).
[28] Code Sec. 641(c); Reg. § 1.641(c)-1.
[29] Code Sec. 1361(d)(2)(A).
[30] Code Sec. 1361(d)(2)(A); Reg. § 1.1361-1(j)(6).
[31] Reg. § 1.1361-1(j)(11).

.01 Sample QSST Election

This is an election under Code Sec. 1361(d)(2). The income beneficiary hereby elects to have Code Sec. 1361(d)(2) apply to the trust.

Effective Date. This election takes effect on _____, which is not earlier than two months and fifteen days before the filing of this election and which is the day on which the Corporation is to make its election under Code Sec. 1362 to be treated as an S corporation.

Stock Transferred to Trust. Stock of the Corporation was transferred to the trust on _____.

Eligibility. The trust which owns stock in the S Corporation meets all the requirements of Reg. § 1.1361-1(j)(6)(ii)(E)(1), (2), and (3) as follows:

1. All trust income (within the meaning of Code Sec. 643(b)) will be distributed (or required to be distributed) currently to the income beneficiary who is a citizen or resident of the United States.
2. The terms of the trust require that there is only one income beneficiary of the trust.
3. Any corpus distributed during the life of the income beneficiary may only be distributed to the income beneficiary.
4. The income interest of the income beneficiary will terminate on the earlier to occur of the death of the income beneficiary or the termination of the trust.
5. If the trust terminates during the life of the income beneficiary, the trust will distribute all its assets to the income beneficiary.
6. No distribution of income or corpus by the trust will be in satisfaction of the grantor's legal obligation to support the Income Beneficiary.

/S/ Income Beneficiary

¶ 1206 ESBT Election

The trustee of the ESBT trust makes the election to have ESBT treatment apply to the trust.[32] The trustee makes the election by signing and filing a statement with the Internal Revenue Service Center where the S Corporation files its income tax return within two months and fifteen days of the effective date.[33] The election is only revocable with the Commissioner's consent.[34]

.01 Sample ESBT Election

The trustee of the trust hereby elects under Code Sec. 1361(e)(3) to treat this trust as an electing small business trust that is qualified to hold S Corporation stock pursuant to Code Sec. 1361(c)(2)(A)(v).

---

[32] Code Sec. 1361(e)(3).
[33] Reg. § 1.1361-1(m)(2).
[34] Code Sec. 1361(d)(2)(C).

Effective Date. This election pursuant to Code Sec. 1361(e)(3) takes effect on _____ which is not earlier than two months and fifteen days before the filing of this election.

Stock Transferred to Trust. Stock of the Corporation was transferred to the trust on _____.

Eligibility. This is an election under Code Sec. 1361(e)(3). The trustee of the trust hereby elects to have Code Sec. 1361(e)(3) apply to the trust: All the potential beneficiaries meet the requirements of Code Sec. 1361(b)(1) and are individuals who are citizens or residents of the United States [or estate or organizations described in Code Sec. 170(c)(2), (3), (4) or (5)]. No interest in the Trust was acquired by purchase and the Trust is neither a qualified subchapter S trust nor a trust exempt from taxation.

/S/ Trustee

Chapter 13

*Foreign Trusts**

¶ 1301   Foreign Trust Defined—In General
¶ 1302   Inbound Foreign Grantor Trusts
¶ 1303   Outbound Foreign Grantor Trusts
¶ 1304   Nongrantor Foreign Trusts
¶ 1305   Reporting Requirements
¶ 1306   FATCA and Other Related Developments Regarding Foreign Trusts
¶ 1307   Offshore Voluntary Disclosure Programs (OVDP)

¶ 1301 Foreign Trust Defined—In General*

The Small Business Job Protection Act of 1996[1] established an objective test to determine the situs of a trust. A trust is classified as a foreign trust unless (1) a court within the United States is able to exercise primary supervision over the administration of the trust (the "Court Test"), and (2) one or more U.S. fiduciaries have the authority to control all substantial decisions of the trust (the "Control Test").[2] Therefore, a trust must pass both tests in order to be excluded from the definition of and treatment as a foreign trust.

For the Court Test, "supervision over the administration" means the authority under applicable law to determine substantially all issues regarding the carrying out of the duties imposed by the terms of the trust instrument and applicable law.[3] A court may have primary supervision notwithstanding the fact that another court has jurisdiction over a trustee, a beneficiary, or trust property.[4]

For the Control Test, "control" means having the power, by vote or otherwise, to make all of the substantial decisions of the trust, with no other person having the power to veto any of the substantial decisions.[5] To determine whether persons have control, it is necessary to consider all persons who have authority to make a substantial decision, not only the trust fiduciaries.[6] The term "substantial decisions" means those decisions that are not ministerial.[7] Decisions that are ministerial include decisions regarding details such as the bookkeeping, the collection of

---

* The author would like to recognize the contribution of Michael T. Mazzone of Pioneer Wealth Partners, LLC, for his input on foreign trusts.

[1] P.L. 104-188, § 1907.

[2] Reg. § 301.7701-7(a)(1).

[3] Reg. § 301.7701-7(c)(3)(iii)-(v).

[4] Reg. § 301.7701-7(c)(3)(iv).

[5] Reg. § 301.7701-7(d)(1)(iii).

[6] *Id.*

[7] Reg. § 301.7701-7(d)(1)(ii).

rents, and the execution of investment decisions.[8] Substantial decisions include, but are not limited to, decisions concerning:
- Whether and when to distribute income or corpus;
- The amount of any distributions;
- The selection of a beneficiary;
- Whether a receipt is allocable to income or principal;
- Whether to terminate the trust;
- Whether to compromise, arbitrate, or abandon claims of the trust;
- Whether to sue on behalf of the trust or to defend suits against the trust;
- Whether to remove, add, or replace a trustee;
- Whether to appoint a successor trustee to succeed a trustee who has died, resigned, or otherwise ceased to act as a trustee; and
- Investment decisions.[9]

¶ 1302 Inbound Foreign Grantor Trusts

The U.S. grantor trust rules[10] generally do not apply to any portion of a trust that would otherwise be deemed to be owned by a foreign person. Rather, the grantor trust rules are generally applied only when the rules result in amounts being taken into account, either directly or indirectly through one or more entities, in computing the income of a U.S. citizen or resident or a domestic corporation. Accordingly, the grantor trust rules apply to the extent that any portion of a trust, upon application of the grantor trust rules without regard to Code Sec. 672(f), is treated as owned by a U.S. citizen or resident or domestic corporation.[11]

The grantor trust rules also apply in the following limited situations:
- revocable trusts where the power to revest is exercisable solely by the grantor and not conditioned on approval or consent of any person, and the grantor has such power for at least 183 days during the tax year of the trust;
- trusts where distributions of income or corpus during the grantor's lifetime are only distributable to the grantor or the grantor's spouse;
- compensatory trusts, such as nonexempt employees' trusts described in Code Sec. 402(b), "rabbi trusts," and any other trusts designated by the IRS; and
- trusts owned by the grantor or another person under Code Sec. 676 or 677 (other than Code Sec. 677(a)(3)) that were in existence on September 19, 1995.[12]

Where the foreign grantor is a controlled foreign corporation as defined in Code Sec. 957, a passive foreign investment company as defined in Code Sec. 1297 or a foreign personal holding company as defined in Code Sec. 522, the grantor

---

[8] *Id.*
[9] *Id.*
[10] For a summary of grantor trust taxation under Code Sec. 671-679, see Chapter 9, Grantor Trusts.
[11] Code Sec. 672(f)(1); Reg. § 1.672(f)-1(a)(1).
[12] Code Sec. 672(f)(2); Reg. § 1.672(f)-3.

trust rules will still apply.[13] In addition, the grantor trust rules continue to apply in determining whether a foreign corporation is characterized as a passive foreign investment company under Code Sec. 1297.[14]

A U.S. donee generally must treat a purported gift from a partnership as ordinary income.[15] Similarly, a purported gift from a foreign corporation generally must be treated as a distribution, includible in the U.S. donee's gross income.[16] However, such purported gifts need not be recharacterized if one of the exceptions from Reg. § 1.672(f)-4(b) applies or if the total transfers to the U.S. donee from all related partnerships or foreign corporations are not in excess of $10,000 for the tax year. The aggregate amount must include gifts or bequests from persons that the U.S. donee knows or has reason to know are related to the partnership or foreign corporation.[17] Similarly, if a U.S. donee receives a gratuitous transfer from a trust to which a partnership or foreign corporation has made a gratuitous transfer, the purported gift generally must be recharacterized unless one of the exceptions set forth in the regulations applies.[18]

If a transferring partnership or foreign corporation receives some consideration from the U.S. donee, but the consideration is less than the fair market value of the property transferred, only the excess will be treated as a purported gift.[19]

A U.S. trust beneficiary who transfers property to a foreign grantor by gift is treated as the grantor of the trust to the extent of the transfer.[20] This rule applies without regard to whether the foreign grantor would otherwise be treated as the owner of the trust.[21] However, the rule does not apply if the transfer is a sale of the property for full and adequate consideration or if the transfer is a gift that qualifies for the gift tax annual exclusion.[22]

¶ 1303 Outbound Foreign Grantor Trusts

Foreign grantor trusts include foreign trusts (other than employee's trusts) with a U.S. beneficiary into which a U.S. person has transferred property. The U.S. person will be treated as the owner of that portion of the trust attributable to the property transferred, and the income generated by the property will be taxable to the transferor under the grantor trust rules.[23]

> ***Example 1:*** Mike Mazzone, a U.S. citizen and calendar-year taxpayer, transfers $50,000 to an existing trust in Country C. Mike's son, who is a U.S. citizen, is a beneficiary of the trust. The transfer increases the trust's principal to $100,000. Mike is required each year to report one-half of the income earned by the trust.

The following transfers are exempt from the above rule: (1) transfers at death; (2) transfers to employee benefit trusts; (3) transfers to charitable trusts; and (4) transfers to the extent they are for fair market value. Transfers for fair market value

---

[13] Code Sec. 672(f)(3)(A); Reg. § 1.672(f)-2(a).
[14] Code Sec. 672(f)(3)(B); Reg. § 1.672(f)-2(c).
[15] Reg. § 1.672(f)-4(a)(1).
[16] Reg. § 1.672(f)-4(a)(2).
[17] Reg. § 1.672(f)-4(f).
[18] Reg. § 1.672(f)-4(c).
[19] Reg. § 1.672(f)-4(d).
[20] Code Sec. 672(f)(5); Reg. § 1.672(f)-5(a)(1).
[21] House Committee Report to the Small Business Job Protection Act of 1996 (P.L. 104-188).
[22] Code Sec. 672(f)(5); Reg. § 1.672(f)-5(a)(1).
[23] Code Secs. 678(b) and 679.

must be evidenced by arm's-length transactions for the use of property or services rendered by the trust.[24]

If a foreign trust acquires a U.S. beneficiary in any tax year and, at the close of the year before the year that the beneficiary is acquired, the trust has undistributed net income (i.e., accumulated income taxable to a beneficiary upon distribution), the transferor of property will be treated as having received additional income in the first year in which he or she becomes subject to the grantor rules. The amount of the additional income will be an amount equal to the undistributed net income attributable to the transferred property remaining in the trust at the end of the last tax year before the trust had a U.S. beneficiary.[25]

A foreign trust will be treated as having a U.S. beneficiary for any tax year unless

- under the terms of the trust, no part of the trust's income or corpus may be paid or accumulated during the tax year to, or for the benefit of, directly or indirectly, a U.S. person; and
- if the trust is terminated at any time during the tax year, no part of the trust's income or corpus may be paid to or for the benefit of, directly or indirectly, a U.S. person.[26]

Generally, for purposes of applying the above rules, income or corpus is considered to be paid or accumulated to or for the benefit of a U.S. person during a tax year of the U.S. transferor if during that year, directly or indirectly, income may be distributed to, or accumulated for the benefit of a U.S. person, or corpus may be distributed to, or held for the future benefit of, a U.S. person. This determination is made without regard to whether income or corpus is actually distributed to a U.S. person during that year, and without regard to whether a U.S. person's interest in the trust income or corpus is contingent on a future event.[27] There is an exception with respect to certain contingent beneficiaries whose interests in the trust are so remote as to be negligible.[28]

A foreign trust may be treated as having a U.S. beneficiary by reference to written and oral agreements and understandings not contained in the trust document. Additionally, reference is made to whether the terms of the trust are actually or reasonably expected to be disregarded by the parties to the trust.[29]

Under attribution rules, the term "U.S. beneficiary" also includes:

- A controlled foreign corporation (as defined in Code Sec. 957(a));
- A foreign partnership that has a U.S. person as a partner, either directly or indirectly; and
- Another foreign trust or a foreign estate that has a U.S. beneficiary.[30]

---

[24] Reg. § 1.679-4(a) and (b).
[25] Code Sec. 679(b).
[26] Code Sec. 679(c)(1); Reg. § 1.679-2(a)(1).
[27] Reg. § 1.679-2(a)(2)(i).
[28] Reg. § 1.679-2(a)(2)(ii).
[29] Reg. § 1.679-2(a)(4).
[30] Code Sec. 679(c)(2).

A beneficiary will not be treated as a U.S. beneficiary if he or she first became a U.S. person more than five years after the date of the property's transfer to the foreign trust.[31]

Generally, to the extent that a U.S. person is not treated as the owner of a foreign grantor trust, a transfer of appreciated property by that U.S. person to the foreign trust results in immediate gain recognition.[32] Exceptions to this general rule include:

- transfers to foreign charitable trusts described in Code Sec. 501(c)(3);[33]
- transfers to foreign trusts by reason of death, if tax basis is determined under Code Sec. 1014(a);[34]
- transfers to unrelated trusts at fair market value;[35]
- transfers of stock by a domestic corporation to a foreign trust not subject to gain recognition under Code Sec. 1032;[36] and
- distributions received from nontrust entities, or from investment, liquidation, or environmental remediation trusts.[37]

Along these lines, a U.S. trust that becomes a foreign trust is considered to have transferred all of its assets to a foreign trust just prior to becoming a foreign trust, which could result in immediate gain recognition.[38]

¶ 1304 Nongrantor Foreign Trusts

.01 United States Taxation of the Trust

If all or a portion of a foreign trust is not taxed as a grantor trust, a nongrantor foreign trust ordinarily is not taxable on non-U.S. source income.[39] However, a nongrantor foreign trust is fully taxable on income effectively connected with the conduct of a U.S. trade or business.[40] Gains from the sale or exchange of U.S. sourced capital gains will be fully taxable to a nongrantor foreign trust if such gains are effectively connected with a U.S. trade or business.[41] Similarly, gains from the sale of U.S. real property interests are fully taxable to a nongrantor foreign trust. A nongrantor foreign trust can elect to have passive income from certain U.S. real estate activities treated as effectively connected with a U.S. trade or business to gain the advantage of deductions and graduated rates.[42] U.S. source "fixed or determinable annual or periodical gains, profits, and income" are taxable to a nongrantor foreign trust at the flat rate of 30% (or lower treaty rate) of the gross amount received.[43] If the nongrantor foreign trust receives such income, the payor to the trust is required to withhold and remit this amount to the United States.[44]

---

[31] Code Sec. 679(c)(3).
[32] Code Sec. 684(a).
[33] Reg. § 1.684-3(b).
[34] Reg. § 1.684-3(c).
[35] Reg. § 1.684-3(d).
[36] Reg. § 1.684-3(e).
[37] Reg. § 1.684-3(f).
[38] Code Sec. 684(c).
[39] Code Sec. 641(b).
[40] Code Sec. 641(b).
[41] Id.
[42] Code Sec. 871(d).
[43] Code Sec. 871(a)(1)(A).
[44] Code Sec. 1441(a).

.02 United States Taxation of the U.S. Beneficiaries

The income of the nongrantor foreign trust is taxed similar to a nongrantor domestic trust insomuch as the income is allocated between the nongrantor foreign trust and its beneficiaries (both domestic and foreign) through the concept of distributable net income (DNI) (see ¶ 702 for a more in-depth discussion of DNI). The U.S. beneficiaries of a nongrantor foreign trust include in their gross income any trust distributions of U.S. and foreign income, to the extent of the beneficiaries' share of the trust's DNI.[45] Further, similar to nongrantor domestic trust, the taxation and application of DNI is dependent on whether the trust is a simple or complex trust (see ¶ 705 for a more in-depth discussion on simple versus complex trusts).

The DNI of a nongrantor foreign trust is computed in the same manner as that of a nongrantor domestic trust, with three general modifications:

1. Inclusion of gross income from sources outside the United States.[46]
2. Inclusion of gross income from sources within the U.S. without regard to Code Sec. 894, which exempts certain income under U.S. tax treaties.[47]
3. Inclusion of capital gains otherwise excluded by Code Sec. 643(a)(3), regardless of whether they are allocated to income or to corpus under the governing instrument or local law, and regardless of whether they are currently distributed.[48]

Further, unlike a nongrantor domestic trust, a nongrantor foreign trust is subject to additional tax on any accumulation distributions. This taxation, known as the throwback rule, is designed to impose on the beneficiaries of a nongrantor foreign trust with accumulation distributions approximately the same income taxes that would have been imposed had the trust distributed its income currently. When they apply, the throwback rules treat accumulation distributions made by complex trusts as if they had been distributed to the beneficiary in the years when the trust income was accumulated. An accumulation distribution is thrown back first to the earliest preceding tax year in which there is undistributed net income.

Although the beneficiary is taxed on the income in the year he or she receives the distribution, the beneficiary's tax liability is computed under special rules. To prevent double taxation of the accumulated income, the beneficiary is entitled to a credit against the tax already paid by the trust.

.03 Accumulation Distributions

When the throwback rules apply, it is necessary to determine whether the trust has made an accumulation distribution in the relevant tax year. An accumulation distribution is the amount by which other amounts properly paid, credited, or required to be distributed for the tax year (other than income required to be distributed) exceed distributable net income reduced (but not below zero) by income required to be distributed currently.[49]

---

[45] Code Sec. 652(a).
[46] Code Sec. 643(a)(6)(A).
[47] Code Sec. 643(a)(6)(B).
[48] Code Sec. 643(a)(6)(C).
[49] Code Sec. 665(b).

.04 Undistributed Net Income

The throwback rules apply to undistributed net income and, thus, the amount thrown back to any one preceding tax year is the amount of the trust's undistributed net income for that year. Income that is currently distributable is not subject to the throwback rules. If the accumulation distribution exceeds the undistributed net income for the trust's earliest preceding tax year, the distribution is thrown back beginning with the next earliest tax year to any of the preceding years of the trust and so on, to the extent of the accumulation distribution.

The undistributed net income of a trust for any tax year is the excess of distributable net income *over* the sum of (1) the taxes imposed on the trust with respect to the distributable net income and (2) required and other distributions.[50] Taxes imposed on the trust are the federal income taxes, before allowance of any income tax credits, which are allocable to the accumulation distribution.[51] This has the effect of passing these credits on to the beneficiary who receives an accumulation distribution, although these credits are not readily identifiable amounts, but, instead, comprise a portion of the federal tax that is used as an offset against the partial tax created by the accumulation distribution.

Income taxes imposed on a trust in the throwback years are considered to be an additional distribution in the accumulation distribution year. For purposes of computing the additional distribution, the term "income taxes" includes the amount of federal income taxes before the allowance of income tax credits. The term, however, does not include taxes imposed under the alternative minimum tax provisions.[52]

.05 How the Throwback Rule Operates

The throwback rules treat an accumulation distribution as though it had been distributed to a beneficiary in the year in which the trust income was earned. These deemed distributions, and the taxes paid by the trust on the distributed accumulated income, are taxed to the beneficiary in the year the distribution is made.

The beneficiary's tax liability in the accumulation distribution year is the sum of:

1. a partial tax on taxable income for the year, computed at the normal rate and in the usual manner, but excluding the accumulation distribution, and
2. a partial tax on the accumulation distribution.

If the trust has no accumulated income, or if the distribution is greater than the income accumulations, then, to this extent, the transaction will be treated as a distribution of corpus and no additional tax will be imposed.[53] The base period for computing the tax on an accumulation distribution consists of the beneficiary's five tax years preceding the year of distribution. However, the years with the highest and lowest taxable income are disregarded and, thus, the partial tax is computed on a three-year base period.[54]

---

[50] Code Sec. 665(a).
[51] Code Sec. 665(d)(1).
[52] Code Sec. 666(b).
[53] Reg. § 1.665(a)-0A.
[54] Code Sec. 667(b)(1).

For purposes of computing the partial tax, the total amount of the accumulation distribution (including taxes considered distributed) is divided by the number of throwback years to which the trust distribution relates, and the result is added to the beneficiary's taxable income for each of the three base years. The partial tax paid by the beneficiary is the excess of (1) the average increase in taxes multiplied by the number of years to which the distribution relates *over* (2) the amount of trust taxes distributed to the beneficiary.

.06 Computation of Beneficiary's Tax

A beneficiary's tax liability for the year in which he or she receives an accumulation distribution is the sum of (1) the partial tax imposed on the accumulation distribution and (2) a partial tax computed in the normal manner on the other income he or she received during the year.[55] "Taxes imposed on the trust" include foreign taxes (income, war profits, and excess profits) paid or accrued by the trust and allocable to the accumulation distribution. Such taxes are deemed distributed as part of the distribution.[56]

A partial tax is computed on the basis of three computation years (arrived at by taking the five immediately preceding tax years and excluding the high-income year and the low-income year), but, subject to foreign tax credit limitations, the distributed foreign taxes deemed included in income in a computation year may be credited against the tax increase only in the computation year. They may not be carried over or back to the other two computation years.[57]

Beneficiaries who elected the foreign tax credit on their computation year return must credit the foreign taxes deemed distributed in computing the year's tax increase. Beneficiaries who did not elect the foreign tax credit on their computation-year return may treat the foreign tax imposed either as a deduction or as a credit in determining that year's increase in tax.[58]

Under a recapture rule,[59] when the beneficiary has sustained an overall foreign loss in a predistribution year, the portion of an accumulation distribution that is out of foreign source income is treated as U.S. source income in computing the credit in the computation year. This rule does not apply to the extent that losses have been recaptured in intervening tax years.[60]

When the income of a foreign trust is not taxed to the grantor under the grantor trust rules, an interest charge is imposed on the beneficiaries receiving taxable accumulation distributions from a foreign trust. This additional, nondeductible interest is computed as compound interest under the rules applicable to general underpayments of income tax.[61] The generally applicable underpayment rate is the federal short-term interest rate plus three percentage points.[62] The period for which interest is charged is determined as a weighted average. For each year in which there is undistributed net income, the undistributed net income for the year is multiplied by the number of tax years between the undistributed net

---

[55] Code Sec. 667(a).
[56] Code Sec. 665(d).
[57] Code Sec. 667(d).
[58] Code Sec. 667(d)(1)(B).
[59] Code Sec. 904(f)(4).
[60] Reg. § 1.904(f)-4(b).
[61] Code Sec. 668(a)(1).
[62] Code Sec. 6621(a)(2).

income year and the year of distribution (including the undistributed net income year, but excluding the year of distribution). The sum of these products is divided by aggregate undistributed net income to arrive at the period for which the interest rate is applied.[63] However, the total interest charge, when added to the partial tax computed, cannot exceed the amount of the distribution.[64]

.07 Anti-Deferral Provisions of the Internal Revenue Code

Although a detailed discussion of the application of the Internal Revenue Code provisions regarding anti-deferral are outside the scope of this book, such provisions, which are applicable to "controlled foreign corporations,"[65] and "passive foreign investment company,"[66] may apply to a U.S. beneficiary of a nongrantor foreign trust.

¶ 1305 Reporting Requirements

The return of a U.S. owner of a foreign trust must be consistent with the information reported by the trust to the beneficiaries, or the Secretary of the Treasury (IRS) must be notified of the inconsistency.[67]

A U.S. person who receives a distribution, directly or indirectly, from a foreign trust must report on Form 3520, Creation of or Transfers to Certain Foreign Trusts, (1) the name of the trust, (2) the aggregate amount of distributions received from the trust during the tax year, and (3) such other information as the Secretary may prescribe.[68] Reporting is required under Code Sec. 6048(c) only if the U.S. person knows or has reason to know that the trust is a foreign trust. A U.S. beneficiary who fails to report a distribution will be subject to a 35 percent penalty on the gross amount of the distribution.[69]

Generally, a distribution from a foreign trust includes any gratuitous transfer of money or property from a foreign trust, whether or not the trust is owned by another person. A distribution from a foreign trust includes the receipt of trust corpus and the receipt of a gift or bequest described in Code Sec. 663(a). In addition, a distribution is reportable if it is either actually or constructively received. Also, if a beneficiary receives a payment from a foreign trust in exchange for property transferred to the trust (or services rendered to the trust), and the fair market value of the payment received exceeds the fair market value of the property transferred (or services rendered), such excess will be treated as a distribution to the U.S. beneficiary that must be reported under Code Sec. 6048(c).

If adequate records are not provided to the IRS to determine the proper treatment of the distribution, any distribution from a foreign trust (whether from income or corpus) to a U.S. beneficiary will be treated as an accumulation distribution includible in the distributee's gross income.[70]

---

[63] Code Sec. 668(a)(3).
[64] Code Sec. 668(b).
[65] See Code Sec. 957.
[66] See Code Sec. 1297(a).
[67] Code Sec. 6048(d)(5).
[68] Notice 97-34, 1997-1 CB 422, modifying in part Notice 97-18, 1997-1 CB 389.
[69] Code Sec. 6677(a).
[70] Code Sec. 6048(c)(2).

¶ 1306 FATCA and Other Related Developments Regarding Foreign Trusts

FATCA (the Foreign Account Tax Compliance Act) was enacted as part of the Hiring Incentives to Restore Employment (HIRE) Act of 2010.[71] The legislation was enacted to identify U.S. taxpayers liable for U.S. tax resulting from non-US investments. Treasury and the IRS issued final regulations on January 17, 2013 related to the Foreign Account Tax Compliance Act (FATCA).[72] Congress passed FATCA on March 18, 2010 in an effort to curb perceived tax abuses by U.S. persons with offshore bank accounts and investments. The final regulations provide some guidelines for the application of the FATCA withholding and reporting rules to foreign trusts.

The withholding and reporting obligations under FATCA depend on the classification of a foreign entity as either a Foreign Financial Institution (FFI) or Non-Financial Foreign Entity (NFFE). An FFI will be subject to 30 percent FATCA withholding by the payor on withholdable payments (primarily U.S.-source income) made to the FFI unless it enters into an FFI agreement with the United States in which the FFI is obligated to comply with certain requirements (e.g., registration, due diligence, and reporting).

.01 Look to Any Applicable IGAs

Several countries have entered into inter-governmental agreements (IGAs) with the United States as an alternative or supplement to the FATCA regime.

.02 Classify Trust In Accordance With Final Regulations

The final regulations define an FFI as any "financial institution," and identify four entities that are considered financial institutions: depository institutions, custodial institutions, investment entities, and insurance companies. Because most trusts use some form of professional money management—sometimes directly when the trustee is a bank or trust company and sometimes indirectly when the trustee is an individual but hires an investment adviser or money manager—the foregoing examples lead to the conclusion that most trusts will be categorized as FFIs.

.03 Determine and Comply With Reporting Requirements

The final regulations allow a trust categorized as an FFI to avoid a 30 percent withholding tax on withholdable payments by entering into an FFI agreement and performing due diligence to identify and report information about certain of its U.S. beneficiaries. The trust may be able to avoid entering into a formal FFI agreement if it qualifies as an owner-documented FFI. An owner-documented FFI is an investment entity with a withholding agent that is a U.S. financial institution or participating FFI that agrees to satisfy the reporting requirements on behalf of the FFI.

---

[71] Hiring Incentives to Restore Employment Act, P.L. No. 111-147.

[72] See Treas. Reg. §§ 1.1471-0 through 1.1474-7, T.D. 9610 (Jan. 17, 2013).

The effective dates for foreign trusts subject to FATCA include July 1, 2014 when required withholding began and March 31, 2015 when the first information report is due.

¶ 1307 Offshore Voluntary Disclosure Programs (OVDP)[73]

An Offshore Voluntary Disclosure Program (OVDP) is a voluntary disclosure program specifically designed for taxpayers with exposure to potential criminal liability and/or substantial civil penalties due to a willful failure to report foreign financial assets and pay all tax due in respect of those assets. The OVDP is designed to provide taxpayers with such exposure (1) protection from criminal liability and (2) terms for resolving their civil tax and penalty obligations.

In 2017, the IRS Large Business and International Division rolled out a campaign for applicants who initially applied for pre-clearance into the OVDP since 2009, but were either (1) denied entry by the IRS Criminal Investigation division, or (2) withdrew prior to acceptance into the OVDP.[74] Taxpayers who opted out of the OVDP, who were removed from an OVDP, or who are currently in an OVDP are not subject to this campaign.

.01 Prior OVDP Campaigns and Administration

The current rendition of the OVDP started in 2012, and the IRS significantly modified the program's terms (including the addition of the streamlined filing procedure) in June 2014.[75] The focus of the 2017 campaign is on noncompliance in any year where the statute of limitation remains open. Typically, the statute of limitations on an individual tax return remains open for three years after the later of the due date or date of actual filing, but can be extended or tolled in certain circumstances, even indefinitely in the case of fraud, tax evasion, or failure to file. One such circumstance includes a taxpayer's failure to file specified information returns relating to certain foreign transfers (e.g., Forms 8621 (PFICs), 5471 (CFCs), 8938 (foreign assets), and 3520 (foreign trusts)). Where a taxpayer fails to file a specified information return for a particular year (and the failure is not due to reasonable cause), the statute of limitation does not begin to run until the required information return is filed, even if the taxpayer has filed his or her individual tax return. While it is unclear whether the Service will aggressively apply this broad rule, it could cause some sleepless nights to a number of the affected applicants under this campaign.

.02 Goals of the Campaign

According to the Service, a taxpayer's current residence will not be a factor in applying the procedures of the OVDP compliance campaign. For those taxpayers falling under this campaign, there are three possible treatment outcomes:

---

[73] The author would like to recognize the contribution of Rodney Read and Daniel W. Hudson, both of Baker McKenzie.

[74] Since 2009, the IRS has effectuated three different OVDPs that, according to recent IRS data, have resulted in more than 55,800 disclosures and $9.9 billion in tax, interest, and penalties.

[75] According to the IRS, there are approximately 6,000 taxpayers affected by this new OVDP compliance campaign, and that number could increase as the OVDP continues.

1. No further action for taxpayers who have become compliant;
2. Soft letters outlining the taxpayer's options, and requiring a taxpayer response in cases of immaterial noncompliance; and
3. Examination for other noncompliant taxpayers.

.03 Selection for Audit

In instances where taxpayers are selected for audit, normal exam procedures will be followed. The current campaign appears to be a strategy shift by the IRS to a more targeted approach to noncompliance. The IRS will review the data it has collected as opposed to allocating its limited resources to collect more. Taxpayers who were denied entry by the IRS Criminal Investigation division or withdrew after submitting an application to the OVDP could ensure that all open years are in compliance and that compliance can be proven. Taxpayers who have yet to resolve their offshore noncompliance could consider entering the OVDP, or one of its ancillary programs currently available.

Chapter 14

Fiduciary Duties and Liabilities

¶ 1401   Fiduciary's Personal Liability for Tax
¶ 1402   Enforcement of Fiduciary Liability
¶ 1403   Executor Can Be Discharged from Liability
¶ 1404   Notice of Fiduciary Relationship
¶ 1405   Identification Numbers
¶ 1406   Claims for Credit or Refund
¶ 1407   Assessment and Collection Period Can Be Shortened
¶ 1408   Transferee Liability of a Beneficiary
¶ 1409   Lien for Taxes—Insurance Proceeds
¶ 1410   Fiduciary Liability for Self-Employment Tax

¶ 1401   Fiduciary's Personal Liability for Tax

A fiduciary is required to make and file a return for an estate or a trust and to pay the tax on its taxable income. A trustee, executor, or administrator may be personally liable for the tax on the estate's taxable income up to and after his or her discharge if, before distribution and discharge, the fiduciary had notice of his or her tax obligations or failed to exercise due diligence in finding out whether such obligations existed. Liability for the tax also follows the assets of the estate distributed to heirs, devisees, legatees, and distributees, who may be required to discharge the amount of the tax due and unpaid to the extent of the distributive shares received by them.[1]

.01 The Federal Priority Statute

The federal law applicable to fiduciary liability for failure to satisfy federal claims is governed by the Federal Priority Statute, Title 31, § 3713 of the United States Code. Under § 3713, every executor, administrator, assignee, or other person who pays, in whole or in part, any debt due by the person or estate for whom or for which he or she acts without first satisfying and paying debts due the United States is personally liable to the extent of such payments. The Statute establishes that the federal government is entitled to have its claims paid first when a person indebted to the government is insolvent, and (i) a debtor without enough property to pay all debts makes a voluntary assignment of property, (ii) property of an absent debtor is

---

[1] Reg. § 1.641(b)-2.

attached, or (iii) an "act of bankruptcy is committed."[2] The Federal Priority Statute covers decedents' estates.[3] The federal government is entitled to have its claims paid first if the estate of the deceased debtor, in the custody of the executor or administrator, is not enough to pay all debts of the debtor. Thus, the government is entitled to be paid before the heirs receive an inheritance from the decedent's estate. Pursuant to the Federal Priority Statute, the fiduciary must pay a federal claim before other claims.

For personal liability to attach, the debts due to the United States must have been determined or determinable at the time the other debts were paid. The fiduciary must also have been "chargeable" with knowledge of the debts due to the United States.[4] However, in the *McCourt* case, the Tax Court pointed out that the knowledge on the part of the fiduciary as to the existence of the liability to the government is not a specific requirement of the law.[5] Moreover, if the government has made a prima facie showing of liability, the burden is on the fiduciary to establish lack of knowledge. Despite receiving notice of an estate's potential income tax liability, an executor's good faith reliance on the advice of counsel that no tax was owed the government can suffice to show lack of knowledge,[6] but not if the executor had actual knowledge of the estate's liability and litigation over the extent of that liability.[7]

According to one Tax Court case,[8] before liability can attach to the fiduciary, he or she must have had a choice between paying the tax owed to the government and paying a debt owed by the estate. If an executor pays a debt of the estate or distributes any portion of the estate before all of its taxes are paid, the executor is personally liable for the unpaid tax to the extent of the payment or distribution, provided the executor had actual or constructive knowledge of its debt to the U.S. government and the estate had sufficient assets to pay the debt at the time this information was known.[9]

A fiduciary may not be held personally liable for amounts paid on debts that have priority over federal taxes. Such debts include (1) probate costs, (2) the decedent's funeral expenses and headstone,[10] and (3) the statutory allowance to a surviving spouse required by local law when the assets used in payment of the allowance are assets of the estate.[11] A distinction was made when the assets used to pay the allowance were assets to which the estate was not entitled, but which, as transferee, it held subject to liabilities of the insolvent transferor.[12]

The Second Circuit liberally construed the federal insolvency statute (31 U.S.C. §3713(b)) when it determined personal liability of an executor of a dece-

---

[2] 31 USC § 3713(a)(1)(A). Note that an "act of bankruptcy" does not refer to cases brought under Bankruptcy Code – here the priorities in the bankruptcy laws apply rather than the Federal Priority Statute.

[3] 31 USC § 3713(a)(1)(B).

[4] *G. Terranova*, 2 TCM 616, CCH Dec. 13,431(M); *F.H.D. Johnson Est.*, 78 TCM 358, CCH Dec. 53,518(M), TC Memo. 1999-284; Rev. Rul. 66-43, 1966-1 CB 291; Rev. Rul. 79-310, 1979-2 CB 404.

[5] *L.T. McCourt*, 15 TC 734, CCH Dec. 17,951.

[6] *W.D. Little*, 113 TC 475, CCH Dec. 53,676.

[7] *E. Bartlett*, DC Ill., 2002-1 USTC ¶ 60,429, 186 F. Supp. 2d 875.

[8] *G.P. Fitzgerald*, 4 TC 494, CCH Dec. 14,291.

[9] *D.S. Beckwith*, 69 TCM 1678, CCH Dec. 50,422(M), TC Memo. 1995-20, citing *L.K. New*, 48 TC 671, CCH Dec. 28,568; Reg. § 20.2002-1.

[10] *K. Weisburn, Exrx.*, DC Pa., 43-1 USTC ¶ 9247, 48 FSupp 393; *E.B. Munroe, Exrx.*, DC Pa., 46-1 USTC ¶ 9219, 65 F. Supp. 213.

[11] *J. Smith, Exrx.*, 24 BTA 807, CCH Dec. 7275 (Acq.).

[12] *L.T. McCourt*, 15 TC 734, CCH Dec. 17,951.

dent's estate who distributed the estate's assets before satisfying its tax debt, thereby rendering the estate insolvent.[13] In this case, the IRS did not issue a notice of estate tax deficiency until after family members entered into an agreement dividing various family businesses among themselves. However, discussions and negotiations between the executor and the IRS about an alleged tax deficiency took place before the signing of the agreement and, thus, were sufficient to put the executor on notice of the tax liability. The Second Circuit found that, while the federal insolvency statute proscribes payment of an estate's *debt* before payment of a claim by the federal government, the executor's distribution of assets to himself and family members was consistent with a broad reading of the statute. Thus, the executor was required to return assets to the estate that he fraudulently transferred out of the estate as part of a scheme to put those assets beyond the reach of the estate's creditors.

The primary duties of the administrator or executor are to (1) collect all the decedent's assets, (2) pay all proper claims of creditors, and (3) distribute the remaining assets to the heirs or beneficiaries. Discharge of the administrator or executor by the probate court does not terminate his or her liability when he or she paid the other debts of the estate without satisfying the prior claim for federal taxes.[14] In order to be indemnified against personal liability for taxes later found due, a fiduciary who distributes property may safeguard his or her interests in doubtful cases by exacting a bond from the distributees.

An executor can obtain a discharge from personal liability for a decedent's income taxes by making a written application for release (see ¶ 1403).

¶ 1402 Enforcement of Fiduciary Liability

Generally, the personal liability of a fiduciary is assessed, collected, and paid in the same way as a deficiency in tax. The Internal Revenue Code provisions for the following are applicable as in the case of any other income tax deficiency:

- delinquency in payment after notice and demand, and the amount of interest attaching because of such delinquency;
- the authorization of distraint and proceedings in court for collection;
- the prohibition of claims and suits for refund;
- the filing of a petition with the Tax Court; and
- the filing of a petition for review of the Tax Court's decision.[15]

Special criminal penalties are incurred when the fiduciary willfully fails to make a return when required by law or regulations to do so, or the fiduciary willfully attempts in any manner to evade or defeat the tax. These penalties are in addition to the civil penalties applicable to the tax due by the estate or trust.

The estate of a decedent is liable for penalties incurred by the decedent during the decedent's lifetime.[16] The penalties provided in the Code are remedial compen-

---

[13] *J.M. Coppola, Jr.*, CA-2, 96-1 USTC ¶ 60,233, 85 F3d 1015.
[14] *M. Viles, Admrx.*, CA-6, 56-1 USTC ¶ 9539, 233 F2d 376.
[15] Reg. § 301.6901-1(a)(3).
[16] *F.P. Kirk, Admr. (Briden Est.)*, CA-1, 50-1 USTC ¶ 9169, 179 F2d 619; *M.J. Reimer*, CA-6, 50-1 USTC ¶ 9189,

sation for loss to the United States, and not personal punishment. Accordingly, they survive the death of the taxpayer.[17]

Estates of mentally disabled, deceased, or insolvent persons are not exempt from penalties for delinquencies or violations. The administrator, executor, or other personal representative is personally liable in such cases.

¶ 1403 Executor Can Be Discharged from Liability

After filing the decedent's return, the executor may apply in writing for discharge from personal liability for tax on the decedent's income. The discharge becomes effective after payment by the executor of any tax of which he or she is subsequently notified, or if nine months have passed since receipt of the application and no notification has been made. This does not discharge the executor from liability as an executor to the extent of the assets of the decedent's estate still in the executor's possession or control.[18]

¶ 1404 Notice of Fiduciary Relationship

The assessment and collection of income and estate taxes from a person acting in a fiduciary capacity are governed by Code Sec. 6903, which provides that the fiduciary give notice that he or she is acting in such capacity. After giving such notice (Form 56, Notice Concerning Fiduciary Relationship, is available for this purpose), the fiduciary assumes the powers, rights, duties, and privileges of the taxpayer for whom he or she acts, and thereafter the IRS will deal directly with the fiduciary until notice is given that the fiduciary capacity has terminated. The tax, however, is payable by the estate or trust and becomes the fiduciary's personal liability only under the conditions discussed at ¶ 1401.

The notice of a fiduciary relationship does not impose any new liability upon the fiduciary. The notice's function is to assure that the fiduciary receives notification of any tax imposed against the estate or trust that he or she represents so that he or she has the opportunity to contest the liability. The failure to file such a notice may result in prejudicing the interests of the estate or trust.

.01 Written Notice

The notice must be in writing, signed by the fiduciary, and filed with the IRS office where the return of the person for whom the fiduciary is acting is required to be filed. It must state the name and address of the person for whom the fiduciary is acting and the nature of the liability of such person; that is, whether it is (1) a liability for tax, and, if so, the year or years involved, (2) a liability at law or in equity of the transferee of property of a taxpayer, or (3) a liability of a fiduciary under 31 U.S.C. § 3713.[19] Proof of the fiduciary's capacity must be retained by the taxpayer but need not be attached to the form.[20]

(Footnote Continued)

180 F2d 159; *W.F. Rau, Sr., Est.*, CA-9, 62-1 USTC ¶ 9339, 301 F2d 51.

[17] *C.E. Mitchell*, SCt, 38-1 USTC ¶ 9152, 303 US 391; Rev. Rul. 73-293, 1973-2 CB 413.

[18] Code Sec. 6905; Reg. § 301.6905-1.

[19] Reg. § 301.6903-1(b).

[20] Reg. § 301.6903-1(b)(2).

¶ 1405 Identification Numbers

An executor or administrator must obtain an employer identification number (trusts also require such a number) to be entered on Form 1041 and on other returns or documents filed for the estate.[21] Such a number is applied for on Form SS-4 (Application for Employer Identification Number). A separate Schedule K-1 (Beneficiary's Share of Income, Deductions, Credits, etc.) to Form 1041 must be filed for each beneficiary. The return should show each beneficiary's taxpayer identification number (TIN), and, absent reasonable cause, an executor or administrator is subject to a $50 penalty (up to an overall ceiling of $100,000 for any calendar year) for each failure (1) to include, if required, a TIN on a return, statement, or other document or (2) to furnish such TIN to another person who, with respect to the taxpayer, is required to file a return, statement, or other document.[22] Failure to provide a TIN to the payer in the manner prescribed may expose a trust or estate to backup withholding.[23]

¶ 1406 Claims for Credit or Refund

The fiduciary is the proper person to make a claim for credit or refund of any overpayment of income tax made by the estate or trust.[24] This is a duty that may be overlooked in the case of an estate because of its short duration and the desire of the heirs or legatees to curtail administrative expenses.

When a taxpayer dies, the administrator or executor of the taxpayer's estate may file claims for refund if he or she is still acting as such, and upon the fiduciary's discharge, the right passes to the beneficiaries entitled to the estate's assets.[25] A beneficiary could be a trustee if the decedent created a testamentary trust. Signature of only one co-executor is required on the claim.[26] When a trust has been terminated, the trust assets distributed, and the trustee discharged, the right to claim a refund of an overpayment of tax made by the trustee passes to the beneficiaries.[27]

If a return is filed by an individual and, after the individual's death, a refund claim is filed by his or her legal representative, certified copies of the letters testamentary, letters of administration, or other similar evidence must be attached to the claim to show the authority of the legal representative to file the claim. If an executor, administrator, guardian, trustee, receiver, or other fiduciary files a return and thereafter a refund claim is filed by the same fiduciary, documentary evidence to establish the legal authority of the fiduciary need not accompany the claim, provided a statement is made in the claim showing that the return was filed by the fiduciary and that the latter is still acting in such capacity. In such cases, if a refund is to be paid, letters testamentary, letters of administration, or other evidence may be required, but they should be submitted only upon receipt of a specific request. If a claim is filed by a fiduciary other than the one by whom the return was filed, the necessary documentary evidence should accompany the claim. A claim may be

---

[21] Code Sec. 6109; Reg. § 301.6109-1.
[22] Code Secs. 6723 and 6724(d)(3)(B).
[23] Code Sec. 3406(a)(1)(A).
[24] Code Sec. 6402.
[25] Rev. Rul. 73-366, 1973-2 CB 408.
[26] Rev. Rul. 54-468, 1954-2 CB 248.
[27] Rev. Rul. 73-366, 1973-2 CB 408.

executed by an agent of the person assessed, but in such cases a power of attorney must accompany the claim.[28]

Except for a surviving spouse filing a joint return, a person claiming a refund on behalf of a taxpayer who has died must attach Form 1310 (Statement of Person Claiming Refund Due a Deceased Taxpayer) to the deceased taxpayer's return.[29]

¶ 1407 Assessment and Collection Period Can Be Shortened

Under a special provision in the law, a fiduciary can shorten the regular three-year period (after a return is filed) for assessment and collection of the tax due from a decedent or his or her estate. The law provides that any tax for which a return is required (except estate taxes) and for which a decedent or an estate of a decedent may be liable is to be assessed, or a court proceeding without assessment for the collection of such tax is to begin, within 18 months after the receipt of a written request for prompt assessment.[30]

The request for prompt assessment is filed by the fiduciary with the IRS office where the regular return was filed. The request may be made on Form 4810 (Request for Prompt Assessment Under Internal Revenue Code Section 6501(d)). The request, to be effective, must set forth the classes of tax and the tax periods for which the prompt assessment is requested and, if the request is not filed on Form 4810, must clearly indicate that it is a request for prompt assessment under the provisions of Code Sec. 6501(d). The request must also be filed after the return in question has been filed and must be sent to the IRS in an envelope separate from any other document.[31] The effect of such a request is to limit the time in which an assessment of tax may be made, or a proceeding in court without assessment for collection of tax begun, to a period of 18 months from the date the request is received by the IRS. The request does not extend the time within which an assessment may be made, or a proceeding in court without assessment begun, beyond three years from the date the return was filed. This special period of limitations will not apply to any return filed after a request for prompt assessment has been made unless an additional request is filed.[32]

The privilege of a request for prompt assessment does not apply if the income tax returns filed by the decedent or estate were fraudulent or failed to report substantial amounts of gross income (defined under Code Sec. 6501(e) as an amount in excess of 25 percent of the gross income reported on the return).[33]

¶ 1408 Transferee Liability of a Beneficiary

The Internal Revenue Code provides that the liability of a transferee of a taxpayer's property for income taxes imposed upon such taxpayer is to be assessed and collected in the same manner as any other deficiency.[34] The term "transferee" is defined as including an heir, a legatee, devisee, donee, or distributee.[35] Thus, a beneficiary, as transferee of a trust, was liable for taxes due from the trust to the

---

[28] Reg. § 301.6402-2(e).
[29] See ¶ 211.
[30] Code Sec. 6501(d); Reg. § 301.6501(d)-1.
[31] Rev. Rul. 57-319, 1957-2 CB 855.
[32] Reg. § 301.6501(d)-1.
[33] Reg. § 301.6501(e)-1.
[34] Code Sec. 6901.
[35] Code Sec. 6901(h); Reg. § 301.6901-1(b).

extent of the assets received upon the trust's termination.[36] In the case of an initial transferee, the assessment must be made within one year after the expiration of the period of limitation for assessment against the transferor.[37] In the case of a transferee, the assessment must be made one year after the expiration of the period of limitation for assessment against the preceding transferee, or three years after the expiration of the period of limitation for assessment against the taxpayer, whichever of such periods first expires.[38] Assessment of a fiduciary's liability must be made within one year after the liability arises or within the limited period for collection of the tax, whichever is later.[39] In the case of the decedent-transferor, it is the period that would have been in effect had death not occurred.[40]

The existence and extent of transferee liability for income tax is determined by state law.[41] In the case of property held by the decedent and others as joint tenants, the IRS has held that a surviving tenant is not liable as a transferee for income tax owed by a deceased joint tenant if, under the laws of the state in which the estate was located, the property that passed directly to the surviving tenant was not subject to the claims of the decedent's creditors.[42] However, depending on the state law involved, the transferees may become subject to transferee liability at the point in time when the decedent originally transferred the property to the joint tenants.[43]

To establish transferee liability under Code Sec. 6901, the IRS has the burden of proving the decedent's insolvency at the time of death.[44] When it fails to do so, the estate is no more liable as a transferee than the decedent would have been if he or she were alive. If the insolvency of the estate is due to the personal representative's failing to observe priority of payment of debts and legacies, it would seem that the IRS has the election of proceeding (1) against the fiduciary under 31 U.S.C. § 3713, (2) against the estate, the fiduciary, or the beneficiary under Code Sec. 6901, or (3) it may invoke both remedies to the extent necessary for the collection of the tax.

¶ 1409 Lien for Taxes—Insurance Proceeds

A lien for taxes may be enforced against the cash surrender value of a life insurance policy that is available to the insured-taxpayer prior to the date of death.[45] According to the U.S. Supreme Court, the cash surrender value of a policy is a property right owned by the insured, and a lien attaching before his or her death is enforceable against the recipient of the policy's proceeds to the extent of the policy's cash surrender value. This is so whether or not state law exempts a beneficiary of life insurance proceeds from taxes owed by the insured. However, state law exemptions will prevail where no tax lien attaches prior to the insured's death. Thus, whether a beneficiary is liable for unpaid federal income taxes of the

---

[36] *E. Yagoda*, CA-2, 64-1 USTC ¶ 9448, 331 F2d 485, cert. denied, 379 US 842.

[37] Reg. § 301.6901-1(c)(1).

[38] Reg. § 301.6901-1(c)(2).

[39] Reg. § 301.6901-1(c)(4).

[40] Reg. § 301.6901-1(e).

[41] *J.F. Stern*, SCt, 58-2 USTC ¶ 9594, 357 US 39, 78 SCt 1047.

[42] Rev. Rul. 78-299, 1978-2 CB 304.

[43] IRS Letter Ruling 9851036, September 15, 1998.

[44] Code Sec. 6902(a).

[45] *Metropolitan Life Insurance Co. (M.A. Gilmore)*, reh'g CA-4, 58-2 USTC ¶ 9630, 256 F2d 17; CA-4, 58-1 USTC ¶ 9230, rev'g and rem'g DC W.Va., 57-1 USTC ¶ 9569, 147 FSupp 902; *Y.S. Duke*, CA-DC, 64-2 USTC ¶ 9831, 343 F2d 294; *L.E. Ball*, CA-4, 64-1 USTC ¶ 9191, 326 F2d 898.

insured in the absence of a lien against the cash surrender value of the policy prior to death depends upon the liability that the state law imposes against the beneficiary.[46]

When the beneficiary pays for and holds the life insurance policy so that the insured cannot defeat his or her rights by executing a change of beneficiary, it has been held that a tax lien against the insured-taxpayer cannot be enforced against the policy.[47]

If a tax lien arises before the insured-taxpayer names an irrevocable beneficiary or assigns the life insurance policy, the United States has a prior right to the cash surrender value of the policy as against the rights of the irrevocable beneficiary or assignee.[48] However, where an insurance policy was assigned after assessment of taxes but no notice of a tax lien was given, the lien was not valid against the proceeds paid to the beneficiary.[49]

¶ 1410 Fiduciary Liability for Self-Employment Tax

Generally, the IRS holds that a professional executor, trustee, or administrator (i.e., one who regularly engages in such services and handles a number of estates and/or trusts) is engaged in a trade or business and, therefore, is subject to the self-employment tax. However, nonprofessional executors, trustees, and administrators who gather the assets of an estate in isolated cases would not ordinarily be engaged in a trade or business and would not be subject to the self-employment tax. A nonprofessional executor or administrator (i.e., a person serving in such capacity in an isolated instance, such as a friend or relative of the decedent) would be subject to self-employment tax only if (1) a trade or business is included in the estate's assets, (2) the executor actively participates in the business, and (3) the fees are related to the business's operation.[50]

In some cases, the activities of the executor of a single estate may constitute the conduct of a trade or business even though the assets of the estate do not include a trade or business as such. If, for example, an executor manages an estate which requires extensive management activities on his or her part over a long period of time, an examination of the facts may show that such activities are sufficient in scope and duration to constitute the carrying on of a trade or business.[51]

Income of an irrevocable testamentary trust that was derived from farming activity and distributed to the spouse and son of a decedent, who were both beneficiaries and trustees of the trust, was considered net earnings from self-employment subject to self-employment taxes, to the extent that the distributions were payments for services that they provided to the trust as part of their trade or business.[52]

---

[46] *J.F. Stern*, SCt, 58-2 USTC ¶ 9594, 357 US 39; *M.G. Bess*, SCt, 58-2 USTC ¶ 9595, 357 US 51.

[47] *J. Burgo*, CA-3, 49-1 USTC ¶ 9307, 175 F2d 196.

[48] *L.E. Knox v. Great West Life Assurance Co.*, CA-6, 54-1 USTC ¶ 9373, 212 F2d 784.

[49] *L. Wintner*, SCt, 64-1 USTC ¶ 9168, 375 US 393.

[50] Rev. Rul. 58-5, 1958-1 CB 322; IRS Publication No. 559, Survivors, Executors, and Administrators (2006), p. 3.

[51] Rev. Rul. 58-5, 1958-1 CB 322.

[52] IRS Technical Advice Memorandum 200305002, July 24, 2002.

Chapter 15

State Fiduciary Income Taxation of Trusts

¶ 1501 Overview of State Fiduciary Income Taxation for Resident and Nonresident Trusts
¶ 1502 The *Linn* Example: Introduction to the Issue
¶ 1503 How Is the "Residence" of a Trust Determined
¶ 1504 Factors the States Apply to Determine State Fiduciary Taxation
¶ 1505 Constitutional Basis for State Taxation—Perspective on Supreme Court Analysis
¶ 1506 The Commerce Clause
¶ 1507 The Due Process Clause
¶ 1508 *Quill Corporation* and Minimum Contacts for State Law Taxing Power
¶ 1509 *Swift*, Founder Criteria and Present Benefit Minimum Contacts for State Trust Laws: Six Points
¶ 1510 *Blue*, Founder Criteria and Ongoing Protection Minimum Contacts Required for State Law Taxing Power
¶ 1511 *Bank of America* and Trust Administration in a State
¶ 1512 *Mercantile Safe Deposit* and Control over the Property Necessary by New York Beneficiaries
¶ 1513 *Kassner* and New Jersey Testamentary Trusts with Undistributed S Corporation Income
¶ 1514 *Pennoyer* and Probate Administration for Testamentary Trust Not Enough
¶ 1515 *D.C. v. Chase Manhattan Bank* and Probate Is Enough to Withstand Challenge
¶ 1516 *McNeil* and the Importance of Discretionary Beneficiaries under the Pennsylvania Statute
¶ 1517 *Gavin* and Treatment of Non-Contingent Beneficiaries
¶ 1518 *Kaestner* and the Residence of the Beneficiary
¶ 1519 Trends Practitioners Should Plan For

¶ 1501 Overview of State Fiduciary Income Taxation for Resident and Nonresident Trusts

Trusts are also subject to particular *state's* tax regime, in addition to federal fiduciary income taxation, if such state imposes a state fiduciary income tax. Currently, 43 states and the District of Columbia impose a state fiduciary income tax.[1] The seven states that do not impose a state-level income tax are: Alaska, Florida, Nevada, South Dakota, Texas, Washington, and Wyoming. The question of whether a state can justify imposing a tax with continued entitlement to its share of fiduciary income tax revenue has become an important and developing issue in fiduciary income taxation. And, the migration of trusts to those states that do not impose a state-level income tax has become a common goal among practitioners.

.01 Resident State Taxation

State fiduciary income taxation is generally based on "residency" within a state, and more broadly, contacts with the state. If a trust is determined to be a "resident" of a particular state, that state's state statute will attempt to tax all of the trust's income. The determination of whether the trust will be treated as a resident trust, and thereby subject a trust to full state taxation, is based on the state statute, and supported by the level of contacts that exist with the state.[2] Five commonly reviewed contacts discussed throughout this chapter include: (1) contacts with the decedent or decedent's estate (i.e., a probate proceeding) that gave rise to a testamentary trust, (2) contacts with the state by the grantor when the grantor created an inter vivos trust in the state, (3) contact through the ongoing administration of the trust in the state, (4) contacts with the trustee of the trust in the state, and (5) contacts with the beneficiary of the trust in the state. Under one or more of these factors, the state statute may deem a trust a statutory resident.

.02 Nonresident State Taxation

Alternatively, if the trust is not determined to be a resident as to a particular state, then a state may apportion tax on trust income based on only that amount of income attributed to such state. Case law has determined apportionment an important aspect of constitutional state taxation as discussed in *Complete Auto Transport* and the "substantial nexus" test of the Commerce Clause (see ¶ 1506). Nonresident state taxation follows the apportionment doctrine, where only state-sourced income is taxed by the state. The New Jersey decision of *Residuary Trust* is an example where the trust in question was determined not to be a resident trust, but New Jersey did tax state-sourced income to the trust as a nonresident trust.[3]

---

[1] *See* Nenno, *Let My Trustees Go! Planning to Minimize or Avoid State Income Taxes on Trusts*, 46th Heckerling Inst. on Est. Pl., ch. 15 (2012) for a thorough review of various states with detailed charts addressing state-by-state application (hereinafter "Nenno").

[2] The issue of resident state taxation was most recently considered in the Supreme Court of North Carolina in *Kaestner v. N.C. Dept. of Revenue*, 814 S.E.2d 43 (N.C. 2018), *aff'g* 789 S.E.2d 645 (N.C. Ct. App. 2016), in Illinois under the decision of *Linn v. Department of Revenue*, 2 NE3d 1203 (Ill. App. Ct. 2013), as well as in Pennsylvania under the decision *McNeil v. Commonwealth*, 67 A3d 185 (Pa. Commw. Ct. 2013), all of which are discussed below.

[3] *Residuary Trust v. Director, Division of Taxation*, 27 NJ Tax 68 (2013).

¶ 1502 The *Linn* Example: Introduction to the Issue

The impact of the above general rules can be illustrated by a review of a 2013 Illinois decision: *Linn v. Department of Revenue*.[4] The statutory residency requirement in *Linn* is the more commonly used amongst the states—the grantor was a resident of Illinois when the trust was created. The *Linn* decision evolved from an irrevocable inter vivos trust created in 1961. Over time, the administration of the trust involved less and less contacts with the state of Illinois, and by 2007 when the underlying proceedings began, where:

- no income was earned in the state of Illinois,
- none of the trust's assets were located in Illinois,
- the trust was administered outside of Illinois, and
- both the trustee and beneficiary resided outside of Illinois (in the state of Texas).

Thus, the trust had no connection with Illinois, *except that* the grantor was a resident of Illinois at the time the trust was created. This fact, under Illinois law, resulted in the premise that the trust would forever be burdened with paying Illinois tax *on all of its worldwide income*, regardless of how brief the grantor was a resident of Illinois.

- Because the grantor was a resident of Illinois when the trust was created, the trust was a deemed Illinois resident trust, and Illinois fiduciary income tax applied on all the income.

If, on the other hand, the grantor of such an inter vivos trust had *not* been resident of Illinois at the time the trust became irrevocable, the trust would be classified as a "nonresident" trust. A nonresident trust in Illinois is taxed on the income apportioned under Illinois law. This is the case even though the trustee may reside in Illinois, the trust offices and trust property may be located in Illinois, and all other domiciliary connections may be exclusively in Illinois.

The Illinois Department of Revenue argued at the trial level that the original trust agreement (which had since been modified) selected Illinois under the choice of law clause, and that this prior choice of law election justified substantial nexus with the state.[5] The Illinois Appellate Court determined that the law subjecting the *Linn* trust to Illinois fiduciary income taxation was unconstitutional—but only as to the *Linn* taxpayer.[6] Thus, inter vivos trusts created by Illinois residents that meet the facts of *Linn* no longer should be subject to Illinois fiduciary income taxation, *based on* the status of the grantor on creating the trust, yet the Illinois Department of Revenue has not conceded the issue, and similarly situated taxpayers must consider a reporting position that may require litigation to achieve the same result.

---

[4] *Linn v. Department of Revenue*, 2 NE3d 1203 (Ill. App. Ct. 2013).

[5] Note that if choice of law was determinative for state taxation as the Illinois trial court concluded, every trust drafted since this case would select one of the seven jurisdictions identified above (Alaska, Florida, Nevada, South Dakota, Texas, Washington, and Wyoming) as the "choice of law" state, regardless of origin or domicile.

[6] Section 304 of the Illinois Income Tax Act. The Illinois Department of Revenue has indicated that they will not appeal the *Linn* decision, yet the State Legislature has no current plans to amend the statute.

¶ 1503 How Is the "Residence" of a Trust Determined

The *Linn* decision is an example of the complexity involved with state fiduciary income taxation where "multi-jurisdictional contacts" are present. The question is: what constitutes sufficient nexus with a state to justify imposing a state fiduciary income tax?

The starting point in the analysis of the state income taxation of a trust is the determination of whether the trust will be treated as a "resident" trust. As discussed above, states that tax the income of a trust generally tax all the income of a resident trust, and only that portion of the state-sourced income of a nonresident trust. If the state taxes all the income of a resident trust, there will be a statute defining what is necessary to reach resident status. The means by which the residence of a trust is determined is not uniform among the states, but the following criteria is commonly recognized to support the residence of a trust.[7]

.01 Mobility and Multi-Jurisdictional Contacts

The state taxation issue is heightened when considering that the mobility of taxpayers increases the mismatch with state fiduciary income tax principles. Consider a family raised in Chicago, with a child that moves to Nevada. Does Illinois still have the power to tax that individual taxpayer? For individual income tax purposes, the answer is generally no, as with corporation taxation and partnership taxation for taxpayers that change situs. But for fiduciary tax purposes, if the taxpayer was originally a resident trust and the trust changed administrative situs as in *Linn*, Illinois would continue to try to tax the taxpayer.

Some initial considerations to be aware of when dealing with multi-jurisdictional trust administration:[8]

- Will the decedent's state of residence before death subject a testamentary trust to state fiduciary income tax?
- Will the grantor's state of residence cause an inter vivos trust to be subject to state fiduciary income tax?
- Will trust administration cause state taxation?
- Will the residence of the trustee cause taxation to that trustee's state?
- Will the residence of the beneficiary cause state taxation of the trust?

As the chart below depicts, most states base the analysis solely on the first two criteria, the residence of either the grantor (for a inter vivos trust) or testator (for a testamentary trust)—also referred to below as the "founder" criteria. Other states either base the analysis on one or both founder criteria, plus some other criteria, such as the place of administration, the residence of the trustee, and/or the residence of the beneficiary.

---

[7] *See* Nenno for more information on how diverse the state determination of residence can be, and note the summary chart below is included for quick reference.

[8] *See* Jeanne L. Newlon and Jennifer A. Birchfield, "*State Income Taxation of Trusts*" for a discussion of the state income taxation of trusts which can be found at: https://www.venable.com/state-income-taxation-of-trusts-at-the-dc-bar-10-18-2010/

¶ 1504 Factors the States Apply to Determine State Fiduciary Taxation

The basis for taxing a trust on the residency of the grantor or testator has been referred to as a "founder criteria" trust, referring to the fact that the founder of the trust was a resident of the state when the trust was created, or became irrevocable, and therefore subject to tax in the state.[9] The trust in *Linn* was such a founder criteria-based residency trust. A number of taxpayers (in addition to Linn) have successfully challenged the founder criteria trust style of state taxation where that is the only basis for taxation.[10] In the chart below, the first two columns depict the founder criteria trust, and are the most commonly used criteria throughout the state taxing regimes. The chart also depicts the other factors various states consider:

Quick Reference Summary Chart of State Fiduciary Income Tax Contacts

	Decedent	Grantor	Admin	Trustee	Beneficiary
Alabama	✓	✓			
Alaska					
Arizona				✓	
Arkansas	✓	✓			
California				✓	✓
Colorado			✓		
Connecticut	✓	✓			
Delaware	✓	✓		✓	
DC	✓	✓			
Florida					
Georgia			✓	✓	✓
Hawaii			✓	✓	
Idaho	✓	✓	✓	✓	
Illinois	✓	✓			
Indiana			✓		
Iowa	✓		✓	✓	

---

[9] Jacob, *An Extended Presence, Interstate Style: First Notes on a Theme From Saenz*, 30 Hofstra L. Rev. 1133 (Summer 2002).

[10] *McNeil v. Commonwealth*, 67 A3d 185 (Pa. Commw. Ct. 2013); *Residuary Trust v. Director, Division of Taxation*, 27 NJ Tax 68 (2013); and *Linn v. Department of Revenue*, 2 NE3d 1203 (Ill. App. Ct. 2013).

	Decedent	Grantor	Admin	Trustee	Beneficiary
Kansas			✓		
Kentucky				✓	
Louisiana	✓		✓		
Maine	✓	✓			
Maryland	✓	✓	✓		
Massachusetts	✓	✓			
Michigan	✓	✓			
Minnesota	✓	✓	✓		
Mississippi			✓		
Missouri	✓	✓			
Montana			✓	✓	
Nebraska	✓	✓			
Nevada					
New Hampshire				✓	
New Jersey	✓	✓			
New Mexico			✓	✓	
New York	✓	✓			
North Carolina					✓
North Dakota			✓	✓	✓
Ohio	✓	✓			
Oklahoma	✓	✓			
Oregon			✓	✓	
Pennsylvania	✓	✓			✓
Rhode Island	✓	✓			
South Carolina			✓		
South Dakota					
Tennessee					✓
Texas					

	Decedent	Grantor	Admin	Trustee	Beneficiary
Utah	✓		✓		
Vermont	✓	✓			
Virginia	✓	✓	✓	✓	
Washington					
West Virginia	✓	✓			
Wisconsin	✓	✓	✓		
Wyoming					

For many states, the ultimate determination rests on a combination of these above criteria, given the recent constitutional challenges to basing residency solely on founder criteria. Thus, an understanding of the constitutional limitations in determining residence is important.

¶ 1505 Constitutional Basis for State Taxation—Perspective on Supreme Court Analysis

One of the first reported Supreme Court cases to test the constitutionality of a state trust related tax law was the *Safe Deposit & Trust Co. v. Virginia* decided in 1929.[11] The *Safe Deposit* case did not involve fiduciary *income* tax, rather it involved a state intangibles tax assessed against a trustee from Maryland. The Supreme Court held that the imposition of an intangibles tax by Virginia was unconstitutional because the situs of the property was in Maryland due to the trustee's residence, and neither the grantor nor the beneficiaries who resided in Virginia had control over the trust estate of the trust. This case highlights the importance of where the trustee resides and where the beneficiaries reside, an issue that continues to impact state taxation.

The *Safe Deposit* case also illustrates one of the complicated aspects of state fiduciary taxation: the premise that you can have a bifurcation of the entity. Note that with corporations, partnerships, LLCs, and individuals, the residency can be changed due to the mobility of the entity or individual. With trusts, many state laws will attempt to cause resident taxation permanent at the onset, regardless of the movement of the parties. From a constitutional perspective, this connection must be purposeful.

In the 2014 decision of *Maryland v. Wynne*, the Supreme Court reviewed a tax case, which is a relatively uncommon occurrence.[12] The issue in *Wynne* was whether Maryland's refusal to grant tax credits to Maryland residents for income taxed out of state was unconstitutional. The Court held that such practice was unconstitutional, based on two popular constitutional premises in tax law chal-

---

[11] *Safe Deposit & Trust Co. v. Virginia*, 280 US 83 (1929).

[12] *Maryland v. Wynne*, 134 SCt 2660 (2014).

lenges: the Commerce Clause and the Due Process Clause, both discussed below.[13] And while *Wynne* is primarily a tax credit case, as we will see, in the field of the administration of trusts in other states, the ability to capture a tax credit will be nearly as important as the state level taxation.

¶ 1506 The Commerce Clause

The Commerce Clause is found under Article I of the U.S. Constitution. Article I provides the basis for our Federal income tax stating in Section 8 that "Congress shall have power to lay and collect taxes."[14] Furthermore, clause three of Section 8 gives Congress the power to "regulate Commerce . . . among the several States." The Supreme Court has historically interpreted from this power, the negative inference that if the Constitution granted to Congress the power to regulate commerce, then the states cannot regulate interstate commerce.[15] Specific to the state taxing power, the Court has ruled that no State may "impose a tax which discriminates against interstate commerce either by providing a direct commercial advantage to local business, or by subjecting interstate commerce to the burden of 'multiple taxation.'"[16]

.01 The Substantial Nexus Test[17]

According to *Complete Auto Transport*, a tax does not violate the Commerce Clause if it (1) is applied to an interstate activity having a substantial nexus with the taxing state; (2) is fairly apportioned; (3) does not discriminate against interstate commerce; and (4) is fairly related to the services provided by the state.[18] These factors discussed in *Complete Auto Transport* represent the "substantial nexus" test of the Commerce Clause, and have been characterized as being more stringent than the minimum contact requirements of the Due Process Clause discussed below.[19]

From a state fiduciary tax perspective, three of the above factors of the substantial nexus test under *Complete Auto Transport* have a direct trust tax impact, because the substantial nexus with the taxing state is directly relevant to the contacts between the trust and the state. For example, if there are no ongoing contacts between the trust and the state, it would follow that the nexus is not

---

[13] In *Wynne*, the Supreme Court also addressed the Internal Consistency, which requires the Court to apply the tax in question to every state to see if interstate commerce would be put at a disadvantage when compared to intrastate commerce. This test allows the Court to distinguish between: (1) tax schemes that are inherently discriminatory to interstate commerce and (2) tax schemes that "create disparate incentives to engage in interstate commerce . . . only as a result of the interaction of two different but nondiscriminatory and internally consistent schemes." Schemes that fall in the first category are generally unconstitutional, while schemes that fall in the second category are generally constitutional.

[14] U.S. Const. art. I, § 8.

[15] *See Oklahoma Tax Comm'n v. Jefferson Lines, Inc.*, 514 US 175, 179 (1995); *Case of the State Freight Tax*, 82 US 232, 279-280 (1873); *Cooley v. Bd. of Warden*, 53 US 299, 318-319 (1852); *Gibbons v. Ogden*, 22 US 1, 209 (1824).

[16] *Northwestern States Portland Cement Co. v. Minnesota*, 358 US 450, 458 (1959).

[17] Noel, Charlotte, *Substantial Nexus: The "Nexus Gap" Over Intangibles*, J. of St. Tax, March-April, 2011 (CCH).

[18] *Complete Auto Transit, Inc. v. Brady*, 430 US 274, 277, 97 SCt 1076, 1079 (1977).

[19] *Quill Corp. v. North Dakota*, 504 US 298, 313 (1992); U.S. Const. art. I, § 8, cl. 3. In reviewing the Commerce Clause, the Supreme Court has imposed an even higher "substantial nexus" standard between the taxpayer and the taxing State. Note that on June 21, 2018, the Supreme Court eliminated the physical presence standard for out-of-state sellers of goods. In *South Dakota v. Wayfair, Inc.*, 138 SCt 2080 (2018), the Court ruled that a state may impose a state sales tax on an in-state consumer, notwithstanding the lack of the seller's physical presence in that state.

substantial. Fairly apportioned is manifested in how the state apportions the tax, especially to certain beneficiaries.[20] And fairly related to the services provided by the state is analogous to the necessary "ongoing nature" of those contacts.

¶ 1507 The Due Process Clause

The Constitution provides that no one shall be "deprived of life, liberty or property without due process of law"—these 11 words are mentioned twice, in the Fifth Amendment and the Fourteenth Amendment.[21] The words of the Due Process clause provide an assurance that all levels of government operate legally and fairly. As applied to states, it empowers states to tax the income of its residents, regardless of the origination of which state the income was derived.[22] A tax allowed under the Due Process clause must still satisfy the requirements of the Commerce Clause to be constitutional.[23] However, to satisfy the Due Process Clause, there must be minimum contacts with the taxing jurisdiction.

.01 Minimum Contacts and Due Process

In *Kaestner*,[24] the North Carolina Supreme Court upheld the appellate court's finding that only relying on the beneficiary's residence in the state was not a sufficient contact. Relying on *Quill* and *International Shoe*, the court noted "it is essential in each case that there be some act by which the [party] purposefully avails itself of the privilege of conducting activities within the forum State."[25]

¶ 1508 *Quill Corporation* and Minimum Contacts for State Law Taxing Power

From a state law perspective, the emphasis of the Due Process Clause as interpreted by *Quill* provides that there must exist "some definite link, some minimum connection, between a state and the person, property or transaction it seeks to tax" as well as a rational relationship between the tax and the "values connected with the taxing State."[26] The connection between the Commerce Clause and the Due Process Clause for state tax law purposes is summarized by the *Quill* Court as "distinct but parallel limitations" on a state's taxing power.[27] *Quill* notes that the Commerce Clause stands for the premise that states should not burden commerce with "multiple or unfairly apportioned taxation." Ultimately, the combination of the Commerce Clause and the Due Process Clause holds that the taxing power exerted by the state must bear some "fiscal relation to protection, opportunities and benefits given by the state."[28]

---

[20] *See Chase Manhattan Bank v. Gavin*, 733 A2d 782 (Conn. 1999), cert. denied, 528 US 965 (1999); Connecticut taxes the income of a trust based on the pro rata share of a non-contingent Connecticut resident beneficiary's share of the trust, (at 790).

[21] U.S. Const. art. V ("nor be deprived of life, liberty, or property, without due process of law"); U.S. Const. art. XIV ("nor shall any state deprive any person of life, liberty, or property, without due process of law").

[22] *Oklahoma Tax Comm'n v. Chickasaw Nation*, 515 US 450, 462-463 (1995).

[23] *Quill Corp. v. North Dakota*, 504 US 298, 305 (1992).

[24] *Kaestner v. N.C. Dept. of Revenue*, 814 S.E.2d 43 (N.C. 2018), aff'g 789 S.E.2d 645 (N.C. Ct. App. 2016).

[25] *Kaestner v. N.C. Dept. of Revenue*, 789 S.E.2d 645 (N.C. 2016), citing *Quill Corp. v. North Dakota*, 504 US 298, 313 (1992), and *International Shoe v. Washington*, 326 US 310, 316 (1945).

[26] *Id.*

[27] *Id.*

[28] *Id.*

Generally, the residence of an individual or decedent's estate in a state provides sufficient connection for taxation. Contact-based connections analysis regarding state trust tax law can be difficult because of the bifurcation between the trustee legal owner and the beneficiary beneficial owner, as well as other contacts related to administration. Some states require more than just the individual or decedent's estate as a contact point, as illustrated in *Swift* below.

¶ 1509 *Swift*, Founder Criteria and Present Benefit Minimum Contacts for State Trust Laws: Six Points

Due Process "minimum contacts" in the context of state income taxation of trusts was concisely interpreted by *In re Swift*. The *Swift* court found that an income tax was justified only when there are benefits and protections provided during the relevant taxing period.[29] The *Swift* court considered "six points of contact" in determining whether a state had sufficient nexus to support the imposition of an income tax on trust income as follows:

1. the domicile of the settlor,
2. the state in which the trust is created,
3. the location of the trust property,
4. the domicile of the beneficiaries,
5. the domicile of the trustees, and
6. the location of the administration of the trust.[30]

The Missouri Supreme Court in *Swift* continued in finding that "[f]or purposes of supporting an income tax, the first two of these factors require the ongoing protection or benefits of state law only to the extent that one or more of the other four factors is present."[31] The first factor was satisfied in *Swift* as the trusts were testamentary trusts created by the will of a Missouri domiciliary. However, the court found that Missouri provided "no present benefit" to the trusts, where none of the beneficiaries or trustees were Missouri residents, the trust property was held, managed, and administered in Illinois, and all trust income-generating business was conducted in Illinois.[32] The court in *Swift* held that, since Missouri law provided no present benefits or protections to the subject trust, beneficiaries, trustees or property, the State of Missouri did not have sufficient connections to impose an income tax—and therefore the tax violated the Due Process Clause.[33]

¶ 1510 *Blue*, Founder Criteria and Ongoing Protection Minimum Contacts Required for State Law Taxing Power

The Michigan decision of *Blue* involved an inter vivos trust established by a Michigan resident, where all beneficiaries, trustees, income-producing assets and administration were located in Florida.[34] The court found that there were "insufficient connections between the trust and the State of Michigan to justify the

---

[29] *In re Swift*, 727 SW2d 880, 892 (Mo. 1987).
[30] *Id.*
[31] *Id.*
[32] *Id.*
[33] *Id.*
[34] *Blue v. Department of Transportation*, 462 NW2d 762 (Mich. Ct. App. 1990).

imposition of an income tax."[35] The Michigan appellate court held that the lack of ongoing protection and benefit of Michigan law resulted in unconstitutional taxation. As a result, Michigan has updated the instructions to the Michigan Form 1041 to alert taxpayers of the outcome in *Blue*, and inform taxpayers that if their fact situation meets with the profile in *Blue*, the trust may not be subject to Michigan state tax.

¶ 1511 *Bank of America* and Trust Administration in a State

In *Bank of America v. Massachusetts Department of Revenue*,[36] the question was whether the bank qualified as an inhabitant of the state subject to the state fiduciary income tax. The bank served as trustee or co-trustee on 34 inter vivos trusts, and maintained 200 branch offices. The record indicated that the trust administration involved employing staff at the branch offices, maintaining relationships with beneficiaries, including timing of distributions, administration of trust assets and records, research for clients and meetings with trust grantors, beneficiaries, and their representatives. Administration outside of the state included "policy and procedures related to administrative investment components of trusts." Ultimately, the Massachusetts Supreme Court looked to whether the trustee's administration of the trusts took place within Massachusetts. The court determined that the permanent offices and the engagement of regular business activities qualified the bank as an inhabitant, and therefore concluded that the trusts were subject to fiduciary income tax in Massachusetts because of the connections with the state.

¶ 1512 *Mercantile Safe Deposit* and Control over the Property Necessary by New York Beneficiaries

In *Mercantile Safe Deposit*, control over the property by New York beneficiaries proved to be the deciding factor for taxation in New York. The grantor and beneficiaries of an inter vivos trust were New York residents and therefore New York taxed the trust as a resident trust.[37] However, the trustee was domiciled in Maryland, the trust was administered in Maryland, and intangibles held in the trust were subject to control of the trustee in Maryland.

The highest court of New York held that taxation by New York on the basis of the residence of the grantor and beneficiaries would be unconstitutional under the Due Process Clause because neither the grantor nor the beneficiaries controlled or had a present right to the possession of the trust estate. Therefore, New York lacked a sufficient constitutional nexus to tax an inter vivos trust where an out-of-state trustee performed all of his duties as trustee outside of New York. The appellate court concluded that taxing the trust's income would "extend the taxing power of the State to property wholly beyond its jurisdiction and thus conflict with the due process clause."[38]

---

[35] *Id.*
[36] 474 Mass 702 (2016). *See* Chapter 15, ¶ 1511.
[37] *Mercantile-Safe Deposit & Trust Co. v. Murphy*, 242 NYS2d 26 (App. Div. 1963), aff'd, 15 NY2d 579 (1964).
[38] *Mercantile-Safe Deposit & Trust Co. v. Murphy*, 242 NYS2d at 28.

¶ 1513 *Kassner* and New Jersey Testamentary Trusts with Undistributed S Corporation Income

Kassner Residuary Trust v. Director, Division of Taxation involved a testamentary trust created by the will of a New Jersey domiciled resident.[39] The trust owned four S Corporations, but the Trust owned no assets in New Jersey. The Division's official guidance publication gave taxpayers unequivocal advice that undistributed trust income would not be taxable if the trustee was not a New Jersey resident and the trust had no New Jersey assets. The trustee was not a New Jersey resident and the trust was administered in another state. The New Jersey Appellate Court affirmed the New Jersey Tax Court holding that New Jersey cannot tax a trust's undistributed non-New Jersey income if the trustee, assets and beneficiaries are all located outside New Jersey. The court noted that in this situation, the trust lacks minimum contacts with the State (relying on the principles recognized in *Potter* and *Pennoyer*).[40]

In the lower court decision, the New Jersey Tax Court specifically rejected the argument that the "lack of a presence [of the trust] in New Jersey [could] be overcome by the Supreme Court's ruling in *Quill Corp.*"[41] The court distinguished *Quill Corp.* on the basis that the taxpayer in that case "actively conduct[ed] a mail order business that targeted the residents of the [taxing] state," whereas the trust at issue was merely a "passive owner of stock" and carried out no business in the state, and the tax at issue in *Quill Corp.* was a use tax, as opposed to an income tax.

¶ 1514 *Pennoyer* and Probate Administration for Testamentary Trust Not Enough

The issue before the court was the New Jersey income taxation of a testamentary trust established under the will of a New Jersey decedent, where the trustee, beneficiaries, and trust assets were all outside of New Jersey.[42] The court held that taxation by New Jersey was unconstitutional. In the view of the court the creation of the trust by the probate process was not a sufficient basis for the required state nexus, benefits, or protection to tax accumulated income of the trust; the court viewed the prior probate administration as merely "an historical fact."[43]

¶ 1515 *D.C. v. Chase Manhattan Bank* and Probate Is Enough to Withstand Challenge

The issue before the court in this case was the District of Columbia resident trust status of a testamentary trust of D.C. decedent where the trustee, beneficiaries, and trust assets were not in the District.[44] The court upheld resident trust status against a constitutional attack, viewing the trust as an entity similar to a corporation (rather than just a form of ownership), and finding that the creation of

---

[39] *Kassner v. Div. of Taxation*, 28 NJ Tax 541 (NJ Super. Ct. App. Div. 2015); *Residuary Trust v. Dir., Div. of Taxation*, 27 NJ Tax 68 (2013).

[40] *Pennoyer v. Dir., Div. of Taxation*, 5 NJ Tax 386 (1983); *Potter v. Dir., Div. of Taxation*, 5 NJ Tax 399 (1983).

[41] *Residuary Trust v. Dir., Div. of Taxation*, 27 NJ Tax 68 (2013).

[42] *Pennoyer v. Dir., Div. of Taxation*, 5 NJ Tax 386 (1983).

[43] *Id.*

[44] *District of Columbia v. Chase Manhattan Bank*, 689 A2d 539 (D.C. 1997).

the trust under the will admitted to probate in the District of Columbia was sufficient to uphold the constitutional challenge to the tax.

¶ 1516 *McNeil* and the Importance of Discretionary Beneficiaries under the Pennsylvania Statute

The Commonwealth Court of Pennsylvania in a 2013 decision with a result similar to *Linn*, decided *McNeil v. Commonwealth*.[45] In *McNeil*, the Pennsylvania grantor created two inter vivos trusts. At the time of the case, the trusts were administered in Delaware, governed by the laws of Delaware, the trustees were located in Delaware and trust assets were held in Delaware. The trust did not have any Pennsylvania source income. The discretionary beneficiaries, however, lived in Pennsylvania.

Pennsylvania assessed fiduciary income tax because the grantor was a resident when the trust was formed.[46] The *discretionary* beneficiaries were residents, and that was the only connection to Pennsylvania. The court found that the imposition of Pennsylvania's fiduciary income tax violated the U.S. Constitution because relying only on resident discretionary beneficiaries lacked the "substantial nexus" necessary under the Commerce Clause.

¶ 1517 *Gavin* and Treatment of Non-Contingent Beneficiaries

The question presented in *Gavin* was whether the Connecticut income taxation of inter vivos or testamentary trusts was proper, where the settlor or testator was a Connecticut resident, but there were no Connecticut trustees and no property in Connecticut.[47] Regarding testamentary trusts, the court held that the creation of testamentary trust through the Connecticut probate process *was* a sufficient contact. For the inter vivos trusts, the residence of a beneficiary in Connecticut was considered a sufficient contact for purposes of taxation. The court in *Gavin* held "the critical link to the undistributed income sought to be taxed is the fact that the non-contingent beneficiary of the inter vivos trust during the tax year in question was a Connecticut domiciliary."[48] The non-contingent beneficiary of that trust was a Connecticut domiciliary receiving advantages of residency and "enjoyed all of the protections and benefits afforded to other domiciliaries. Her right to the eventual receipt and enjoyment of the accumulated income was, and so long as she is such a domiciliary will continue to be, protected by the laws of the state."[49]

Connecticut also taxes the income of a trust based on the pro rata share of a non-contingent Connecticut resident beneficiary's share of the trust.[50] This provides additional constitutional protections. Because there was only one non-contingent beneficiary in *Gavin*, and she was a Connecticut resident, therefore 100% of the trust income was taxable by Connecticut.

---

[45] *McNeil v. Commonwealth*, 67 A3d 185 (Pa. Commw. Ct. 2013).
[46] 72 P.S. § 7301(s).
[47] *Chase Manhattan Bank v. Gavin*, 733 A2d 782 (Conn. 1999), cert. denied, 528 US 965 (1999).
[48] *Gavin*, 733 A2d at 802.
[49] *Id.*
[50] *Gavin*, 733 A2d at 790.

¶ 1518 *Kaestner* and the Residence of the Beneficiary

In *Kaestner*, the North Carolina Supreme Court found that *only* relying on the beneficiary's residence in the state was not a sufficient contact to "purposefully avail" the trust of the privilege of conducting activities within the State.[51] A potentially unresolved issue in North Carolina, where the state has not amended the limited unconstitutional nature of the statute, is the distinction between primary beneficiaries versus contingent beneficiaries.[52]

¶ 1519 Trends Practitioners Should Plan For

In each of the *Linn* and *McNeil* decisions, the analysis holds that the traditional "founder residence" alone is not constitutionally sufficient to support the fiduciary income tax of the trust to the state. These decisions challenged the state nexus on constitutional grounds, that the state taxing regime violated the Commerce Clause of the U.S. Constitution. Given the constitutional scrutiny to founder-state based residency, the other criteria considered may play an increased role in the determination of residency.

The other criteria typically used by states include the place of administration of the trust, the residence of the trustee, and the residence of the beneficiary—discretionary or otherwise. While it is difficult to plan around where the beneficiaries will locate, and what type of beneficiaries a trust has, the choice of trustee is somewhat within the control of the administration.

Approximately 19 states (based on the Nenno research reproduced in the chart), base the state fiduciary taxation of trusts on the place of administration of the trust.[53] With an individual trustee, the determination of where the trust is being administered may be straightforward—it is where the individual trustee is administering the trust. If a corporate trustee is acting, and the corporate fiduciary has trust operations in multiple states where administration takes place, the trust administration will likely be a fact-intensive analysis, and perhaps favor utilization of a corporate trustee because of this flexibility.

---

[51] *Kaestner v. N.C. Dept. of Revenue*, 814 S.E.2d 43 (N.C. 2018), *aff'g* 789 S.E.2d 61 (N.C. Ct. App. 2016).

[52] The holding and its "unconstitutional" determination was limited to the particular taxpayer, and was not a blanket "unconstitutional" determination.

[53] *See* the Nenno article for detailed state law information. Examples of states with a "place of administration" tax system include Colorado, Georgia, Hawaii, Idaho, Indiana, Iowa, Kansas, Louisiana, Maryland, Minnesota, Mississippi, Montana, New Mexico, North Dakota, Oregon, South Carolina, Utah, Virginia, and Wisconsin.

Case Table

Case Name	Paragraph
A	
Abell, W.W.	616.02
Arrott, L.R.	616.02
Avery, S.L.	403
B	
Ball, L.E.	1409
Bank of America v. Massachusetts Department of Revenue	107; 1511
Bankhead, E., Est.	603
Bartlett, E.	1401.01
Bausch, E., Est.	309
Beatty, T.R.	616.02
Beckwith, D.S.	1401.01
Bell, F.S., Est.	812
Benson, L.W.	906.01; 906.02
Bernard, A.V.	303
Bess, M.G.	1409
Bisbee, F.D.	616.02
Blair, E.	813
Blair	901
Blue	1410; 1510
Bluestein	1105
Bradley, A., Exr.	310.02
Brewster, E.F.	603.03
Brigham, Jr., P.L., Exr.	806
Britten, E.F., Jr.	502.02
Brockamp, M.	211
Brown Jr., E.A., Est.	502.01
Burgo, J.	1409
Bunting, C.E.	801.01
Burnett v. Wells	901
C	
Carkhuff, S.G.	903.02
Carol, S.	614.01
Chase Manhattan Bank	1410; 1515
Chase Manhattan Bank v. Gavin	1506.01; 1517
Cherry, W., Est.	314
Chichester, C.H.	308.01
Clifford	901.01; 901.02; 901.03
Clifford, Helvering v.	901.01
Cohen, B.B., Est.	603.02
Coleman, J.C.	309
Commissioner v. Wemyss	909.03
Complete Auto Transit, Inc. v. Brady	1506.01
Complete Auto Transport	1501.02; 1506.01
Consolidated Edison Co. of N.Y.	612
Cooley	1506
Coppola, Jr., J.M.	1401.01
Corliss	901
Craig, G.L.	603.02
Crummey	910.01
D	
Davis, C.S.	609
Davidson, H., Est.	307.01
Davison, H., Est.	603.05
Deutsch, R.	806
Dickinson, J.L., Testamentary Trust	510
Diedrich, V.P.	909.03
Doumakes, J.J., Est.	309
Duberstein, M.	309
Duke, Y.S.	1409
DuPont, A.I., Testamentary Trust	709
E	
Enright, J.M.	309
Erdman, C.P.	609; 709.01
Estate of Kite v. Commissioner	909.03
Ewald, O.A.	903.02
F	
Ferber, J., Est.	603.03
First National Bank & Trust Co. in Macon	812

Case Name	Paragraph
First Trust & Deposit Co., Exr.	603
Fitzgerald, G.P.	1401.01
Flato, F.	801.01
Fleming, W., Trustee	615
Flitcroft, W.	908
Frank Aragona Trust	105
Frankel, G.E.	309

G

Case Name	Paragraph
Gavin	1410; 1517
Gavin, V., Est.	301
Gibbons v. Ogden	1506
Goodman, S., Est.	308.01
Goodwyn Estate	903.03
Grant, A.I.	801.01
Greentree, E.F.	309
Gregg, H.A., Est.	308.01
Grinstead, A.P.	309
Guaranty Trust Co. of N.Y.	603.02
Gunther, M.J.	411

H

Case Name	Paragraph
Haden, W.D., Est.	605
Haeri, F.	903.02
Hallowell, B.N.	801.01
Hanover Bank	501
Hargis, J.F., Est.	502.01
Harrison v. Commissioner	909.03
Hoffman, J.S., Est.	616.03
Horst, Helvering v.	901
Hubert, O., Est.	609

I

Case Name	Paragraph
International Shoe Co. v. Washington	107; 1507.01

J

Case Name	Paragraph
J.A. Love Charitable Foundation	1104
Jenn, L.J.	909.02
Johnson, F.H.D., Est.	1401.01

K

Case Name	Paragraph
Kaestner v. N.C. Dept. of Revenue,	107; 1501.01; 1507.01; 1518
Kassner	1410; 1513
Kasynski, H.B.	309
Keil Properties, Inc.	612
Kellahan, W.N., Jr.	413
Kenan, W.R., Jr.	604; 711.03
Kimberly Rice Kaestner 1992 Family Trust v. North Carolina Department of Revenue	107
Kirk, F.P., Admr. (Briden Est.)	1402
Knight	608
Knox, L.E.	1409
Kuntz, Sr., M., Est.	309

L

Case Name	Paragraph
LaFargue, E.	909.05
Lavery, U.A.	302
Lazarus, S.M.	909.05
Linde, R.J.	603.05
Linn	107; 1410; 1501.01; 1502; 1503; 1503.01; 1504; 1516; 1519
Little, W.D.	1401.01
Long, M.L.	604
Loose, E.C., Exrx.	302
Lowenstein	1105
Loyd, F.S.	609
Lucas	901

M

Case Name	Paragraph
Mallinckrodt, E.J., Jr.	801.01
Manufacturers Hanover Trust Co.	609; 709.01
Maryland v. Wynne	1505
Mattie Carter Trust	105; 616.02
McAllister, B.E.	812
McCourt, L.T.	1401.01
McIlvaine, W.B.	510
McIntosh, C.L.F.	614.01
McNeil	107; 1410; 1501.01; 1504; 1516; 1519
Mellinger, J.S., Exr.	609
Mellon Bank, NA	608
Mercantile Safe Deposit	1410; 1512

Case Name	Paragraph
Metropolitan Life Insurance Co. (M.A. Gilmore)	1409
Miller, A.T.	502.01
Mitchell, C.E.	1402
Moore, H.A., Trust	609
Morgan	501
Morris, J.E., Est.	308.01
Morton, S.	903.02
M.T. Straight Trust	510
Munroe, E.B., Exrx.	1401.01

N

Case Name	Paragraph
Napolitano, E.G.	301
Narischkine, S.L., Est.	603
Nemser, A.	813
New, L.K.	1401.01
Northwestern States Portland Cement Co.	1506

O

Case Name	Paragraph
O'Bryan, F.M.	619.01
O'Daniel, E., Est.	309
Oklahoma Tax Comm'n v. Chickasaw Nation	1507
Oklahoma Tax Comm'n v. Jefferson Lines, Inc.	1506
Old Colony Trust Co	1104
Old Virginia Brick Co.	502.01; 1202.02
Olsen, W.R., Est.	309
O'Neill, Jr., W.J., Irrevocable Trust	608

P

Case Name	Paragraph
Paxton, F.G., Est.	903.02
Penick, M.H.D.	309
Pennoyer	1410; 1513; 1514
Peterson, C.W., Est.	301
Potter	1513
Putnam, H.W., Est.	302; 403

Q

Case Name	Paragraph
Quill Corp	1410; 1506.01; 1507; 1508; 1513

Case Name	Paragraph
Quill Corp. v. North Dakota	107; 1507.01

R

Case Name	Paragraph
Rath, V.D.	1201.05
Rau, Sr., W.F., Est.	1402
Reimer, M.J.	1402
Reinecke, M.G.	903.02
Rollert, E.D., Residuary Trust	301
Rosen, L., Est.	309
Roth, J.	603

S

Case Name	Paragraph
Safe Deposit	1505
Sapirstein, J.	903.02
Savage	903.01
Schaefer, M.H.	621
Schaffner, S.H.	813
Scheft, W.	909.06
Schwan, M.	611
Scott, J.H.	608
Sheaffer, C.R.	909.01
Sidles, H.B., Est.	301
Smith, F.W.	510
Smith, J., Exrx.	1401.01
South Dakota v. Wayfair, Inc.,	1506.01
Spiegel, M.J., Est.	310.02
Steinberg v. Commissioner	909.03
Stern, J.F.	1408; 1409
Stewart, J.	502.01
Studebaker, G.M.	616.03
Suisman, S.P.	604; 711.03
Sullivan, J.A., Exr.	612
Swift, In re	1509
Swift	1410; 1508; 1509

T

Case Name	Paragraph
Taproot Administrative Services, Inc.	1202.03
Terranova, G.	1401.01
Trust Co. of Georgia	301
Trust of M.L. Bingham	609
Tucker, M.B.	709.01

Case Name	Paragraph
U	
United States Trust Co.	613
United States Trust Co. of New York	510
V	
Van Buren	1103
Viles, M., Admrx.	1401.01
W	
Weisburn, K.,Exrx.	1401.01
Westphal, M.C.	309
Widener, J.E.	616.04
William L. Rudkin Testamentary Trust	608
Wilson, M.S., Exr.	616.02
Wintner, L.	1409
Witherbee, M.S.	903.02
Witt, E.B., Est.	310.02
Wylie, C.H., Exr.	502.01
Wynne	1505
Y	
Yagoda, E.	1408
Yetter, O.F., Est.	613
Z	
Zwerner	217.03

Table of Internal Revenue Code Sections

Code Sec.	Paragraph
IRC Section	
1(c)	912.01
1(e)	911.02
1(g)	902
1(h)(1)	605.04
1(h)(1)(B)	605.01
1(h)(1)(D)	605.02
1(h)(4)	605.03
1(h)(6)	605.02
2(a)	212
27	310.01
49	1002
53	202.05
54	202.05
55(b)(1)(A)(i)	504.05
55(b)(2)	504.05
55(d)	202.01
55(d)(1)(D)	504.05
55(d)(3)(C)	504.05
56	504.05
57	504.05
58	504.05
59(c)	504.05
61	309; 909.03
61(a)(4)	102.01; 401
61(a)(12)	603
62(a)(19)	412.02
63(c)(6)(D)	504.02
67	104; 608
67(a)	104; 608; 619.01
67(b)	619.01
67(b)(4)	608
67(e)	104; 608
67(e)(1)	608
67(g)	104; 608; 619.01
68	1002
68(b)	202.01; 215
71(b)(1)(B)	408
71(b)(1)(D)	408
72	309; 316; 409.02
72(b)(3)(A)	409.06
72(c)(2)	409.06
72(s)	304
79(a)(1)	410
79(d)	410
79(d)(6)	410
79(d)(8)	410
83	404
83(a)	404.05
83(c)(3)	404.05
101(a)(1)	409
101(a)(2)	409.03
101(c)	409.02
101(f)	409.04
101(g)	409.01
101(g)(2)(B)	409.01
101(g)(2)(b)(i)(II)	409.01
101(g)(3)(B)	409.01
101(g)(3)(C)	409.01
101(g)(3)(D)	409.01
101(g)(4)(A)	409.01
101(g)(4)(B)	409.01
101(j)(1)	409.07
101(j)(2)	409.07
101(j)(2)(A)	409.08
101(j)(3)	409.07
101(j)(4)	409.08
102	309
102(a)	621
102(b)(2)	621
112	216
121(a)	308.02
121(b)(2)	308.02
121(c)	308.02
121(d)(2)	308.02
121(d)(7)	308.02
121(d)(10)	308.02
136l(b)(l)	102.02
151(d)	214
162(l)(1)	410
163	611
163(d)	611
163(d)(4)	611
164(a)	612

Code Sec.	Paragraph
164(d)	612
165	311; 616
165(h)	311
165(h)(1)	616.01
165(h)(2)	616.01
165(h)(4)(C)	616.01
165(h)(4)(D)	616.01
165(h)(4)(E)	311
166(d)	616.03
167(d)	313; 614.01; 614.02
170(a)	413; 1101; 1107
170(b)(1)(B)	1108.05
170(c)	1101; 1109.01; 1111.01; 1115
170(c)(2)	1206.01
170(c)(2)(A)	1101
170(c)(2)(B)	103.02
170(d)(1)(A)	1108.05
170(e)(1)(B)	413
170(f)(2)(B)	1112.01
170(f)(8)	413
170(f)(8)(B)	1107
170(f)(10)	413.01
170(f)(11)	413; 1107
170(f)(11)(A)(ii)(II)	1107
170(f)(11)(B)	1107
170(f)(11)(C)	413; 1107
170(f)(11)(D)	413; 1107
170(f)(11)(F)	1107
170(f)(12)	413
170(f)(12)(E)	413
170(h)	613
172	617; 618; 1111.06
172(b)(1)(A)	311; 618
172(b)(1)(F)	311
172(b)(1)(G)	311; 618
172(b)(1)(H)	618
172(b)(3)	311
172(i)	311
172(j)	618
175	619.01
179	607; 614.02
179(d)(4)	607; 614.02
212	607.02; 612

Code Sec.	Paragraph
213	412.02
213(a)	312
213(c)	102; 102.01; 312; 312.01; 312.02
213(c)(1)	312.02; 610
213(c)(2)	312.01; 312.02
213(d)	412.02
213(d)(5)	312.02
220(f)(8)(A)	412.01
220(f)(8)(B)(i)	412.01
220(f)(8)(B)(ii)	412.01
220(i)	412.01
223	412.02
223(c)(1)	412.02
223(f)(1)	412.02
223(f)(6)	412.02
223(f)(8)	412.02
266	612
267	102.02; 616.04; 711.02; 711.03
267(b)	616.04; 711.02
267(b)(3)	102.02
273	616.03
275	612
401(a)	103.03; 409.07
401(c)(1)	409.07
402(b)	1302
402(c)(3)	411
402(c)(9)	411
403(b)	411
408(d)(3)	411
408A(d)(2)(B)	411
416(i)	410
421(c)(1)	404.01; 404.04
421(c)(3)	404.04
422	404.01
422(b)	404.03
422(d)	404.03
423	404.01
423(b)	404.02
424(c)(1)(A)	404.04
441	102.02
441(e)	507.01
444	1004
451(a)	302

Table of Internal Revenue Code Sections

Code Sec.	Paragraph
451(b)	301
453B(b)	306
454(a)	102.01; 602.01
454(c)	602.01
457	411
461(b)	310
461(g)	611
465	617.01; 1002; 1201.03
469	103.03; 105; 317; 504.04; 1002; 1201.04
469(a)(2)(A)	616.02
469(c)(1)	105
469(c)(2)	105
469(g)	317.02
469(g)(1)(A)	317.02
469(g)(2)(A)	317.02
469(g)(2)(B)	317.02
469(h)(1)	317
469(i)(4)	102.02
501	103.02; 808
501(a)	409.07; 504; 802
501(c)(3)	1108; 1202.03; 1303
512(b)(11)	1114
513	1114
522	1302
530(b)(1)	412.03
530(b)(1)(A)(iii)	412.03
530(b)(1)(E)	412.03
530(c)(1)	412.03
530(d)(7)	412.03
611(b)(3)	615
611(b)(4)	615
641	504.05; 505
641(a)	601
641(b)	1304.01
641(c)	1204
641(c)(1)(A)	501
641(c)(2)(A)	501
641(c)(2)(C)	501
641(c)(2)(C)(iv)	501
642	619.01; 1114
642(b)	504.02; 504.03; 608; 911.02
642(b)(2)(C)	504.03
642(c)	102.02; 108; 504.02; 608; 613; 617; 707; 810; 1102; 1103; 1104; 1105; 1106; 1114; 1115
642(c)(1)	102.02; 1101; 1115
642(c)(3)	1101
642(c)(4)	1102
642(d)	617; 1111.06
642(e)	614
642(g)	102.02; 312.02; 613
642(h)	605
642(h)(1)	618
642(h)(2)	619
642(i)	912.03
643	703; 707
643(a)(3)	707; 1304.02
643(a)(6)(A)	1304.02
643(a)(6)(B)	1304.02
643(a)(6)(C)	1304.02
643(b)	1108.06; 1205.01
643(e)(1)	711.01
643(e)(1)(B)	711.02
643(e)(2)	711.01
643(e)(3)	711.02; 711.04
643(e)(3)(A)(ii)	711.02
643(e)(3)(A)(iii)	711.02
643(e)(3)(B)	711.02
643(e)(4)	711.02
643(f)	504.01; 510; 814
643(g)	102.02; 507.02
643(g)(2)	102.02
644	504; 802; 808
644(a)	102.02; 507.01
644(b)	507.01
645	102.02; 503
645(a)	102.02; 507.01; 802; 808
645(b)(1)	102.02
645(b)(2)	503

Table of Internal Revenue Code Sections

Code Sec.	Paragraph
646	912.01
646(b)	912.01
646(c)	912.01
646(d)	912.01
646(f)	912.01
646(f)(1)	912.01
646(g)	708; 709
646(i)	912.01
651	501; 707; 708; 811
651(a)	701
651(b)	708
652	707
652(a)	801.01; 801.02; 1304.02
652(b)	801.02
652(c)	802
661	310.01; 707; 708; 709; 809; 810; 811; 1106
661(a)	701; 708; 709; 710.03
661(a)(2)	613
661(b)	709.01
661(c)	709.02; 710.03
662	707; 806; 808; 810; 811; 1106
662(a)	605.01; 803
662(b)	803.02
662(c)	808
663(a)	1305
663(a)(1)	711; 809
663(a)(2)	810; 1106
663(a)(3)	811
663(b)	102.02; 712
663(c)	807
664	103.02; 1110
664(b)	1111.06
664(c)	1101; 1110.05
664(d)(1)	1110.01
664(d)(1)(D)	1110.01
664(d)(2)	1110.01
664(d)(2)(D)	1110.01
664(f)	1110.01
665(a)	816; 1304.04
665(b)	815; 1304.03
665(c)(2)	814
665(d)	818.02; 1304.06
665(d)(1)	816; 1304.04
666(b)	816; 1304.04
667(a)	818; 1304.06
667(b)(1)	817; 1304.05
667(b)(6)	816
667(c)	818.01
667(d)	818.02; 1304.06
667(d)(1)(B)	818.02; 1304.06
668(a)(1)	818.02; 1304.06
668(a)(3)	818.02; 1304.06
668(b)	818.02; 1304.06
671	902
671-677	1112.01
671-678	918; 920
671-679	1302
672	818.02; 903; 903.02
672(a)	903.01
672(b)	903.02
672(c)	903.02; 903.03
672(e)	102.02
672(e)(1)	902
672(e)(2)	902
672(f)	1302
672(f)(1)	1302
672(f)(2)	1302
672(f)(3)(A)	1302
672(f)(3)(B)	1302
672(f)(5)	1302
673	818.02; 901.03; 902; 904; 905.02; 910
673(a)	901.02; 904; 908.01; 909.06
673(b)	904
673(c)	904
673(d)	904
674	818.02; 901.03; 902; 905
674(a)	905
674(b)	905.02
674(c)	905.01
674(d)	905.01

Table of Internal Revenue Code Sections   17,005

Code Sec.	Paragraph
675	818.02; 901.03; 902; 906
675(1)	906
675(2)	906
675(3)	906; 906.02
675(4)	818.02; 902; 907; 910
676	102.02; 818.02; 902; 908; 1302
676(a)	908
676(b)	908.01
677	818.02; 901; 902; 904; 909
677(a)	909.06; 909.07
677(a)(1)	909
677(a)(2)	909
677(a)(3)	909; 1302
677(b)	909; 909.07
678	818.02; 902; 910; 910.01
678(a)	910; 910.01
678(b)	910; 910.01
679	818.02; 911; 911.01
679(b)	1303
679(c)(1)	1303
679(c)(2)	1303
679(c)(3)	1303
681	1114
684(a)	1303
684(c)	1303
685	504.05; 911.02
685(a)(2)	504.03; 911.02
685(b)	911.02
685(c)	911.02
685(c)(2)	911.02
685(d)	911.02
685(e)	911.02
691	305; 314; 402; 601; 602.01; 603.05; 802.01; 808; 1001; 1008
691(a)(1)	301; 303; 1104
691(a)(2)	305; 616.03
691(a)(3)	304
691(a)(4)	306
691(b)	102.02; 610
691(b)(1)	310.01; 310.02
691(b)(2)	313
691(c)	102.01; 314; 403; 412.01; 412.02; 504.05; 1008
691(c)(1)	314
691(c)(1)(B)	314
691(c)(2)	314
691(c)(4)	403
691(d)	316
692(a)	216.01; 216.03
692(a)(1)	216
692(a)(2)	216
692(b)	216.02
692(c)	216; 216.01; 216.03
692(d)	216; 216.01
692(d)(2)	216
692(d)(3)	216
692(d)(4)	409.07
692(d)(5)	216
704(c)(1)(C)(i)	1011
704(c)(1)(C)(ii)	1011
706(a)	1001.02
706(b)	1004
706(c)(2)	1005
706(c)(2)(A)	1001
706(d)	1001.02
708(b)	1010.02
708(b)(1)	1001
731	1006
734(b)	1011
736	1006
736(a)	1006; 1007
736(b)	1006; 1007
736(b)(3)	1009.01
743	1010.01; 1010.03; 1011
743(b)	1010; 1010.03
743(d)	1010.03
753	1008

Table of Internal Revenue Code Sections

Code Sec.	Paragraph
754	1010; 1010.01; 1010.02; 1010.03; 1011
771-777	1002
772(c)(1)	1002
773(a)(3)(B)	1002
871(a)(1)(A)	1304.01
871(d)	1304.01
894	1304.02
904(f)(4)	818.02; 1304.06
911	202.02
931	213
957	1302; 1304.07
957(a)	1303
1001(e)	812
1012	711.03
1014	305; 317.02; 1010.01
1014(a)	603.02; 1303
1014(a)(4)	606
1014(b)(1)	606
1014(c)	305
1014(f)	110; 207.05; 315
1015(d)(6)	606.01
1016	606.01
1017	606.01
1032	1303
1033	308
1033(a)	308
1202	605.01
1202(a)	707; 1102
1211(b)	616.04; 618
1212	605.01; 618; 1111.06
1223(2)	711.04
1223(10)	404.04; 605
1231	605
1244	1201.05
1250	605.01; 605.02
1250(a)	605.02
1250(b)(1)	605.02
1252	603.04
1297	1302
1297(a)	1304.07
1361(b)(1)	1206.01
1361(b)(1)(A)	1201; 1204
1361(b)(1)(B)	406; 1201; 1202; 1202.02
1361(b)(3)	1202.05
1361(c)	1111.05
1361(c)(1)(A)	1202.01
1361(c)(2)(A)	911.03
1361(c)(2)(A)(ii)	1202.03
1361(c)(2)(A)(iv)	1202.03
1361(c)(2)(A)(v)	1206.01
1361(c)(6)	1202.03
1361(d)	1111.05; 1203
1361(d)(1)	1201.04
1361(d)(2)	1203; 1205.01
1361(d)(2)(A)	1205
1361(d)(2)(C)	1206
1361(d)(3)	920
1361(e)	1111.05
1361(e)(3)	1206; 1206.01
1361(f)	1202
1362	1205.01
1362(a)	1201
1366(a)	1201.01
1366(a)(1)	406
1366(b)	1201.01
1367(b)(4)(A)	304
1367(b)(4)(B)	304
1402(a)(1)	504.04
1402(f)	1001.03
1411	103.01; 103.05; 103.06; 105; 504.04
1441(a)	1304.01
2031(c)	606
2032	606; 1110.02
2032A	606
2035	909.03
2035(b)	909.03
2037	904
2051	102.02; 613
2053	102.02; 312.02; 613
2056(b)(10)	604
2105(d)(1)	407
2105(d)(2)	407
2105(d)(3)	407

Table of Internal Revenue Code Sections 17,007

Code Sec.	Paragraph
2502(c)	909.03
2503(c)	904
2512(b)	909.03
3406(a)(1)(A)	1405
4943	1111.01
4947	1110.06; 1113
4947(a)(1)	1115
4947(a)(2)	1115
4947(b)(3)	1111.01
6012(a)	202.01
6012(a)(4)	913
6012(b)(1)	201
6012(b)(2)	505.03
6012(b)(5)	505
6012(c)	202.02
6013	922.03
6013(a)(2)	206
6013(a)(3)	206
6013(b)	206.02
6013(b)(2)(A)-(D)	206.02
6013(d)(2)	206.01
6013(f)	216.02
6013(g)	213
6013(g)(4)	206
6018(a)	207.05
6018(b)	207.05
6034	1115
6034A(a)	915
6035	110; 315
6037	1201.02
6039H	912.01
6039H(a)	912.01
6048(c)	1305
6048(c)(2)	1305
6048(d)(5)	1305
6072(a)	506
6103(e)	204.02
6109	1405
6166	611; 613
6212	206.02
6213	206.02

Code Sec.	Paragraph
6223	1003
6401(b)(1)	202.05
6402	1406
6501(d)	1407
6501(e)	1407
6511	211
6511(a)	216
6511(h)	211
6621(a)(2)	818.02; 1304.06
6651(a)(1)	508.02
6652(c)(2)(A)	1115
6652(c)(2)(C)	1115
6654	213
6654(d)(1)(B)	507.02
6654(d)(1)(C)(i)	507.02
6654(e)(1)	507.02
6654(e)(2)(B)	507.02
6654(i)	102.02
6654(l)(2)	102.02; 507.02
6662(b)(8)	110; 315
6677(a)	1305
6721	110; 207.05; 315
6722	110; 207.05; 315
6901	310.02; 1408
6901(h)	1408
6902(a)	1408
6903	1404
6905	1403
7121	206.02
7122	206.02
7508(a)	216
7508(a)(1)	508
7508A(a)	508
7520	1109.01; 1109.02
7520(a)	1109.02
7701(a)(1)	1111.01
7701(a)(30)(E)	505
7701(a)(31)(A)	505
7702B(g)	409.01
7805(b)(2)	110; 315

Table of Treasury Regulations

Regulation	Paragraph
Regulations	
1.2-2	212
1.67-4	608
1.72-9	316
1.79-3(d)(2)	410
1.83-1(d)	404.05
1.83-7	404.05
1.83-7(b)	404.05
1.121-2(a)(4)	308.02
1.165-1(d)	311
1.165-8	311
1.167(h)-1(b)	614.01
1.167(h)-1(c)	614.02
1.170A-1	413
1.170A-1(c)(2)	413
1.170A-1(h)(2)	413
1.170A-6(c)(2)	1112.02; 1112.04
1.170A-8(a)(2)	1112.01
1.170A-13(c)(4)(iv)(F)	413
1.170A-13(f)	413
1.170A-13(f)(2)	413
1.212-1(i)	607.02
1.213-1(d)	312.02
1.213-1(d)(1)	610
1.213-1(d)(2)	102.01
1.267(a)-1(c)	616.04
1.273-1	616.03
1.301-1(b)	403
1.421-1(a)	404
1.421-2(c)	404.01; 404.04; 605
1.423-2(k)	404.04
1.424-1(c)(1)(i)	404.04
1.443-1(a)(2)	214; 202.01
1.446-1(c)(1)	401
1.451-1(b)(1)	301
1.451-2(a)	302; 401
1.454-1	102.01
1.611-1(c)	615
1.611-1(c)(4)	615
1.611-1(c)(5)	615
1.641(a)-2	601
1.641(b)-1	607
1.641(b)-2	505; 1401
1.641(b)-3(a)	502.01
1.641(b)-3(b)	502.02
1.641(b)-3(c)(1)	502.02
1.641(b)-3(d)	502.03
1.641(c)-1	501; 1204
1.642	1115
1.642(a)(1)-1	603.01
1.642(b)-1	504.03
1.642(c)(5)	1115
1.642(c)-1(b)	1115
1.642(c)-2	1115
1.642(c)-2(c)	1115
1.642(c)-3(b)(2)	1115
1.642(c)-5(c)(1)	1115
1.642(d)-1	617
1.642(e)-1	614; 615
1.642(g)-1	613
1.642(g)-2	613
1.642(h)-1	605.01; 618
1.642(h)-1(c)	618
1.642(h)-2	619; 619.01
1.642(h)-4	620
1.643(a)-1– 1.643(a)-7	707
1.643(a)-3(a)	705; 707
1.643(a)-3(b)	705; 707
1.643(a)-7	707
1.643(b)-1	702; 703; 1108.06
1.643(b)-2	702
1.645-1(e)(2)	503; 507.01
1.645-1(f)(1)	503
1.645-1(f)(2)(ii)	503
1.645-1(f)(2)(iv)	503
1.651(a)-1	706; 801
1.651(a)-2	502.02
1.651(a)-2(a)	706.01
1.651(a)-2(c)	706.03
1.651(a)-2(d)	706.04
1.651(a)-3(a)	706.02
1.651(a)-3(b)	706.02

Table of Treasury Regulations

Regulation	Paragraph
1.651(b)-1	707
1.652(a)-1	801.01
1.652(a)-2	801.02
1.652(b)-1	801.02
1.652(b)-2(b)	801.02
1.652(b)-3	709.01; 801.02
1.652(c)-1	802
1.652(c)-2	802.01
1.652(c)-3	802.01
1.661(a)-1	706.05
1.661(a)-2(b)	709
1.661(a)-2(c)	709
1.661(a)-2(e)	621; 709
1.661(a)-2(f)	709; 711.01; 711.03
1.661(b)-1	709.01
1.661(b)-2	709.01
1.661(c)-1	709.02
1.662(a)-1	803
1.662(a)-2(b)	803.01
1.662(a)-2(c)	621; 803
1.662(a)-3(b)	621; 711
1.662(a)-3(c)	803.02
1.662(b)-1	803.02
1.662(b)-2	803.02
1.662(c)-1	808
1.662(c)-2	808
1.662(c)-3	808
1.662(c)-4	804.08
1.662-2(c)	1110.02
1.663(a)-1(b)	809
1.663(a)-1(c)	809
1.663(a)-2	810
1.663(a)-3	811
1.663(b)-1	712
1.663(b)-2	712
1.663(c)-1(a)	807
1.663(c)-4(a)	807
1.663(c)-6	806
1.664-1	1110; 1110.01; 1110.05
1.664-1(a)(3)	1110.01
1.664-1(c)	1110.05
1.664-1(d)(1)(i)	1111.06
1.664-1(d)(1)(ii)(a)	1111.06
1.664-1(d)(1)(iv)	1111.06
1.664-1(d)(1)(vi)	1111.06
1.664-1(d)(viii)	1111.06
1.664-1(e)	1111.06
1.664-2	1110; 1110.01
1.664-3	1110; 1110.01; 1110.03
1.664-3(a)(1)(i)(b)	1110.03
1.664-3(a)(1)(i)(b)(3)	1108.06
1.664-3(a)(1)(i)(c)(3)	1110.03
1.664-4	1111.04; 1112.05
1.665(a)-0A	817; 1304.05
1.671-1(a)(1)	902
1.671-1(a)(2)	902
1.671-1(a)(3)	902
1.671-1(a)(4)	902
1.671-1(a)(5)	902
1.671-2(a)	902
1.671-2(e)(1)	902
1.671-2(e)(5)	902
1.671-3(b)(2)	904
1.671-4(a)	902.01; 913; 918
1.671-4(b)	913
1.671-4(b)(2)(i)(A)	921
1.671-4(b)(2)(ii)	915
1.671-4(b)(2)(ii)(B)	915; 916; 917
1.671-4(b)(2)(iii)	915; 917
1.671-4(b)(2)(iv)(Ex.2)	917
1.671-4(b)(3)(ii)	922.04
1.671-4(b)(5)(i)	917
1.671-4(b)(6)	920
1.671-4(b)(8)	922.04
1.671-4(g)	919.01
1.671-4(g)(1)	919.01
1.671-4(g)(2)	919.03
1.671-4(g)(3)(i)	919.04
1.671-4(g)(3)(ii)	919.05
1.672(a)-1(a)	903.01
1.672(a)-1(c)	903.01
1.672(a)-1(d)	903.01
1.672(f)-1(a)(1)	1302
1.672(f)-2(a)	1302
1.672(f)-2(c)	1302
1.672(f)-3	1302
1.672(f)-4(a)(1)	1302

Table of Treasury Regulations 18,003

Regulation	Paragraph
1.672(f)-4(a)(2)	1302
1.672(f)-4(b)	1302
1.672(f)-4(c)	1302
1.672(f)-4(d)	1302
1.672(f)-4(f)	1302
1.672(f)-5(a)(1)	1302
1.673(a)-1(a)	909.06
1.674(a)-1	905
1.674(b)-1(a)	905.02
1.674(b)-1(b)(5)	905.01
1.674(c)-1	905.01
1.674(d)-1	905.01
1.675-1(a)	906
1.675-1(b)(1)-(4)	906
1.675-1(b)(2)	906.01
1.675-1(b)(3)	906.02
1.675-1(b)(4)	907
1.676(b)-1	908.01
1.677(a)-1(c)	909.01
1.677(a)-1(d)	909.02
1.677(a)-1(f)	909.06
1.677(b)-1	909.07
1.677(b)-1(c)	909.07
1.677(b)-1(d)	909.02; 909.07
1.677(b)-1(e)	909.07
1.677(b)-1(f)	909.07
1.678(a)-1	910
1.678(d)-1	910
1.679-2(a)(1)	1303
1.679-2(a)(2)(i)	1303
1.679-2(a)(2)(ii)	1303
1.679-2(a)(4)	1303
1.679-4(a)	1303
1.681(a)(2)	1114
1.684-3(b)	1303
1.684-3(c)	1303
1.684-3(d)	1303
1.684-3(e)	1303
1.684-3(f)	1303
1.691(a)-1(b)	405
1.691(a)-2	301; 603.05
1.691(a)-2(a)	303
1.691(a)-2(b)	301; 309; 405
1.691(a)-3	304

Regulation	Paragraph
1.691(a)-4(a)	305
1.691(a)-5	306
1.691(b)-1	310.01
1.691(b)-1(b)	313
1.691(c)-1	403
1.691(c)-1(a)(1)	314
1.691(d)-1(a)	316
1.691(d)-1(e)	316
1.692-1	216.01
1.692-1(a)	216
1.692-1(a)(1)	216.01
1.692-1(b)	216.01; 216.03
1.692-1(c)	216.01
1.706-1(b)	1004
1.706-1(b)(2)(ii)	1004
1.706-1(b)(4)(ii)(B)	1004
1.706-1(c)(3)(ii)	1001.02
1.706-1(c)(3)(iii)	1005
1.706-1(c)(3)(vi), *Example 1*	1001.03
1.706-1(c)(3)(v)	1001.03
1.708-1(b)(1)(i)	1001.01
1.736-1(a)(5)	1006
1.736-1(a)(6)	1001.01
1.736-1(b)(5)	1007
1.743-1(k)(1)	1011
1.743-1(k)(2)	1011
1.753-1(a)	1008
1.753-1(b)	1001.03; 1008
1.904(f)-4(b)	818.02; 1304.06
1.1001-1(f)	812
1.1014-1	405
1.1014-1(a)	603.02
1.1014-1(c)(1)	305
1.1014-2(a)(5)	603.05
1.1014-4	606.01
1.1014-4(a)(3)	711.03
1.1014-4(c)	606.01
1.1015-4	606
1.1252-2(b)	603.04
1.1361-1(e)(3)	1202.01
1.1361-1(h)(1)(v)	1202.03
1.1361-1(j)	1203
1.1361-1(j)(6)	1205
1.1361-1(j)(6)(ii)(E).(1)	1205.01

Table of Treasury Regulations

Regulation	Paragraph
1.1361-1(j)(11)	1205
1.1361-1(j)(12)	1203
1.1361-1(m)(2)	1206
1.1361-1(m)(7)	1204
1.1362-6	1201
1.1366-1(a)	406; 1201.01
1.1366-1(b)	1201.01
1.1377-1	1201.01
1.1377-1(a)(2)(ii)	406
1.1402(f)-1	1001.03
1.1411-3(c)(1)	504.04
1.1474-7	109; 1306
1.6012-3(a)(1)	505
1.6012-3(a)(2)	510
1.6012-3(a)(3)	509
1.6012-3(a)(4)	510
1.6012-3(b)(1)	201; 202.01
1.6012-3(b)(2)	505.01
1.6012-3(b)(2)(i)	505.02
1.6012-3(b)(3)	505.03
1.6012-3(c)	505
1.6013-1(d)	206
1.6013-1(d)(2)	206
1.6013-1(d)(5)	206.01
1.6013-2(a)(3)	206.02
1.6013-4(a)	206.01
1.6014-2	208
1.6015(b)-1(b)	213
1.6015(b)-1(c)	213
1.6034-1(d)	1115
1.6072-1(a)(1)	506
1.6072-1(a)(2)	506
1.6072-1(b)	207
1.6072-1(c)	505.01
1.6161-1(b)	508
1.6654-2(e)(5)(i)	213
1.6654-2(e)(5)(ii)	213
1.6654-2(e)(7)	213
1.6654-5	213
1.7520-2(a)(2)	1109.01
20.2002-1	1401.01
20.2056(a)-1(c)(3)	604
20.7520-2(b)	1109.02
25.2511-1(g)(1)	909.03
25.2512-8	909.03
301.6109-1	921; 922; 1405
301.6109-1(a)(2)(i)(A)	921
301.6109-1(a)(2)(i)(B)	921
301.6402-2(e)	1406
301.6501(d)-1	1407
301.6501(e)-1	1407
301.6651-1(c)(3)	207.01
301.6901-1(a)(3)	1402
301.6901-1(b)	1408
301.6901-1(c)(1)	1408
301.6901-1(c)(2)	1408
301.6901-1(c)(4)	1408
301.6901-1(e)	1408
301.6903-1(b)	1404.01
301.6903-1(b)(2)	1404.01
301.6905-1	1403
301.7508-1	508
301.7508A-1	411
301.7701-7	505
301.7701-7(a)(1)	1301
301.7701-7(c)(3)(iii)-(v)	1301
301.7701-7(c)(3)(iv)	1301
301.7701-7(d)(1)(ii)	1301
301.7701-7(d)(1)(iii)	1301
301.9100-8(a)(1)	1109.02
301.9100-8(a)(4)(i)	102.02; 507.02

Proposed Regulations

Regulation	Paragraph
1.1411-3	504.04
1.1411-3	504.04
1.1411-3(b)(5)	504.04
1.1411-4(e)	504.04

Temporary Regulations

Regulation	Paragraph
1.71-1T(e)	912.02
1.469-1T(b)(2)	616.02
1.1474-7T	109; 1306
1.6081-4T	207.01
1.6081-6T(b)(3)	508
1.6081-6T(c)	508.02

Table of Revenue Rulings and Other IRS Releases

Field Service Advice

FSA	Paragraph	FSA	Paragraph
200011023	314	200140080	1105

Letter Rulings

LTR	Paragraph	LTR	Paragraph
8144001	409	199910067	411
9232006	102.01	200108035	1111.01
9323039	1111.01	200210002	807; 809
9452026	1110	200236052	411
9615043	411	200316008	314
9703036	411	200325008	411
9714101	1111.05	200329018	912.01
9811008	411	200546052	903.03
9851036	1408	200637025	903.03
		201235006	910.01

Notices

Notice	Paragraph	Notice	Paragraph
89-60	1115	2004-2	412.02
97-18	1305	2005-32	1011
97-34	1305	2006-15	1110.01
98-6	911.02	2008-63	903.03
98-66	911.02	2011-37	104; 608
		2012-67	410

Revenue Procedures

Rev. Proc.	Paragraph	Rev. Proc.	Paragraph
83-32	1110.06	2007-45	1112
84-80	211	2007-46	1112
88-53	1115	2007-56	411
94-27	611	2008-45	1112
2003-16	411	2008-46	1112
2004-26	216.03	2011-52	409.01
2005-24	1110.01	2013-15	202.01; 504.03
2007-39	1112	2013-35	214
		2018-18	202.01

Revenue Rulings

Rev. Rul.	Paragraph	Rev. Rul.	Paragraph
54-143	402	54-516	909.02
		55-38	813
54-207	311	55-117	604
54-468	1406	55-229	309

Table of Revenue Rulings and Other IRS Releases

Rev. Rul.	Paragraph
55-457	603
55-463	603
56-145	612
56-222	616.04
56-270	604
57-31	619
57-133	603.02; 1104
57-310	312.02
57-319	1407
57-544	303
58-5	1410
58-69	310.01
58-191	619
58-435	402
58-436	307.01
59-32	613; 709.01
59-64	309
59-375	603.02
60-47	615
60-87	604
60-227	303
61-20	618
61-86	612
61-134	409
62-147	801.01
63-27	613; 709.01
64-62	813
64-104	402; 602.03
64-289	307.01; 603.05
66-43	1401.01
66-160	903.03
67-74	711; 711.03
67-400	313
67-461	413
68-145	102.01; 402; 602.03
68-609	1009.01; 1009.02
70-361	613
71-154	309
71-159	214
72-243	812
72-409	612
73-64	612
73-293	1402

Rev. Rul.	Paragraph
73-322	611; 805
73-366	1406
73-397	502.01
74-94	909.07
74-175	311
75-61	603.02; 621
75-72	909.03
76-7	1111.02
76-8	1111.02
77-355	707
77-357	102.01; 312.02
77-466	801.02
78-1	216.01
78-81	612
78-203	314
78-292	312.02
78-299	1408
79-409	102.01
80-148	604
80-165	707
80-335	310.02
81-287	613
82-4	604
82-177	505
82-206	505.03
85-116	801.01
86-82	906.02
86-109	309
90-55	504
90-56	103.03
92-47	411
92-48	1110.01; 1112.05; 1202.03
92-51	505
92-73	1202.02
1976-1	1114.02
2002-82	409.01
2003-102	412.02
2003-123	613
2004-5	108; 1105
2004-64	901.04; 909.04
2004-77	923
2005-30	304
2008-41	1110.04

Technical Advice Memoranda

TAM	Paragraph	TAM	Paragraph
200305002	1410	200733023	616.02

Treasury Decisions

T.D.	Paragraph	T.D.	Paragraph
5488	901.03	9229	508
8633	914	9582	703; 810; 1103; 1106; 1114
8690	1107		
9102	703		

Index

References are to paragraph (¶) numbers.

A

Accumulation distributions815, . . . 1304.03

Administration expenses . . . 607.02

Administrative powers of a grantor, . . . 906
. actual borrowing from the trust . . . 906.02
. grantor as owner of any portion of a trust . . . 906-906.03
. to make loans . . . 906.01
. other powers . . . 906.03
. power of substitution, . . . 907

Adverse parties . . . 903.01

Alaska Native Claims Settlement Act . . . 912.01

Alaska Native Settlement Trusts . . . 912.01
. beneficial interest, limitation on transfer of . . . 912.01
. distribution deduction not allowed708, . . . 709
. election . . . 912.01
. loss disallowance rule . . . 912.01

Alimony408, 621, . . . 912.02

Allocation
. partnership payments, . . . 1007
. unused loss carryovers and excess deductions, . . . 620

Alternative minimum tax (AMT)
. exemption amounts for . . . 202.01
. fiduciary income tax return . . . 504.05

Amended returns
. for decedent's medical expenses . . . 312.01
. Form 1040X211, . . . 216.03

American Bar Endowment, . . . 413

American Jobs Creation Act of 2004, . . . 1011

American Opportunity Credit . . . 412.03

American Safe Deposit Association (TASDA) . . . 204.06

American Taxpayer Relief Act of 2012 (ATRA)214, . . . 412.03, 504.03

AMT. *See* Alternative minimum tax (AMT)

Ancillary representatives, . . . 509

Annuity
. charitable remainder trust . . . 1110.01
. charitable trust lead interest . . . 1108.04
. deferred annuity, . . . 304
. payments to charitable recipients . . . 1112.03
. private annuity . . . 909.05

Anti-deferral provisions of the Internal Revenue Code . . . 1304.07

Armed forces members, decedent's final income tax return, . . . 216
. joint returns . . . 216.01
. missing in action status . . . 216.02
. procedure for claiming relief . . . 216.03

Assignment of trust interest vs. trust income, . . . 813

Astronauts, death benefits for . . . 409.08

ATRA. *See* American Taxpayer Relief Act of 2012 (ATRA)

At-risk limitations, net operation loss deduction . . . 617.01

At-risk rules, S corporation . . . 1201.03

B

Bank of America and Trust Administration in State, . . . 1511

Bankruptcy estate, . . . 501

Basis adjustment rules . . . 606.01, 1010.03, 1011

Basis of estate or trust property606, . . . 606.01

Basis reporting rules, consistency of110, . . . 315

Beneficial enjoyment
. grantor
. . independent trustees . . . 905.01
. . overview, . . . 905

Beneficial enjoyment—continued
. grantor—continued
.. permissible powers . . . 905.02
. postponement of . . . 907.01

Beneficiary
. beneficiary-transferee liability, . . . 1408
. charitable remainder trust, . . . 1111
.. assets for funding a CRT . . . 1111.05
.. generally, . . . 1111
.. income beneficiary . . . 1111.01
.. ordering rules of distributions . . . 1111.06
.. remainder beneficiary . . . 1111.02
.. trust term . . . 1111.03
.. valuation of the remainder interest . . . 1111.04
. complex trust, levels of beneficiaries, . . . 704
. computation of tax, . . . 818
.. foreign trusts . . . 818.02
.. multiple trust distributions . . . 818.01
. control over property for New York beneficiaries, . . . 1512
. deduction for distributions to, . . . 709
. discretionary beneficiaries under Pennsylvania statute (*McNeil*), . . . 1516
. estates and complex trusts, taxation of 803-803.02
. foreign trusts . . . 1304.06
. non-contingent (*Gavin*), . . . 1517
. qualified non-grantor charitable lead trust . . . 1112.02
. simple trust, taxation of 801-801.02, 802, . . . 802.01
. taxation of foreign trusts . . . 1304.02

Bequests
. fractional formula, . . . 807
. tax exemption for, . . . 809

Blue, founder criteria and ongoing protection minimum contacts for state law taxing power, . . . 1510

Bundled fiduciary fees, . . . 104

C

Calendar-year requirement, . . . 808

Capital gains
. collectibles . . . 605.03

Capital gains—continued
. depreciable real estate . . . 605.02
. distributable net income 106, . . . 707
. distributions . . . 1111.06
. distributions in kind . . . 711.01
. in excess of capital losses . . . 1111.06
. fiduciary income tax return . . . 605-605.04
. long-term 605, . . . 1111.06
. netting of . . . 605.04
. from sale of life interest, . . . 812
. short-term . . . 605.04, 1111.06
. tax rates . . . 605.01

Capital losses
. collectibles . . . 605.03
. deductible losses of an estate or trust . . . 616.02
. depreciable real estate . . . 605.02
. distributions in kind . . . 711.01
. fiduciary income tax return 605-605.04
. long-term . . . 605.04
. netting of . . . 605.04
. short-term . . . 605.04
. tax rates . . . 605.01

Casualty losses. *See also* Losses . . . 616.01

Cemetery perpetual care trust . . . 912.03

Charitable contributions
. deduction limited to sums paid out of gross income, . . . 1102
. deductions for 413, . . . 413.01
. distribution deduction not allowed 810, . . . 1106
. fiduciary income tax return, . . . 1101
.. flow-through entities, . . . 1105
.. substantiation requirements, . . . 1107
. made after year end . . . 102.02
. pass-through entities, . . . 108
. tax elections affecting estate and trust income tax return . . . 102.02

Charitable lead annuity trust (CLAT) . . . 1011.02, 1108.03

Charitable lead trust (CLT) . . . 1108.03
. assets for funding a CLT . . . 1112.06
. charitable lead annuity trust . . . 1011.02
. charitable lead unitrust . . . 1011.02
. distribution income ordering regulations, . . . 1114
. generally . . . 1011.02, 1112
. grantor charitable lead trusts . . . 1112.01

Index

Charitable lead trust (CLT)—continued
. payments of annuity or unitrust amounts . . . 1112.03
. present value, . . . 1109.02
. qualified non-grantor charitable lead trust . . . 1112.02
. tax reporting, . . . 1113
. trust term . . . 1112.04
. valuation of the remainder interest . . . 1112.05

Charitable lead unitrust (CLUT) . . . 1011.02

Charitable remainder annuity trust (CRAT)
. characteristics . . . 1108.02
. generally, . . . 1110
. payments to charitable recipients . . . 1108.02, 1110.02

Charitable remainder trust (CRT)
. beneficiaries, distributions to, . . . 1111
. . assets for funding a CRT . . . 1111.05
. . generally, . . . 1111
. . income beneficiary . . . 1111.01
. . ordering rules of distributions . . . 1111.06
. . remainder beneficiary . . . 1111.02
. . trust term . . . 1111.03
. . valuation of the remainder interest . . . 1111.04
. charitable remainder annuity trust
. . characteristics . . . 1108.02
. . generally, . . . 1110
. . payments to charitable recipients . . . 1108.02, 1110.02
. charitable remainder unitrust
. . characteristics . . . 1108.02
. . generally, . . . 1110
. . payments to charitable recipients . . . 1112.03
. generally . . . 1108.02, 1110
. IRS requirements, . . . 1110
. present value, . . . 1109.02
. qualification
. . division of trust . . . 1110.04
. . reporting . . . 1110.06
. . sum certain annuity or fixed percentage unitrust . . . 1101.01
. . taxation . . . 1110.05

Charitable remainder unitrust (CRUT)
. characteristics . . . 1108.02
. generally, . . . 1110

Charitable remainder unitrust (CRUT)—continued
. payments to charitable recipients . . . 1110.03, 1112.03

Charitable trusts
. pooled income trusts, . . . 1115
. present value, . . . 1109.02
. split-interest charitable trusts, . . . 1108
. . additional contributions, prohibition of, . . . 1108.05
. . annuity and unitrust interest, . . . 1108.04, 1110
. . charitable lead trust (CLT), . . . 1108.03
. . charitable remainder trust (CRT), . . . 1108.02
. . current 7520 rate and two months preceding, . . . 1109.01
. . funding of, . . . 1109
. . grantor v. non-grantor trust status, . . . 1108.01
. . trust income, definition of, . . . 1108.06
. testamentary CRT, . . . 1109.02

CLAT. *See* Charitable lead annuity trust (CLAT)

Clifford Trusts . . . 901.01, 901.02, 901.03

CLT. *See* Charitable lead trust (CLT)

CLUT. *See* Charitable lead unitrust (CLUT)

Code Sec. 672, adverse and nonadverse parties . . . 903-903.03

Code Sec. 673, reversionary interests in grantor trusts, . . . 904

Code Sec. 674, power to control beneficial enjoyment . . . 905-905.02

Code Sec. 675, exercise of administrative powers . . . 906-906.03

Code Sec. 675(4), power of substitution, . . . 907

Code Sec. 676, power to revoke grantor trusts907, . . . 907.01

Code Sec. 677, income for benefit of grantor . . . 909-909.07

Code Sec. 678, income taxable to person other than grantor910, . . . 910.01

Code Sec. 679, foreign grantor trusts . . . 911.01

Index

Code Sec. 685, qualified funeral trust ... 911.02

Code Sec. 691, charitable deduction for IRD property, ... 1104

Code Sec. 754 Election, ... 1010
. coordination with mandatory basis adjustment rules ... 1010.03
. the election ... 1010.01
. termination of the election ... 1010.02

Collectibles ... 605.03

Columbia space shuttle disaster, ... 216

Commerce Clause, ... 1506
. substantial nexus test ... 1506.01

Complex trust
. beneficiary levels, ... 704
. beneficiary's tax liability
.. accumulation distributions, ... 815
.. assignment of trust interest vs. trust income, ... 813
.. calendar-year requirement, ... 808
.. charitable contributions, ... 810
.. comprehensive example ... 804-804.08
.. computation of tax ... 818-818.02
.. double deductions denied, ... 811
.. elective shares, ... 806
.. gain from sale of life interest, ... 812
.. gifts and bequests may be exempt, ... 809
.. interest paid on deferred legacies, ... 805
.. separate shares treated as separate trusts, ... 807
.. throwback rules814, ... 817
.. "tier" basis of income taxed ... 803-803.02
.. undistributed net income, ... 816
. deduction for distributions to beneficiaries
.. character of amounts distributed ... 709.01, 710.03
.. computation illustration ... 710-710.04
.. income required to be distributed709, ... 710.01
.. limitations709, ... 709.02
.. taxable income ... 710.04
. distributable net income706, ... 710.02
.. capital gains, distribution of, ... 705
.. decedent's estate ... 706.05

Complex trust—continued
. distributable net income—continued
.. distributions in kind ... 706.04
.. any principal distributed ... 706.02
.. income accumulated ... 706.03
. distributions ... 709-709.02
. simple vs., ... 706

Conservation easement, ... 606

Constructive distributions ... 909.01

Constructive receipt rule, ... 302

Contributions. *See* Charitable contributions

Corpus
. distributions ... 1111.06
. trust corpus ... 603.02

Costs. *See* Expenses

Coverdell education savings account ... 412.03

CRAT. *See* Charitable remainder annuity trust (CRAT)

Credits
. decedent's final income tax return ... 202.05
. estates and trusts ... 607.01
. fiduciary claims for, ... 1406

Crop sales ... 603.05

CRT. *See* Charitable remainder trust (CRT)

Crummey Powers ... 910.01

CRUT. *See* Charitable remainder unitrust (CRUT)

D

D.C. v. Chase Manhattan Bank and probate is enough to withstand challenge, ... 1515

Death. *See* Post mortem elections

Debt in respect of a decedent, not allowed on final return ... 310.02

Decedent's final income tax return ... 201-217.03
. accounting method, ... 301
. armed forces members and terrorist victims, ... 216
.. joint returns ... 216.01

Index

Decedent's final income tax return—continued
- armed forces members and terrorist victims,—continued
  - missing in action status . . . 216.02
  - procedure for claiming relief . . . 216.03
- basis consistency rules for taxpayers, . . . 315
- checklist for handling tax matters, . . . 201
- constructive receipt rule, . . . 302
- deductions
  - charitable contributions413, . . . 413.01
  - education savings accounts . . . 412.03
  - health savings accounts . . . 412.02
  - medical savings accounts . . . 412.01
  - self-employed decedent's health insurance expenses . . . 412.01
- deductions not allowable, . . . 310
  - debt in respect of a decedent . . . 310.02
  - expenses . . . 310.01
  - interest . . . 310.01
  - taxes . . . 310.01
- dependency exemptions, . . . 215
- depreciation and depletion, . . . 313
- determining whether a return must be filed, . . . 202
  - additional taxes due . . . 202.04
  - dependents . . . 202.03
  - filing requirements . . . 202.01
  - Form 1310 claim for refund . . . 202.06
  - gross income threshold . . . 202.02
  - refunds or credits . . . 202.05
- due date . . . 207-207.05
- estate tax deduction for recipient of income, . . . 314
- estimated tax payments . . . 102.02, 213, 213.01
- filing by personal representative, . . . 201
- filing requirements . . . 202.01
- filing the final returns, . . . 203
- financial information, gathering . . . 204
  - decedent's income tax returns . . . 204.02
  - financial institutions . . . 204.03
  - insurance and annuities . . . 204.04
  - monitor mail . . . 204.05
  - safe deposit box . . . 204.06
  - sources of information . . . 204.01
- foreign assets, tax obligations, . . . 217
  - FinCEN reporting and FBAR . . . 217.03
  - foreign bank accounts . . . 217.02

Decedent's final income tax return—continued
- foreign assets, tax obligations,—continued
  - W-2 filers . . . 217.01
- form to file, . . . 205
- income in respect of a decedent, . . . 305
- income to report
  - agreements to sell stock at stockholder's death, . . . 405
  - alimony, . . . 408
  - dividends401, . . . 403
  - employee's group-term life insurance, . . . 410
  - individual retirement accounts, . . . 411
  - interest, . . . 401
  - life insurance proceeds not subject to tax . . . 409-409.08
  - qualified retirement plans, . . . 411
  - regulated investment company stock, . . . 407
  - S corporation income, . . . 406
  - stock options . . . 404-404.04
  - U.S. Savings Bond interest, . . . 402
- income treatment by recipient, . . . 304
- installment obligations from a decedent, . . . 306
- joint returns206-206.02, . . . 216.01
- losses
  - of decedent, . . . 311
  - passive activity losses . . . 317-317.02
  - suspended losses . . . 317.01
- mailing address, . . . 210
- medical expenses . . . 312-312.02
- passive activity losses . . . 317-317.02
- payment of tax, . . . 208
- payments by employers to surviving spouse or estate, . . . 309
- personal exemptions, . . . 214
- post mortem tax elections, . . . 102
  - installment sales . . . 102.01
  - medical expenses . . . 102.01
  - savings bond interest . . . 102.01
- postponement-of-gain benefits, . . . 308
  - post-death transactions . . . 308.01
  - principal residence, sale of . . . 308.02
- refunds, . . . 211
- signing the return, . . . 209
- surviving spouse, special benefit for, . . . 212
- survivor annuitant deduction, . . . 316

DEC

Index

Decedent's final income tax return—continued
- tax elections affecting estate and trust income tax return . . . 102.02
  - charitable contributions made after year end . . . 102.02
  - disallowance of double deductions . . . 102.02
  - estimated tax payments . . . 102.02
  - fiscal year end . . . 102.02
  - qualified revocable trust . . . 102.02
  - 65-day election rule . . . 102.02
- taxable amounts to estate or survivors, . . . 303
- unrealized profits not taxed 307, . . . 307.01

Deductions
- decedent's final income tax return
  - charitable contributions 413, . . . 413.01
  - education savings accounts . . . 412.03
  - health savings accounts . . . 412.02
  - medical savings accounts . . . 412.01
  - self-employed decedent's health insurance expenses . . . 412.01
- disallowance of double deductions . . . 102.02
- for distributions
  - complex trust . . . 709-710.04
  - estate . . . 709-710.04
  - simple trust, . . . 708
- distributions to beneficiaries, . . . 708
- double . . . 102.02, 613
- double deductions denied, . . . 811
- estate tax deduction for recipient of decedent's income, . . . 314
- excess deductions on termination . . . 619
  - limitation on deductibility of . . . 619.01
- fiduciary income tax return
  - alimony and separate maintenance payments, . . . 621
  - charitable contributions, . . . 1101
  - depletion, . . . 615
  - depreciation . . . 614-614.02
  - double, . . . 613
  - excess 619, . . . 620
  - generally, . . . 601
  - interest, . . . 611
  - litigation expenses, . . . 609
  - losses . . . 616-616.04
  - miscellaneous itemized deductions and Section 67, . . . 608

Deductions—continued
- fiduciary income tax return—continued
  - net operating loss 617, . . . 617.01
  - in respect of a decedent, . . . 610
  - taxes, . . . 612
  - unused loss carryovers, . . . 618
- limitations . . . 312.02
- not allowed on final return, . . . 310
  - debt in respect of a decedent . . . 310.02
  - expenses . . . 310.01
  - interest . . . 310.01
  - taxes . . . 310.01
- for survivor annuitant, . . . 316
- trusts and estates, . . . 104

Deductions in respect of a decedent (DRD)
- disallowance of double deductions . . . 102.02
- fiduciary income tax return, . . . 610

Deferred annuity, . . . 304

Deferred legacies, interest paid on, . . . 805

Dependents
- on decedent's final income tax return . . . 202.03, 215
- support allowance as income required to be distributed, . . . 709

Depletion
- on decedent's final income tax return, . . . 313
- on fiduciary income tax return, . . . 615

Depreciation
- capital gains and losses . . . 605.02
- estates . . . 614.02
- treatment on decedent's final income tax return, . . . 313
- trusts . . . 614.01

Disallowance of double deductions . . . 102.02

Distributable net income (DNI)
- adjustments, . . . 707
- capital gains, . . . 106
- defined, . . . 704
- determination of, . . . 707

Distributions
- accumulation distributions 815, . . . 1304.03
- charitable contributions not deductible as, . . . 810

DED

Distributions—continued
. CLT income ordering regulations, ... 1114
. complex trust
. . any principal distributed ... 706.02
. . character of amounts distributed ... 709.01, 710.03
. . computation illustration ... 710-710.04
. . decedent's estate ... 706.05
. . distributions in kind ... 706.04
. . income accumulated ... 706.03
. . income required to be distributed709, ... 710.01
. . limitations709, ... 709.02
. . taxable income ... 710.04
. constructive ... 909.01
. estate
. . character of amounts distributed ... 709.01, 710.03
. . computation illustration ... 710-710.04
. . income required to be distributed709, ... 710.01
. . limitations709, ... 709.02
. . taxable income ... 710.04
. multiple trust distributions, taxation of ... 818.01
. ordering rules of ... 1111.06
. property in kind
. . defined, ... 711
. . election to recognize gain ... 711.02
. . gain or loss ... 711.01
. . issues, ... 711
. . mandatory recognition of gain or loss ... 711.03
. pursuant to the terms of the governing instrument, ... 1103
. simple trust, deduction for, ... 708

Dividends
. income to report, ... 401
. taxation of, ... 403

DNI. *See* Distributable net income (DNI)

DRD. *See* Deductions in respect of a decedent (DRD)

Due date of tax returns
. decedent's final income tax return, ... 207
. . extensions for income tax returns ... 207.01

Due date of tax returns—continued
. decedent's final income tax return,—continued
. . longer extension of time for Form 1040 ... 207.02
. fiduciary income tax returns, ... 506

Due Process clause, ... 1507
. minimum contacts and ... 1507.01

E

Easement, conservation, ... 606

Education savings accounts ... 412.03

Electing large partnerships, ... 1002

Electing Small Business Trust (ESBT)
. charitable remainder trust funding ... 1111.05
. election, ... 1205
. as S corporation shareholder, ... 1204
. S corporation stock501, 1206, ... 1206.01
. sample election ... 1205.01

Elective shares, ... 806

Employee
. group-term life insurance, ... 410
. key employee, ... 410

Employee stock purchase plans ... 404.02

ESBT. *See* Electing Small Business Trust (ESBT)

Estate
. administration ... 502.01
. bankruptcy, ... 501
. basis of property606, ... 606.01
. beneficiary's tax liability
. . accumulation distributions, ... 815
. . assignment of trust interest vs. trust income, ... 813
. . calendar-year requirement, ... 808
. . charitable contributions, ... 810
. . comprehensive example ... 804-804.08
. . computation of tax ... 818-818.02
. . double deductions denied, ... 811
. . elective shares, ... 806
. . gain from sale of life interest, ... 812
. . gifts and bequests may be exempt, ... 809

Estate—continued
- beneficiary's tax liability—continued
  - interest paid on deferred legacies, . . . 805
  - separate shares treated as separate trusts, . . . 807
  - throwback rules 814, . . . 817
  - "tier" basis of income taxed . . . 803-803.02
  - undistributed net income, . . . 816
- deductible losses . . . 616-616.04
- deduction for distributions to beneficiaries
  - character of amounts distributed . . . 709.01, 710.03
  - computation illustration . . . 710-710.04
  - income required to be distributed 709, . . . 710.01
  - limitations 709, . . . 709.02
  - taxable income . . . 710.04
- defined, . . . 501
- depreciation deduction apportioned . . . 614.02
- distributable net income 706, . . . 710.02
- distributions . . . 709-709.02
- Medicare tax . . . 504.04
- personal exemptions . . . 504.03
- as S corporation shareholder . . . 1202.02
- tax computation . . . 504.02
- tax deduction for recipient of income, . . . 314
- tax rates . . . 504.03
- taxation of . . . 504-504.05
- term of . . . 502-502.03
- U.S. Savings Bond interest reported . . . 602-602.03

Estimated tax payments
- decedent's final income tax return 213, . . . 213.01
- fiduciary income tax return . . . 507.01
- tax elections affecting estate and trust income tax return . . . 102.02

Excess deductions 619, . . . 620
- limitation on deductibility of . . . 619.01

Executor discharged from tax liability, . . . 1403

Exempt organizations as S corporation shareholders . . . 1202.04

Exemptions
- AMT . . . 202.01
- bequests, . . . 809
- dependency, . . . 215
- gifts, . . . 819
- personal 214, . . . 504.03

Expenses
- administration . . . 607.02
- fees
  - bundled fiduciary fees, . . . 104
  - investment advisory . . . 104
  - for trusts and estates, . . . 104
- investment expenses . . . 103.04
- litigation, . . . 609
- medical. *See* Medical expenses
- not allowed on final return . . . 310.01

Extensions for filing
- decedent's final income tax return . . . 207.01, 207.02
- fiduciary income tax return . . . 508-508.02

F

Farming
- crop sales . . . 603.05
- loss property and farm land . . . 603.04
- losses, . . . 311

FATCA. *See* Foreign Account Tax Compliance Act (FATCA)

Federal Priority Statute . . . 1401.01

Federal Revenue Act, . . . 501

Fees
- bundled fiduciary fees, . . . 104
- investment advisory, . . . 104
- for trusts and estates, . . . 104

Fiduciary
- assessment and collection period can be shortened, . . . 1407
- beneficiary-transferee liability, . . . 1408
- claims for credit or refund, . . . 1406
- defined, . . . 101
- executor discharged from liability, . . . 1403
- identification numbers, . . . 1405
- income tax of 101, 107. *See also* State fiduciary income taxation of trusts

Index 20,009

Fiduciary—continued
. income tax returns. *See* Fiduciary Income tax returns
. liability enforcement, . . . 1402
. lien for taxes, insurance proceeds, . . . 1409
. material participation, . . . 105
. notice of fiduciary relationship1404, . . . 1404.01
. passive activity losses, . . . 105
. personal liability for tax1401, . . . 1401.01, 1402
. self-employment tax, liability for, . . . 1410

Fiduciary accounting income701, . . . 702
. total return legislation, . . . 703

Fiduciary income tax returns
. alternative minimum tax . . . 504.05
. ancillary representatives, . . . 509
. basis of property606, . . . 606.01
. capital gains and losses . . . 605-605.04
. credits . . . 607.01
. deductions
. . administration expenses . . . 607.02
. . alimony and separate maintenance payments, . . . 621
. . charitable contributions, . . . 1101
. . depletion, . . . 615
. . depreciation . . . 614-614.02
. . double, . . . 613
. . excess619, . . . 620
. . generally, . . . 601
. . interest, . . . 611
. . litigation expenses, . . . 609
. . miscellaneous itemized deductions and Section67, . . . 608
. . losses . . . 616-616.04
. . net operating loss617, . . . 617.01
. . in respect of a decedent, . . . 610
. . taxes, . . . 612
. . unused loss carryovers, . . . 618
. due date for return, . . . 506
. estate
. . basis of property606, . . . 606.01
. . deductible losses616, . . . 616.04
. . depreciation deduction . . . 614.02
. . taxation of . . . 504-504.05
. . term of . . . 502-502.03
. . U.S. Saving Bond interest reported by an estate . . . 602-602.03
. estimated tax . . . 507.01

Fiduciary income tax returns—continued
. expenses of administration . . . 607.02
. excess deductions on termination . . . 619
. . limitation on deductibility of . . . 619.01
. farms . . . 603.04, 603.05
. filing extensions . . . 508-508.02
. gain or loss when legacy satisfied in property, . . . 604
. guardian fiduciary capacity . . . 505.03
. income test for filing . . . 505-505.03
. income to report, . . . 601
. interest income received . . . 603.01
. nonresident aliens . . . 505.01, 505.02
. overview, . . . 501
. personal exemptions . . . 504.03
. personal property income . . . 603.03
. qualified revocable trusts, . . . 503
. real property income . . . 603.02
. revocable trust, . . . 503
. tax rates . . . 504.03
. tax to be paid, . . . 507
. trust
. . basis of property606, . . . 606.01
. . creation of . . . 502.02
. . deductible losses . . . 616-616.04
. . depreciation deduction . . . 614.01
. . rule against perpetuities . . . 502.03
. . separate return for each, . . . 510
. . taxation of . . . 504-504.05
. . term of . . . 502.03
. . trust corpus . . . 603.02

Final income tax return. *See* Decedent's final income tax return

Fiscal year end, tax elections affecting estate and trust income tax return . . . 102.02

Fixed percentage unitrust . . . 1110.01

Flow-through entities, charitable contribution deduction for distributions from, . . . 1105

Foreign Account Tax Compliance Act (FATCA), . . . 109
. Foreign Financial Institution . . . 109.02
. foreign trusts, . . . 1306
. . applicable IGAs . . . 1306.01
. . classification in accordance with final regulations . . . 1306.02
. . reporting requirements . . . 1306.03
. inter-governmental agreements . . . 109.01
. reporting requirements . . . 109.03

FOR

Foreign assets, tax obligations for, . . . 217
. FinCEN reporting and FBAR . . . 217.03
. foreign bank accounts . . . 217.02
. W-2 filers . . . 217.01

Foreign trusts
. computation of beneficiary's tax . . . 818.02
. Control Test, . . . 1301
. Court Test, . . . 1301
. defined, . . . 1301
. Foreign Account Tax Compliance Act (FATCA) 109, . . . 1306-1306.03
. grantor trusts . . . 911.01
. inbound foreign grantor trusts . . . 921.01, 1302
. nongrantor foreign trusts
. . accumulation distributions . . . 1304.03
. . anti-deferral provisions of the Internal Revenue Code . . . 1304.07
. . beneficiary's tax, computation of . . . 1304.06
. . throwback rules . . . 1304.05
. . undistributed net income . . . 1304.04
. . U.S. taxation of the trust . . . 1304.01
. . U.S. taxation of U.S. beneficiaries . . . 1304.02
. offshore voluntary disclosure programs (OVDP), . . . 1307
. . audit, selection for . . . 1307.03
. . campaigns and administration . . . 1307.01
. . goals of campaign . . . 1307.02
. outbound foreign grantor trusts . . . 921.01, 1303
. reporting requirements, . . . 1305

Form 56 (Notice Concerning Fiduciary Relationship)
. charitable lead trust reporting, . . . 1113
. for charitable remainder trusts . . . 1110.06
. fiduciary duties and responsibilities, . . . 1404
. filed by the representative . . . 204.02

Form 114 (Report of Foreign Bank and Financial Accounts) . . . 217.03

Form 706, federal estate tax return . . . 207.05
. deduction limitations . . . 312.02

Form 706, federal estate tax return—continued
. disallowance of double deductions . . . 102.02
. double deductions for certain items not allowed, . . . 613
. estate tax return . . . 207.04
. medical expenses . . . 102.01
. savings bond interest . . . 102.01

Form 706-CE . . . 207.05

Form 706-GS(D) . . . 207.05

Form 706-NA . . . 207.05

Form 706-QDT . . . 207.05

Form 709 (U.S. Gift and Generation-Skipping Transfer Tax Return)
. charitable lead trust reporting, . . . 1113
. for charitable remainder trusts . . . 1110.06
. extensions . . . 207.02
. gift tax return . . . 207.03

Form 843 (Claim for Refund and Request for Abatement), . . . 211

Form 990, . . . 1115

Form 990-EZ, . . . 1115

Form 1040 (U.S. Individual Income Tax Return)
. armed forces members . . . 216.03
. for decedent's final tax return 201, . . . 205
. extensions for income tax returns . . . 207.01
. fiduciary capacity of guardian . . . 505.03
. fiduciary income tax return . . . 505.01
. for grantor trusts . . . 902.01
. longer extension of time . . . 207.02
. medical expenses . . . 102.01, 312.02
. savings bond interest . . . 102.01
. Schedule A, . . . 413
. terrorist victims . . . 216.03

Form 1040A, decedent's final return 205, . . . 207.01

Form 1040EZ, decedent's final return 205, . . . 207.01

Form 1040NR (U.S. Nonresident Alien Income Tax Return)
. for decedent's final tax return, . . . 205

Index

Form 1040NR (U.S. Nonresident Alien Income Tax Return)—continued
. extensions for income tax returns . . . 207.01
. fiduciary income tax return . . . 505.01, 505.02
. income test for filing, . . . 505
. mailing address for, . . . 210

Form 1040NR-EZ, extensions for . . . 207.01

Form 1040X (Amended U.S. Individual Income Tax Return) 211, . . . 216.03

Form 1041 (U.S. Income Tax Return for Estates and Trusts)
. alternative minimum tax . . . 504.05
. ancillary representative duties, . . . 509
. for bankruptcy estates, . . . 501
. cemetery perpetual care funds . . . 912.03
. charitable lead trust reporting, . . . 1113
. due date for return, . . . 506
. expense deduction, . . . 613
. fiduciary income tax return . . . 505.02
. filing extensions, . . . 508
. grantor tax letter statement with, . . . 918
. income test for filing, . . . 505
. interest income received . . . 603.01
. Net Investment Income Tax . . . 103.04
. not for grantor trusts . . . 902.01
. perpetual care fund . . . 912.03
. pooled income trusts, . . . 1115
. reporting estate or trust income, . . . 504
. Schedule K-1 . . . 1110.06, 1405
. 65-day election rule . . . 102.02
. taxpayer identification numbers, . . . 1405

Form 1041-A (Trust Accumulation of Charitable Amounts) 1113, . . . 1115

Form 1041-B, unrelated business taxable income reporting . . . 1110.06

Form 1041-ES (Estimated Income Tax for Estates and Trusts) . . . 507.01

Form 1041-N (U.S. Income Tax Return for Electing Alaska Native Settlement Trusts) . . . 912.01

Form 1041-QFT (U.S. Income Tax Return for Qualified Funeral Trusts) . . . 911.02

Form 1041-T (Allocation of Estimated Tax Payments to Beneficiaries) . . . 102.02, 507.01

Form 1042 (Annual Withholding Tax Return for U.S. Source Income of Foreign Persons) . . . 505.02

Form 1099 (Interest Income) 217, . . . 401

Form 1099-DIV (Dividends and Distributions) 401, . . . 505

Form 1099-INT (Interest Income), . . . 401

Form 1127 (Application for Extension of Time for Payment of Tax), . . . 508

Form 1300, Department of Defense certification . . . 216.03

Form 1310 (Statement of Person Claiming Refund Due a Deceased Taxpayer)
. applicability of 208, . . . 211
. fiduciary duties for filing, . . . 1406
. filing procedure . . . 216.03
. refunds or credits 201, . . . 202.06, 211

Form 2120 (Multiple Support Declaration), . . . 215

Form 2553, S corporation election, . . . 1201

Form 2758 (Application for Extension of Time To File Certain Excise, Income, Information, and Other Returns), . . . 508

Form 3520 (Creation of or Transfers to Certain Foreign Trusts), . . . 1305

Form 4506 (Request for Copy of Tax Return) . . . 204.02

Form 4506-T, request for transcript . . . 204.02

Form 4720 (Return of Certain Excise Taxes on Charities and Other Persons) . . . 1110.05, 1110.06, 1113

Form 4768 (Application for Extension of Time to File a Return and/or Pay U.S. Estate and Generation-Skipping Transfer) Taxes . . . 207.04

Form 4810 (Request for Prompt Assessment Under Internal Revenue Code Section 6501(d)), . . . 1407

Form 4868 (Application for Automatic Extension of Time to File U.S. Individual Income Tax Return) . . . 207.01, 207.02, 207.03

FOR

Form 5227 (Split-Interest Trust Information Return) ... 1110.05, 1110.06, 1113, 1115

Form 7004 (Application for Automatic 6-Month Extension of Time To File Certain Business Income Tax, Information, and Other Returns), ... 508

Form 8282 (Donee Information Return) ... 1110.06, 1113

Form 8283 (Noncash Charitable Contributions) ... 1110.06, 1113

Form 8736, extensions, ... 508

Form 8814 (Parents' Election To Report Child's Interest and Dividends) ... 505.03

Form 8821 (Tax Information Authorization) ... 216.03

Form 8855 (Election to Treat a Qualified Revocable Trust as Part of an Estate), ... 503

Form 8868 (Application for Extension of Time to File an Exempt Organization Return) ... 1110.06, 1113

Form 8869, QSSS filing ... 1202.05

Form 8892, extensions ... 207.02, 207.03

Form 8938 (Statement of Foreign Financial Assets) ... 217.02

Form 8971 (Information Regarding Beneficiaries Acquiring Property from a Decedent) ... 207.05

Form SS-4 (Application for Employer Identification Number) ... 102.02, 1405

Form W-2 (Wage and Tax Statement) ... 216.03, 217

Form W-4 (Employee's Withholding Allowance Certificate), ... 215

Fractional formula bequest, ... 807

Funeral trust ... 911.02

G

Gains. *See* Capital gains

Gavin and treatment of non-contingent beneficiaries, ... 1517

Gift tax, payment of ... 909.03

Gifts, tax exemption for, ... 809

Goodwill
. defined, ... 1009
. formula for valuing ... 1009.02
. payments for ... 1009.01

Grantor trusts
. administrative powers, ... 906
. . actual borrowing from the trust ... 906.02
. . grantor as owner of any portion of a trust ... 906-906.03
. . to make loans ... 906.01
. . other powers ... 906.03
. adverse parties ... 903.01
. Alaska Native Settlement Trusts ... 912.01
. alimony and separate maintenance payments ... 912.02
. alternative filing methods for, ... 915
. . Form 1099 with statement, ... 917
. . grantor directly on Form 1040, ... 916
. blank Form 1041 with grantor tax letter, ... 918
. cemetery perpetual care funds ... 912.03
. charitable lead trust ... 1108.01, 1112.01
. charitable remainder trust ... 1108.01
. Crummey Powers ... 910.01
. disregarded entities922, ... 923
. foreign trusts
. . Code Sec. 679 ... 911.01
. . inbound foreign grantor trusts, ... 1302
. . outbound foreign grantor trusts, ... 1303
. generally, ... 901
. history of, ... 901
. . Clifford regulations ... 901.03
. . Clifford trusts ... 901.02
. . contemporary planning and rate compression ... 901.04
. . *Helvering v. Clifford* ... 901.01
. income for benefit of grantor
. . constructive distributions ... 909.01
. . discharge of legal obligation ... 909.07
. . overview, ... 909
. . payment of gift tax and net gifts ... 909.03
. . payment of income taxes and Revenue Ruling 2004-64 ... 909.04
. . private annuity ... 909.05

Index

Grantor trusts—continued
. income for benefit of grantor—continued
.. reversionary interests in excess of 5%... 909.06
.. uses of trust income... 909.02
. income taxable to person other than grantor910, ... 910.01
. nonadverse parties... 903.02
. overview of rules, ... 902
. power of substitution, ... 907
. power to control beneficial enjoyment
.. independent trustees... 905.01
.. overview, ... 905
.. permissible powers... 905.02
. power to revoke, ... 907
.. postponement of beneficial enjoyment... 907.01
. pre-need funeral trusts... 911.02
. related or subordinate parties... 903.03
. reporting methods, changes to... 919-919.05
. reporting regulations, ... 914
. reversionary interests, ... 904
. tax identification numbers, ... 921
. tax reporting913, ... 922
.. irrevocable life insurance trust... 922.01
.. joint return... 922.03
.. revocable joint trust... 922.04
.. revocable transfers... 922.05
.. term trusts... 922.02
. tax returns... 902.01
. trusts not report under alternative method, ... 920
. trusts holding S corporation stock... 911.03
. use of, ... 902

Guardian
. fiduciary capacity of... 505.03
. income tax returns. *See* Fiduciary income tax returns

Gulf Opportunity Zone, ... 508

H

Health Care and Education Reconciliation Act of 2010... 504.04

Health insurance, self-employed... 412.01

Health savings accounts... 412.02

Helvering v. Clifford... 901.01

Hurricane Katrina, ... 508

Hurricane Rita, ... 508

Hurricane Wilma, ... 508

I

Identification numbers, ... 1405

Inbound foreign grantor trusts... 911.01, 1302

Incentive stock options... 404.03

Income
. beneficiary... 1111.01
. for benefit of grantor
.. constructive distributions... 909.01
.. discharge of legal obligation... 909.07
.. overview, ... 909
.. payment of gift tax and net gift... 909.03
.. payment of income taxes and Revenue Ruling 2004-64... 909.04
.. private annuity... 909.05
.. reversionary interests in excess of 5%... 909.06
.. uses of trust income... 909.02
. decedent's final income tax return
.. agreements to sell stock at stockholder's death, ... 405
.. alimony, ... 408
.. dividends401, ... 403
.. employee's group-term life insurance, ... 410
.. individual retirement accounts, ... 411
.. interest, ... 401
.. life insurance proceeds not subject to tax... 409-409.08
.. qualified retirement plans, ... 411
.. regulated investment company stock, ... 407
.. S corporation income, ... 406
.. stock options... 404-404.04
.. U.S. Savings Bond interest, ... 402
. distributable net income
.. adjustments, ... 707
.. capital gains, ... 106
.. defined, ... 704
.. determination of, ... 707

INC

Income—continued
. estate tax deduction for recipient of decedent's, . . . 314
. fiduciary accounting income, . . . 702
. fiduciary income tax return, . . . 603
. interest income received . . . 603.01
. ordinary income . . . 1111.06
. from personal property . . . 603.03
. from real property . . . 603.02
. simple trusts, beneficiary's gross income amounts, . . . 801
. from stock options . . . 404-404.05
. taxable to estate or survivors, . . . 303
. test for filing . . . 505-505.03
. treatment of decedent's income by recipient, . . . 304
. trust interest vs. trust income, . . . 813
. undistributed net income816, . . . 1304.04

Income in respect of a decedent (IRD)
. charitable deduction of IRD property, . . . 1104
. decedent's final income tax return, . . . 305
. fiduciary income tax return, . . . 610
. partnerships, . . . 1008
. types of estate income, . . . 603
. . farm loss property and farm land . . . 603.04
. . income from personal property . . . 603.03
. . income from real property . . . 603.02
. . interest income received . . . 603.01
. . sales of crops . . . 603.05

Individual retirement accounts (IRAs)
. inherited, . . . 411
. separate shares, . . . 807
. tax-free rollovers, . . . 411

Installment obligations acquired from decedent, . . . 306

Installment sales, post mortem tax elections . . . 102.01

Insurance
. health, self-employed . . . 412.01
. lien for taxes on proceeds, . . . 1409
. life. *See* Life insurance

Inter vivos trust501, . . . 606

Interest
. on deferred legacies, . . . 805

Interest—continued
. fiduciary income tax return . . . 603.01, 611
. on filing extensions . . . 508.01
. income to report401, . . . 402
. not allowed on final return . . . 310.01
. U.S. Savings Bonds . . . 102.01, 402

Internal Revenue Code, anti-deferral provisions . . . 1304.07

Investment advisory fees, . . . 104

IRAs. *See* Individual retirement accounts (IRAs)

IRD. *See* Income in respect of a decedent (IRD)

J

Joint returns, decedent's final income tax return
. armed forces members and terrorist victims . . . 216.01
. change to joint return . . . 206.02
. disaffirmance of joint returns . . . 206.01
. filing of, . . . 206

K

Kassner and New Jersey testamentary trusts, . . . 1513

L

Land
. conservation easement, . . . 606
. farm . . . 603.04

Legacies, interest paid on, . . . 805

Legal obligations, discharge of . . . 909.07

Life insurance
. accelerated death benefits . . . 409.01
. astronauts, death benefits for . . . 409.08
. defined . . . 409.05
. employee's group-term life insurance, . . . 410
. flexible premium policies . . . 409.04
. installment payments . . . 409.02
. not subject to tax, . . . 409

Life insurance—continued
. policy transfers . . . 409.03
. split-dollar . . . 413.01
. terrorist attacks, death benefits from . . . 409.07
. unrecovered investment in annuity contracts . . . 409.06

Life interest, treatment of gain from sale of, . . . 812

Lifetime Learning Credit . . . 412.03

Linn example, . . . 1502

Litigation expenses, . . . 609

Loans
. from the trust . . . 906.02
. trustee power to make . . . 906.01

Loss disallowance rule . . . 912.01

Losses
. capital. *See* Capital losses
. casualty losses . . . 616.01
. decedent's final income tax return, . . . 311
. of an estate or trust . . . 616-616.04
. . capital losses . . . 616.02
. . casualty losses . . . 616.01
. . deductible losses . . . 616-616.04
. . losses sustained by decedent or estate . . . 616.03
. . related parties . . . 616.04
. net operating loss617, . . . 617.01
. passive activity, . . . 317
. . disposals of taxpayer's entire interest . . . 317.02
. . suspended losses . . . 317.01
. unused loss carryovers, . . . 618

M

Mandatory basis adjustment rules . . . 1010.03, 1011

Material participation for fiduciaries and beneficiaries, . . . 105

McNeil and discretionary beneficiaries under Pennsylvania statute, . . . 1516

Medical expenses
. deduction on decedent's final income tax return, . . . 312
. . amend prior returns . . . 312.01
. . limitations . . . 312.02
. health savings accounts . . . 412.02
. medical savings accounts . . . 412.01
. post mortem tax elections . . . 102.01

Medicare tax
. applicability to estates and trusts . . . 504.04
. Net Investment Income Tax . . . 103.01-.06
. . Affordable Care Act, status of . . . 103.06
. . basics of . . . 103.01
. . estates and trusts not subject to . . . 103.02
. . income for estate and trusts . . . 103.03
. . investment expenses deductible . . . 103.04
. . regulations . . . 103.05

Mercantile Safe Deposit property control by New York beneficiaries, . . . 1512

Mortality tables, . . . 1109

N

Net gifts . . . 909.03

Net Investment Income Tax . . . 103.01-.06
. Affordable Care Act, status of . . . 103.06
. basics of . . . 103.01
. estates and trusts not subject to . . . 103.02
. income for estate and trusts . . . 103.03
. investment expenses deductible . . . 103.04
. regulations . . . 103.05

Net operating loss (NOL)
. carryback period, . . . 311
. deduction by an estate or trust617, . . . 617.01

New Jersey testamentary trusts, *Kassner* and, . . . 1513

New York beneficiaries, *Mercantile Safe Deposit* property control by, . . . 1512

NOL. *See* Net operating loss (NOL)

Nonadverse parties . . . 903.02

Non-grantor charitable lead trust . . . 1112.02

Index

Nonresident aliens. *See* Form 1040NR (U.S. Nonresident Alien Income Tax Return)

Nonresident state taxation . . . 1501.02

O

Offshore voluntary disclosure programs (OVDP), . . . 1307
. audit, selection for . . . 1307.03
. campaigns and administration . . . 1307.01
. goals of campaign . . . 1307.02

Oklahoma City terrorist attack, . . . 216

Ordinary income . . . 1111.06

Outbound foreign grantor trusts . . . 911.01, 1303

P

Partnerships
. accounting periods, . . . 1004
. allocation of payments, . . . 1007
. Code Sec. 754 election . . . 1010-1010.03
. death of member 1001-1011
. electing large partnerships, . . . 1002
. goodwill, . . . 1009
. . formula for valuing . . . 1009.02
. . payments for . . . 1009.01
. income in respect of a decedent, . . . 1008
. income on deceased partner's final return, . . . 1001
. . final 1040 reporting . . . 1001.02
. . 50% partner, death of . . . 1001.01
. . self-employment tax, treatment of . . . 1001.03
. mandatory basis adjustment rules . . . 1010.03, 1011
. partnership representative, . . . 1003
. payments to deceased partner's successor in interest, . . . 1006
. transfer of interest to spouse, . . . 1005

Passive activity losses
. decedent's final return . . . 317-317.02
. fiduciaries and beneficiaries, . . . 105

Passive activity rules, S corporation . . . 1201.03, 1201.04

Pass-through entities, charitable deduction for contributions, . . . 108

Patriot Act . . . 204.06

Payment of tax, . . . 208

Penalty, on filing extensions . . . 508.02

Pennoyer and probate administration for testamentary trust not enough, . . . 1514

Pennsylvania statute, *McNeil* and discretionary beneficiaries under, . . . 1516

Pension Protection Act of 2006, . . . 411

Perpetual care fund . . . 912.03

Personal exemptions. *See also* Exemptions
. decedent's final income tax return, . . . 214
. fiduciary income tax return . . . 504.03

Personal property, income from . . . 603.03

Personal representative, . . . 201

Pooled income trusts 1101, . . . 1115

Post mortem elections
. effects of . . . 102.01
. income taxes, . . . 102
. installment sales . . . 102.01
. medical expenses . . . 102.01
. savings bond interest . . . 102.01

Postponement-of-gain benefits, . . . 308
. post-death transactions . . . 308.01
. principal residence, sale of . . . 308.02

Power of administration . . . 906-906.03

Power of substitution, . . . 907

Power to control beneficial enjoyment . . . 905-905.02

Power to revoke grantor trusts 907, . . . 907.01

Pre-need funeral trusts . . . 911.02

Present value, . . . 1109.02

Property
. basis of 606, . . . 606.01
. distributions in kind . . . 711-711.03
. farm loss property and farm land . . . 603.04
. gain or loss when legacy satisfied in, . . . 604
. personal property income . . . 603.03

Property—continued
. property in kind
.. defined, . . . 711
.. election to recognize gain . . . 711.02
.. gain or loss . . . 711.01
.. issues, . . . 711
.. mandatory recognition of gain or loss . . . 711.03
. real property income603, . . . 603.02

Q

QFT. *See* Qualified funeral trust (QFT)

QSSS. *See* Qualified subchapter S subsidiary (QSSS), as shareholder

QSST. *See* Qualified Subchapter S Trust (QSST)

Qualified funeral trust (QFT) . . . 911.02

Qualified non-grantor charitable lead trust . . . 1112.02

Qualified retirement plans, . . . 411

Qualified revocable trust . . . 102.02, 503

Qualified subchapter S subsidiary (QSSS), as shareholder . . . 1202.05

Qualified Subchapter S Trust (QSST)
. charitable remainder trust funding . . . 1111.05
. election, . . . 1205
. sample election . . . 1205.01
. as shareholder, . . . 1203

Quill Corporation and minimum contacts for state law taxing power, . . . 1508

R

Real estate, capital gains and losses . . . 605.02

Real property, income from603, . . . 603.02

Refunds
. decedent's final income tax return . . . 202.05
. fiduciary claims for, . . . 1406
. forms to claim, . . . 211

Regulated investment company stock, . . . 407

Related party
. grantor trusts . . . 903.03
. losses of an estate or trust . . . 616.04

Remainder beneficiary . . . 1111.02

Residence
. determination of residence of trust, . . . 1503
.. mobility and multi-jurisdictional contacts . . . 1503.01
. *Kaestner* and residence of beneficiary, . . . 1518
. sale of principal . . . 308.02

Resident state taxation . . . 1501.01

Retirement plans
. individual retirement accounts
.. inherited, . . . 411
.. separate shares, . . . 807
.. tax-free rollovers, . . . 411
. qualified retirement plans, . . . 411

Reversionary interests in grantor trusts904, . . . 909.06

Revocable trust503, . . . 901

Rule against perpetuities . . . 502.03

S

S corporation
. at-risk rules . . . 1201.03
. duty of consistency . . . 1201.02
. electing small business trust501, 1206, . . . 1206.01
. general rules, . . . 1201
. grantor trusts . . . 911.03
. income to report, . . . 406
. New Jersey testamentary trusts (*Kassner*), . . . 1513
. passive activity rules . . . 1201.03, 1201.04
. qualified subchapter S subsidiary election1205, . . . 1205.01
. shareholders, . . . 1202
.. Electing Small Business Trust, . . . 1204
.. estates . . . 1202.02
.. exempt organizations . . . 1202.04
.. individuals . . . 1202.01

S corporation—continued
- shareholders,—continued
  - qualified subchapter S subsidiary . . . 1202.05, 1203
  - taxation of . . . 1201.01
  - trusts . . . 1202.03
- small business stock . . . 1201.05
- treatment of decedent's income by recipient, . . . 304

Safe-deposit boxes . . . 204.03, 204.06

Savings bond interest, post mortem tax elections . . . 102.01, 402

Savings Bonds, . . . 402

Securities Exchange Act of 1934 . . . 404.05

Self-employment tax, . . . 1410

Separate maintenance payments, . . . 621

Separate shares, . . . 807

September 11, 2001, terrorist attack 216, . . . 508

Shareholder
- exempt organizations as . . . 1202.04
- QSST as . . . 1202.05, 1203
- S corporation, . . . 1202
  - Electing Small Business Trust, . . . 1204
  - estates . . . 1202.02
  - exempt organizations . . . 1202.04
  - individuals . . . 1202.01
  - qualified subchapter S subsidiary . . . 1202.05, 1203
  - taxation of . . . 1201.01
  - trusts . . . 1202.03

Shares. *See also* Stock
- elective, . . . 806
- fractional formula bequest, . . . 807
- separate shares treated as separate trusts, . . . 807

Signing the return, . . . 209

Simple trust
- all income distributed . . . 706.01
- beneficiary's gross income, amounts included in, . . . 801
- character of income and allocation of expenses . . . 801.02
- complex vs., . . . 706
- death of beneficiary . . . 802.01

Simple trust—continued
- deduction for distributions to beneficiaries, . . . 708
- distributable net income, . . . 707
- income required to be distributed . . . 801.01
- tax years, . . . 802

65-day election rule
- distributions under Section 663(b), . . . 712
- tax elections affecting estate and trust income tax return . . . 102.02

Small Business Job Protection Act of 1996, . . . 1301

Social Security Act . . . 504.03

Space shuttle disaster, Columbia, . . . 216

Split interest trusts *See* Charitable trusts

Split-dollar insurance . . . 413.01

State fiduciary income taxation of trusts
- Commerce Clause, . . . 1506
  - substantial nexus test . . . 1506.01
- constitutional basis for, . . . 1505
- discretionary beneficiaries under Pennsylvania statute (*McNeil*), . . . 1516
- Due Process clause, . . . 1507
  - minimum contacts and . . . 1507.01
- factors to determine state fiduciary taxation, . . . 1504
- founder criteria and present benefit minimum contacts for state trust laws (*Swift*), . . . 1509
- founder criteria and ongoing protection minimum contacts for state law taxing power (*Blue*), . . . 1510
- *Linn example*, . . . 1502
- minimum contacts for state law taxing power (*Quill Corporation*), . . . 1508
- New Jersey testamentary trusts (*Kassner*), . . . 1513
- non-contingent beneficiaries (*Gavin*), . . . 1517
- nonresident state taxation . . . 1501.02
- probate administration for testamentary trust not enough (*Pennoyer*), . . . 1514
- probate is enough to withstand challenge (*D.C. v. Chase Manhattan Bank*), . . . 1515

State fiduciary income taxation of trusts—continued
- property control by New York beneficiares (*Mercantile Safe Deposit*), . . . 1512
- Residence of beneficiary (*Kassner*), . . . 1518
- residence of trust, determination of, . . . 1503
- - mobility and multi-jurisdictional contacts . . . 1503.01
- resident state taxation . . . 1501.01
- summary chart of income tax contacts, . . . 1504
- trust administration in state (*Bank of America*), . . . 1511
- trends for practitioners to plan for, . . . 1519

Stock. *See also* Shares
- agreements to sell stock at stockholder's death, . . . 405
- small business stock . . . 1201.05
- stock options
- - employee stock purchase plans . . . 404.02
- - held by a decedent . . . 404.04
- - incentive stock options . . . 404.03
- - income from, . . . 404
- - nonstatutory stock options . . . 404.05
- - statutory stock options . . . 404.01
- voting power of grantor or trustee . . . 906.03

Subchapter J, . . . 501

Subordinate parties, grantor trusts . . . 903.03

Substantial nexus test . . . 1506.01

Substitution, power of, . . . 907

Sum certain annuity . . . 1110.01

Surface Transportation and Veterans Health Care Choice Improvement Act of 2015110, . . . 315

Surviving spouse
- income required to be distributed, . . . 709
- payments by employers to, . . . 309
- special benefit for, . . . 212

Survivor annuitant, . . . 316

Swift, founder criteria and present benefit minimum contacts for state trust laws, . . . 1509

T

Tax Cuts and Jobs Act (TCJA) . . . 202.01, 408, 504.05, 608

Tax elections affecting estate and trust income tax return . . . 102.02
- charitable contributions made after year end . . . 102.02
- disallowance of double deductions . . . 102.02
- estimated tax payments . . . 102.02
- fiscal year end . . . 102.02
- qualified revocable trust . . . 102.02
- 65-day election rule . . . 102.02

Tax rates
- capital gains and losses . . . 605.01
- fiduciary income tax return . . . 504.03

Tax year
- of beneficiaries and trusts, . . . 802
- calendar-year requirement, . . . 808
- fiscal year end . . . 102.02

Taxes
- Alternative Minimum Tax . . . 202.01, 504.05
- computation of, . . . 818
- - foreign trusts . . . 818.02
- - multiple trust distributions . . . 818.01
- deduction by an estate or trust, . . . 612
- fiduciary personal liability for1401, . . . 1401.01, 1402
- foreign trusts . . . 1304.01, 1304.02
- grantor payment of income taxes . . . 909.04
- lien for, . . . 1409
- not allowed on final return . . . 310.01
- self-employment, . . . 1410
- "tier" basis of income taxed . . . 803-803.02

Taxpayer identification number, . . . 1405

Taxpayer Relief Act of 1997, . . . 814

Terrorism
- death benefits resulting from . . . 409.07

Terrorism—continued
. decedent's final income tax return, . . . 216
. . joint returns . . . 216.01
. . missing in action status . . . 216.02
. . procedure for claiming relief . . . 216.03
. Oklahoma City attack, . . . 216
. September 11, 2001, attack216, . . . 508

Testamentary charitable remainder trust, . . . 1109.02

Testamentary trusts
. creation of, . . . 501
. New Jersey (*Kassner*), . . . 1513
. probate administration not enough (*Pennoyer*), . . . 1514

Throwback rules
. accumulation distributions, . . . 815
. distributions from trusts, . . . 814
. foreign trusts
. . accumulation distributions . . . 1304.03
. . operation of . . . 1304.05
. . undistributed net income . . . 1304.04
. operation of, . . . 817
. undistributed net income, . . . 816

"Tier" basis of income taxed . . . 803-803.02

Transferee liability, . . . 1408

Trust
. Alaska Native Settlement Trusts . . . 912.01
. . beneficial interest, limitation on transfer of . . . 912.01
. . distribution deduction not allowed708, . . . 709
. . election . . . 912.01
. . loss disallowance rule . . . 912.01
. basis of property606, . . . 606.01
. business, . . . 501
. cemetery perpetual care funds . . . 912.03
. charitable. *See* Charitable trusts
. Clifford Trusts . . . 901.01, 901.02, 901.03
. complex. *See* Complex trust
. corpus . . . 603.02
. creation of . . . 502.02
. defined, . . . 501
. depreciation deduction apportioned . . . 614.01
. electing small business trust. *See* Electing Small Business Trust (ESBT)

Trust—continued
. foreign trusts. *See* Foreign trusts
. funeral trusts . . . 911.02
. grantor. *See* Grantor trusts
. income, definition of . . . 1108.06
. *inter vivos*501, . . . 606
. interest vs. income, . . . 813
. living trust, . . . 501
. Medicare tax . . . 504.04
. multiple . . . 504.01
. nonresident aliens . . . 505.01, 505.02
. personal exemptions . . . 504.03
. pooled income trusts, . . . 1115
. pre-need funeral trusts . . . 911.02
. QSST. *See* Qualified Subchapter S Trust (QSST)
. qualified funeral trust . . . 911.02
. qualified non-grantor charitable lead trust . . . 1112.02
. qualified revocable trust . . . 102.02
. revocable trust503, . . . 901
. as S corporation shareholder . . . 1202.03
. separate return for each, . . . 510
. separate shares treated as separate trusts, . . . 807
. simple. *See* Simple trust
. state fiduciary income taxation
. . resident and nonresident trusts, . . . 107
. . trusts. *See* State fiduciary income taxation of trusts
. tax computation . . . 504.02
. taxation of, . . . 504
. term of . . . 502.03, 1111.03
. testamentary
. . creation of, . . . 501
. . New Jersey (*Kassner*), . . . 1513
. . probate administration not enough (*Pennoyer*), . . . 1514
. testamentary charitable remainder trust, . . . 1109.02

Trustees, independent, power to control beneficial enjoyment . . . 905.01

U

Undistributed net income816, . . . 1304.04

Uniform Principal and Income Act, . . . 702

Uniform Prudent Investor Act, . . . 702

Unitrust . . . 1108.04

Unitrust—continued
. characteristics . . . 1110.01

Unrealized profits not taxed307, . . . 307.01

U.S. Savings Bonds, interest on
. decedent's final return, . . . 402
. estate reporting, . . . 602
. . estate holding the bonds . . . 602.03
. . individual beneficiary receiving bonds from estate . . . 602.02
. . Section 454 election . . . 602.01
. post mortem tax elections affecting the decedent's final income tax return . . . 102.01

V

Valuation
. present value, . . . 1109.02
. of remainder interest . . . 1111.04, 1112.05

Vietnam service member tax abatement . . . 216.02

W

Working Families Tax Relief Act of 2004, . . . 403